CIPS Study Matters

Level 6

Graduate Diploma in Purchasing and Supply

Finance for Purchasers

Second Edition

Richard Herman
Financial training consultant
(Study sessions 1–8, 11–12, 17 and 19–20)

and

David L Loseby
Vault Consulting Ltd
(Study sessions 9–10, 13–16 and 18)

THE
CHARTERED INSTITUTE OF
PURCHASING & SUPPLY®

Published by

The Chartered Institute of Purchasing and Supply
Easton House, Easton on the Hill, Stamford, Lincolnshire PE9 3NZ
Tel: +44 (0) 1780 756 777
Fax: +44 (0) 1780 751 610
Email: info@cips.org
Website: http://www.cips.org

© The Chartered Institute of Purchasing and Supply 2007, 2009

First published January 2007
Second edition published June 2009

All rights reserved. No part of this publication may be reproduced, stored in
a retrieval system, or transmitted, in any form or by any means, electronic,
mechanical, photocopying, recording or otherwise without permission of
the copyright owner.

While every effort has been made to ensure that references to websites
are correct at time of going to press, the world wide web is a constantly
changing environment and CIPS cannot accept any responsibility for any
changes to addresses.

CIPS acknowledges product, service and company names referred to in this
publication, many of which are trade names, service marks, trademarks or
registered trademarks.

CIPS, The Chartered Institute of Purchasing & Supply and its logo are all
trademarks of the Chartered Institute of Purchasing & Supply.

The right of Richard Herman and David Loseby to be identified as authors
of this work have been asserted by them in accordance with the Copyright,
Design and Patents Act, 1988 in force or as amended from time to time.

Technical reviewer: David L Loseby, Vault Consulting Ltd

Instructional design and publishing project management by Wordhouse Ltd,
Reading, UK

Content management system, instructional editing and pre-press by Echelon
Learning Ltd, London, UK

Index prepared by Indexing Specialists (UK) Ltd, Hove, UK

ISBN 978-1-86124-185-6

Finance for Purchasers

Contents

Introduction **vii**

Unit content coverage **xi**

Study session 1: Management accounting v financial accounting **1**
  The difference between management accounting and financial
    accounting **2**
  What different types of accountant do **7**

Study session 2: Assessing the impact of external factors **13**
  Assess the impact of macro-economic factors (including taxation) upon
    decision-making processes **14**
  Describe the procurement regulatory framework with particular
    reference to EU Directives for Procurement **18**
  Describe recent developments in CSR and corporate governance **24**

Study session 3: Finance and accounting terminology **33**
  Accounting standards and their role **34**
  International issues in accounting standards **38**
  The effects of the convergence of accounting standards and practices **39**

Study session 4: Capital v expense items **43**
  Capital expenditure and the impact of depreciation **44**
  Expense items and their impact on profitability. **47**
  Why the difference between capital and revenue is important **49**

Study session 5: Key financial statements **55**
  The profit and loss account **56**
  The balance sheet **60**
  The cash flow statement **64**
  Other financial statements **68**

Study session 6: Descriptive and inferential statistics **75**
  Descriptive statistics and the circumstances in which they are useful **76**
  Inferential statistics and the circumstances in which they are useful **84**

Study session 7: Contribution analysis and marginal costing **91**
  Analysing cost–volume–profit and break-even data **92**
  Contribution, and marginal costing, as an aid to decision making **99**
  Limiting factors and their effect on decision-making **102**
  The limitations and assumptions involved in the use of contribution
    analysis and marginal costing. **104**

Study session 8: Pricing strategies **111**
  Market pricing **112**
  Cost-plus pricing **115**
  Transfer pricing **118**

Study session 9: Different types of expenditure **125**
  The principal drivers of capital projects **126**
  Making the choice between Capex and Opex **129**

iii

Public facilities with private money **132**

Study session 10: Evaluating project decision-making tools **141**
Whole life costing **142**
Target costing **145**
Value analysis – tear-down **149**
Value management and value engineering **153**
Value for money (VFM) **156**

Study session 11: Sources of finance **167**
Internal sources of finance **168**
External sources of finance – non-equity **172**
External sources of finance – equity **180**
Public sector sources of finance **183**

Study session 12: Developing and managing budgets **191**
Setting and controlling budgets to achieve performance targets **192**
Creating and presenting a budget to support a business plan **195**
The benefits and limitations of using budgets **200**

Study session 13: Assessing resource requirements **207**
How to identify the tasks or projects (business needs) that will provide
the best use of human capital (people) **208**
Categorising people and matching them to the business needs to deliver
optimum value **212**
Project costing and cash flow forecasting of people resources **215**

Study session 14: Communicating findings and recommendations **225**
Effective presentation and communication of key data **226**
How to prepare and deliver a business case. **231**

Study session 15: Managing costs **241**
Base estimates and change control for capital projects **242**
Project/programme evaluation by benchmarking **249**
Key review stages **253**
Procurement spend authority levels **256**

Study session 16: Managing the cost base of the purchasing function **263**
The process of budgeting, apportionment and the need for
forecasting **264**
Forecasting **267**
Reporting and management actions **269**

Study session 17: Investment decision making using a range of
methods **279**
Profit-based techniques **280**
Payback period (PP) **283**
Discounted cash flow (DCF) techniques **285**
The cost of capital and other issues **290**
The impact of depreciation on running costs **295**

Study session 18: Functions of an organisation – reduction and control of costs **299**
Understanding the key functions of an organisation and how they relate to purchasing **300**
The importance of cross-functional team working **303**
The monitoring and control cycle **306**
Cost coding and reporting:c cost overruns **308**

Study session 19: Evaluating risks and their impact **315**
Different types of risk **316**
Financial appraisal, using a range of financial performance and efficiency ratios **318**
Investment ratios and their usefulness in the purchasing context **326**

Study session 20: Evaluate and select risk management options **333**
The risks presented by debt **334**
Futures and derivatives **338**
Insurance **340**

Revision questions **345**

Feedback on revision questions **349**

References and bibliography **367**

Index **371**

Finance for Purchasers

Introduction

This course book has been designed to assist you in studying for the CIPS Finance for Purchasers unit in the level 6 Graduate Diploma in Purchasing and Supply. The book covers all topics in the official CIPS unit content document, as illustrated in the text beginning on page xi.

An understanding of finance is a vital part of any purchaser's knowledge base. Finance impacts directly on many aspects of purchasing activity – such as planning, cost awareness, pricing policies, supplier appraisal, risk management and project evaluation.

This course book covers a wide range of finance-related topics, all of which have some bearing on purchasing activities, and will encourage you where possible to consider finance in a context that is relevant to the purchasing professional.

How to use this book

The course book will take you step by step through the unit content in a series of carefully planned 'study sessions' and provides you with learning activities, self-assessment questions and revision questions to help you master the subject matter. The guide should help you organise and carry out your studies in a methodical, logical and effective way, but if you have your own study preferences you will find it a flexible resource too.

Before you begin using this course book, make sure you are familiar with any advice provided by CIPS on such things as study skills, revision techniques or support and how to handle formal assessments.

If you are on a taught course, it will be up to your tutor to explain how to use the book – when to read the study sessions, when to tackle the activities and questions, and so on.

If you are on a self-study course, or studying independently, you can use the course book in the following way:

- Scan the whole book to get a feel for the nature and content of the subject matter.
- Plan your overall study schedule so that you allow enough time to complete all 20 study sessions well before your examinations – in other words, leaving plenty of time for revision.
- For each session, set aside enough time for reading the text, tackling all the learning activities and self-assessment questions, and the revision question at the end of the session, and for the suggested further reading.

vii

Guidance on roughly how long you should set aside for studying each session is given at the beginning of the session.

Now let's take a look at the structure and content of the individual study sessions.

Overview of the study sessions

The course book breaks the content down into 20 sessions, which vary from three to six or seven hours' duration each. However, we are not advising you to study for this sort of time without a break! The sessions are simply a convenient way of breaking the syllabus into manageable chunks. Most people would try to study one or two sessions a week, taking one or two breaks within each session. You will quickly find out what suits you best.

Each session begins with a brief **introduction** which sets out the areas of the syllabus being covered and explains, if necessary, how the session fits in with the topics that come before and after.

After the introduction there is a statement of the **session learning objectives**. The objectives are designed to help you understand exactly what you should be able to do after you've studied the session. You might find it helpful to tick them off as you progress through the session. You will also find them useful during revision. There is one session learning objective for each numbered subsection of the session.

After this, there is a brief section reproducing the learning objectives and indicative content from the official **unit content document**. This will help you to understand exactly which part of the syllabus you are studying in the current session.

Following this, there are **prior knowledge** and **resources** sections if necessary. These will let you know if there are any topics you need to be familiar with before tackling each particular session, or any special resources you might need, such as a calculator or graph paper.

Then the main part of the study session begins, with the first of the numbered main subsections. At regular intervals in each study session, we have provided you with **learning activities**, which are designed to get you actively involved in the learning process. You should always try to complete the activities – usually on a separate sheet of your own paper – before reading on. You will learn much more effectively if you are actively involved in doing something as you study, rather than just passively reading the text in front of you. The feedback or answers to the activities are provided at the end of the session. Do not be tempted to skip the activity.

We also provide a number of **self-assessment questions** in each study session. These are to help you to decide for yourself whether or not you have achieved the learning objectives set out at the beginning of the session. As with the activities, you should always tackle them – usually on a separate sheet of paper. Don't be tempted to skip them. The feedback or answers are again at the end of the session. If you still do not understand a topic having attempted the self-assessment question, always try to re-read the relevant passages in the textbook readings or session, or follow the advice on further reading at the end of the session. If this still doesn't work, you should contact the CIPS Membership and Qualification Advice team.

For most of the learning activities and self-assessment questions you will need to use separate sheets of paper for your answers or responses. Some of the activities or questions require you to complete a table or form, in which case you could write your response in the course book itself, or photocopy the page.

At the end of the session are three final sections.

The first is the **summary**. Use it to remind yourself or check off what you have just studied, or later on during revision.

Then follows the **suggested further reading section**. This section, if it appears, contains recommendations for further reading which you can follow up if you would like to read alternative treatments of the topics. If for any reason you are having difficulty understanding the course book on a particular topic, try one of the alternative treatments recommended. If you are keen to read around and beyond the syllabus, to help you pick up extra points in the examination for example, you may like to try some of the additional readings recommended. If this section does not appear at the end of a session, it usually means that further reading for the session topics is not necessary.

At the end of the session we direct you to a **revision question**, which you will find in a separate section at the end of the course book. Feedback on the questions is also given.

Reading lists

CIPS produces an official reading list, which recommends essential and desirable texts for augmenting your studies. This reading list is available on the CIPS website or from the CIPS Bookshop. This course book is one of the essential texts for this unit. In this section we describe the main characteristics of the other essential text for this unit, which you are strongly urged to buy and use throughout your course.

The other essential text is: *Financial Management for Decision Makers*, 4th edition, by Peter Atrill, published by Pearson in 2009.

This book covers a wide range of financial management topics in a practical way, using many real-world examples to illustrate points. One important aspect to note, though, is that the book does not precisely match the syllabus. Certain aspects of the syllabus are not covered by this book, and significant sections of the book are beyond the scope of the course syllabus – especially in certain corporate finance areas.

The bibliography includes other texts that would be useful to access for particular elements of the syllabus. Of these, the book by Holmes et al (2005) is particularly useful for the financial accounting areas of the course, and the book by Colin Drury (2005) sits well with the management accounting sections.

Finance for Purchasers

Second edition amendments

There have been three amendments of note in the second edition of this course book, following the introduction of the revised unit content by CIPS in spring 2009. These occur in study session 10 on the topic of value for money, in study session 11 on factoring and also in study session 15 on procurement spend authority limits.

Unit content coverage

In this section we reproduce the whole of the official CIPS unit content document for this unit. The overall unit characteristics and statements of practice for the unit are given first. Then, in the table that follows, the learning objectives and indicative content are given in the left-hand column. In the right-hand column are the study sessions in which you will find coverage of the various topics.

Unit characteristics

Purchasing managers are responsible for specific activities and processes which can contribute to achieving corporate strategic goals.

This unit is designed to provide students with an understanding of strategic aspects of finance in relation to the decision-making process and detailed analysis necessary to deliver effective procurement.

Students will understand how to navigate around the world of finance in an effective and efficient manner so they can identify the where, when, how, and what a professional purchaser needs, in order to use and interpret the key financial models and tools required to deliver robust and sustainable procurement solutions.

Students will be expected to propose a range of both tried and tested models, as well as innovative tools and techniques, which will allow key business stakeholders to effectively interact and contribute towards developing and exploiting opportunities to grow and expand the business, through new supply arrangements, channels to market, diversification, outsourcing and differentiation strategies.

It will help students to develop an understanding of the terminology and differentiated sectors within the financial and accounting profession which allows an engagement and exchange that will guide and benefit the decision-making process in an effective and efficient manner.

Statements of practice

On completion of this unit, students will be able to:

- Evaluate the appropriate cost and benefit models for a wide variety of scenarios
- Evaluate and assess reports that have their origins in finance and accounting and relate them back to the business
- Compare the value and relevance of financial information in the context of the decision-making process for evaluation and selection of supplier and service providers
- Use the wide variety of finance and accounting terminology

Finance for Purchasers

- Propose financial management tools and techniques and be able to apply these in relation to the total procurement and supply chain process
- Evaluate the elements that make up a complex business case for a capital acquisition, including downstream maintenance, service provisions for the life of the acquisition, and disposal
- Assess the non-financial factors that are interrelated with financial modelling and analysis, and predict their impact

Learning objectives and indicative content

1.0 Financial management tools (Weighting 10%)

1.1 Evaluate the difference between management accounting and financial accounting.
Study session 1
- Management accounts
- Company secretaries
- Financial accountants
- Cost accountants

1.2 Assess the importance of corporate governance, regulation and corporate social responsibility (CSR) and sustainability in relation to economic performance and value creation.
Study session 2
- Examples of CSR and sustainability in practice
- Importance of CSR and sustainability to customer satisfaction
- Contemporary developments in the area of CSR and sustainability
- Regulatory mechanisms – EU Directives for Procurement

1.3 Understand and use the terminology associated with finance and accounting.
Study session 3
- Accounting standards and their role
- International issues in accounting standards
- Effects of the convergence of accounting standards and practices

1.4 Identify which goods and services can be categorised as capital and which will be expense items.
Study session 4
- Capital items – plant and equipment, building vehicles, high value office equipment, construction
- Expense items – cleaning materials, stationery, office suppliers, consumables, cleaning services, services contracts

2.0 Financial and non-financial factors in decision making (Weighting 20%)

2.1 Analyse key financial statements to inform decisions.
Study session 5
- Profit and loss accounts/income statements
- Balance sheet
- Cash flow statement
- Five-year summary

2.2 Use descriptive and inferential statistics.
Study session 6
- Definitions
- How and when to use them
- Assess the outcomes of analysis

2.3	Determine alternative pricing strategies and assess their impact upon transfer pricing within an organisation.	Study session 8

- Market price
- Total cost
- Transfer pricing
- Variable cost
- Negotiated price

2.4	Use contribution analysis and marginal costing to evaluate a range of decision-making situations.	Study session 7

- Cost–volume–profit analysis and break-even analysis
- Make or buy decisions
- Deciding on product range
- The analysis, and most profitable use, of limiting factors

3.0 Sources of finance available for business and major capital acquisitions and projects (Weighting 10%)

3.1	Analyse the use of different types of expenditure.	Study session 9

- Capital expenditure (Capex)
- Operational expenditure (Opex)
- Public sector expenditure

3.2	Evaluate and select a range of sources of finance to assessing funds for capital acquisitions and projects.	Study session 11

- Retained profit
- Controlling working capital
- Sale of assets
- Factoring
- Overdraft
- Grants
- Venture capital
- Debentures
- Share issues
- Bank loans – medium or long term
- Leasing
- PPP/PFI
- Public borrowing for public sector (Bank of England and HM Treasury)

4.0 Budget and cost management control procedures (Weighting 25%)

4.1	Explain how to develop and manage budgets to achieve target performance.	Study session 12

- The importance of setting and controlling budgets to achieve performance targets
- The importance of setting a realistic budget
- Financial objectives
- Motivational objectives
- SMART objectives
- How to create and present a budget to support a business plan
- The importance of financial forecasting

4.2	Analyse resource requirements and their application in purchasing activities.	Study session 13

Finance for Purchasers

- Time
- Peoples
- Money
- Quality

4.3 Communicate findings and recommendations effectively.　　Study session 14
- Target audience: finance professionals and other parts of the business
- Budget presentation
- Presenting the business case

4.4 Develop process and plans for managing costs.　　Study session 15
- Estimating
- Controls
- Review stages
- Contingency planning
- Who should be involved
- Tools and techniques
- Procurement spend authorities

4.5 Develop a plan to manage the cost base of the purchasing function.　　Study session 16
- The principles of cost management
- Planning
- Co-ordination
- Control
- Reporting
- Effective programme/project management

5.0 Effective capital purchasing plans (Weighting 20%)

5.1 Evaluate the nature and importance of investment decision making for home and international markets.　　Study session 17
- Accounting rate of return (ARR)
- Payback period (PP)
- Discounted cash flow (DCF)
- Net present value (NPV)
- Internal rate of return (IRR)
- Opportunity costs of capital
- The impact of depreciation on running costs

5.2 Assess the impact of external factors upon the decision-making process and how these might be factored into the modelling and ultimate business case.
- Inflation
- Customs and Excise
- Taxation
- Exchange rates and currency management
- Social and political factors
- CSR and sustainability
- PESTLE and regulatory factors

5.3 Evaluate the most appropriate decision-making tools for projects　Study session 10
across a variety of sectors.
- Whole life costing
- Target costing
- Value engineering
- Value for money (VFM)

5.4	Evaluate the roles of the functions of an organisation in the reduction and control of costs.	Study session 18

- Design and engineering
- Purchasing
- Marketing
- Distribution
- Finance

6.0 Financial risk in procurement (Weighting 15%)

6.1	Assess the different types of risk and their impact on each of the following.	Study session 19

- Supplier
- Own organisation
- Customers

6.2 Carry out a financial appraisal and risk analysis of suppliers, own organisation, and customers, using a range of financial performance ratios.

- Profitability ratios
- Efficiency ratios
- Liquidity ratios
- Investment ratios

6.3	Evaluate and select financial risk management options.	Study session 20

- Debt
- Futures and derivatives
- Insurance

Finance for Purchasers

Study session 1
Management accounting v financial accounting

Introduction

This study text is written to help you successfully complete the Finance module of the CIPS Level 6 Graduate Diploma in Purchasing and Supply.

This opening session will introduce you to the world of finance, and in particular will provide an overview of what accountancy is all about, and what accountants do.

Many different aspects of accountancy and finance are introduced in this session. As the course progresses, you will be able to explore some of these different strands in more depth and consider more fully how they impact on purchasing and procurement.

This course is also designed to help you communicate with accountants. Accountancy – like many other specialist areas of work – has its own language, its own acronyms and its own jargon. These may at times appear unfathomable, and designed specifically to exclude non-accountants. This book will try to help you overcome any barriers that may exist in this area.

Q: How many accountants does it take to change a light bulb?
A: Eight – one to change the light bulb, one to sign that it has been changed, one to check that someone has checked and signed that it has been changed, one to update the stock records, one to accurately price and charge for the light bulb, one to work out whether it is cost-effective for accountants to change light bulbs, one to reclaim the VAT and one to count the accountants.

Session learning objectives

After completing this session you should be able to:

1.1 Describe the difference between management accounting and financial accounting.
1.2 Give examples of the roles of different 'accountants' within an organisation.

Unit content coverage

This study session covers the following topics from the official CIPS unit content document:

Learning objective

1.1 Evaluate the difference between management accounting and financial accounting.
   • Management accounts
   • Company secretaries
   • Financial accountants
   • Cost accountants

Finance for Purchasers

Resources

Very useful background information can be accessed from the websites of the various UK professional accountancy institutes:

Association of Chartered Certified Accountants (ACCA): http://www.accaglobal.com

Institute of Chartered Accountants in England and Wales (ICAEW): http://www.icaew.co.uk

Chartered Institute of Management Accountants (CIMA): http://www.cimaglobal.com

Timing

You should set aside about 4 hours to read and complete this session, including learning activities, self-assessment questions, the suggested further reading (if any) from the essential textbook for this unit and the revision question.

1.1 The difference between management accounting and financial accounting

A good starting point would be to understand what accountants do, and learn more about some of their main activities and responsibilities.

Accountancy has a somewhat staid image, but, as with many other areas of business activity, it has undergone much recent change. This session will outline the different aspects of accountancy, but will also highlight how these aspects have changed in recent years. It will also introduce aspects of accounting which have a direct bearing on the purchasing function, and these will be developed further in later sessions.

In the UK, anybody can be called an 'accountant'. No formal qualifications are required for the term to be used, for example, in a job title. However, to be legally able to carry out certain professional work, for example performing a statutory audit, one does need formal professional accountancy qualifications. These can be achieved through different professional institutes, of which there are six in the UK:

- Institute of Chartered Accountants in England and Wales (ICAEW): ICAEW: http://www.icaew.co.uk
- Institute of Chartered Accountants in Ireland (ICAI)
- Institute of Chartered Accountants in Scotland (ICAS): ICAS: http://www.icas.org.uk
- Association of Chartered Certified Accountants (ACCA): ACCA: http://www.accaglobal.com
- Chartered Institute of Management Accountants (CIMA): CIMA: http://www.cimaglobal.com
- Chartered Institute of Public Finance and Accountancy (CIPFA): CIPFA: http://www.cipfa.org.uk.

Members of the first three institutes above – the 'chartered accountants' – are likely to have trained with an accountancy firm and during their training will have been mainly involved with audit and taxation services provided by those firms. The ACCA qualification – the 'certified accountants' – may also train with an accountancy practice, but that is not a requirement.

The CIMA qualification is obtained while working in business itself, rather than in an accounting practice, and therefore has much more of a managerial emphasis. This is an important distinction, and one that we shall consider in more detail later in this chapter.

CIPFA has a different emphasis again. Its members will specialise in central and local government activity.

Visiting the different institutes' websites will give you a good overview of the different emphasis each one has. They also all provide a wealth of useful information on many topics to be covered in this course.

Financial accounting v management accounting

Historically, and rather unkindly, accountants have often been referred to as 'bean counters'. This suggests that all they do is add up figures. The reality is that there are many different types of accountant, as is highlighted by the different qualification routes.

A useful starting point for considering these differences is the distinction between what is known as **financial accounting** and **management accounting**. Accountants, especially in larger organisations, will tend to work in one or the other of these areas. That is because the whole emphasis of financial accounting is very different to that of management accounting.

Financial accounting is all about what companies must do by law. One important legal requirement is the production by companies of financial accounting statements. These are the documents that include, among other data, a profit and loss account, a balance sheet and a cash flow statement. The make-up of these statements will be covered in study session 5. Suffice to say at this stage that companies must produce these financial reports, which are distributed to shareholders and made available to the public.

The law also requires companies to comply with accounting standards, which are issued by a regulatory body for the accounting profession. This aspect will also be covered in more depth in study session 3, and is highly topical, as companies in the UK are currently being required to switch from UK accounting standards to International Accounting Standards – requiring the financial accounting community to develop additional skills and knowledge.

Financial accountants prepare these statements for the outside world. They form part of the annual report and accounts, which is prepared for shareholders of the company. Although the report is addressed to shareholders, it is used by a much wider group of interested parties or 'stakeholders' – for example, suppliers, customers, competitors, staff, government and analysts.

Finance for Purchasers

When reporting externally, a financial accountant must therefore have the technical skills to ensure that the financial statements comply with:

- statutory requirements
- professional requirements (that is, they adopt appropriate accounting standards)
- Stock Exchange requirements (if the company is 'listed' on the stock market).

The contents of the reports themselves are very tightly defined, in terms of exactly what has to be produced. The statements must be drawn up in line with what are known as Generally Accepted Accounting Principles (GAAP for short) . For companies above a certain size (currently those with a turnover of over £5.6 million) the accounts have to be externally audited. The audit process requires that the accounts are signed off by an independent firm of external auditors. The auditors must be satisfied that the accounts represent what is known as 'a true and fair view' of the business. However, what constitutes 'true and fair' has always been a matter of some debate and the term has never been defined in UK legislation.

Financial accounts have to be filed at Companies House – where the information becomes publicly available – within seven months of the financial year end for a public limited company (PLC) or within 10 months of the financial year end for a private limited company (LTD).

The reports themselves describe what has already happened, with very little reference to future events. They cover a particular financial period – normally a year – and they describe the activities of the whole company, with little if any reference to departmental or divisional data.

How useful such financial accounting reports actually are is a regularly debated issue. Some recent initiatives have tried to widen the usefulness by, for example, considering more fully the needs of parties other than shareholders and by trying to introduce some legally required forward-looking data.

In summary, financial accounting is mainly concerned with what is legally required to be communicated to external parties. It has to conform to various principles and standards. It is historic, covering a period of time that has passed, and it is concerned with the whole of a company rather than individual parts of it.

Effectively, management accounting is the opposite of this. There are no legal requirements, no set formats, no rules or regulations. The data produced tends to be forward-looking and involve smaller parts of a business rather than the whole entity. Table 1.1 summarises these differences:

Table 1.1

	Financial accounting	**Management accounting**
Main purpose	Reporting to shareholders	Aiding management decision-making
Users	External (shareholders)	Internal (managers)
Legal requirement	For example the requirement to produce and file annual financial accounts	No legal requirement

(continued on next page)

1 Management accounting v financial accounting

Table 1.1 *(continued)*

	Financial accounting	**Management accounting**
Focus	Focus tends to be on the whole business	Focus tends to be on separate parts of the business
Accounting principles	Must conform to GAAP	No requirement to adhere to particular principles. Emphasis is on providing useful information, whatever the form.
Time horizon	Historical, backwards-looking, reports what has happened	Includes some historical data, but main emphasis is on future events
Reporting frequency	Annually, sometimes half-yearly depending on company size	More frequent – e.g. monthly, weekly, even daily – as appropriate to particular business

Learning activity 1.1

Search out some management accounting data and financial accounting data from within your own organisations and compare the two.

Consider in particular whether the data is:

1   for external or internal use
2   historic or projected
3   the frequency of the report
4   meeting any legal or regulatory need
5   useful as a basis for making any decisions.

Explain why the data is either 'management' or 'financial' accounting data.

For the management accounting data, suggest three ways in which the information is of practical use to management.

Feedback on page 11

Recent developments in financial accounting

Financial accounting, as we have seen, is driven by legislation and the setting of accounting standards. The most significant recent development in financial accounting has been the transition to International Accounting Standards (IAS). (You will also come across the abbreviation IFRS – International Financial Reporting Standards. This describes more recently developed standards.) All EU-listed companies now report using international standards, with the likelihood that non-listed companies will eventually follow.

It is perhaps too early to say whether the switch has been successful. There have been practical difficulties, and some of the new standards are controversial. However, the logic of having an international set of standards is well founded. It is important that users of accounts can make direct

Finance for Purchasers

comparisons between companies around the world, and it is also sensible that global companies can prepare their accounts against a single set of rules.

From a purchasing perspective, and in particular in the area of supplier appraisal, it should in theory represent a useful development. This will be considered in more detail in study session 3.

Management accountants also produce financial reports, but because there are no statutory reporting constraints the reports can be tailored to the needs of the organisation and to the recipients of reports. Thus the reports need to be:

- relevant to the user
- presented in a timescale that allows decisions to be made
- reliable, complete and fair.

The interface between users and providers of management accounting is an important one. Users need to identify what information they need, and what decisions they might base on the information. They need to discuss this with the information providers, the management accountants, who in turn need to design an appropriate and understandable report, which uses measurable information.

Management accounting, then, involves the provision of accounting data to management, in order to facilitate managerial activity.

The UK business environment has changed radically in recent years. There is less manufacturing industry, and far more service businesses. Technological developments have allowed ever more sophisticated data to be available instantaneously.

Many organisations have also placed greater emphasis than before on non-financial factors in the measurement of performance, and a commonly used model is the 'balanced scorecard'. This considers performance against a range of indicators, which are not necessarily financial in nature. The role of the management accountant has not, however, been diminished by this development – rather it has been expanded to include involvement in the development and measurement of more wide-ranging performance indicators.

Some observers therefore draw a distinction between 'traditional' and 'innovative' management accounting practices. Traditional aspects tend to focus on cost control and, in particular, what is known as 'variance analysis' and which involves comparing forecast outcomes with actual outcomes – for example for costs such as materials and labour. The types of activity, therefore, that management accountants have traditionally involved themselves with include:

- cost analysis
- cost control
- budget preparation
- budgetary control processes
- cost/benefit analysis
- investment appraisal.

More modern, 'innovative' approaches include initiatives such as:

- business process re-engineering: which is about re-thinking and re-designing business processes as a means of reducing costs and improving delivery
- zero-based budgeting: re-thinking budgets in a way that involves justifying and prioritising all items of expenditure
- activity-based management: looking at what actually causes costs to be incurred, and being better able to forecast and control costs
- life cycle costing : considering a product's costs over its entire life cycle (rather than just, for example, the initial building costs)
- total quality management: the process of continuous quality improvement
- 'beyond budgeting': a challenge to traditional budgeting techniques via the use of more flexible and wide-ranging processes
- balanced scorecards: the use of key performance indicators within four different perspectives – financial, customer, internal business process and learning/growth.

You may have come across some of these in your own work experience. They all have direct links with management accounting and the way information is reported, presented and used, and we shall be considering in more detail those that have most relevance to purchasing later in this book.

Self-assessment question 1.1

Identify whether each of the following is this an aspect of financial accounting or management accounting (or both, or neither):

- Preparing budgetary control reports: FA/MA/Both/Neither
- Working out the company's tax bill: FA/MA/Both/Neither
- Declaring a dividend: FA/MA/Both/Neither
- Analysing last year's pay increases: FA/MA/Both/Neither
- Evaluating a new production line: FA/MA/Both/Neither
- Reporting last year's profit performance by division: FA/MA/Both/Neither
- Revaluing the company's buildings: FA/MA/Both/Neither
- Appraising a potential supplier's financial status: FA/MA/Both/Neither
- Reporting on material wastage over the last 12 months: FA/MA/Both/Neither
- Assessing the bad debt position at the year end: FA/MA/Both/Neither

Feedback on page 11

1.2 What different types of accountant do

Having looked at the different aspects of management and financial accounting, we can now turn our attention to some more specific roles within those areas.

Finance for Purchasers

Learning activity 1.2

We have considered the activities of financial accountants and management accountants, and we are about to consider in more detail the particular roles of financial controllers, tax accountants, cost accountants and company secretaries.

With reference to what we have looked at so far, and also from considering the way things are done in your own organisation, what job function is most likely to be involved in the following activities? (NB you may include more than one at a time.)

- Putting together the cost/benefit analysis for a new IT system.
- Submitting the company's accounts to Companies House.
- Establishing what outstanding loans exist at the end of the year.
- Designing a new budgetary control report.
- Appraising the financial status of an existing supplier.
- Determining what price to charge for a new service.
- Assessing whether to make a component in-house, or buy it in from elsewhere.

Feedback on page 11

Financial controllers

The role of the financial controller often bridges the financial/management accounting gap, as it is involved in both aspects of accounting.

For example, a financial controller is likely to be responsible for coordinating and finalising both internal and external reporting of results. This could therefore involve managing the gathering of financial information for internal management accounting needs – to aid management decision making and the budgeting process, for example. It might equally involve responsibility for the provision of information to aid the year-end external audit and the company's tax and VAT positions.

The role essentially involves the management of financial information.

Cost accountants

Cost accounting falls under the overall management accounting umbrella, but is focused specifically on costs. How much a product or service costs is a vital piece of information. It can also be a difficult figure to identify and, as we shall see in later sections of this book, different approaches to costing can be useful in different scenarios.

For example, costing data can be used in financial accounting reports to arrive at profit figures. It can also be used in a different way to make key decisions about whether to make something in-house, or to buy it from an external source – something we will be looking at in a later chapter.

Costing data can also be used as a fundamental part of an organisation's pricing strategy, including situations where one division or subsidiary of a group is selling to another. It can also form a vital part of the data that goes into a major investment proposal or purchasing contract. Again, both these areas are to be explored at a later stage of this course.

So, understanding costs, where they come from, what drives them, how they can be controlled, how best they should usefully be reported, is key. For a larger organisation, this is a specialist role.

Tax accountants

Tax accountants specialise in the very technical area of taxation. All organisations will want to minimise their tax bills. This can be done perfectly legally, and is referred to as 'tax avoidance'. A tax accountant would advise on the most appropriate, legal ways of reducing tax liabilities.

However, not declaring income on which tax would be due is not legal, and such practice is known as 'tax evasion'.

Taxation impacts organisations in a number of ways, which we shall look at in more detail in a later chapter. In summary, though, corporation tax is paid by businesses and affects how much profitable is available for distribution to shareholders. Other key points, which we will be developing at different later stages, include:

- Most business expenditure is 'tax-deductible' – i.e. it reduces profit but by doing so it also reduces the tax liability.
- Interest paid is also tax-deductible, and this impacts on how a company finances its activities.
- Some areas of expenditure, particularly investment in plant and equipment, attract additional favourable tax treatment.
- The tax impact on major project expenditure can have a major bearing on investment decisions.
- Companies with operations around the world will need to plan activities carefully to minimise their tax liabilities

Most large companies will employ an in-house team of tax professionals. The alternative approach is to buy the expertise in from external firms.

Company secretaries

All UK limited companies must have a company secretary, but for a smaller company the role may be carried out by one of the directors. In larger companies, the role would normally be carried out by an accountant, or by a lawyer.

Their main role is administrative. They will be responsible for doing all the necessary administrative tasks associated with the legal requirements of being a limited company. This will include important activities such as completing the annual return required by Companies House, and 'filing' – i.e. making available for public inspection – the financial accounts there.

It will also, for larger companies, involve making sure the company complies with all appropriate corporate governance requirements and meets any

Finance for Purchasers

'listing' requirements. Listing requirements are the additional administrative and legal obligations involved if a company is listed on a stock market. How onerous these listing requirements are will depend on which market the company's shares are traded on. In the UK, for example, the listing requirements for AIM ('Alternative Investment Market') are less onerous than those for a full UK listing.

Building on this administrative role, company secretaries also concern themselves with the *conduct* of the organisation – is it doing things properly, legally, ethically?

Corporate governance is an important and growing feature of business life, and considers ways that businesses should behave. Recent developments in corporate governance will be covered in the next chapter, but companies – especially larger ones – are currently faced with the need to comply with various codes of practice and other requirements. Such compliance activity is likely to be the responsibility of the company secretary.

Given that aspects of corporate governance are a mandatory element of an annual report, and that a lot of a company secretary's work involves liaising with external parties, they are more closely linked to financial accounting than management accounting.

A company secretary should be directly accountable to the board of directors (through the chairman) on all core duties. It is an important and sensitive role, and there is therefore a need to report direct to the top of an organisation.

Current trends

A frequently discussed issue regarding the role of accountants is the extent to which they are – or should be – guardians of business ethics. Much of what accountants (and company secretaries) do involves ensuring that various codes of practice are followed. Given the increasingly high profile of business ethics, accountants may find that their already varied roles become wider still.

Self-assessment question 1.2

A company is considering the launch of a new product. It involves acquiring major new production facilities, and sourcing a new supply of raw materials.

Try to identify an aspect of the product launch that would involve:

- a financial accountant
- a management accountant
- a cost accountant
- a tax accountant
- a company secretary.

Feedback on page 12

1 Management accounting v financial accounting

Revision question

Now try the revision question for this session on page 345.

Summary

This session has looked at the role of accountants. First it considered the broad distinction between management accounting and financial accounting, outlining the very different perspectives that the two accounting areas focus on.

The session then went on to discuss some additional different aspects of the accountant's role, and how they link to particular job functions.

Suggested further reading

Dyson, JR (2004) *Accounting for Non-accountants*, 6th edition, chapter 1. Harlow: FT Prentice Hall

Feedback on learning activities and self-assessment questions

Feedback on learning activity 1.1

You should be able to contrast the two types of data along the lines highlighted above. Internally used management accounting data is likely to include information that is more detailed at a micro level – for example, any internal income statements and budget reports are likely to include much more detail in terms of, for example, different cost items.

Feedback on self-assessment question 1.1

- Preparing budgetary control reports: management accounting
- Working out the company's tax bill: financial accounting
- Declaring a dividend: relates to financial accounting
- Analysing last year's pay increases: perhaps management accounting
- Evaluating a new production line: management accounting
- Reporting last year's profit performance by division: management accounting
- Revaluing the company's buildings: financial accounting
- Appraising a potential supplier's financial status: uses financial accounting data
- Reporting on material wastage over the last 12 months: management accounting
- Assessing the bad debt position at the year end: financial accounting

Feedback on learning activity 1.2

Putting together the cost/benefit analysis for a new IT system will be essentially carried out by management accounting staff, with cost accountants' expertise likely to be required for the 'cost' aspect.

Finance for Purchasers

The company secretary is most likely to submit the company's accounts to Companies House. The account themselves will have been prepared by financial accountants.

Establishing what outstanding loans exist at the end of the year will be part of the financial accounting process.

Appraising the financial status of an existing supplier may be done by a specialist in analysing companies, though the role will involve assessment of financial accounting data.. However, it is possible that management accounting data is also provided by the supplier. This does assume that the supplier is willing to divulge information that is not in the public domain. Availability of such data would depend on the relationship with the supplier.

Designing a new budgetary control report is a management accounting role.

Determining what price to charge for a new service is likely – in part, at least – to involve cost accountants. We shall look at pricing in study session 8, but it is likely that the pricing for this new product is set with some reference to the cost of producing it.

Assessing whether to make a component in-house, or buy it in from elsewhere is, again, the type of analysis that is done by management accountants, who are likely to refer to internal, detailed and necessarily relevant data to aid the decision.

Feedback on self-assessment question 1.2

A financial accountant is more likely to have direct involvement in the project after the event – i.e. after the product has been launched it will have a direct impact on the financial results of the company. However, financial accountants would want to consider the potential impact of the launch on future profitability, and its likely impact on shareholders.

A management accountant is likely to be involved in putting together a business case, and evaluating the financial benefits involved in project investment of this type (this is something we will be looking at in more detail in later chapters).

A cost accountant would be involved more specifically in the preparation of the costing schedules and forecasts that would be used to develop the business case.

A tax accountant would be needed to assess the tax implications of the product launch. What tax allowances might be available, how would taxation impact on the cost of funding the project.

A company secretary is less likely to be directly involved in the launch process.

Study session 2
Assessing the impact of external factors

Introduction

Purchasers need to be aware of the external environment that influences them, and the other organisations they are exposed to.

This session will outline some of the more important external factors that impact on purchasing work. It will first look at the main macro-economic factors, including aspects such as interest rates and economic growth. It will then consider legal aspects, with particular reference to EU procurement directives. Finally, it will address the increasingly significant areas of corporate governance and corporate social responsibility (CSR).

Business does not exist in a vacuum. It operates within an external environment, and it needs to be aware of developments and trends taking place in that environment. Corporate governance and corporate social responsibility both involve doing business with fairness and integrity. But does it improve the bottom line?

Session learning objectives

After completing this session you should be able to:

2.1 Assess the impact of macro-economic factors (including taxation) upon decision-making processes.
2.2 Describe the procurement regulatory framework with particular reference to EU Directives for Procurement.
2.3 Describe recent developments in CSR and Corporate Governance.

Unit content coverage

This study session covers the following topics from the official CIPS unit content document:

Learning objective

1.2 Assess the importance of corporate governance, regulation and corporate social responsibility (CSR) and sustainability in relation to economic performance and value creation.
   • Examples of CSR and sustainability in practice
   • Importance of CSR and sustainability to customer satisfaction
   • Contemporary developments in the area of CSR and sustainability
   • Regulatory mechanisms – EU Directives for Procurement

Prior knowledge

Study session 1 plus awareness of external factors in the business press (eg *Financial Times, Economist, Wall Street Journal*, etc).

Finance for Purchasers

Resources

Business press, as suggested above.

Corporate annual reports for real-world reporting of corporate governance and corporate social responsibility reporting (accessible within 'investor relations' sections of most large company websites).

Timing

You should set aside about 6 hours to read and complete this session, including learning activities, self-assessment questions, the suggested further reading (if any) from the essential textbook for this unit and the revision question.

2.1 Assess the impact of macro-economic factors (including taxation) upon decision-making processes

Purchasers need to understand how major economic factors are likely to impact on their markets and suppliers. Being able to forecast the likely impact of, for example, interest rates, inflation and exchange rates will enable a purchaser to be better placed to make informed choices and decisions. Being aware of the history of relevant commodity price movements, and what expectations are of future trends, will also be of great practical use.

This wider, external environment – the macro-economic environment – is directly influenced by government monetary and fiscal policy. This section will describe what the main macro-economic indicators are, and will then outline how government action can influence these factors.

Before looking at some of these factors in more detail, it might be worth considering a real-world example:

Learning activity 2.1

British Airways is a UK-based international airline. How might the following external factors impact on the company's ability to make a profit? In particular, say how the company might be affected by:

- inflation
- interest rates
- taxation
- gross domestic product (GDP)
- commodity prices.

Feedback on page 30

The main economic indicators are:

- economic growth
- employment
- inflation
- balance of payments
- imports/exports.

A fundamental economic statistic is the growth rate of the economy. The measure of total economic activity is normally referred to as **GDP (gross domestic product)**. Other similar terms and measures that you may have encountered include **GNP (gross national product)** and **national income**. All three of these indicators are similar, and involve adding up the country's total economic output for a particular period of time. The actual monetary figure is perceived to be less important than the trend – is the figure growing or shrinking, and what is the rate of growth?

These growth rate measures are reported on a quarterly basis and expressed in percentage terms. Two or more consecutive reductions in GDP are officially classed as a 'recession'.

Economic growth is desirable, as it means that the overall wealth of the nation has increased. Recent UK GDP growth figures published by the Government statistics office are as follows:

Table 2.1 UK GDP growth

2004 Q2	0.8%
2004 Q3	0.3%
2004 Q4	0.6%
2005 Q1	0.2%
2005 Q2	0.5%
2005 Q3	0.5%
2005 Q4	0.6%
2006 Q1	0.8%

Unemployment

Unemployment is a measure of the number of people out of work. A low rate of unemployment is deemed a good thing. If unemployment increases it means the country will suffer:

- loss of output (GDP will be lower than it might have been)
- increased costs – government, instead of receiving tax revenues, will have to pay out unemployment benefits
- reduction in the skills base of the country.

Inflation

The term 'inflation' describes an increase in price levels. The inflation rate, which is measured using a basket of representative items, is a measure of how much prices have risen over a given period (usually a year). The measure used in the UK has changed quite recently, and is now referred to as the **CPI (consumer prices index)**. This measure replaced **RPI (the retail prices index)** in 2003, as a means of comparing rates across Europe.

High inflation causes a number of problems:

- It reduces the purchasing power of money. This has a particularly damaging effect on those with fixed incomes and those with cash savings.
- It makes planning and forecasting difficult. In particular, long-term investment decisions (see study session 17) become harder to assess in a confident and efficient way.
- It has a damaging effect on the 'balance of payments'. As inflation rises, so do the prices charged for exported goods, making them more difficult to sell. By the same token, imported goods will become relatively cheaper for consumers. Wealth will therefore flow out of the country.

A small amount of inflation is, however, generally considered a good thing, as it is a driver of economic activity. If, for examples, prices are not rising at all – or are actually falling (a situation known as 'deflation') – then purchasing decisions are more likely to be postponed. Some economies, have experienced deflation in recent times. A high profile example has been Japan, where deflation took place in the seven years to 2005.

So, given that a low level of inflation is desirable, the UK government sets a target rate. In 2006 the target was 2%.

Balance of payments

The balance of payments records the flows of money between one country and the rest of the world. If the position is negative, it means more money is going out than coming in. This may mean that a country is importing too much, or exporting too little. Either way, the country's wealth will be reducing.

There are ways in which a government can attempt to manage an economy. The two main economic policy frameworks are monetary policy and fiscal policy.

Monetary policy

Governments need to manage economic activity. They need to be able to influence the key economic variables discussed above, and the two main approaches to managing the economy involve **monetary policy** and **fiscal policy**.

Monetary policy has historically involved action in three main areas:

- **Money supply**: by restricting the amount of money in an economy, a government may be able to control economic activity and, as a consequence, keep inflation under control
- **Interest rates**: by raising or lowering interest rates, a government can affect the levels of demand in an economy. Thus growth, and in particular inflationary growth, can be curbed if required, while a reduction in interest rates may increase demand if that is desirable. Interest rates also have a direct impact on exchange rates. If, for example, UK interest rates rise, then demand for sterling might increase – pushing up its value. That makes exported goods more difficult to

sell (they become relatively more expensive) and it makes imports more attractive to the UK buyer.

- **Credit availability**: by restricting the amount of credit available, inflationary demand could be controlled.

In recent times, the UK government has made little direct use of monetary policy as described above. Credit has been freely available, and money supply has not had the high profile it had in the 1980s. Interest rates are still used as a means of managing inflation, but this is now a task delegated by the UK government to the Bank of England Monetary Policy Committee (MPC). The MPC decides on interest rate levels, which are set at a level intended to achieve the Government's single objective – meeting the target inflation rate (currently 2%). Remember that the 2% is a target, not a ceiling, and interest might feasibly be reduced as a means of actually *increasing* inflation.

Fiscal policy

Fiscal policy involves managing the economy via government spending and raising money. The spending part – often referred to as 'pubic expenditure' – involves all the money the government spends on goods and services. This will include major items such as the NHS, road building and education provision. The raising money part is achieved in two main ways – by collecting taxes and by borrowing. If money raised from taxes is insufficient to meet public expenditure requirements, the government may borrow to finance the spending.

To give you an idea of the magnitude of figures, and how public expenditure is split, the following figures may be useful. Total spending by the UK government in 2005/6 was expected to be over £500 billion, and major components of this figure were as shown in table 2.2.

Table 2.2

Area of expenditure	£ billion
Social protection (pensions, child benefit, jobseekers' allowance, etc)	146
Other personal and social services	23
Health	90
Transport	20
Education	68
Defence	28
Debt interest	26
Industry, agriculture, employment and training	20
Public order and safety	31
Housing and environment	16

Fiscal policy therefore gives the government some scope for managing the economy. If it wants to boost demand, it can increase spending – thereby generating economic activity and creating jobs.

The government raises taxation either directly or indirectly. Direct taxation includes taxes such as income tax (on individuals) and corporation tax (on companies) where the tax cannot be avoided. It also includes personal taxes such as capital gains tax and inheritance tax. National insurance is also, effectively, another form of direct taxation.

Finance for Purchasers

Indirect taxation is, theoretically at least, voluntary. It is added to the cost of goods and services, so is only paid if those goods and services are bought. Examples include VAT and excise duty.

Table 2.3 sets out the approximate figures that were expected to raised from different types of taxation in 2005/06:

Table 2.3

Tax source	£ billion
Income tax	138
National insurance	83
VAT	76
Corporation tax	44
Excise duties	41
Council tax	21
Business rates	19
Other	65

Now complete self-assessment question 2.1 below.

Self-assessment question 2.1

- A small amount of inflation is deemed to be good for an economy: true/false.
- As the UK government is responsible for managing the economy, it decides on what interest rates should be: true/false.
- An accepted way of reducing inflation is to reduce interest rates: true/false.
- An increase in interest rates tends to be good news for exporters, because it boosts their local currency: true/false.

Feedback on page 30

2.2 Describe the procurement regulatory framework with particular reference to EU Directives for Procurement

In study session 13 of Legal Aspects in Purchasing and Supply you will have looked in detail at the legal aspects of EU Procurement Directives. This session is a refresher for that knowledge gained there.

Tendering procedures can apply to private and public sectors. However, the major difference is that public sector bodies are subject to the European Union (EU) Directives on Public Procurement. You will look at these Directives in this session. The Directives are legal rules that only apply to public sector bodies in the European Community. The legal rules stipulate how public sector bodies should approach the award of high-value contracts for the supply of goods and services. What is meant by high-value is dictated by the threshold levels applied and will be subject to amendment.

Total public expenditure in the EU, of goods, services and public works by governments and public utilities, was estimated at about €1,500 billion in 2002. Public procurement varies significantly between member states and the opening of public procurement within the internal market has increased cross-border competition and improved prices by public authorities.

The European Commission adopted a package of amendments to simplify and modernise the public procurement Directives. Directive 2004/18/EC coordinates the procedures for the award of public works contract, public supply contracts and public service contracts.

EU key objective

The key objective of the EU was and is the establishment of a free market without trade barriers between member states. It follows that the aims of the EU Public Procurement Directives are intended to guarantee fair and non-discriminatory international competition in bidding for goods, services and works above specified threshold values. The threshold values are reviewed on a regular basis, normally every two years. It is recommended that as a procurement professional you should regularly check the levels of the thresholds. The current levels of thresholds can be viewed on the internet at government websites. These levels are available on the government website OGC: http://www.ogc.gov.uk.

Learning activity 2.2

Search the website OGC: http://www.ogc.gov.uk to find the current thresholds for procurements. List or draw in table form the current levels applicable to the Supplies Directive, Services Directive and the Works Directive.

Feedback on page 31

Background to EU Public Procurement Directives

In many countries the public sector accounts for much of the economic activity in the economy. The Treaty of Rome (Article 86) establishing the European Community aimed to establish freedom of movement of goods, persons, services and capital by the existence of a single market in which there are no internal borders, which could be barriers to free trade and competition within the external boundaries of the European Union. There were a series of Directives introduced to implement the provisions of the Treaty of Rome.

There are six Directives constituting the Public Procurement Directives that are applicable to contractor authorities. The contracting authorities are:

- the state
- regional authorities
- local authorities
- bodies governed by public law
- associations formed by one or more bodies governed by public law.

The first two Directives (Council Directive 89/665/EEC – December 1989 and 92/13/EEC – February 1992) provide for remedies in the event of non-

Finance for Purchasers

compliance with the set procedures laid down in the other four Directives. These four Directives lay down the procedures to be followed in tendering and award of relevant contracts. The regulations were amended by the Public Contracts (Works, Services and Supply) (Amendment) Act 2000.

Just as the thresholds differ between sectors so does the effect of the EU procurement directives. For the full extent of the effect of the directives we recommend the further reading suggested at the end of this session. In brief, the Directives have opened up supply markets in areas where competition had been restricted.

The policy of the EU is to open up public procurement and encourage member states to take tenders from firms throughout the community and to award contracts to the best contender, which may or may not be in their own country.

EU Public Sector Directives

These include:

- Public Works Directive
- Public Supplies Directive
- Public Services Directive
- Utilities Directive
- Compliance Directive) - Public Purchasing Remedies Directive 1989 amended by the Services Directive 1992.

There are features that are common to all Directives and are discussed in more detail below. The main provisions of the **EU Directives** include:

- thresholds (supplies, services, works)
- advertisements and prior indicative notices (PIN)
- technical standards and specifications
- timescales
- framework arrangements which are discussed in the next section below
- procedures (open, restricted, negotiated), which are discussed in the last section of this session
- evaluation criteria.

Thresholds (supplies, services, works)

The Directives apply to procurements above specified threshold values. By following learning activity 2.2 above, you should already be familiar with the levels. Also, from the information at the beginning of this session, you know that they are reviewed on a regular basis, normally every two years.

Despite the levels of threshold, all Directives allow certain exceptions. For the EU services exceptions table, you can go to the internet and find out through the government website.

Advertisements and prior indicative notices (PINs)

One of the main provisions of the Directives is that contracts are published EU-wide to give firms across the EU Community the opportunity to participate in the submission of a tender.

The individual public sector bodies, that is, the contracting authorities, must publish a notice giving brief details of prospective contracts that are likely to be let in the following 12 months. This includes contracts within each category, which individually or in aggregate are expected to exceed the threshold level. Where such a prior indicative notice (PIN) is given, then the open and restricted procedures may be shortened.

Technical standards and specifications

All Directives provide that specifications for contracts subject to the Directives must refer to a British Standard that implements a European Standard where possible. The words used after British Standard within a tender are 'or equivalent' to indicate if a European Standard is not used. Exceptions can be made where the use of a European Standard is not possible owing to national binding rules, such as health and safety, or the European Standard being incompatible, too costly, technical difficulties arising, etc. In such cases reasons must be given in the contract.

Specifications should not refer to proprietary brands but if this is not possible then the appropriate words 'or equivalent' should be inserted after the brand name.

Timescales

There are minimum timescales laid down by the Directives. These are aimed at providing prospective suppliers with sufficient time to respond to notices. Timescales can be reduced for urgent requirements under restricted and negotiated procedures. The reason for the urgency must be stated in the notice. Reducing the timescale is done through an accelerated procedure, which can be challenged by the Commission.

Timescales must be built into projections for contract awards. After a notice has been sent to the *Official Journal of the European Communities* (OJEC), the Department of Trade and Industry (DTI) can alert companies who have shown an interest in tendering. These companies should be sent a copy of the notice. No additional information should be given to these companies.

Under Directive (2001/78/EC), the European Commission has made the use of standard forms for notices to be published mandatory. As the standard forms are complex and time-consuming, it is DTI policy that a web-based software package is used to generate OJEC notices and to transmit them to the OJEC in Luxembourg. Information on this can be obtained through the government internet site.

Framework arrangements and tender procedures are discussed later in this session.

Evaluation criteria

The main criterion is to award the contract to the economically most advantageous bid. Detailed evaluation must be provided within the invitation to tender; this includes quality, experience and resources.

Finance for Purchasers

Good practice information

It is worthwhile noting some good practice points. To improve the procurement process, development of suppliers and future competitiveness, the purchasing organisation should debrief all suppliers so that those who were unsuccessful will understand why they were not selected and failed to win the contract. Experienced professionals should do debriefing and it must be accurate.

We will now look at each of the Directives in turn.

Public Works Directive

This Directive consolidates previous directives on public works contracts. The Directive redefines public words to include those with 50% public funding. The contract value threshold refers to contracts valued at more than specific amounts of European Currency Units (ECUs; now renamed Euros). The threshold is re-assessed every two years.

Two important changes were made relating to the requirement of purchasers. These were:

- to give more notice of construction projects and
- to provide reasons for refusing a contractor's application or bid.

Public Supplies Directive

As with the Public Works Directive, this consolidated all previous directives and set out procedures to be followed where a public body wanted to enter into a contract for the rental, lease, purchase or hire purchase of goods worth more than the specific amount of ECUs. The threshold levels differ depending on whether the contract relates to matters covered by the General Agreement on Tariffs and Trade (GATT) or World Trade Organization (WTO) agreements on government procurement. In this Directive, three types of tender procedure were set out. These tender procedures are, briefly:

- open tender procedure: a procedure when anyone can apply. This procedure is used when the main criteria is lowest price
- restricted tender procedure: where applications have been pre-vetted. This procedure is used where only suppliers who are pre-qualified are invited to make a bid. This is the procedure used for most tenders
- negotiated tender procedure: where contractors are chosen. This procedure is used in certain circumstances only, such as an emergency or in the case of a supplier who must be used again because they have retained some design or intellectual property right.

These tender procedures have been discussed in Legal Aspects in Purchasing and Supply study session 12. We recommend that you return to that session to ensure you understand the different tender procedures.

The Public Supplies Directive included details of the following:

- when each type of tender procedure should be used
- advertising requirements
- time limits
- publication of results

- the use of European standards and technical specifications
- strict award criteria.

Member states are required to report annually on contracts awarded by public bodies in their territory.

Public Services Directive

This covers most contracts that are not classified as public works or supplies. It applies where contracts have a bid value of over a specified number of ECU's. This Directive divides contracts into 'priority' and 'residual' categories with different procedures applying in each case. The Directive is also concerned with contracts relating to:

- advertising services
- computer and maintenance services
- financial services
- transport (except rail)
- some telecommunications
- refuse disposal and sewage
- design contests to award contracts
- defence services unless they fall within national security provisions.

Utilities Directive and Utilities Regulations 2006

The Public Supply Directive does not include public utilities. They were governed by the Excluded Sector Directive 1990, also referred to as the Utilities Directive, which has since been further developed by a new Directive 2004/17/EC. This new Directive came into force on 30 April 2004 and was implemented on 31 January 2006. The Utilities Contracts Regulations 2006 coordinates the procurement of utilities such as energy, water, transport and postal services sectors.

The Utilities Directive is a vast subject area. In developing its policy for the new Directive, the OGC consulted widely including utilities, the Chartered Institute of Purchasing and Supply, Confederation of British Industry, Department for Environment, Food and Rural Affairs, Northern Ireland Office, Heads of Procurement in other government departments, Office of the Deputy Prime Minister, Small Business Service and Trades Union Congress. The full text of the new Utilities Directive (2004/17/EC) is available at EU: http://www.europa.eu.int.

In addition to implementing the new Directive (2004/17/EC), the European Court of Justice (ECJ) ruled in *Alcatel Austria* v *Bundesministerium für Wissenshaft und Verkehr* [C-81/98], known as the 'Alcatel case [1998]', that for procurements caught by the EU Procurement Directives a contract award decision must in all cases be open to review before contract conclusion to enable the award decision to be set aside by a court where an aggrieved bidder has been prejudiced by a breach of the rules, notwithstanding the possibility of damages being awarded after contract conclusion. To comply with this judgment the UK government agreed on a 10-day mandatory standstill period to be introduced in the UK between the communication of award decision and contract conclusion for procurements subject to the EU Directives.

Impact of the new Directive on public sector bodies

The Directive does not impose any burdens on business generally as in the main it clarified, simplified and modernised existing legislation. It was also anticipated that the savings from increased competition and structured procurement would outweigh the costs of compliance. There should be no disproportionate effect on any particular business sectors and public sector bodies in other EU member states as they will all be subject to the rules in the same way.

Compliance Directive (as amended by Services Directive 1992)

This Directive governs compliance with public procurement procedures for public works and supply contracts. It set up a national appeals procedure for infringements. It provided for damages for victims.

The study of EU Directives is challenging as it is not only a vast subject area but always evolving and developing. It is recommended that as a procurement professional you should continue to seek out information from the appropriate government websites.

Self-assessment question 2.2

Describe in short paragraphs the main provisions that are common to all the EU Directives.

You should provide a short paragraph on each of the main provisions as described in the text of this part of the session. This will include short description of each of the following:

- thresholds (supplies, services, works);
- advertisements and prior indicative notices (PIN)
- technical standards and specifications
- timescales
- framework arrangements
- procedures (open, restricted, negotiated)
- evaluation criteria.

Feedback on page 31

2.3 Describe recent developments in CSR and corporate governance

Corporate governance and **CSR** are two fast-developing areas. They both address the way that companies should conduct their business.

Corporate governance

What is corporate governance, and why do we need it?

It is useful to go back to basics. Companies are owned by their shareholders. In many cases, however, the very large number of different shareholders means it is impractical for them to have a direct role in running the business. The task of running the business is therefore delegated to the directors of the company, who have a duty to manage the business in a way that maximises the long-term returns to the shareholders.

Increasingly in recent times, though, directors have been criticised for the way in which they have run companies. There have been some high-profile cases where directors have seemingly put their own interests ahead of those of the wider body of shareholders.

Corporate governance guidelines primarily exist to ensure that, among other things:

- directors are maximising returns to shareholders
- business risk is set at a reasonable level
- no director becomes too dominant
- remuneration of directors is kept within reasonable bounds.

The current UK corporate governance framework has evolved over the past 15 years or so, via a number of different reports. The reports have been named after the chairman of the committee that looked into various aspects of corporate activity, and the first of these was the Cadbury Report (1991).

Cadbury produced a *voluntary* code of best practice. It included guidance on:

- the workings and make-up of boards of directors
- the role of non-executive directors
- the disclosure and nature of executive director remuneration
- internal control reporting
- the establishment of audit committees.

This was followed by the Greenbury Report (1995), which issued a four-part code on directors' remuneration including good practice guidance on:

- the establishment of remuneration committees
- disclosure of executive directors' remuneration
- suitable remuneration policies
- appropriate service contracts.

The Hampel Report (1998) fine-tuned the Cadbury and Greenbury reports, and came up with the following main provisions:

- the chairman and chief executive should be separate roles
- directors' contracts should be one year or less
- remuneration committees should be made up of independent non-executive directors.

The Higgs Report (2003) reviewed the role and effectiveness of non-executive directors, while the Smith Report considered further the role of audit committees.

The Combined Code on Corporate Governance (2003) has built on these, and other, reports to set out standards of good practice in:

- board composition and development
- remuneration

- accountability and audit
- relations with shareholders.

All UK listed companies have to report on how they have applied the Combined Code in their annual report and accounts.

Companies are required to report on how they have applied the broader principles of the Code. They must also confirm that they have complied with the Code's more specific provisions. Where they have not complied with provisions, they must provide an explanation as to why not.

The Combined Code incorporates aspects of the earlier reports mentioned above (the Turnbull guidance on Internal Control, the Smith guidance on Audit Committees and elements of good practice guidance from the Higgs report).

The focus of the above corporate governance initiatives has been UK-based. However, corporate governance has also been developing globally, often in response to local financial scandals that have taken place. The highest profile example has been in the USA, where major scandals such as Enron and Worldcom have prompted a robust response from the US Government and the New York Stock Exchange. The main result has been the Sarbanes-Oxley Act (commonly referred to as 'SOX'). This enforces the independence of external auditors, and reinforces the duties of chief executive officers (CEOs) and chief financial officers (CFOs) by imposing very strict penalties for misrepresenting the financial position of their companies in financial reports.

The Organisation for Economic Co-operation and Development (OECD) has developed and published a non-binding but widely used set of Corporate Governance principles. In 2004 the principles were revised, and they cover the following areas:

- ensuring the basis for an effective corporate governance framework
- the rights of shareholders and key ownership functions
- the equitable treatment of shareholders
- the role of stakeholders in corporate governance
- disclosure and transparency
- the responsibilities of the board.

There is some way to go before genuinely global convergence can take place, but recent developments have been moving in that direction. Some economies clearly have better developed governance frameworks than others, and that can help attract investment. However, the introduction of Sarbanes-Oxley in the USA has resulted in some companies de-listing from US stock markets, to avoid the onerous requirements of that particular piece of legislation.

Corporate social responsibility

What is corporate social responsibility (CSR) and why do we need it?

While much of the emphasis of corporate governance is on shareholders and their needs, it must also be recognised that the duties and responsibilities of a company go far beyond keeping that one particular group happy.

Formally, of course, shareholders own companies and provide capital for them. They are important, and their rights have to be protected.

There are, however, many other parties who have an interest in the activities of a business. This interest can be large or small, it can be direct or indirect, and it can be financial or non-financial. These interested parties are often referred to collectively as 'stakeholders'.

Examples of stakeholders include:

- customers
- suppliers
- government
- employees/potential recruits
- retirees
- local residents
- environmental groups
- lenders and bondholders
- regulators.

Shareholders are 'stakeholders' too, but the point is that they are only one of a number of interested parties. And stakeholders are taking an increasing interest in the activities of companies, and want to be assured that the company is managing its operations in a socially responsible way.

Learning activity 2.3

Select a company of which you have some prior knowledge. Visit their website and explore their CSR policies. Most large companies will have a separate CSR area, and the annual report and accounts should also report CSR activities.

To what extent might there be a commercial justification for the policies in place?

Feedback on page 32

The focus of a company's external reporting has traditionally been financial. This is something that we considered in study session 1 when we discussed financial accounting, and is something we will return to when we look at the content of financial reports.

Given the wide range of other types of stakeholder, we need to consider two questions. What is a company's responsibility to these stakeholders, and how should these responsibilities be reported?

One way of looking at this issue is to consider what it is that drives the CSR initiatives of an organisation. The following list highlights what are sometimes referred to as the 'Top Ten Drivers for CSR':

1 reputation and trust
2 values
3 the environment (climate change, pollution, resource use)

4 health and well-being (disease, malnutrition, quality of life)
5 population and demographics (affluence, education, consumer trends)
6 human rights and diversity (labour standards, working conditions)
7 transparency and accountability (reporting and engagement)
8 governance (leadership, function of the board)
9 shareholder activism and pressure groups
10 regulation.

Social responsibility, and the need to report it, might for some companies begin and end with what the law requires them to do. Some stakeholders can exert significant power, however, and companies may therefore see it as commercially sensible to respond to the needs and interests of such stakeholders.

A useful grid is set out in figure 2.1, which plots the power of stakeholders against the extent to which they have an active interest in the activities of a company. The boxes contain what the company's likely approach will be in different circumstances.

For example, if a stakeholder has neither power nor interest, there is little a company needs to do other than monitor the situation. On the other hand, if the stakeholder is powerful and is taking an active interest, then clearly their needs need to be closely managed.

Figure 2.1: The stakeholder power/interest matrix

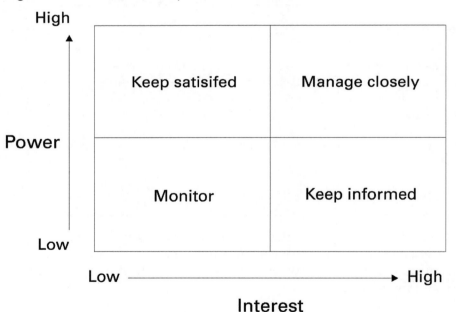

It would not be possible to set out a list of all the potential content areas that could be included within corporate social responsibility. Many models and frameworks exist in this area, and one can usefully categorise the various areas of CSR under four broad headings:

- community
- environment
- marketplace
- workplace.

2 Assessing the impact of external factors

Within these four areas, all sorts of different issues and initiatives may emerge (see table 2.5 for some examples). No two companies are identical, and each business will therefore have its unique set of needs and priorities in the CSR arena.

Table 2.5

	Community	Environment	Marketplace	Workplace
Description	Relationship between business and society	Responsible management of activities that impact on the environment	Maintaining high standards when developing, purchasing and selling products and services	Creating a responsible and fulfilling work environment
Examples	Sponsorship of local education initiatives Charitable donations	Reducing harmful emissions Recycling old equipment	Screening suppliers based on CSR record Customer health and safety initiatives	Diverse workforce initiatives Employee training

Self-assessment question 2.3

Take as an example a company (ideally a supplier) with whose activities you are familiar.

Draft a report outlining suggestions of five key CSR criteria that the supplier should meet before being shortlisted. Describe why you believe the criteria should be met, and whether at present the chosen supplier does meet your selected criteria at the present time.

Feedback on page 32

Revision question

Now try the revision question for this session on page 345.

Summary

This session has looked at various ways in which organisations interact with a changing external world.

We first looked at the more general external environment, and how it might impact on an organisation. In particular, we considered the impact of major macro-economic variables such as interest rates, economic growth and inflation.

We then turned our attention to more specific external influences including regulatory developments in the procurement field, in particular EU Procurement Directives.

Finance for Purchasers

In recent years, organisations have been paying ever more attention to the need for improved corporate governance and corporate social responsibility reporting. This session has outlined the background to and recent development in these aspects of corporate reporting

Suggested further reading

Holmes, G, A Sugden and P Gee (2004) *Interpreting Company Reports and Accounts*, 9th edition, chapter 26. Harlow: FT Prentice Hall.

Feedback on learning activities and self-assessment questions

Feedback on learning activity 2.1

All the above will have an impact on BA's profitability, although some of them are interlinked. Inflation is likely to increase the company's costs, although the term 'inflation' is a generic one and what will concern BA will be price inflation of those items to which it is most exposed (especially oil, which links to the commodity prices question). General inflation will, however, impact on salary expectations of staff.

Interest rate movements will impact BA in various ways. Most directly, it will increase its cost of borrowing. Even if it is borrowing mainly at fixed rates, these borrowings will mature and need to be replaced at prevailing rates. Rising interest rates will also impact on the ability of consumers and businesses to spend, and so could impact on demand for flights. Interest rates will also partially drive exchange rates, which will have a direct impact on BA as an international business.

Like interest rates, tax rates will impact on business and consumer disposable income, as well as having a direct influence on how much tax BA has to pay out of its profits. Specific tax changes can have more direct impact – for example, changes to the scope of insurance and airport taxes. GDP growth reflects the rate of growth in the economy as a whole. A good growth rate signals growing business activity, which is likely to lead to more demand for air travel.

The main commodity prices that BA will be interested in will be the oil price. Recent increases in the price have led BA to add a surcharge to their fares. The company will also need to protect itself against the risk of further adverse price movements.

Feedback on self-assessment question 2.1

A small amount of inflation is deemed to be good for an economy. *This is true. Zero inflation or, even worse, deflation tends to curtail economic activity. Why buy something now if the price will be lower in the future?*

The UK government is responsible for managing the economy, so it decides on what interest rates should be. *Technically this is false. The UK government is responsible for managing the economy, but its decisions about interest rates are*

2 Assessing the impact of external factors

made by the Bank of England's Monetary Policy Committee. They do set rates, however, in response to a government set inflation target.

An accepted way of reducing inflation is to reduce interest rates. _False – the opposite is the case. Increasing interest rates reduces demand, which tends to slow down price increases._

An increase in interest rates tends to be good news for exporters, because it boosts their local currency. _This is false. An increase in local interest rates will attract investment into that currency, putting its relative price up. That will therefore make exports more expensive for overseas buyers who may therefore buy from elsewhere._

Feedback on learning activity 2.2

This learning activity is firstly to get you used to looking outside your organisation for threshold information and not just relying on internal information. This is necessary as the threshold levels are reviewed regularly. You should then show the levels as you have identified them to be in each of the following areas: the levels at 31 January 2006 are shown in table 2.4.

Table 2.4

	Supplies	Services	Works
Central government bodies subject to the World Trade Organization (WTO) and Government Procurement Agreement (GPA)	£93,738 or €137,000	£93,738[1] or €137,000	£3,611,319[2] or €5,278,000
Other public sector contracting authorities	£144,371 or €211,000	£144,371 or €211,000	£3,611,319[2] or €5,278,000
Indicative notices	£513,166 or €750,000	£513,166 or €750,000	£3,611,319[2] or €5,278,000
Small lots	£54,738 or €80,000	£54,738 or €80,000	£684,211 or €1,000,000

[1]With the exception of the following services that have a threshold of £144,371 (€211,000):

- Part B (residual) services.
- Research and development services – category 8.
- Telecommunications services – category 5, that is, TV and radio, interconnection, integrated telecommunications.
- Subsidised services contracts under regulation 34.

[2]Includes subsidised services contracts under regulation 34.

Utilities are not included in this learning activity, but information on thresholds is available on the government website.

Feedback on self-assessment question 2.2

Check your response against the summaries and descriptions given earlier in the session.

Feedback on learning activity 2.3

While most large organisations adopt CSR policies, and report their activities in these fields, there is a danger that they are perceived to be merely paying lip service to initiatives that are currently popular.

There is clearly, though, benefit to be derived from adopting policies that are in line with stakeholders' expectations. Stakeholders' best interests need to be a priority – especially those high-power, high-interest stakeholders – otherwise simply carrying out the business is going to be difficult. For example, given that an increasing number of organisations are selecting and monitoring their suppliers against CSR criteria, it is ever more important to be able to demonstrate a serious and comprehensive approach to CSR issues.

Although difficult to quantify in terms of financial benefits, especially on a shorter term basis, many CSR initiatives should improve longer term profitability and in practice, many elements of CSR will go through a business case appraisal before being implemented.

Feedback on self-assessment question 2.3

There is no right answer to this exercise, but – using the community, environment, marketplace and workplace headings as illustrated above – it might be that environment and marketplace aspects are given a higher priority than the workplace and (especially) community ones.

Study session 3

Finance and accounting terminology

Introduction

Accounting standards have existed for many years, and guide the way in which financial reporting is carried out throughout the world. The standards environment has, however, experienced much change in recent years. In the UK many new standards have been introduced to meet the needs of a changing business environment. Additionally, the move towards a global set of international standards has made significant progress. This session looks at the background to accounting standards, and outlines the significant recent developments.

Session learning objectives

After completing this session you should be able to:

3.1 Explain accounting standards and their role.
3.2 Give examples of international issues in accounting standards.
3.3 Demonstrate the effects of the convergence of accounting standards and practices.

Unit content coverage

This study session covers the following topics from the official CIPS unit content document:

Learning objective

1.3 Understand and use the terminology associated with finance and accounting.
- Accounting standards and their role
- International issues in accounting standards
- Effects of the convergence of accounting standards and practices

Prior knowledge

Study sessions 1 and 2.

Resources

Suggested websites:

- ACCA IFRS information: http://www.accaglobal.com/ifrs
- IFRS: http://www.ifrs.co.uk

'International Financial Reporting Standards were adopted across the EU on 1 January 2006 and are now required or permitted in nearly 100 countries. The US and Japan are seeking to narrow differences between their standards and IFRS, and China will adopt an accounting system based on IFRS next year.' (*Financial Times*) The move to IFRS continues to be controversial, and meet opposition in some quarters. But the rate of adoption – as highlighted above – suggests that they are here to stay.

Finance for Purchasers

- FT.com: http://www.ft.com/indepth/accountingstandards (may require subscription)
- The International Accounting Standards Board: http://www.iasb.org/standards/summaries.asp
- The Accounting Standards Board: http://www.frc.org.uk/asb/
- It is also worth visiting corporate websites and viewing recently published annual reports which, for EU listed companies, are likely to include commentary on the switch to IFRS.
- Holmes, G, Sugden, A and Gee, P (2005) *Interpreting Company Reports and Accounts*, 9th edition. Harlow: FT/Prentice Hall.

Timing

You should set aside about 5 hours to read and complete this session, including learning activities, self-assessment questions, the suggested further reading (if any) from the essential textbook for this unit and the revision question.

3.1 Accounting standards and their role

The background

As outlined in the previous session, companies are required by law to prepare and publish their accounts. This is a requirement of the Companies Act 1985.

Two aspects of this are key to understanding the content of a set of company accounts. First, the Companies Act determines what the accounts should contain, and in what form they should be presented. Second, the Act requires that the accounts comply with **accounting standards** as issued by a regulatory body for the accounting profession.

Within the UK, accounting standards are now known as Financial Reporting Standards (FRSs), and have been produced since 1990 by the Accounting Standards Board (ASB). Prior to 1990 the standards were known as SSAPs (Statements of Standard Accounting Practice), and in fact the current body of UK accounting standards consists of a mix of the older SSAPs that have stood the test of time, and the newer FRSs which have been introduced since 1990.

The Accounting Standards Board sits within the Financial Reporting Council, which independently oversees the regulatory framework for UK accounting. The regulatory framework for accounting in the UK has evolved over many years, and consists of many regulations – some statutory, some mandatory and some merely statements of best practice.

The standards-related aspects of the Council's activities are set out in figure 3.1.

Figure 3.1: Structure of standards-related activities

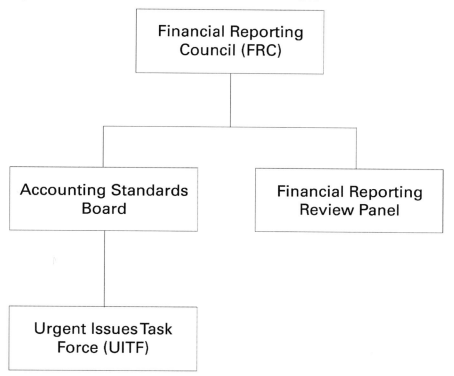

The FRC oversees the standard-setting process, and ensures that the process is carried out efficiently and economically. The ASB is the organisation that actually sets the standards. It has done so at the same time as developing a set of *principles*. These principles, alongside a changing business environment, have directed the development of new standards and the amendment of existing ones.

The UITF separately looks at urgent issues that are not covered by existing standards. Its aim is to assist the ASB in developing good standards and best practice in financial reporting.

The role of the Review Panel is to ensure that companies are preparing their accounts in line with applicable standards. It does not itself actually monitor companies, but will look into cases that are drawn to its attention. This reactive, as opposed to proactive, approach has met with criticism.

Other roles of the FRC not included in the above diagram include the Auditing Practices Board, the Professional Oversight Board for Accountancy, and the Accountancy Investigation and Disciplinary Board.

The 'principles' approach referred to above is important, and it is an aspect of standard-setting that distinguishes the UK from other accounting regimes, particularly the USA. The ASB has drawn up a 'Statement of Principles' which is at the heart of current UK standards. Any new standards, or any revision to existing standards, will be driven by the principles.

Different chapters in the Statement of Principles cover:

- *The objectives of financial statements*, this is, that they are mainly about reporting on the financial performance and financial status of the organisation in question.

Finance for Purchasers

- *The reporting entity*, which highlights the fact that the accounts may cover the activities of a single company or a group of companies – and in the latter case what are known as 'consolidated accounts' have to be prepared.
- *The qualitative characteristics of financial information*, highlighting the fact that for financial information to be useful it needs to be:
    - relevant
    - reliable
    - comparable
    - understandable.
- *The elements of financial statements* – that is, what they should contain. In particular, there is guidance on how the following are defined and how they should be presented:
    - assets
    - liabilities
    - ownership interest
    - gains
    - losses.
- *Recognition in financial statements*, which considers how and when transactions should be recognised.
- *Measurement in financial statements*, which describes how, for example, assets should be valued in the accounts.
- *Presentation of financial information*, which highlights the need for simple and concise presentation, without compromising reliability or relevance.
- *Accounting for interests in other entities*, which is about how to deal with situations where one company has control or influence over another. Much depends here on how much influence or control exists – the extent will determine the way in which financial results are reported and presented.

Learning activity 3.1

Consider the 'qualitative characteristics' of financial information from a purchaser's point of view. When looking at the accounts of a potential supplier, identify how each of the characteristics might play a part in rendering the accounts useful.

The four characteristics are:

- relevance
- reliability
- comparability
- understandability.

Feedback on page 41

This statement of principles is not, itself, an accounting standard. It serves to influence and guide the development of new standards, and the revision of existing ones. The IASB uses a similar document to underpin its own standards, the *Framework for the Preparation and Presentation of Financial Statements*.

The ASB/IASB approach contrasts with the American one, which is 'rules-based', and this difference in approach is currently seen as a potential stumbling block in the move towards full global harmonisation. The Federal Accounting Standards Board is the US standard setter. US standards are more numerous and more detailed and prescriptive than their UK/International counterparts.

However, the benefits of a genuinely global set of standards are potentially very significant. Users of accounts would be able to compare any company with another, regardless of their domicile. And the companies themselves would only have to publish one set of figures – something that is not always the case at present, as they have to, for example, submit accounts that follow different standards to meet stock market listing requirements in different countries.

Another direct link concerns the fact that the ASB is conducting a phased replacement of existing UK standards with new standards that are aligned with existing international standards. So, although some UK companies – typically the larger ones, listed on the Stock Market – now report using international standards, while others still apply UK standards, the differences between the two should reduce over time.

For non-expert users of accounts, one very noticeable difference that has arisen from the switch to IFRS concerns layout and terminology. We will look at this in more detail when examining individual financial statements in the next chapter.

Key differences include the use of the term 'income statement' (as opposed to 'profit and loss account'). Other significant terminology differences include the following:

UK term	IAS term
Fixed assets	Non-current assets
Stock	Inventories
Debtors	Receivables
Creditors	Payables

The layout of the statements is also slightly different, and this is a topic that will be explored in more detail in study session 5.

The scope of this course does not include detailed coverage of individual accounting standards. However, students may find it useful to visit the websites of the ASB and the IASB, which both contain a large amount of useful information, including summaries of all the current accounting standards.

Self-assessment question 3.1

1   Who is responsible for accounting standards in the UK? Is it

(continued on next page)

Finance for Purchasers

> **Self-assessment question 3.1** *(continued)*
> - (a) the Financial Reporting Council
> - (b) the Institute of Chartered Accountants
> - (c) the Accounting Standards Board
> - (d) the Financial Reporting Review Panel.
> 2 True or false. International Accounting Standards:
>   - (a) Follow a 'rules-based' approach to accounting standards: true/false
>   - (b) Are mandatory throughout the world: true/false
>   - (c) Are mandatory throughout the EU: true/false
>   - (d) Have superseded UK GAAP: true/false.
>
> *Feedback on page 41*

3.2 International issues in accounting standards

Historically, just as the UK has had its own standards, so have many other countries – for example the Federal Accounting Standards Board produces accounting standards for the US. As a first step towards global standards, the International Accounting Standards Committee was set up in 1973, and began to develop a set of International Accounting Standards (IASs).

> **Learning activity 3.2**
>
> What do you consider to be the main benefits of having a uniform set of accounting standards around the world? Why do you think such a situation does not yet exist?
>
> *Feedback on page 41*

Over the years, many countries adopted these standards – or, at least, used them as the basis for developing their own standards – and the International Accounting Standards Board ('IASB') was set up in 2001 to develop the harmonisation process further. As well as adopting the IASs in existence, the IASB is responsible for developing and issuing new international standards. These are known as International Financial Reporting Standards (IFRS).

The first IFRS was IFRS1 – 'The First Time Adoption of International Reporting Standards'. This standard was directly linked to the decision that all listed companies in the European Union should, for financial periods ending after 1 January 2005, prepare their financial statements in accordance with International Accounting Standards.

It is too early to judge the full impact of the switch to International Standards, although a commonly held view is that once users become familiar with the changes, the switch will be seen as having been worthwhile. They are certainly here to stay and are already in use in over 100 different countries.

There are differences between UK and International Standards, although it is not within the scope of this book to get into the detail of individual standards. The underlying principles are very similar, and the way most transactions are treated is identical. A comparison of UK GAAP and IFRS can be found on page 259 of Holmes et al (2005).

The most important single innovation of IFRS is to move away from historical cost principles. Whereas companies used, in most cases, to value their long-term assets at their historical cost less depreciation (something we will specifically looking at in later chapters), they now have the option to value their long-term assets based on their original cost or alternatively at 'fair value', a concept similar to market value.

A major area of contention is linked to this. International standards require that changes in 'fair value' are included in the calculation of profit. This gives rise to concerns about volatility and misleading reporting of profits – particularly when revaluing items such as financial derivatives.

More general concerns include the idea that IFRS accounts are just too complex for the non-expert user.

One important area of common ground is that both the Accounting Standards Board in the UK and the London-based International Accounting Standards Board adopt a 'principles-based' approach to standard-setting. As highlighted earlier in this session, this means that the standards themselves are more open to interpretation, but are underpinned by a set of agreed principles which should be followed.

The principles that underpin the ASB's standard-setting are very similar to those used by the IASB.

Self-assessment question 3.2

Which one of the following statements correctly describes the primary role of the International Accounting Standards Board?

1   Reviewing Financial Reporting Standards for international acceptance.
2   Identifying problems in international application of Financial Reporting Standards.
3   Issuing accounting standards for international application.
4   Converting financial statements from UK GAAP to International GAAP.

Feedback on page 41

3.3   The effects of the convergence of accounting standards and practices

There have been many recent developments in the field of accounting standards, with the ultimate objective of a harmonised set of global accounting standards. Proponents of such standards believe that, in an increasingly global economy, a single set of standards is essential. How can

Finance for Purchasers

one compare the performance of different global organisations, if their accounts are drawn up using different rules?

Learning activity 3.3

Carry out some research into accounting standards. Identify one area of accounting that is covered by a standard and establish:

- how the issue is treated by current UK standards
- how the issue is treated by IAS
- how it might be of relevance to purchasers.

Feedback on page 42

Self-assessment question 3.3

'In five years' time you'll find US accounts and international accounts are almost identical.'

List three key reasons why those involved in international purchasing activity would benefit from accounts that are 'almost identical' across the world.

Suggest three potential stumbling blocks to the achievement of this goal.

Feedback on page 42

Revision question

Now try the revision question for this session on page 345.

Summary

This session has looked at the background to accounting standards, and how they fit into the overall regulatory framework in the UK. The session has also outlined the significant recent developments and some different approaches to standard-setting. It is a fast-changing environment, with further major developments expected in the future, including progress towards a fully global set of standards.

Suggested further reading

Black, G (2003) *Students' Guide to Accounting and Financial Reporting Standards*, 8th edition. Harlow: FT Prentice Hall.

Elliot, BJ and J Elliot (2005) *Financial Accounting and Reporting*, 7th edition. Harlow: FT Prentice Hall.

Holmes, G, A Sugden and P Gee (2004) *Interpreting Company Reports and Accounts*, 9th edition. Harlow: FT Prentice Hall.

Feedback on learning activities and self-assessment questions

Feedback on learning activity 3.1

The four characteristics are important from a purchasers' point of view when it comes to reviewing a supplier's accounts.

The data will be relevant if it is able to influence economic decisions – for example a decision regarding a potential supplier. Timeliness is an issue here – the information should be available within a sensible time period. The more time that has elapsed since the events described by the figures, the less relevant the data becomes.

That the data is reliable is essential, if it is to form the basis of an important decision about awarding or continuing with a major contract. Comparability is also key – the data provided by one supplier needs to be directly comparable with that provided by another – if not, drawing meaningful conclusions will be difficult. Understandability is also important, and the idea is that accounts are understandable to someone with a reasonable knowledge of business and accounting.

Feedback on self-assessment question 3.1

1   Who is responsible for accounting standards in the UK? The answer is (c).
2
   (a)   False – the approach is more principles-based.
   (b)   False – though adoption is becoming widespread.
   (c)   False – though they are now mandatory for listed companies in Europe.
   (d)   False – UK GAAP still exists, although new standards will fall in line with IFRS.

Feedback on learning activity 3.2

The main benefit would be the ability to compare one company with another using the same set of rules. At present, comparing a US company with a European one can be difficult, as the application of different standards can result in key differences in apparent performance.

The situation does not yet exist partly because harmonisation of various well-established sets of standards is fraught with potential difficulties. There are also strongly held views about whether IFRS represents an improvement to existing standards. While the EU is making the transition, the US has so far not done so.

Feedback on self-assessment question 3.2

The correct answer is 3.

Feedback on learning activity 3.3

Your research here could have covered any number of areas. You might, for example, have looked at the way assets are valued as this is a particularly thorny area, with the more frequent use of 'fair value' accounting under IAS causing some concern. Alternatively, you might have selected an area where the differences are minimal – for example accounting for R&D, which we shall be looking at in the next session, but for which the accounting treatment remains broadly unchanged.

The detail of individual standards is outside the scope of this syllabus for this course, but an awareness of some of the related issues is useful background knowledge.

Feedback on self-assessment question 3.3

Purchasing activity, and especially international purchasing activity would benefit from having one set of rules:

- It would allow them to make better comparisons between companies.
- It would requite them only to be familiar with one set of rules.
- It would make assessing accounts easier – at present some companies have to present different sets of accounts to describe the same business.

Potential stumbling blocks include:

- The principles v rules issues described above.
- The practical difficulties of carrying out such a major change.
- Resistance to more change following the recent switch to IFRS.

Study session 4
Capital v expense items

Introduction

Whenever a company incurs expenditure, it is classified as either 'capital' expenditure, or else treated as an 'expense' (also known as 'revenue' expenditure).

The distinction is important, as it directly impacts on how much profit a business reports, and the value of its assets. This in turn can influence a company's perceived financial status, so the correct treatment of expenditure is vital if financial results are to be meaningful.

This session will start by looking at capital expenditure, and will also illustrate how depreciation works. It will then consider revenue expenditure, and finally illustrate why the distinction between the two is important.

A US company recently over-reported its profits to the tune of more than $3 billion – having wrongly categorised 'revenue expenses' items as 'capital'. The distinction between the two types of expenditure is an important facet of profit reporting, but is not always straightforward.

Session learning objectives

After completing this session you should be able to:

4.1 Give examples of capital expenditure, and explain the implications of categorising an item as capital.
4.2 Give examples of expense items, and explain the implications of categorising an item as an expense.
4.3 Describe the difference between capital and expense items, and why the difference is important.

Unit content coverage

This study session covers the following topics from the official CIPS unit content document:

Learning objective

1.4 Identify which goods and services can be categorised as capital and which will be expense items.
   • Capital items – plant and equipment , building vehicles, high value office equipment, construction
   • Expense items – cleaning materials, stationery, office suppliers, consumables, cleaning services, services contracts

Prior knowledge

Study sessions 1 to 3.

Finance for Purchasers

Timing

You should set aside about 4 hours to read and complete this session, including learning activities, self-assessment questions, the suggested further reading (if any) from the essential textbook for this unit and the revision question.

4.1 Capital expenditure and the impact of depreciation

Capital expenditure essentially relates to longer-term investment. As a general rule, if expenditure is likely to be of benefit in more than one accounting period, it should be classed as capital. There are, though, other likely attributes of capital expenditure:

- It is likely to involve a large amount.
- Its benefits will be spread over a number of years.
- It is likely to be linked to an organisation's longer-term goals.

Investment is a necessity if a company wants to grow, and if the existing assets base is not replaced or enhanced, growth is unlikely to be achievable.

An important financial term to be aware of at this stage is 'fixed asset'. The word 'asset' in a financial context describes something that a company owns. A 'fixed asset' is something that a company owns, and is using, on a long-term basis. 'Long-term' is usually understood to mean more than one year.

It is also worth pointing out at that companies preparing their accounts under IFRS will use the term 'non-current asset' instead of 'fixed asset'. Whatever the term used, however, fixed assets can be found in a company's balance sheet – something we will look at in detail in study session 6.

In summary, money spent on acquiring new fixed assets, or enhancing existing ones, is classed as capital expenditure.

All other expenditure is money spent on items from which no ongoing longer-term value is derived. This is classed as revenue expenditure, or simply termed as 'expensed' items.

The distinction is crucially important when it comes to working out how much profit has been achieved in a given period.

If an item is treated as revenue, or 'expensed' as it is sometimes referred, then it is charged against profits at the time the expenditure is incurred.

If, however, the item in question is being treated as capital expenditure, then the expenditure will not be deducted from profits in the year it is incurred – or at least not all of it. The cost will be spread over a number of years via a concept known as depreciation.

The number of years will normally relate to the expected life of the asset being bought. This spreading of the expenditure is known as **depreciation**, and is a measure of the loss in value of an asset due to use, the passage of time or obsolescence.

Different types of depreciation

There are several different types of depreciation. The two most commonly used are:

- straight-line depreciation
- reducing balance depreciation.

For straight-line depreciation, a company must decide what the expected useful life of the asset will be, and also what it is likely to be worth at the end of that useful life.

For example, a company might acquire some equipment for £235,000. The expected useful life of the equipment is five years, after which time the company expects to be able to sell the asset for £55,000.

The annual depreciation charge over the next five years will be as shown in table 4.1.

Table 4.1

Cost of asset	£235,000
Residual value	£55,000
Depreciable amount	£180,000
Expected useful life	5 years
Annual depreciation charge	£180,000/= £36,000

An amount of £36,000 will therefore be recorded as an expense each year for the next five years, and will therefore reduce the reported profit by the same amount. Additionally, the asset value shown on the balance sheet will reduce by the same amount:

- balance sheet value at purchase £235,000
- balance sheet value after 1 year £199,000
- balance sheet value after 2 years £163,000

and so on.

The main alternative to the above method is known as 'reducing balance' depreciation. Here, we also start with the capital cost of £235,000, but we do not need to concern ourselves with any estimate of a residual value. Instead, we reduce the asset value by a certain percentage each year. Let us say, for this example, that a reducing balance charge of 25% is appropriate:

Table 4.2

Cost of asset	235,000
Year 1 depreciation	58,750
Net book value after 1 year	176,250
Year 2 depreciation	44,063
Net book value after 2 years	132,188
Year 3 depreciation	33,047
Net book value after 3 years	99,141
Year 4 depreciation	24,785
Net book value after 4 years	74,355
Year 5 depreciation	18,589
Net book value after 5 years	55,767

Finance for Purchasers

You will see in table 4.2 that a different amount of depreciation is charged each year, and that it is more heavily loaded towards the earlier years. This may be particularly logical if a company gets more use out of an asset in its earlier years of use – a common scenario. The first year's depreciation is £58,750, but by year 5 the charge has fallen to under £20,000.

There are other methods of depreciation which also build in higher levels of depreciation in earlier years. The **sum of the years' digits** would, using the depreciable amount from the above straight-line example, involve adding up the digits of each of the eight years – so:

$5 + 4 + 3 + 2 + 1 = 15$

The first year's depreciation would be $5/15 \times £180,000 = £60,000$

The fifth and final year's depreciation would be $1/15 \times £180,000 = £12,000$

There are no actual rules for depreciation, and what a company's depreciation policy should be. There is a need, however, for a company's accounts to be independently audited. The auditor must sign off the accounts on the basis that they represent a 'true and fair view' of the company – and clearly an unrealistic depreciation policy would undermine such a view.

Figure 4.1 shows an extract from the most recently published accounts of a major packaging company, Rexam, showing a very typical outline of a depreciation policy:

Figure 4.1: Rexam depreciation policy

Freehold land and buildings are not depreciated. For all other property, plant and equipment, depreciation is calculated on a straight line basis to allocate cost less residual values of the assets over their estimated useful lives as follows.

Freehold buildings	Up to 50 years
Leasehold buildings	Shorter of 50 years or lease term
Manufacturing machinery	7 to 17 years
Furnaces in glassworks	Up to 12 years
Computer hardware	Up to 8 years
Fixtures, fitting and vehicles	4 to 10 years

Residual values and useful lives are reviewed at each financial year end.

Source: Rexam Plc Annual Report 2005

Learning activity 4.1

Identify some recent major capital item expenditure in your own organisation.

Establish why, with reference to the study material, it is a capital item.

(continued on next page)

4 Capital v expense items

Learning activity 4.1 *(continued)*

Over what period and by what method is the asset being depreciated in the accounts?

Feedback on page 52

Self-assessment question 4.1

A company buys new equipment costing £500,000.

Calculate in table 4.3 the annual depreciation and the balance sheet value at the end of the year for the next four years using straight-line depreciation. The equipment has an expected life of four years, and a residual value £120,000.

Table 4.3

	Opening balance	Year's depreciation deducted from profits	Closing balance ('NBV')
Year 1			
Year 2			
Year 3			
Year 4			

Recalculate in table 4.4 using reducing balance depreciation, 30%

Table 4.4

	Opening balance	Year's depreciation deducted from profits	Closing balance (NBV)
Year 1			
Year 2			
Year 3			
Year 4			

Feedback on page 52

4.2 Expense items and their impact on profitability.

We have so far concentrated on capital items, and the way they are treated. Expense items are a lot more straightforward, in that their costs are deducted from the profit and loss account at the time they are incurred (see table 4.8).

Table 4.8

	Revenue expenditure ('expense')	Capital expenditure
Definition	Spending on assets that are used up or 'consumed' within the financial year	Spending (acquiring or improving) on assets being used on a long-term basis
Examples	Buying materials	Buying equipment

(continued on next page)

Finance for Purchasers

Table 4.8 *(continued)*

	Revenue expenditure ('expense')	Capital expenditure
	Hiring a car	Buying a car
	Maintaining a power station	Building a power station
Effect on financial statements	Included in P&L in the period incurred	Value of asset shown in balance sheet, at cost less depreciation to date. Depreciation of asset included in P&L.
Potential impact on profit	Unless controlled, can have a direct bearing on profitability	Profits only impacted via depreciation – but investment is necessary for longer term profitability.

Learning activity 4.2

Identify three circumstances in which the purchase of exactly the same item could be treated as:

1 a capital purchase and
2 an expense – depending on the nature of the business, and the use to which the item will be put.

Feedback on page 53

Examples of areas where the capital v revenue distinction can be a little blurred include:

Finance costs

Finance costs *can* be capitalised where the interest can be specifically linked to a project that is expected to generate revenue in the future. The interest costs involved, for example, while constructing an asset such as a major building can be included in the capital cost of the asset, and then depreciated once the building is completed (even if it is not yet operational).

R&D

The rules on the treatment of research and development expenditure are quite rigid. While many would naturally view R&D expenditure as an investment, it can only be classified as such in certain clearly defined circumstances.

Broadly speaking, all **research** costs have to be expensed. **Development** costs can be capitalised (that is to say, treated as a fixed asset) but only if certain criteria have been met. These are:

- There is a clearly defined project.
- The project expenditure is separately identifiable.
- There is reasonable certainty about the project's feasibility and viability.
- Revenues earned from the project will exceed its costs.

4 Capital v expense items

- Resources are in place to enable the project to be completed.

All the above criteria have to be met for the expenditure to be treated as capital.

Leasing

With leases, it depends on the nature of the lease. Accountants will classify a lease as one of the following:

- finance lease
- operating lease.

A finance lease is one where the lessee has use of the asset for most of its life, and therefore bears the risks and enjoys the benefits of the asset as if they actually owned it. An operating lease tends to be shorter term, and would describe a situation where a particular asset would be leased by a number of different lessees over a period of years.

Accounting for leases is quite complex, but in essence a finance lease is treated as if it were a capital asset, whereas an operating lease is effectively treated as an expense.

Marketing/advertising

One might argue that certain marketing and advertising initiatives should be deemed investment. For example, money spent on advertising to create brand awareness might logically fit the investment description. However, under current UK and international accounting regimes, such expenditure should not be treated in this way – or at least not in the first instance. If subsequently either a brand, or a company that has invested in such brands, gets sold, then an 'intangible' fixed asset may be created and its value then depreciated.

Self-assessment question 4.2

List the circumstances in which purchased items should be treated as (a) capital and (b) expense.

- staff costs
- interest costs
- developing a new drug
- leasing costs
- purchase of IT equipment.

Feedback on page 53

4.3 Why the difference between capital and revenue is important

We have so far looked at the difference between capital and expense items, considered how they are treated, and explored some areas where appropriate classification can be difficult.

Finance for Purchasers

It would be useful here to demonstrate, using some figures, exactly why the distinction is important.

To take the example used in section 4.1 a stage further, let us consider the impact on profitability if the £235,000 expenditure was treated as 'capital', but also if it was treated as revenue. Let us assume that the company, before accounting for this £235,000 investment, made annual profits shown in table 4.9.

Table 4.9

	Year 1	Year 2	Year 3	Year 4	Year 5
Profit before £235,000 purchase	100,000	120,000	140,000	160,000	180,000

How would the profit position look if Coyx was able to treat the £235K item as capital, and used the straight-line method as illustrated above, with annual depreciation of £36,000? It would look like table 4.10.

Table 4.10

	Year 1	Year 2	Year 3	Year 4	Year 5
Profit before £235,000 purchase	100,000	120,000	140,000	160,000	180,000
Depreciation	(36,000)	(36,000)	(36,000)	(36,000)	(36,000)
Net profit	64,000	84,000	104,000	124,000	144,000

This shows the profits reduced by the additional annual depreciation charge, but still showing a gradual improvement over the five-year period. If, however, the item had been treated as revenue, the profit stream would look very different (see table 4.11).

Table 4.11

	Year 1	Year 2	Year 3	Year 4	Year 5
Profit before £235,000 purchase	100,000	120,000	140,000	160,000	180,000
Additional revenue expenditure	(235,000)	0	0	0	0
Net profit	(135,000)	120,000	140,000	160,000	180,000

One additional point worth making at this stage is that the figures above – where the item is treated as revenue expenditure – also broadly reflect the cash flow movements in the business. We will be looking at cash flow statements in study session 5, and cash budgets in study session 12.

Learning activity 4.3

Read this extract from the BBC website following the collapse of the US telecoms company, MCI Worldcom:

> WorldCom's dodge was relatively simple. In 2001 and 2002 the company pretended that $3.8bn (£2.5bn) in normal operating expenses – in fact, routine maintenance – qualified as investment.

That allowed the company to spread the cost over a number of years, instead of having to account for it all at once. Unsurprisingly, that made its profits

(continued on next page)

Learning activity 4.3 *(continued)*

look much, much better than they were. It also artificially inflated the company's value.

> It is as if a company pretended its outlay on paperclips and stationery – necessary, certainly, but by no means adding value – was in fact used to buy new equipment or build a new factory.

So instead of making a $1.3 billion profit in 2001, WorldCom was deeply in the red.

Discussion questions

What safeguards should have stopped the above happening?

As well as boosting profits, the actions taken by Worldcom 'artificially inflated the company's value'. Why would this be?

How would the above have affected the cash position of the company?

Feedback on page 54

One aspect of the capital v expense topic that we have not considered yet is taxation. In the UK tax is levied on profits that companies make. It might therefore seem possible for a company, by choosing the way it treats its expenditure, to manipulate its profits and therefore its tax bill.

It is important to note, therefore, that depreciation is not itself a tax-deductible expense. The amount of depreciation charged, therefore, will not affect the company's tax bill. Instead, the tax authorities will apply their own rules for the acquisition of assets and grant a company what are called tax allowances. This means that the company can offset the cost of fixed assets against their tax bill, but can only do so using the rules provided by the Inland Revenue.

While the calculations are often similar to the reducing method approach described earlier, the government will sometimes change the rates and time periods to encourage or discourage certain types of expenditure. It may also grant more attractive allowances to smaller companies, to encourage their development.

In recent years, for example, smaller companies have been able to claim 100% allowances on certain IT spending. That means that qualifying companies have been able to offset 100% of their IT spend against tax in the year the cost was incurred.

Self-assessment question 4.3

Identify whether the following items should be treated as capital expenditure, or just 'expensed':

- Leasing IT equipment over a four-year period: capital/expense
- Building a new power station: capital/expense

(continued on next page)

Finance for Purchasers

> **Self-assessment question 4.3** *(continued)*
> - Interest on money borrowed to finance the above: capital/expense
> - A one-off major repair to manufacturing equipment: capital/expense
> - The cost of training staff to use a newly acquired IT system: capital/expense
> - Refurbishing a head office reception area: capital/expense
>
> *Feedback on page 54*

Revision question

Now try the revision question for this session on page 345.

Summary

This session has outlined the important distinction between capital and revenue expenditure. It has looked at the criteria that are used to determine whether an item should be capitalised or expensed, and has summarised the different depreciation treatments that can be applied to capital items, and the resulting impact on profitability.

Feedback on learning activities and self-assessment questions

Feedback on learning activity 4.1

Specific feedback here will depend on the asset identified. It is important that you understand why it is a capital item and the logic of then depreciating the asset via the P&L. It would also be useful if you understand and agree with the depreciation method being used.

Feedback on self-assessment question 4.1

First, using straight-line depreciation, we need to work out the depreciable amount (table 4.5).

Table 4.5

Cost of asset	£500,000
Less Residual value	£120,000
= Depreciable amount	£380,000
Divided by 4 years =	£95,000 per year for 4 years

The schedule will therefore look like table 4.6.

Table 4.6

	Opening balance	Year's depreciation deducted from profits	Closing balance (NBV)
Year 1	500,000	95,000	405,000
Year 2	405,000	95,000	310,000
Year 3	310,000	95,000	215,000
Year 4	215,000	95,000	120,000

Using reducing balance, the schedule will be as shown in table 4.7.

Table 4.7

	Opening balance	Year's depreciation deducted from profits	Closing balance (NBV)
Year 1	500,000	150,000	350,000
Year 2	350,000	105,000	245,000
Year 3	245,000	73,500	171,500
Year 4	171,500	51,450	120,050

Here the depreciation is loaded more towards the earlier years, although, in this particular example, the amount of depreciation charged over the four-year period is almost identical in both cases.

Feedback on learning activity 4.2

When a business acquires a fixed asset, it will usually do so by buying the item from a supplier of those assets. By definition, therefore, the buyer will treat the asset as a capital item, but it will have been part of the day-to-day business of the supplier and thus treated as a short-term asset by them (usually as 'stock' or inventory').

So, for example, a car is likely to be a fixed asset for the buyer, but would simply have been part of the stock of the seller (the garage or the manufacturer). IT equipment and machinery would be treated in a similar way.

More contentiously – staff salaries, finance costs and aspects of R&D could be treated by one company as capital and by another as revenue, depending on the prevailing circumstances.

Feedback on self-assessment question 4.2

Staff costs would ordinarily be expensed. However, they may be treated as capital where work is specifically linked to a capital project. For example, work carried out in the design of a power station could be legitimately considered part of the capital cost of the asset.

Interest costs will usually be expensed at the time of payment. Interest can be capitalised, though, if it can be directly attributed to the cost of an asset that is being constructed.

The cost of developing a new drug could be treated as capital, if all the criteria outlined on page 53 have been met – i.e. that the drug represents a separately defined project which is technically feasible, commercially viable, potentially profitable and adequately resourced. If any of these do not apply – for example if the drug is being developed but there is no certainty that it will meet with the necessary regulatory approval – then the costs should be expensed.

Leasing costs

If the lease is a finance lease, i.e. where the lessee takes on the risks and rewards of ownership, even though not technically the owner, then the lease will be treated as a fixed asset which will be depreciated as other assets. Where it is an operating lease – i.e. more akin to a shorter-term rental – the cost will be expensed.

Purchase of IT equipment

Will normally be capitalised. Historically, IT equipment has sometimes had a shorter useful life than was originally anticipated, which has caused accounting problems.

Feedback on learning activity 4.3

In terms of safeguards, the company's internal control processes should have ensured that such mis-classification of expenditure should have been avoided. Additionally, the external audit process should have been independent and robust enough to have picked up the problem. Changes in US legislation, in particular the **Sarbanes-Oxley Act of 2002**, are attempting to address these, and other, control issues.

The company's value would be 'artificially inflated' as a direct result of the short-term profit boost. One way of valuing a company is on the basis of its earnings (or profits) per share. The treatment of costs as capital will also inflate the balance sheet position – the fixed assets will be higher than they should be as they will include items that shouldn't be there. The retained profits of the business – forming part of its 'equity' will also be similarly overstated.

The cash position, however, would be unaffected. The decision to treat an item as capital or as expense has no bearing on the cash going out of the business. It is simply a decision about how to treat something in the accounts.

Feedback on self-assessment question 4.3

- Leasing IT equipment over a four-year period will probably be capital expenditure. The three-year period, for IT equipment, is likely to represent the bulk of its useful life
- Building a new power station will be capital expenditure.
- Interest on money borrowed to finance the above can be treated as capital, but does not have to be.
- A one-off major repair to manufacturing equipment will be an expense. Regardless of how major the amount is, it is repair and therefore should not be treated as a capital item.
- The cost of training staff to use a newly acquired IT system will probably be treated as capital expenditure, as training in the use of the asset can be included in its cost, More general training – management training for example – would have to be treated as an expense.
- Refurbishing a head office reception area would probably be treated as capital expenditure. It would depend on precisely what was involved, but if the work involves improving the area (rather than just maintaining it) then it could justifiably be treated as capital.

Study session 5
Key financial statements

Introduction

In previous sessions we have considered some of the background to financial accounting statements. Now we shall turn our attention to the actual contents of the statements, and what they tell users about the reporting organisation.

We will look first at the profit and loss account – also known as the income statement. We will then consider the balance sheet, followed by the cash flow statement. These are the three main statements that companies publish as part of their annual report and accounts.

We will also consider other elements of a set of accounts, including the five-year summaries that many organisations provide.

'Published accounts are absolutely and utterly useless.'
This was said at a TUC conference some years ago. Attempts have since been made to make them more useful – but do they really contain what their users want?

Session learning objectives

After completing this session you should be able to:

5.1 Explain and appraise a profit and loss account/income statement.
5.2 Explain and appraise a balance sheet.
5.3 Explain and appraise a cash flow statement.
5.4 Explain and appraise a five-year summary.

Unit content coverage

This study session covers the following topics from the official CIPS unit content document:

Learning objective

2.1 Analyse key financial statements to inform decisions.
- Profit and loss accounts/income statements
- Balance sheet
- Cash flow statement
- Five-year summary

Prior knowledge

Study sessions 1 to 4, especially study sessions 1, 2 and 4.

Resources

As for study session 3, it will be worth visiting corporate websites and viewing recently published annual reports (usually within the 'Investor Relations' part of the site).

Holmes, G, Sugden, A and Gee, P (2005) *Interpreting Company Reports and Accounts*, 9th edition, especially chapters 5–19. Harlow: FT Prentice Hall.

Timing

You should set aside about 7 hours to read and complete this session, including learning activities, self-assessment questions, the suggested further reading (if any) from the essential textbook for this unit and the revision question.

5.1 The profit and loss account

The profit statement or profit and loss account (P&L) shows the results of a company's financial performance *over a period of time*. The statement will address questions such as:

- How much has the business sold during the period?
- What have its costs been?
- How much tax will it have to pay as a result?
- How much of the profit will it pay out to shareholders, and how much is it keeping in the business?

The statement is also often referred to as the 'income statement'. It includes the following major elements:

- **Turnover**, also known as **sales**. This represents the total value of all goods and/or services sold by the company during the period in question. Sales can include goods or services invoiced, or cash sales. In other words, cash does not have to be received before a sale is deemed to have taken place. Revenue recognition – the issue of when an organisation can and should record something as a sale – can be a contentious area of accounting.
- **Operating costs.** From the turnover figure are deducted all costs incurred in creating the sales. Again, the costs incurred need not have been paid out in cash to be recorded in the profit statement. An important underlying concept in accounting is the 'accruals' or 'matching' concept. This involves matching income to its relevant expenditure, regardless of when the expenditure is paid out in cash. It also means that the cost of materials, for example, is accounted for in expenditure terms when the product for which the materials are used has actually been sold. The cost of unused materials in any given period is included in the value of an asset – stock – and is not deducted in the P&L until that stock is sold.

The costs on the P&L do *not* directly include capital expenditure – the costs involved in the purchase or creation of fixed assets such as buildings, machinery and equipment. In such cases the relevant cost to the business is depreciation, which – as we looked at in the previous session – is the cost of a fixed asset spread over its expected useful life. Costs are shown in different ways in a profit and loss account – it depends on the format being used. Where it is an appropriate split, however, a company is likely to state separately its 'cost of sales' or 'cost of goods sold'. These amounts represent those costs directly incurred in getting the goods that have been sold into a saleable condition. These would typically include for a manufacturing business the purchase of raw materials consumed and direct manufacturing costs. Deducting these costs from the turnover figure would then give us what is known as **gross profit**.

From the gross profit are deducted other operating expenses such as distribution and administration. These represent what are normally described as indirect costs, or overheads. Once these costs have been deducted, we arrive at the operating profit.

- **Operating profit** tells us how much profit a company has made on its normal operating activities. If the costs exceed the turnover figure, the difference would represent an operating loss.

Operating profit is a key measure of performance. However, in terms of published financial accounts, further deductions have to be made:

- **Interest**. If a company is borrowing money, the year's interest is deducted from the operating profit to give us what is known as profit before tax (or pre-tax profit). If, over the course of the year, the company has earned interest, this amount will be added to the operating profit rather than deducted from it.
- **Taxation**. Companies may also pay corporation tax, calculated as a percentage of what is known as 'taxable profit'. The figure for taxable profit is not shown on a published profit and loss account, but is one that takes account of the fact that some expenses are not tax-deductible. The taxation figure in the P&L Account represents the tax based on that year's activities – not necessarily the amount actually paid out that year. Corporation tax includes capital gains tax.
  The remaining figure is known as **profit after tax** or **profit attributable to shareholders**, and it represents the amount of profit left over for the owners of the business to use as they see fit.
  This figure forms the basis of a measure known as **earnings per share**, which is commonly abbreviated to **eps**. It is calculated by dividing the profit attributable to shareholders by the number of shares in the company – thereby arriving at a figure that represents the amount of profit that has been made in the period for each share that exists. Such profits are either paid out to shareholders as dividends or 'ploughed back' into the company as retained profits.
- **Dividends** represent the amount that will be paid out to shareholders in proportion to the size of their shareholding in the company.
- **Retained profit** is what is left after all the elements mentioned above have been deducted, and represent the amount of profit that the

Finance for Purchasers

shareholders are leaving in the business, which could be used to finance future growth.

The example set out below is a simple one. Additional aspects of a profit and loss account that you are likely to encounter in practice include:

- *Continuing/discontinued operations:* where aspects of operations that are not ongoing are separately stated to allow for better year-on-year comparisons.
- *Exceptional items:* where major one-off items are stated separately, which again can help with year-on-year comparisons
- *Profit/loss on the sale of fixed assets:* where an asset has been sold for more (or less) than the value shown in the balance sheet.

The P&L account is a very useful document for a purchaser to see. It gives an indication of the level of business activity, via the turnover figure. Are sales increasing or decreasing? If we place an order, how relatively big will that be for the seller? What sort of margins are they making on their sales (eg gross profit/sales and operating profit/sales as a percentage).

Learning activity 5.1

Consider the example profit and loss account set out in table 5.1.

Table 5.1 UK Enterprise Plc profit and loss account

UK Enterprise Plc	2006	2005
Profit and loss account Y/E 31 March		
	£000	£000
Turnover	20,874	17,238
Cost of sales	(16,156)	(13,256)
Gross profit	4,718	3,982
Distribution expenses	(1,962)	(1,604)
Administration expenses	(898)	(724)
Operating profit	1,858	1,654
Interest payable	(598)	(488)
Profit before tax	1,260	1,166
Taxation	(416)	(386)
Profit for the year	844	780
Dividends	(308)	(262)
Retained profit	536	518

1. From the perspective of an external purchaser, what useful information does the statement provide?
2. Why might the information contained in a published P&L be considered of limited use?
3. Given that the example is a 'financial accounting' statement, how might similar information be presented differently in a management accounting context?

Feedback on page 70

For companies that are now reporting their financial results using International Accounting Standards, the 'profit and losss account' is referred to as the 'Income Statement', but essentially similar data is shown.

It is also worth noting, however, that the ordinary dividend payable does not appear on the IAS Income Statement. This is because of a technical difference in approach towards when a dividend actually becomes a liability. Under UK GAAP, dividends are accrued in the period to which they relate regardless of when they are declared and approved. Under IAS, dividends are accrued only when declared and appropriately approved.

So the UK Enterprise profit and loss account might look like table 5.3 if presented using International Standards and its associated terminology:

Table 5.3

UK Enterprise Plc	2006	2005
Income Statement Y/E 31 March		
	£000	**£000**
Revenue	20,874	17,238
Cost of sales	(16,156)	(13,256)
Gross profit	4,718	3,982
Operating expenses	(2,860)	(2,328)
Operating profit	1,858	1,654
Interest payable	(598)	(488)
Profit before tax	1,260	1,166
Taxation	(416)	(386)
Profit for the year	844	780

This is not telling us anything different – it is merely using slightly different terminology. In practice there would, in all likelihood, be some differences in the figures due to the adoption of different standards.

Self-assessment question 5.1

Company X has reported the information shown in table 5.4.

Table 5.4

	£ million
Sales	200
Direct costs	110
Interest	20
Administrative and other expenses	30
Taxation	15
Dividend	10

A total of 160 million ordinary shares have been issued by Company X.

Calculate the company's:

Gross profit

(continued on next page)

Finance for Purchasers

> **Self-assessment question 5.1** *(continued)*
> Operating profit
>
> Earnings per share (eps)
>
> *Feedback on page 71*

5.2 The balance sheet

The balance sheet is very different to the P&L account. It gives a snapshot of a company's financial position at one particular point in time, while the P&L, as we have seen, is a summary of activities that have taken place over a period of time, such as a month or a year. It states what the company owns (assets) and what it owes (liabilities) at that point in time.

Put in another way, the balance sheet is a cumulative picture of where a company's money has come from, and where it has gone to.

Where the money comes from is usually limited to three basic sources:

- *share capital:* being money put up by the owners (or shareholders) of the business.
- *reserves:* being (most frequently) profits retained in the business rather than paid out as dividends.
- *debt (or loan capital):* being money borrowed from other sources to help run the business.

Where the money goes to can similarly be split into three categories:

- *fixed assets:* represent things a company owns on a longer-term basis
- *working capital:* representing money being used to run the business on a short-term basis
- *investments:* representing money invested elsewhere, long-term or short-term.

The first items shown are the assets of the business. Assets are those things that a company owns, and are classified as being either fixed or current.

Fixed assets are those that are used in the course of running the business on a longer term basis. They are therefore mainly represented by such items as buildings and machinery. The purchase of such assets is normally referred to as capital expenditure.

Fixed assets are usually included in the balance sheet at their original cost less the total amount of depreciation charged since their purchase. Depreciation involves spreading the cost of an asset over its expected useful life.

Some fixed assets – such as land – are not depreciated at all, but are periodically re-valued. Fixed assets are classified as being either tangible or intangible. Tangible fixed assets have a physical form, for example machinery or buildings, whereas intangible fixed assets, such as brand names and goodwill, do not.

Accounting for intangible assets has been the subject of much debate and change. For example, if a company develops a brand identity, should its value appear on the balance sheet? And, if so, how might the value be calculated?

Goodwill occurs when one business acquires another, and when the price paid exceeds the fair value of the net assets of the acquired business. For example, Company A pays £10 million for Company B. If the 'fair value' of the net assets of Company B were £8 million, then the value of the goodwill acquired will be £2 million. This represents an intangible fixed asset which, depending on the accounting standards being adopted, will either be depreciated over a number of years or regularly reviewed to ensure its value is still fair.

Current assets, on the other hand, are those that are constantly on the move – i.e. shorter term in nature and typically comprise:

- stock (raw materials, work-in-progress, finished goods)
- debtors (money owing to the company following the sale of products or services)
- cash (money held in the bank, petty cash).

The next stage in looking at a balance sheet is to see how much the company owes to others – represented by liabilities.

Current liabilities (or 'creditors due in less than one year') are those amounts that the company owes – and will normally have to pay out within the next 12 months. They would typically include:

- trade creditors (amounts owed to the company's suppliers)
- tax payable (tax liabilities due to be paid within the next year)
- proposed dividend (payable to shareholders)
- bank overdrafts (in theory, repayable on demand and therefore deemed to be 'current').

Deducting current liabilities from the current assets creates what is known as net current assets, or **working capital**. It is an important figure – in terms of measuring a company's liquidity – its ability to keep going on a day-to-day basis.

Long-term liabilities (or long-term creditors) represent amounts repayable in more than one year. Typically, this will include term loans from a bank, but would also include any long-term provisions that a company has made – setting money aside now (in the accounts) to cover something it expects to have to pay in later years.

Net assets represent the difference between all the company's assets and all its liabilities. They represent the company's worth – in accounting terms only. A balance sheet is not a reliable guide to market value (the amount that somebody else would pay for the business) nor to break-up value (the

Finance for Purchasers

amount that could be generated by closing down the business and selling off the assets). Net assets will have a value which equals the shareholders' funds figure.

The **shareholders' funds** figure comprises the value of the share capital put into the business by its shareholders, together with any reserves that have accumulated – the most significant of which is normally retained profit. This represents the total amount that the company's owners have 'ploughed back' into the business since it started.

A balance sheet is based at least in part on opinion. The value ascribed to fixed and current assets contains at least an element of opinion – for example how long the fixed assets will last, how much the stock is worth, the expectation that debtors will pay. Such subjectivity can give rise to a lack of credibility in terms of the usefulness of a balance sheet.

Table 5.6 UK Enterprise Plc, balance sheet as at 31 March

	2006	2005
	£000	£000
Fixed assets		
Tangible assets	10,652	8,890
Current assets		
Stock	2,482	1,906
Debtors	3,122	2,382
Cash	30	40
	5,634	4,328
Creditors due in less than 1 year		
Creditors	(2,246)	(1,838)
Bank overdraft	(1,774)	(1,226)
Taxation	(416)	(386)
Proposed dividend	(308)	(262)
	(4,744)	(3,712)
Net current assets	890	616
Total assets less current liabilities	11,542	9,506
Long-term liabilities (Loans)	(6,000)	(4,500)
Net assets	5,542	5,006
Shareholders' Equity		
Share capital (Ordinary £1 shares)	2,000	2,000
Share premium	650	650
Retained profit	2,892	2,356
Shareholders' Funds	5,542	5,006

For companies that are now reporting their financial results using International Accounting Standards, the balance sheet looks a little different.

Again, as an example and so that we can consider the IAS layout and terminology that will become increasingly prevalent, we can represent the UK Enterprise balance sheet as shown in table 5.7.

5 Key financial statements

Table 5.7

UK Enterprise Plc	2006	2005
Balance sheet as at 31 March		
	£000	£000
Non-current assets		
Property, plant and equipment	10,652	8,890
Current assets		
Inventories	2,482	1,906
Trade receivables	3,122	2,382
Cash and cash equivalents	30	40
	5,634	4,328
Current liabilities		
Trade payables	(2,246)	(1,838)
Bank overdraft	(1,774)	(1,226)
Tax liabilities	(416)	(386)
	(4,436)	(3,450)
Net current assets	1,198	878
Total assets less current liabilities	11,850	9,768
Non-current liabilities	(6,000)	(4,500)
Net assets	5,850	5,268
Shareholders' Equity		
Share capital (Ordinary £1 shares)	2,000	2,000
Share premium	650	650
Retained profit	3,200	2,618
Equity/Shareholders' Funds	5,850	5,268

You may note some new terminology in the above example, and that there is no longer a dividend as a liability in the statement. The retained profit is still a cumulative figure, though it is now based on the latest profits less the dividend *paid out* during the period.

Learning activity 5.2

The example financial statements covered so far have been set out using the UK GAAP format and terminology and IFRS format and terminology.

Using these examples, or any other examples you wish, highlight five significant terminology differences that a user of accounts faces.

(If you do want to look at a range of other examples, most stock market listed companies make their accounts freely available on their websites, usually within a section entitled 'Investor relations' or similar.)

Feedback on page 72

Now attempt self-assessment question 5.2 below.

Finance for Purchasers

Self-assessment question 5.2

True or false?

- Assets minus liabilities = capital and reserves: true/false
- A balance sheet describes the financial position at one moment in time: true/false
- A balance sheet includes a figure for sales made on credit during the year: true/false
- A balance sheet includes both tangible and intangible assets: true/false
- A company's share price at the balance sheet date is reflected in the 'share capital' section of the statement: true/false

Feedback on page 72

5.3 The cash flow statement

The third financial statement that companies produce is known as the 'cash flow statement'. It deals with cash only – where it came from and where it went – and differs in this respect from the P&L and balance sheet, which take into account non-cash items (eg depreciation, trade credit, etc).

Aspects of a cash flow statement would include:

- *Cash flows generated from operating activities:* The starting point for calculating this figure is the operating profit – but this needs to be adjusted for two main reasons.
  Firstly, some items in the P&L will not have involved a cash movement during the year. The best and most commonly seen example is depreciation. Having deducted depreciation to arrive at a profit figure, we now need to add it back again – as it wasn't a cash deduction and we are trying to get to a cash figure.
  Secondly, we need to make what are known as 'working capital adjustments'. This involves reflecting the cash impact of changes in certain balance sheet items – debtors, creditors and stock. If, for example, debtors have increased over the year, this will have a negative effect on the company's cash position – because more of its money is owed by customers. The same logic apples to stock – if stock goes up, the cash position goes down (because more cash is now tied up in stock). The opposite applies to creditors – if they increase, it has a beneficial impact on the cash position.
  All this is merely reflecting the fundamental differences between profit and cash flow. Depreciation is an amount that is deducted from the profit statement – but it is not a cash flow. Also, the sales figure included in the profit statement represents the value of goods or services sold – but not necessarily paid for.

The cash flow statement, then, looks at the amount of cash received during the period. It highlights movements of cash under several different headings:

- Cash movements in or out relating to dividends paid or received, and interest paid or received.

5 Key financial statements

- Cash movements in respect of taxation.
- Cash spent on fixed assets or realised from the sale of fixed assets.
- Cash spent or received from the management of liquid resources.
- Cash flows in respect of financing the business – for example, cash going out to repay loans or to buy back shares, or cash coming in as a result of new loans or a share issue.

The main usefulness of any cash flow statement involves being able to see where cash is coming from and going to during the year (see table 5.9 for an example). For example, is it mainly used to service borrowing, or is it being used to acquire fixed assets and other investments for the future?

Table 5.9

UK Enterprise Plc cash flow statement	2006	2005
Y/E 31 March		
	£000	£000
Operating activities		
Operating profit	1,858	1,654
Depreciation	990	804
Increase in stock	(576)	(344)
Increase in debtors	(740)	(482)
Increase in creditors	408	150
Net cash flow from operating activities	1,940	1,782
Returns on investment and servicing of finance	(598)	(488)
Taxation	(386)	(380)
Capital expenditure	(2,752)	(2,408)
Equity dividend paid	(262)	(226)
Net cash flow before financing	(2,058)	(1,720)
Financing		
Increase in short-term borrowings	548	200
Increase in long-term borrowings	1,500	1,500
Net cash inflow from financing	2,048	1,700
Change in cash position	(10)	(20)

From the above cash flow statement, we can pick out a few important points:

- UK Enterprise is making an operating profit (something we already saw from the P&L) but it is also making a positive cash flow from its operations – in fact this has gone up from £1,782,000 to £1,940,000.
- UK Enterprise is investing in fixed assets. The capex figure is the largest single item on the statement, and has risen from £2,408,000 to £2,752,000.
- UK Enterprise is not generating sufficient cash internally to be able to finance its investment activities. Although they made an operating cash flow of £1,940,000, the fact is that that they have made significant investment and also had to pay a tax bill, a dividend and some interest on borrowings. This has left the company with a shortfall of over £2m. This amount has to be financed, and in this case the finance has been borrowed – partly on a short-term basis (overdraft) and partly via

long-term borrowings, which have risen by £1.5 million. This extra borrowing is also reflected in the balance sheet – where you will see liabilities increasing by the same amounts.

Referring again to the UK/International differences, with cash flow statements the key difference is in the number of headings used in the statement. Under IFRS the number of categories of cash flow is limited to just three:

- Cash flows from operating activities
- Cash flows from investing activities
- Cash flows from financing activities

This perhaps makes for a simpler statement, with items such as taxation and interest included in the 'operating' section, and dividends usually appearing under the 'financing' heading.

Once again, we can adjust the UK Enterprise statement to reflect these differences (see table 5.10).

Table 5.10

UK Enterprise Plc cash flow statement	2006	2005
Y/E 31 March		
	£000	£000
Cash flows from operating activities		
Cash generated from operations*	1,940	1,782
Interest paid	(598)	(488)
Tax paid	(386)	(380)
Net cash from operating activities	956	914
Cash flows from investing activities		
Purchase of property, plant and equipment	(2,752)	(2,408)
Net cash flows from investing activities	(2,752)	(2,408)
Cash flows from financing activities		
Increase in short-term borrowings	548	200
Increase in long-term borrowings	1,500	1,500
Payment of dividend to shareholders**	(262)	(226)
Net cash inflow from financing activities	1,786	1,474
Net decrease in cash and cash equivalents	(10)	(20)

* The cash flow from operations figure is as calculated as per the UK layout statement.

** The dividend payment may alternatively be shown as part of the operating activities cash flow.

Note that there are just the three classes of activity listed – operating, investing and financing. The statement will also be followed by a reconciliation with the changes in cash and debt levels in the balance sheet.

5 Key financial statements

Learning activity 5.3

For each of the following transactions, describe what the impact would be on the organisation's current year profit and cash position?

- Investment in a new IT system
- Issue of new shares
- Downpayment on the purchase of an item to be delivered in the subsequent financial year
- Capital repayment of a bank loan
- Loan interest
- Purchase of raw materials

Feedback on page 72

Now attempt self-assessment question 5.3 below.

Self-assessment question 5.3

Table 5.11 shows the most recently published cash flow statement of Company X.

Table 5.11 Company X cash flow statement for the year ended 31 March 2006

	£000	£000
Cash flows from operating activities		
Profit before taxation	380	
Depreciation	130	
Interest expense	85	
Increase in receivables	(92)	
Increase in inventories	(63)	
Increase in payables	35	
Cash generated from operations	475	
Interest paid	(95)	
Taxation	(102)	
Net cash from operating activities		278
Cash flows from investing activities		
Purchase of property, plant and equipment	(395)	
Investment income received	13	
Net cash used in investing activities		(382)
Cash flows from financing activities		
Proceeds from issue of share capital	200	
Loans advanced	120	
Loans repaid	(85)	
Dividend paid	(105)	

(continued on next page)

Self-assessment question 5.3 *(continued)*

	£000	£000
Net cash used in financing activities		**130**
Net increase in cash and cash equivalents		**26**
Cash and cash equivalents at beginning of period		**38**
Cash and cash equivalents at end of period		**64**

1 Is this a profitable company?
2 Why has the depreciation figure been added to arrive at an operating cash flow figure?
3 Why does the increase in receivables represent a cash outflow?
4 Did the company have more cash at the end of the year, or the beginning?
5 Why might the above statement be deemed more reliable than either a balance sheet or a P&L (income statement)?

Feedback on page 73

5.4 Other financial statements

STORGLs

A fourth primary financial statement that you will see presented by larger companies id the 'Statement of total recognised gains and losses', or STORGL for short. This is a statement that is used to show gains and losses that have been made in the year, but which are not recorded on the P&L.

Five-year: summary

Many larger companies provide a summary of financial results over a longer period of time than just the two most recent years. Typically, this will be a five-year summary, although sometimes companies cover a longer timespan. The inclusion of such information is entirely at the company's discretion, and its content and form are not governed by any accounting standard or other regulation.

Some companies go into far more detail than others. The two examples below are adapted versions of real five-year summaries that have been presented by UK companies recently. The first example (table 5.12) is fairly low on detail.

Table 5.12 Example A – Five-year summary

	2005	2004	2003	2002	2001
Revenue (£ million)	1130.1	819.9	777.7	662.9	570.6
Profit before tax (£ million)	45.7	35.6	33.5	28.5	22.6
Earnings per share (p)	7.05	5.73	5.51	4.79	4.12
Dividend per share (p)	1.49	1.31	1.16	1.04	0.93
Free cash flow (£ million)	36.9	27.9	23.5	4.85	4.45

Whereas the table 5.13 provides a lot more information – including balance sheet information – to the reader of the accounts:

5 Key financial statements

Table 5.13 Example B – Five-year summary

	2005	2004	2003	2002	2001
Turnover (£ million)	1410	1402	1377	1375	1347
Pre-tax profit (£ million)	86	80	70	68	82
Earnings per share (p)	3.25	3.00	2.70	3.15	3.90
Dividend per share (p)	2.50	2.50	2.50	2.50	2.55
Fixed assets (£ million)	793	749	760	690	673
Stocks (£ million)	197	206	191	172	172
Debtors (£ million)	242	227	232	208	253
Cash and securities (£ million)	43	28	32	45	70
Creditors short (£ million)	352	325	335	302	338
Creditors long (£ million)	592	583	651	588	559
Shareholders' funds (£ million)	361	352	342	337	368
Market capitalisation (£ million)	654	714	310	570	763

This example covers a range of data from both the income statement and the balance sheet. Other companies will provide more data still.

In summary, there are no rules or standards regarding the presentation of a five-year summary, so it is up to the organisation to present what it sees as appropriate. The statement can, however, be an extremely useful one to look at as it picks up figures over an extended timeframe, and allows the user to consider longer-term trends.

Learning activity 5.4

Obtain the five-year summary of a large listed company. How comprehensive is the information provided? Are there key figures that would be particularly useful in the purchasing context? Are these figures included in the example you have selected?

Comment on the performance over the five-year period – is it improving or deteriorating?

Feedback on page 73

Now attempt self-assessment question 5.4 below.

Self-assessment question 5.4

Multiple choice questions

1   The amount owed to a company by its customers would be found in:
(a)   the balance sheet
(b)   the income statement
(c)   the cash flow statement
(d)   the balance sheet *and* the cash flow statement

(continued on next page)

Finance for Purchasers

Self-assessment question 5.4 (continued)

2 The amount a company has newly borrowed in the last 12 months will be shown in:
   - (a) the balance sheet
   - (b) the income statement
   - (c) the cash flow statement
   - (d) the balance sheet *and* the cash flow statement
   - (e) all three statements.

3 How much a company has spent on new fixed assets will be shown in:
   - (a) the balance sheet
   - (b) the income statement
   - (c) the cash flow statement
   - (d) the balance sheet *and* the cash flow statement
   - (e) all three statements

4 A five-year summary contains:
   - (a) anything the company wants it to contain
   - (b) certain key figures, as prescribed by the Accounting Standards Board
   - (c) a summary of the all three financial statements over the past five years
   - (d) a narrative review of the past five years' results.

Feedback on page 73

Revision question

Now try the revision question for this session on page 345.

Summary

This session has covered some very important ground, covering as it has the main financial accounting statements. The profit and loss account describes the company's performance – in profit terms – over the past year. The cash flow statement is similar in that it reports what happened over the past year, but does so in terms of movements of cash. The balance sheet looks at the financial status of the organisation as at the end of the financial year, in terms of its assets and liabilities.

Feedback on learning activities and self-assessment questions

Feedback on learning activity 5.1

The P&L is a useful statement for a purchaser to assess. The first figure in the statement – the 'sales' or 'turnover' figure – immediately gives an indication of the size of the business, and therefore (if a major purchase is being considered) how much of the seller's business volume that might represent.

We will be looking at ratio analysis in a later chapter, but from the P&L we can calculate key 'margin' ratios – measures that look at profit as a percentage of sales.

From the example above we could calculate the margin ratios shown in table 5.2.

Table 5.2

	2006	2005
Gross margin (gross profit/turnover)	22.6%	23.1%
Operating margin (operating profit/turnover)	8.9%	9.6%

These profitability ratios have declined a little, indicating a weakening performance. This might represent falling sales prices, and/or less effective control of costs. If purchasing on a longer-term contract basis, a weakening supplier financial performance may be a concern.

The information is of limited use on its own. In reality, we would like to see more than two years' data, and we would like to see it alongside the other financial statements such as the balance sheet and the cash flow statement. It is also limited in that it is historic – it doesn't give us any information about the future, which is something a purchaser would be interested in. It also doesn't go into much detail – the cost figures, for example, are very broad in nature.

Which brings us to the third question. A company's internal – management accounting – reporting will include profit statements, but the data within them will be much more detailed and practically useful. Sales figures, for example, will be broken down by product, by customer, by geographical location. Cost will be shown in much greater detail and in a way that will enable users to assess performance in a meaningful way, or make key business decisions. This, again, is an aspect we will be studying at a later point in this course.

Feedback on self-assessment question 5.1

First it would be useful to restate the data in a more meaningful way (see table 5.5).

Table 5.5

	£ million
Sales	200
Less direct costs	110
Gross profit	90
Less administrative and other expenses	30
Operating profit	60
Less interest	20
Profit before tax	40
Less taxation	15
Profit after tax	25
Dividend	10
Retained profit	15
So the required figures are:	
Gross profit	£90 million
Operating profit	£60 million
Earnings per share (eps)	£25 million/160 million = 15.6p

Finance for Purchasers

Feedback on learning activity 5.2

Table 5.8

UK Term	IFRS Term
Profit and loss account	Income statement
Fixed assets	Non-current assets
Debtors	Receivables
Stock	Inventory
Creditors	Payables

Feedback on self-assessment question 5.2

- True. This is the basic balance sheet equation. Assets minus liabilities = net assets. The shareholders own the net assets. The 'share capital and reserves' part of the balance sheet describes how the shareholders' ownership of the net assets has been financed – typically through shares having been issued and profits having been retained in the business.
- True. As opposed to the P&L, which looks at what has happened over a period of time.
- False. None of the published statements directly gives the user this information, although the sales figure itself will be the first figure in a P&L.
- True, although not all intangibles assets will be shown.
- False. The balance sheet expresses the share capital at its 'nominal' value, rather than market value. If shares are issued at more than their nominal value, the amount raised is expressed as a share premium and this will be reflected in the balance sheet. However, the market value at the balance sheet date is not taken into account.

Feedback on learning activity 5.3

- Investment in a new IT system. The impact on cash flow would depend on how it was being paid for. Assuming it is bought outright, the cash flow would be reduced by the same amount. The profit, however, would only be reduced by whatever the current year's depreciation of that asset was.
- Issue of new shares. This will nor affect the P&L, other than indirectly perhaps by an increased dividend payment. It will, though, have a direct impact on the cash position of the company – with cash coming in from the share issue.
- Downpayment on the purchase of an item to be delivered in the subsequent financial year. This will have a negative effect on cash flow, but will not impact on the current year's profitability.
- Capital repayment of a bank loan. This will impact on the cash flow directly, as cash goes out of the business. There will be no corresponding impact on P&L, although indirectly the interest charge will reduce.
- Loan interest. In most circumstances this will affect profit and cash flow in the same way – that is, it is a deduction from the P&L and it also reflects cash going out of the business.
- Purchase of raw materials. The P&L will reflect this amount in its calculation of direct costs, although only the materials actually used

5 Key financial statements

during the year will be charged. There will be an outflow of cash to the extent that the purchased materials are actually paid for.

Feedback on self-assessment question 5.3

1   Yes, it made a £380,000 pre-tax profit.
2   The depreciation is added back because the starting point is a *profit* figure, and we are trying to convert it to a *cash flow* figure. As depreciation is not a cash item, we add it back to the profit figure (effectively to cancel it out).
3   Because 'receivables' describes amounts owed by customers. If this amount has gone up, it means Company X is owed more by its customers than it had been. This has an adverse effect on the cash position.
4   More. The cash (and cash equivalents) position has increased from £38,000 to £64,000.
5   Any of the statements on their own are of very limited use. However, of the three, the cash flow statements has some particular strengths – mainly concerning the fact that cash is 'real'. The other two statements include many figures that are based, at least in part, on opinions. For example, figures representing asset values, depreciation charges and bad debt provisions all require judgements to be made. Cash is cash, and it is something that cannot easily, or legally, be manipulated.

Feedback on learning activity 5.4

Given that the five-year summary is a voluntary statement, and has no prescribed format, the data you will be presented with is at the company's discretion. One may therefore be advised to take a fairly sceptical view of this. Are they just highlighting the best parts? Are there aspects that they are not divulging? How comprehensive is the information? How well would it meet a purchaser's needs?

Feedback on self-assessment question 5.4

1   (a) The 'debtors' or 'receivables' figure is shown in the balance sheet. The income statement shows the annual sales figure. The cash flow statement shows *changes* in the debtors figure, but not the actual amount owed.
2   (c) The cash flow statement shows what additional borrowing has been taken out, and/or what loans have been repaid during the year. The balance sheet described the loans outstanding at the end of the year. This could be compared to the previous year's figure, and might therefore suggest an amount of loans that have been repaid (so answer (d) might be arguable – but the cash flow statement confirms the actual movements).
3   (c) It is the cash flow statement that explicitly states what has been spent on fixed assets. The balance sheet shows the asset values, but these could have changed for reasons other than purchases/sales – for example depreciation charges, asset write-downs, revaluations.
4   (a) The five-year summary is not a formal requirement.

Finance for Purchasers

5

Study session 6
Descriptive and inferential statistics

Introduction

We have all heard the quote about 'lies, damned lies and statistics'. The quote is driven by the idea that statistics can be used to suggest more or less anything.

In this context an important distinction can be drawn between what are known as **descriptive** and **inferential** statistics. The first part of this session will look at descriptive statistics, and the second will consider inferential statistics.

Descriptive statistics just involve summarising some data. Inferential statistics take it further by allowing us to draw some conclusions (ie to 'infer something') from the data.

'The main problem with statistics is that people like favourable numbers to back up a decision.'

Session learning objectives

After completing this session you should be able to:

6.1 Define 'descriptive statistics', and explain the circumstances in which they are useful.
6.2 Define 'inferential statistics', and explain the circumstances in which they are useful.

Unit content coverage

This study session covers the following topics from the official CIPS unit content document:

Learning objective

2.2 Use descriptive and inferential statistics.
   • Definitions
   • How and when to use them
   • Assess the outcomes of analysis

Prior knowledge

None.

Finance for Purchasers

Timing

You should set aside about 3 hours to read and complete this session, including learning activities, self-assessment questions, the suggested further reading (if any) from the essential textbook for this unit and the revision question.

6.1 Descriptive statistics and the circumstances in which they are useful

Descriptive statistics covers any of the many techniques that can be used to summarise data. Among the approaches are:

- tabular description (i.e. using tables to present and summarise data)
- graphical description (i.e. using graphs to present and summarise data)
- summary statistics (which involves calculating certain 'values' – for example, an average value).

Learning activity 6.1

The data in table 6.1 is taken from a fictional European country's tourist board. The data shows the number of visitors to the country, and the amount spent by those visitors during their stay.

Table 6.1

Year	Number of visitors (millions)	Amount spent (€ millions)
1995	18.2	6,750
1996	22.3	7,500
1997	23.9	7,800
1998	21.0	7,425
1999	20.5	7,350
2000	20.6	7,275
2001	17.5	6,450
2002	20.0	7,050
2003	15.8	6,600

How might this data be better presented in order to be more useful?

What additional information would be required before conclusions about the data could be drawn?

Feedback on page 88

Let us now consider some different data, and apply some different descriptive measures to it. The data concerns the amount of business investment made by the UK distribution services industry since 1995, quarter by quarter. The figures are expressed in chained volume measures, which means that they are not distorted by inflationary factors. They are also seasonally adjusted, to avoid seasonal distortions (see table 6.2).

Table 6.2

Year and quarter	Investment (£ million)
1995 1	1,966
1995 2	2,006
1995 3	2,278
1995 4	2,246
1996 1	1,998
1996 2	2,060
1996 3	2,119
1996 4	2,245
1997 1	2,495
1997 2	2,590
1997 3	2,589
1997 4	2,765
1998 1	3,120
1998 2	3,430
1998 3	3,551
1998 4	3,364
1999 1	2,982
1999 2	2,789
1999 3	2,852
1999 4	2,950
2000 1	3,049
2000 2	3,000
2000 3	2,912
2000 4	2,883
2001 1	3,005
2001 2	3,026
2001 3	3,074
2001 4	3,206
2002 1	3,071
2002 2	3,153
2002 3	3,395
2002 4	3,270
2003 1	3,036
2003 2	3,213
2003 3	2,842
2003 4	3,018
2004 1	3,047
2004 2	2,799
2004 3	3,178
2004 4	3,064
2005 1	3,603
2005 2	3,392
2005 3	3,316
2005 4	3,157
2006 1	3,063
2006 2	3,527

An alternative approach would be to present the data graphically – and the most descriptive approach might be to use a bar chart, as shown in figure 6.2.

Figure 6.2: Data presented in bar chart

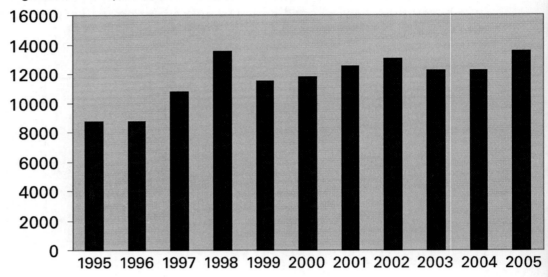

The above chart presents the data on an annual basis, keeping it simple and thus easily highlighting a general trend.

We might also want to present the data in a way that summarises it in another way. Often what is used is known as a 'measure of central tendency' which is represented by one of:

- mean
- median
- mode.

The **mean** is also known as the average, and involves dividing the sum of the observations by the number of observations.

So, by adding up all the quarterly spend amounts dividing by the number of quarters we get:

133,694/46 = £2,906 million (to the nearest million)

The **median** is the middle value in a sorted distribution, sample or population.

Firstly, we need to rearrange the spend amounts in order of value, as shown in table 6.3.

Table 6.3

1,966	1,998	2,006	2,060
2,119	2,245	2,246	2,278
2,495	2,589	2,590	2,765
2,789	2,799	2,842	2,852
2,883	2,912	2,950	2,982
3,000	3,005	3,018	3,026
3,036	3,047	3,049	3,063
3,064	3,071	3,074	3,120
3,153	3,157	3,178	3,206
3,213	3,270	3,316	3,364
3,392	3,395	3,430	3,527
3,551	3,603		

The formula for working out the median is:

$$\frac{n+1}{2}$$

Where 'n' is the number of different values. So in this example, there are 46 values, so the median will be between the 23rd and 24th value. We take the mean of the two values.

The median value is therefore 3,018 + 3,026 = 6,044/2 = 3,022

An extension of this idea is to establish the upper quartile and lower quartile values.

The lower quartile is calculated from the formula:

$$\frac{n+1}{4}$$

So it is 47/4 = 11.75 i.e. between the 11th and 12th value =

2590 + 2765 = 5355/2 = 2677.5.

The upper quartile is calculated from the formula:

$$\frac{3(n+1)}{4}$$

So it is 141/4 = 35.25, i.e. between the 35th and 36th value = 3,192.

The **mode** is the most frequently occurring number in a distribution, population or sample. This measure might not be particularly useful with the data being used – but we can work it out as long as we group the figures within bands, for example as shown in table 6.4.

Table 6.4

£ million bands	No of values
1900–1999	2
2000–2099	2
2100–2199	1
2200–2299	3
2300–2399	0
2400–2499	1
2500–2599	2
2600–2699	0
2700–2799	3
2800–2899	3
2900–2999	3
3000–3099	11
3100–3199	4
3200–3299	3
3300–3399	4
3400–3499	1
3500–3599	2
3600–3699	1

In this example, the most frequently appearing value is within the band 3000–3099 (it appears 11 times).

Finance for Purchasers

The mean is more sensitive to outliers than the median or mode. If in one particular quarter the capital spend was only £500 million, the mean would be reduced but the median and mode values would remain the same.

As well as the measure of central tendency, it is also useful to be aware of how widely spread the different values are. This is known as spread or variability, and there are a number of different measures including the following:

Range

This simply measures the distance between the highest value and the lowest. In our example, the range will be between £1,966 million (the lowest quarterly spend) and £3,603 million (the highest), i.e. a range of £1637 million.

Interquartile range

For this we have to work out the interquartile values, and establish the distance between them. It looks at the middle half of the values – and again using our data, and the interquartile figures calculated earlier, we can work out the interquartile range of $3,192 - 2,677.5 = £514.5$ million.

Whereas the range includes extreme values, the interquartile range excludes them.

Mean deviation

This establishes the average deviation from the mean of each value. Returning to our original data, we know that the mean is £2,906 million – or, to be more precise, it is £2,906.391 million. We then need to calculate the difference between the mean and each value – the deviation from the mean – and express it as an absolute value (ie don't worry about whether it is a positive or negative figure) (see table 6.5).

Table 6.5

Period	£ million	Deviation
1995 1	1,966	940.3913
1995 2	2,006	900.3913
1995 3	2,278	628.3913
1995 4	2,246	660.3913
1996 1	1,998	908.3913
1996 2	2,060	846.3913
1996 3	2,119	787.3913
1996 4	2,245	661.3913
1997 1	2,495	411.3913
1997 2	2,590	316.3913
1997 3	2,589	317.3913
1997 4	2,765	141.3913
1998 1	3,120	213.6087
1998 2	3,430	523.6087
1998 3	3,551	644.6087
1998 4	3,364	457.6087
1999 1	2,982	75.6087
1999 2	2,789	117.3913
1999 3	2,852	54.3913
1999 4	2,950	43.6087

(continued on next page)

Table 6.5 *(continued)*

Period	£ million	Deviation
2000 1	3,049	142.6087
2000 2	3,000	93.6087
2000 3	2,912	5.608696
2000 4	2,883	23.3913
2001 1	3,005	98.6087
2001 2	3,026	119.6087
2001 3	3,074	167.6087
2001 4	3,206	299.6087
2002 1	3,071	164.6087
2002 2	3,153	246.6087
2002 3	3,395	488.6087
2002 4	3,270	363.6087
2003 1	3,036	129.6087
2003 2	3,213	306.6087
2003 3	2,842	64.3913
2003 4	3,018	111.6087
2004 1	3,047	140.6087
2004 2	2,799	107.3913
2004 3	3,178	−271.609
2004 4	3,064	157.6087
2005 1	3,603	696.6087
2005 2	3,392	485.6087
2005 3	3,316	409.6087
2005 4	3,157	250.6087
2006 1	3,063	156.6087
2006 2	3,527	620.6087

If we add up all the deviations we get 15,230.09. Divide this by 46 (the number of values) and we get a mean deviation – how much, on average, do the figures stray from the overall mean – of £331.09 million.

Variance and standard deviation

Here we have to:

1 Calculate the overall mean (we know this is £2,906.391 million).
2 Work out the deviations (and we can express these as positive or negative).
3 Square the deviations.
4 Calculate the mean of the squared deviations. This is the **variance**.
5 Calculate the square root of the variance. This is the **standard deviation**.

See table 6.6.

Table 6.6

Period	£ million	Deviation from mean	Deviation squared
1995 1	1,966	−940.391	884,335.8
1995 2	2,006	−900.391	810,704.5
1995 3	2,278	−628.391	394,875.6
1995 4	2,246	−660.391	436,116.7
1996 1	1,998	−908.391	825,174.8
1996 2	2,060	−846.391	716,378.2
1996 3	2,119	−787.391	619,985.1

(continued on next page)

Finance for Purchasers

Table 6.6 *(continued)*

Period	£ million	Deviation from mean	Deviation squared
1996 4	2,245	−661.391	437,438.5
1997 1	2,495	−411.391	169,242.8
1997 2	2,590	−316.391	100,103.5
1997 3	2,589	−317.391	100,737.2
1997 4	2,765	−141.391	19,991.5
1998 1	3,120	213.6087	45,628.67
1998 2	3,430	523.6087	274,166.1
1998 3	3,551	644.6087	415,520.4
1998 4	3,364	457.6087	209,405.7
1999 1	2,982	75.6087	5,716.675
1999 2	2,789	−117.391	13,780.72
1999 3	2,852	−54.3913	2,958.414
1999 4	2,950	43.6087	1,901.718
2000 1	3,049	142.6087	20,337.24
2000 2	3,000	93.6087	8,762.588
2000 3	2,912	5.608696	31.45747
2000 4	2,883	−23.3913	547.1531
2001 1	3,005	98.6087	9,723.675
2001 2	3,026	119.6087	14,306.24
2001 3	3,074	167.6087	28,092.67
2001 4	3,206	299.6087	89,765.37
2002 1	3,071	164.6087	27,096.02
2002 2	3,153	246.6087	60,815.85
2002 3	3,395	488.6087	238,738.5
2002 4	3,270	363.6087	132,211.3
2003 1	3,036	129.6087	16,798.41
2003 2	3,213	306.6087	94,008.89
2003 3	2,842	−64.3913	4,146.24
2003 4	3,018	111.6087	12,456.5
2004 1	3,047	140.6087	19,770.81
2004 2	2,799	−107.391	11,532.89
2004 3	3,178	271.6087	73,771.28
2004 4	3,064	157.6087	24,840.5
2005 1	3,603	696.6087	485,263.7
2005 2	3,392	485.6087	235,815.8
2005 3	3,316	409.6087	167,779.3
2005 4	3,157	250.6087	62,804.72
2006 1	3,063	156.6087	24,526.28
2006 2	3,527	620.6087	385,155.2
			8,733,261
		Variance (stage 4 above)	189,853.5
		Standard deviation (stage 5)	435.7218

So – applying to the data:

1   The overall mean is £2906.391 million.
2   The deviations from the mean are set out in the third column.
3   Square the deviations – see fourth column.
4   Turning to the bottom of the table, calculate the mean of the squared deviations = 49.5875. This is the **variance**.
5   Calculate the square root of the variance = £435.7 million. This is the **standard deviation**.

The point about standard deviation is that it is a more meaningful measure than the variance, and it can be more easily grasped as a concept. It measures the dispersion of the data – the bigger the standard deviation, the more widely dispersed the data is.

Any collected data can be plotted on a graph to provide a visual display of the distribution of that data. Figure 6.3 below is an example of normally distributed data.

Figure 6.3: Normal distribution

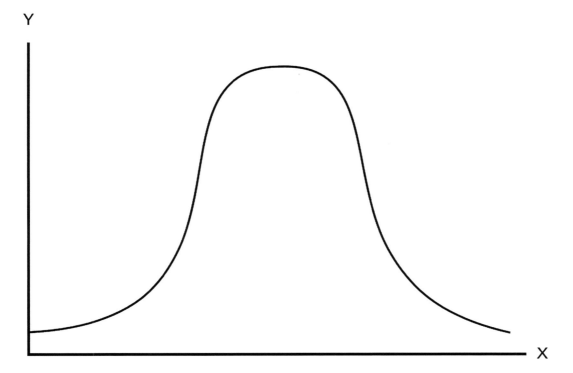

Where normal distribution exists, there are fixed percentages of scores falling between points on the scale represented in standard deviation units.

If you are using a large number of observations, and they are normally distributed, then 68% should be within one standard deviation of the mean, and 95% will be within two standard deviations. In our case, 75% are within one standard deviation, and all the observations are within two standard deviations. So, the lower the standard deviation, the more consistent are the data.

The steps that are usually taken with descriptive statistics are as follows:

- collect
- classify
- summarise
- present data
- draw conclusions from data (inferential statistics).

Finance for Purchasers

Self-assessment question 6.1

The data in table 6.7 describes the average number of US dollars that could be bought for £1 for the 20 years to 2003:

Table 6.7

Year	Rate
1984	1.3366
1985	1.2962
1986	1.4672
1987	1.6392
1988	1.7812
1989	1.6397
1990	1.7850
1991	1.7699
1992	1.7661
1993	1.5023
1994	1.5321
1995	1.5782
1996	1.5619
1997	1.6378
1998	1.6570
1999	1.6183
2000	1.5162
2001	1.4400
2002	1.5026
2003	1.6344

For this data, work calculate:

- the mean value
- the median value
- the range
- the interquartile range
- the standard deviation.

NB: The various calculations can all be quickly carried out using a spreadsheet, which have functions designed to work out the mean, median, quartiles and standard deviation. However, carrying out the exercise manually may be more useful from a learning point of view, as it will require an understanding of how the figures are derived.

Feedback on page 89

6.2 Inferential statistics and the circumstances in which they are useful

Inferential statistics do more than just describe data. They, as the name suggests, infer causes. In other words, the data can be used to make informed guesses about a situation, even where a complete set of information is unavailable.

6 Descriptive and inferential statistics

Where a full set of data is available, it is referred to as the **population** (and this, of course, doesn't just refer to people). Where only part of the information is available, it is called a **sample**.

A sample should be a representative subset of the population. If the sample is too small, it may not be fully representative of the population, but using a very large sample can be expensive and time consuming. Choosing a sample size can therefore involve a trade-off between cost and accuracy.

The sample size that is used is typically driven by the following factors:

- Margin of error, which represents the extent to which the sample used may differ from the population as a whole.
- Variability – the range of values derived from the sample, and usually measured by standard deviation. The greater the variability, the more the need for a larger sample.
- Confidence level – how likely are the results from the sample to represent the whole population?
- Population size – only really relevant when the sample is relatively large (e.g. greater than 5% of population) and than can be reduced in size.

Learning activity 6.2

From within your working environment, or from the media, identify a report that contains some statistics and draws some conclusions.

- What samples have been used?
- How have the samples been determined?
- What conclusions have been drawn?
- How have inferential statistics been derived?

Feedback on page 89

There are also many different methods of sampling, including:

- *Random sampling:* where every item in the population is equally likely to be selected.
- *Cluster sampling:* involves splitting the population into definable clusters (eg geographical areas) and then using a random selection of clusters.
- *Convenience sampling:* where willing volunteers are used (eg for a survey.
- *Judgement sampling:* effectively the opposite of random sampling, where the sample is chosen on some subjective basis.
- *Quota sampling:* where the sample is selected against some predetermined criteria, so that the sample contains a minimum number of examples that show certain characteristics.
- Systematic sampling – where every nth item is selected.

These different methods will be used to meet the needs of the organisation using them, and how precise the results need to be. Some are more robust than others in terms of achieving a statistically valid result.

85

Inferential statistics use samples to draw conclusions about the whole population.

By comparing different samples, we can establish whether the idea that we are testing is likely to be true or not.

It is very difficult to calculate directly the probability of a conclusion being true. An easier approach is to turn this on its head, and try to establish how likely it is *not* to be true. In other words, how likely is it that we can't draw the conclusions that we want from the data?

This neutral conclusion is known as the 'null hypothesis'. It is then relatively easy to calculate the probability of data being different from the 'neutral' (ie 'no effect') conclusion.

There are various stages that have to be gone through in order to test the null hypothesis, and we can illustrate the process with a simple and well-used example.

Suppose we toss a coin six times, and on each occasion it turns up 'heads'. How can we prove that the coin is biased or double-sided?

Step 1: Establish what we need to know.

We need to identify precisely what it is that we are trying to prove. In this case, we need to know that the coin is biased. This is sometimes known as the 'alternative hypothesis' – in that it is the alternative to the null hypothesis outlined above.

Step 2: Assume the 'null hypothesis'.

The null hypothesis is that there is no conclusion that can be drawn from the data – for example that there is no difference between two groups of people, or no relation between two factors. We need to find evidence against the null hypothesis.

In our example, the null hypothesis is that the coin has no bias, and that there is therefore a 50% of it turning up 'heads' with each toss. Remember – we are trying to prove that the coin is biased, but we are going to do so establishing how likely it is to be *unbiased*.

Step 3: Work out the probability that the difference from the null hypothesis could have occurred by chance.

In other words, in our example, how likely is it that a coin tossed six times will turn up 'heads' each time (or, indeed, 'tails')?

The probability of six consecutive heads is:

$0.5 \times 0.5 \times 0.5 \times 0.5 \times 0.5 \times 0.5 = 0.15625$

The probability of six consecutive tails is also 0.15625

So the probability that this could have occurred simply by chance is:

$0.15625 + 0.15625 = 0.3125$

6 Descriptive and inferential statistics

In other words, the chances of a tossed coin turning up with the same result from six consecutive tosses is just over 3%.

Step 4: Set the significance level.

A level of probability has to be set that gives us confidence that we can reasonably reject the null hypothesis.

A probability level of 0.05 (i.e. 5%) is often used. If the chances of the null hypothesis being correct are less than 1 in 20, we can reject it. A lower threshold might be used in circumstances where a greater degree of certainty is deemed appropriate.

In our coin example, the null hypothesis has a probability of just over 3%. We might reasonably conclude that the coin is biased.

If the coin had turned up heads 4 times in a row, and we went through the same process, we could work out that the probability of the null hypothesis was 0.125 (12.5%). If our threshold was 5%, we would not be able to reject the null hypothesis and the data would be insufficient for us to say that the coin was biased.

It is important to appreciate that the probability value is not about the chances of the null hypothesis being true, but about how likely it could have happened by chance.

Self-assessment question 6.2

The following are quotes from media reports.

Are they derived from descriptive or inferential statistics?

1   In a study of 10,000 people carried out in Tokyo, office workers who spend all day looking at screens were found to have a one in 20 chance of risking eye problems, especially in people who are short-sighted.
2   Almost a quarter of UK A-level entries were awarded the top grade this year, amidst claims that the A-level exams are getting easier. The proportion of exam entries that achieved an A was 24.1%, up 1.3 percentage points on last year.
3   Retail sales fell last month as the searing heat and a drop-off in demand for electrical goods following the end of the World Cup curtailed spending. The Office for National Statistics said the volume of retail sales declined by 0.3% between June and July. This compared to growth of 0.7% recorded in June, a figure revised down from 0.9%.
4   Obese people are up to 80 times more likely to develop Type 2 diabetes than those who maintain a healthy weight.

Feedback on page 89

Revision question

Now try the revision question for this session on page 346.

Summary

In this session we have looked at statistics. We first considered descriptive statistics – the use of data which provides information but which does not in itself attempt to infer any additional findings. In this context we covered measures of central tendency – including mean, median and mode – and measures of variation including the standard deviation.

We then looked at inferential statistics, and the idea of using statistical data to try to draw conclusions and the commonly used approach of using the null hypothesis.

Feedback on learning activities and self-assessment questions

Feedback on learning activity 6.1

Firstly the data would be better presented graphically, to show trends and to give scale. A bar chart and line chart might be most effective. The trends can be shown in terms of both numbers of visitors and spend. The graph could also be shown to highlight the extent to which the trends coincide – in other words to highlight whether spend **per visitor** is changing, and if so, in what way, and what the average spend per visitor trends are.

In order to do this, we have to re-base one set of data, and you will see that the 'Amount spent (€ millions)' starts at 6,000 to achieve this.

While the graphical presentation tells us nothing new, it makes some interpretation of the data more straightforward.

Figure 6.1

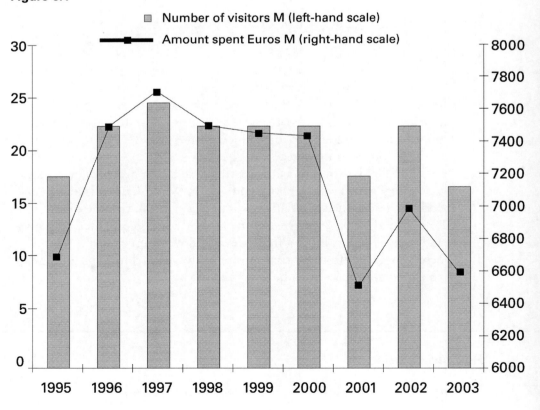

6 Descriptive and inferential statistics

Also, useful additional data would include:

- inflation data (are the amounts of spend adjusted for inflation?)
- comparative data for other countries
- breakdown of who the visitors are, where they have come from, age groups, and so on.

Feedback on self-assessment question 6.1

The answers are as shown in table 6.8.

Table 6.8

Mean	1.583095
Median	1.59825
Lower Quartile	1.50245
Upper Quartile	1.64835
Range	0.4888
Interquartile range	0.1415
Standard deviation	0.138528

Feedback on learning activity 6.2

It is important, when presenting statistics and drawing conclusions, to be able to back the latter up.

If a conclusion has been drawn, this needs to be supported with statistically valid data. The question of what is 'valid' can in itself be contentious, and a week rarely passes by without some media report or other making claims about how good (or bad) for you a particular activity or food product is.

Work-based reports might similarly wish to 'prove' something. It is important, therefore, to be able to ascertain the basis for any claims of conclusions that are being made.

Feedback on self-assessment question 6.2

1 Inferential – there has clearly been some analysis done from a sample (10,000) of people working in offices.
2 Although there is some suggestion of a link between improved results and easier exams, the data is descriptive only. 'Claims' and research data are not the same thing.
3 Descriptive again. The fall-off in sales might have had something to do with the weather and the World Cup, but the statistics quoted simply describe a fall-off in sales.
4 Inferential.

Finance for Purchasers

Study session 7
Contribution analysis and marginal costing

Introduction

Understanding costs is key for any business decision maker. This session will look at costs from a number of different angles – how they are classified, measured and reported, and how they can be used – if presented in a particular way – to help make a number of business decisions.

Decision-making is at the heart of all management activity.

Session learning objectives

After completing this session you should be able to:

7.1 Analyse cost–volume–profit and break-even data.
7.2 Apply the concept of contribution, and marginal costing, as an aid to decision making.
7.3 Analyse limiting factors and demonstrate their effect on decision making.
7.4 Describe the limitations and assumptions involved in the use of contribution analysis and marginal costing.

Unit content coverage

This study session covers the following topics from the official CIPS unit content document:

Learning objective

2.4 Use contribution analysis and marginal costing to evaluate a range of decision-making situations.
   • Cost–volume–profit analysis and break-even analysis
   • Make or buy decisions
   • Deciding on product range
   • The analysis, and most profitable use, of limiting factors

Prior knowledge

Study sessions 1 to 5.

Timing

You should set aside about 6 hours to read and complete this session, including learning activities, self-assessment questions, the suggested further reading (if any) from the essential textbook for this unit and the revision question.

7.1 Analysing cost–volume–profit and break-even data

Costing background

Key business decisions – about pricing, production levels, whether to make or buy in components, optimal levels of output – can be aided by understanding more about costs.

In order to run a business properly, managers need prompt, accurate and understandable information about the costs of different activities. Without this information:

- they will not know if the business is operating at a profit or a loss
- they will not be able to plan for the future
- they will not be able to set correct selling prices or control expenditure.

During this session, and the next one which looks at pricing, we will consider the ways in which an understanding of costs can aid decision making.

Costs represent the total expenditures involved in running a business. They can then broken down in ways that help managers understand different aspects of the business. There are many different ways in which they can be broken down, reported and analysed. Different approaches will be taken, and these will depend on the different objectives that the organisation is trying to achieve.

Traditional financial reporting has involved splitting costs in terms of whether they are **direct** or **indirect.**

Direct costs are those that can be specifically associated with a particular product or activity. A good example would be raw material costs in a manufacturing process.

Indirect costs are, by contrast, those costs that can *not* be specifically identified to a product or activity. They might include some production costs, if they are of a general nature and so cannot be immediately linked to a particular product. Other examples would include health and safety, purchasing, accounts, HR and marketing. Indirect costs are often referred to as **overheads**.

The **total cost** of a product can therefore be defined as its direct cost plus its indirect cost. A difficult issue, though, concerns a company's ability to determine the cost of an individual product. Identifying the direct cost of a product may be relatively straightforward, but how do we allocate the overheads to different products? If an company has six different product lines, and an HR department that costs £1 million a year to operate, how much of that £1 million should be allocated to each of the different products?

The traditional way of dealing with this has been to require each product or service to absorb their share of the overhead. For example, the HR costs in the first instance have been allocated to the HR function, but these might then be allocated to other departments on the basis of how many employees each department has. Ultimately, each product or service will have to absorb the total overheads on some predetermined but possibly arbitrary basis (often, traditionally, on the basis of direct labour hours or machine hours consumed by that product line). The process is known as **full absorption costing**.

The problem with this approach is that it is often quite arbitrary, and this has been compounded in more recent times by the changing nature of business – with less emphasis on manufacturing. An increasingly large proportion of costs are of an indirect, overhead nature. Thus an accurate and reliable way of apportioning overheads has become a pressing issue.

Activity-based costing (ABC) represents what many believe to be a more sophisticated approach, as it attempts to get to the root of overhead costs and, most importantly, understand why they are being incurred.

ABC identifies **activities** that cause costs to be incurred. It then assigns the cost of the activities to the product or service that uses them. This – in theory – enables firms to pinpoint the sources of indirect costs and allocate them precisely to specific activities rather than just spreading them evenly across all products or departments in a company.

Fixed and variable costs

The major benefit of producing and analysing cost data is the ability to make more effective business decisions. Areas in which cost information can prove useful are:

- *Pricing:* A business needs to know how much any product or service costs before it can decide what price to charge. This will be explored in more detail in the next chapter.
- *Make or buy situations:* for example should a company buy in components, or manufacture its own? A cost comparison of the two would help it to make the right decision.
- *Setting up or closing down decisions:* for example should the company keep a particular part of its business in operation?

In these contexts, an awareness of how costs 'behave' is vital. **Cost behaviour** highlights the extent to which costs change with sales volumes, and this can directly impact on the types of decision highlighted above.

Some costs will not change in the short run. In other words, regardless of the level of business activity, the costs will stay the same. Examples would include business rates, office rental or salary costs for full-time administrative staff. Such costs are known as **fixed costs**.

Other costs are likely to move in line with business activity levels. For example, raw material costs will be directly linked to sales volumes, as will the hiring of temporary staff at busy periods. These are known as **variable costs**.

The reality, though, is that many costs are neither purely fixed, nor purely variable. They sit somewhere between the two. Telecoms costs, for example, may involve a fixed fee element and then some usage-based charges. Such costs are known as semi-variable costs.

The three main cost behaviour patterns are illustrated below in graphical form. The left-hand graph illustrates fixed costs, which have the same financial value regardless of activity levels. The middle graph shows variable costs, which increase in line with activity. The third graph illustrates semi-variable costs, which start at a fixed level and then increase with activity.

Figure 7.1: Cost behaviour patterns

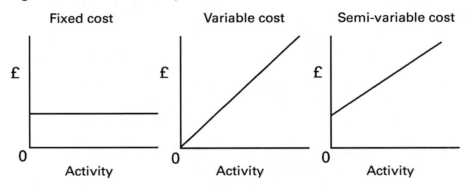

Engineering companies tend to have high fixed costs because of the need for large-scale plant and machinery. Telecoms companies have a big network which has to be depreciated (and depreciation is a fixed cost). Transport companies have the fixed costs associated with flying a plane or running a train.

Where fixed costs are relatively high, as in the examples above, a company is said to have high **operational gearing**. What this means is that these businesses are very sensitive to changes in business volume.

Learning activity 7.1

Woolly Plc makes jumpers.

Its latest summarised P&L is shown in table 7.1.

Table 7.1

	£
Sales	500,000
Cost of sales	225,000
Gross profit	275,000
Other expenses	195,000
Net profit	80,000

Cost of sales include labour, materials and production overheads. Other expenses include administration expenses, and selling and distribution expenses. This is how a traditional profit and loss account is presented.

(continued on next page)

7 Contribution analysis and marginal costing

Learning activity 7.1 (continued)

Presenting the same data using a fixed v variable cost split, it looks as shown in table 7.2.

Table 7.2

	£
Sales	500,000
Variable costs	290,000
Contribution	210,000
Fixed costs	130,000
Net profit	80,000

Identify a cost that would be part of the 'cost of sales', but which is likely to be a fixed cost.

Identify a cost that would fall under 'other expenses' but which would be a variable cost when using the format above.

Comment on how and when the two different presentations would be useful.

Feedback on page 106

This approach is sometimes referred to as **marginal costing**, and it looks at costs in terms of their behavioural characteristics rather than their functional aspects (which absorption costing is geared towards).

The focus is therefore on separating costs into variable elements (where the cost per unit remains the same with total cost varying in proportion to activity) and fixed elements (where the total cost remains the same in each period regardless of the level of activity). This is not easily achieved with accuracy, and is an oversimplification of reality.

Let us look at some new figures:

A summary income statement, classified according to patterns of cost behaviour, is set out below. At present, the company is selling 60 units per year, at £1,000 per unit (see table 7.3).

Table 7.3

Sales	60,000	
Less variable costs	36,000	variable costs are 60% of sales
Contribution	24,000	the 'contribution' margin is 40%
Less fixed costs	20,000	
Net profit	4,000	

From the information above, we can see that the company is making a profit – in this case a net profit of £4,000 after all operating costs (both variable and fixed) have been deducted.

But by splitting the costs into 'variable' and 'fixed' categories we can use the resulting data to make key decisions.

A key figure in the above data is the 'contribution'. Contribution describes the amount of profit that is being made *before fixed costs are taken into account.* Or, put another way, it is the excess of sales revenue over variable costs. Figure 7.2 shows the idea graphically:

Figure 7.2: Contribution in relation to fixed costs and profit

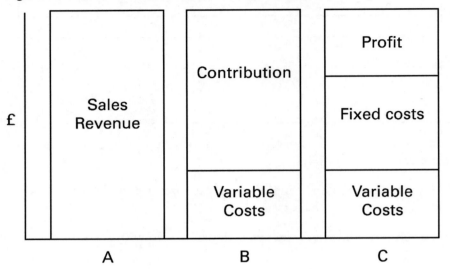

Columns A and B represent the basic equation that tells us:

Contribution = sales revenue minus variable costs

Column C represents the idea that contribution equals (or 'contributes to') the fixed costs and the profits of a business.

In our numerical example, it means that, if this business can sell 60 units, it will be making a contribution of £24,000 to the fixed costs and profits of the overall business. As the fixed costs are £20,000, we are left with a profit of the remaining amount, which is £4,000.

To be even more useful, however, we should look at the data in more detail, and consider it in the context of one single unit.

We can sell one unit for £1,000. We can also see that the variable cost of one unit is £600. (£36,000/60 units). So the contribution per unit is as shown in table 7.4.

Table 7.4

Sales price per unit	£1,000
Variable cost per unit	£600
Contribution per unit	£400

In other words, each time the company sells a unit for £1000, it is making a contribution of £400 towards the fixed costs and overall profitability of the business.

This can then help us to answer important questions. For example, what is the break-even point of this operation? The answer is that the break-even point will be that point at which the contribution made will be enough to cover the fixed costs – and no more.

This can be calculated by dividing the total fixed costs by the contribution per unit, as shown in table 7.5.

Table 7.5

Fixed costs	£20,000
Contribution per unit	£400
Break-even point	£20,000/£400 = 50 units

Another question might involve establishing the sales volume needed to achieve a particular level of profit. Let us say that this business needs to achieve annual profits of £10,000. This will require the contribution figure to cover both the fixed costs of £20,000 and the required profit of £10,000 – a total of £30,000.

If we divide this £30,000 figure by the £400 contribution per unit figure, we get a sales volume of 75 units.

Sometimes it is easier to present this type of information graphically, as demonstrated in figure 7.3. Where the sales revenue curve crosses the total cost curve is the break-even point.

Figure 7.3: Break-even point

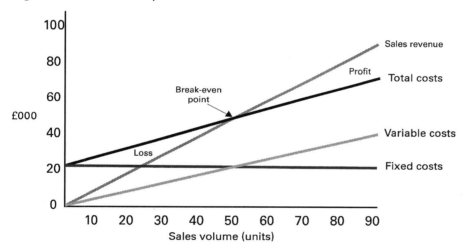

Earlier, we worked out that the break-even output was 50 units or £50,000 sales. From the graph above, we can see that this is the case. The break-even point occurs where the 'sales' and 'total costs' curves intersect.

The level of total **contribution** at any point is represented by the area between the sales curve and the variable costs curve.

Using the same data we can assess – and chart – how much profit will be made at a variety of different levels of sales. This is known as cost–volume–profit analysis.

At different levels of sales, Company X will show the profit results in table 7.6.

Table 7.6

Sales revenue	0	10,000	20,000	30,000	40,000	50,000	60,000	70,000	80,000
Variable costs	0	6,000	12,000	18,000	24,000	30,000	36,000	42,000	48,000
Contribution	0	4,000	8,000	12,000	16,000	20,000	24,000	28,000	32,000

(continued on next page)

Table 7.6 *(continued)*

Fixed costs	20,000	20,000	20,000	20,000	20,000	20,000	20,000	20,000	20,000
Net profit	(20,000)	(16,000)	(12,000)	(8,000)	(4,000)	0	4,000	8,000	12,000

Thus we can see that, if the company doesn't sell anything it will lose £20,000 (its fixed costs), but if it can sell 80 units at £1,000 a time, it will make a profit of £12,000. The break-even point is identifiable here too – at sales revenue of £50,000 (that is 50 units at £1,000 each).

This data can also usefully be presented graphically as shown in figure 7.4.

Figure 7.4: Cost–volume–profit graph

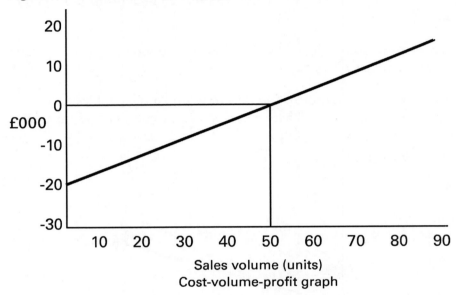

Cost-volume-profit graph

Marginal costs are extra costs incurred with each additional unit of output, or costs which will only be incurred if it is decided to continue with an activity. Variable costs are usually marginal – that is they will not be incurred if an activity doesn't take place.

Some fixed costs could also be marginal – for example rent could be, if a building could be vacated immediately a decision is made to cease operations.

The concept of marginal costing is helpful when considering production volumes – and indeed expansion – and asking the question 'What would happen if we made one more unit?' The variable cost of a product will often be similar to its marginal cost, though sometimes the marginal cost will be a lot higher – for example if an operation is working at full capacity, the making of one more unit may trigger some significantly increased investment costs.

There are some major weaknesses and limitations associated with this type of analysis, and its value as a decision-making tool.

In practice no costs remain permanently fixed, so the classification of costs into a fixed category can only be applied for a limited and shorter-term time span.

A further complication, as highlighted above, is that costs may not be fixed or variable, but somewhere between the two. For example, some contracts

7 Contribution analysis and marginal costing

may involve a fixed fee, with additional charges for use over a certain level of activity. If this is the case, then an attempt must be made to split them into their variable or fixed elements if any use is to be made of these behaviour patterns.

Another limitation is the fact that variable costs will not, in practice, have a precisely linear relationship with volumes of output. For example, with raw materials there are likely to be discounts available for larger volumes, which would reduce the variable cost per unit.

These limitations apart, an understanding of cost behaviour and its impact on profitability can be very useful for short-term planning, control and decision-making, especially in a multi-product business.

Self-assessment question 7.1

The information in table 7.7 relates to Company Y, a bottled drinks maker.

Table 7.7

Selling price per crate of 12 bottles	£6
Variable costs per crate	£3.50
Monthly fixed costs	£7,500

1. How many crates must it sell per month if it wants to break even?
2. How many crates must it sell per month if it wants to make a monthly profit of £5,000?

If it increased the selling price to £6.50, how would the above answers differ?

Feedback on page 107

7.2 Contribution, and marginal costing, as an aid to decision making

In section 7.1 we introduced the idea of contribution and marginal costing, and we looked at the way in which it can help a business understand its break-even point. We also looked at cost–volume–profit analysis.

This section will expand on these ideas, and consider ways in which these techniques can be used as a basis for decision making.

Learning activity 7.2

A company operates a national chain of 30 off-licence stores. Profits are calculated for each store before allocating any of the head office costs. All stores are profitable at the pre-head office level, but once a suitable allocation of head office costs has been deducted (on the basis of each store's square footage), five of them become loss-making.

(continued on next page)

Finance for Purchasers

> ### Learning activity 7.2 *(continued)*
>
> On the basis that head office costs are real, and they are allocated on a perfectly fair basis, it has been suggested that the five loss making stores should be closed down.
>
> Why is this suggestion likely to be flawed, and what additional information about the head office costs is required before a proper analysis can be conducted?
>
> *Feedback on page 107*

The key decisions that can be made using contribution analysis and marginal costing are:

- decisions about ceasing certain activities
- decisions about 'one-off' contracts
- 'make or buy' decisions
- decisions involving scarce resources, or 'limiting factors'.

Decisions about ceasing, or closing down, certain operations concern situations such as the one briefly outlined in the above learning activity. To explore the idea further, we should look at a different scenario and put some figures to it.

Company X makes beds, and has a range of three products – the Pine, the Metallic and the Luxury. The following figures represent one month's figures. The beds are all made in the same factory, and at present all fixed overheads (total £540,000 per month) are split equally between the three lines. The latest set of monthly figures is shown below in Table 7.8

Table 7.8

	Pine	Metallic	Luxury	Total
	£000	£000	£000	£000
Sales	320	400	200	920
Variable costs	112	152	80	344
Contribution	208	248	120	576
Fixed costs	180	180	180	540
Net profit	**28**	**68**	**–60**	**36**

The key question is whether the company should close down the luxury bed line, as it is making a monthly loss of £60,000.

The most important figure to consider is the contribution figure, and a better way of presenting the data might involve not spreading the overheads (see table 7.9).

Table 7.9

	Pine	Metallic	Luxury	Total
	£000	**£000**	**£000**	**£000**
Sales	320	400	200	920
Variable costs	112	152	80	344
Contribution	208	248	120	576
				540
				36

7 Contribution analysis and marginal costing

It may be that the Luxury line should be closed down – but only if the resource that it frees up would mean that sales of the Pine and/or the Metallic lines would more than compensate. This is possible, and they both have higher contribution margins than the Luxury.

Other considerations involve whether closure of the Pine might upset customers, who might buy from each of the three ranges.

Make or buy decisions are based on similar grounds. An example would be a maker of a range of lawn mowers, company X, that use a number of common components manufactured in-house. Company X is considering buying one particular component externally. The current cost of the component part is £45, made up as shown in table 7.10.

Table 7.10

	£
Direct labour	13
Direct materials	15
Variable overheads	2
Fixed overheads	15
	45

This compares with the price of an identical part available externally at £35. Should the company buy in the part, or continue to make it in-house?

The decision would need to be based on a comparison of the external price and the relevant variable cost of making the component. Thus we need to compare the £35 price with our current cost *without the fixed overhead* as that will have to be paid anyway. Thus the cost of making the part comes down to 13 + 15 + 2 = £30 and, on the face of it, the company should continue to make the component in-house.

Self-assessment question 7.2

A car manufacturer is considering the purchase of some component parts that it currently manufactures in-house. It currently makes 5,000 units of the components it needs per year, and the costs involved in making this volume are set out in table 7.11.

Table 7.11

Direct materials	60,000
Direct labour	50,000
Variable manufacturing costs (power, utilities, etc)	5,000
Fixed manufacturing costs	40,000
General overheads	25,000
Total costs	180,000

The total cost per unit is therefore is £36 (£180,000/5000)

The external component maker has offered to supply an annual 5,000 units at a price of £30 per unit.

(continued on next page)

Finance for Purchasers

Self-assessment question 7.2 *(continued)*

Assume that:

(a) there would be no other use for the released manufacturing capacity, and
(b) using an external supplier would reduce the fixed manufacturing costs by £5,000 per annum
(c) no additional costs (e.g. redundancy) would be incurred if the work was outsourced

Is the £30 per unit quoted price acceptable?

Feedback on page 107

7.3 Limiting factors and their effect on decision-making

Another decision-making situation for which the contribution approach can be useful is where a business faces a scarce resource or 'limiting factor'. The term limiting factor describes a situation where there is some overriding constraint on the activity of a business. It could be production capacity, it could be available skilled people, it could be availability of materials.

Learning activity 7.3

Select a company that is known to you – ideally a supplier.

Identify some scarce resources or limiting factors that may constrain the activities they are involved with.

What impact are these limiting factors having on their operations?

Feedback on page 108

Now consider the following example.

Company X has projected the data for the month of May shown in table 7.13.

Table 7.13

Product	A	B	C
Selling price (£ per unit)	24	60	90
Variable cost (£ per unit)	12	50	60
Estimated sales demand	400	200	190
Assembly labour hours (per unit)	10	4	15

We also know that there is a limit to the amount of assembly labour available and for May the maximum such labour available is 3,000 hours.

As we have the sales price and the variable costs, we can easily work out the contribution per unit as shown in table 7.14.

Table 7.14

Product	A	B	C
Selling price (£ per unit)	24	60	90
Variable cost (£ per unit)	12	50	60
Contribution per unit (£)	12	10	30

From this data, we might conclude that C is our most profitable product, and that we should make as much of that as we can before perhaps moving on to Product A, which shows the second highest contribution.

Alternatively, given that Product A has the greatest demand, we might conclude that we could maximise our overall contribution by prioritising its production.

But these ideas ignore the limiting factor of assembly labour hours. For whatever reason, we are limited to 3,000 hours of assembly labour in May. We therefore need to work out how much profit we will make per unit of limited resource. This involves dividing the unit contribution figures by the amount of limited resource consumed:

Table 7.15

Product	A	B	C
Contribution per unit (£)	12	10	30
Assembly labour hours (per unit)	10	4	15
Contribution per limiting factor (£)	1.2	2.5	2

This will influence our approach. Product B now becomes the most attractive product to make, given its less demanding use of the limited resource – labour. We will therefore maximise profitability if we first of all produce product B, and then shift production to the next best product – C.

Given our limited resource, we could satisfy all the demand for Product B. This would involve making 200 units and therefore using up 200 × 4 = 800 hours of labour. If we then move to product C, we will plan to produce as much as the remaining labour resource will allow:

Each C consumes 15 hours of labour

We have 3000 – 800 = 2200 hours of labour available

We can plan to make 2200/15 = 146 units

This will not meet all the demand for C, nor any of the demand for A, but we will have adopted the most profitable production plan given the labour constraints we are presented with.

Now have a go at self-assessment question 7.3 below below.

Self-assessment question 7.3

A company manufactures and sells two products (X and Y).

(continued on next page)

Finance for Purchasers

Self-assessment question 7.3 (continued)

Both products use the same skilled labour.

For the coming month, supply of the required labour is limited to 2,000 hours.

Data relating to each product is as shown in table 7.16.

Table 7.16

Product	X	Y
Selling price per unit	£20	£40
Variable cost per unit	£12	£30
Skilled labour hours per unit	2	4
Maximum demand (units) per period	800	400

In order to maximise profit in the coming month, how many units of each product should the company plan to make and sell?

(a) 200 units of X and 400 units of Y
(b) 400 units of X and 300 units of Y
(c) 600 units of X and 200 units of Y
(d) 800 units of X and 100 units of Y

Feedback on page 108

7.4 The limitations and assumptions involved in the use of contribution analysis and marginal costing.

While very useful as a decision-making aid, there are a number of limitations associated with contribution analysis and marginal costing.

Learning activity 7.4

We have looked at contribution analysis and marginal costing from a number of angles. You may have noticed some weaknesses and limitations to the concept as you have worked through the examples.

Summarise what assumptions the underlying concept requires.

Outline what you think some of the practical limitations might be.

It might be useful, when carrying out this activity, to think about the following:

- the fixed v variable cost split
- the role that the price of the product has to play
- the fact that most companies sell more than one product or service.

Feedback on page 108

If we look at the practical application of contribution analysis, the often-cited weaknesses can be split into two main aspects – the assumptions that have to be made and the limitations that make useful application difficult.

The assumptions that have to be made include:

- The selling price is constant at different levels of activity. This is unlikely in practice, as greater sales volumes, for example, may either encourage, or be a result of, discounting activities. The important concept of price elasticity of demand is also overlooked. This is something we will cover in study session 8, and is about the sensitivity of sales volumes to the price being charged.
- Costs behave in a linear way (for example, the variable cost curve on the CVP graph is a straight line). This is similar to the above point, in that unit variable costs are likely to fall as volume increases. The price of a component, for example, is likely to be different if you buy 10 compared to buying 10,000. Clearly, costs per unit will decrease with volume buying, as discounts will be available.
- Costs can easily be categorised as either fixed or variable. As we have seen, the idea that some costs are absolutely fixed, while others are conveniently variable, rather ignores the idea that many costs in reality fall somewhere between the two descriptions. In practice, it is not that easy to identify cost behaviour.
- In multi-product examples, the sales mix is constant.
- The production facilities anticipated for the purpose of contribution and cost–volume–profit analysis do not undergo any change.

Other weaknesses include the following:

- There is the question of whether the relationships between costs and income will hold true beyond the very short term. The contribution concept is used to aid decision making, but will the assumptions made hold true into the future?
- Use of contribution analysis for decision making involves making estimates and extrapolating into the future. This involves a great deal of subjectivity and uncertainty.
- The concept assumes that what is manufactured is sold. In reality, not everything that is manufactured will be sold.
- Where a cost is neither fixed, nor variable, it cannot easily be fitted into the contribution model. It may be possible to develop a model that can build in costs that don't strictly fit either the fixed or variable label – but often the behaviour can be quite complex.

Now answer the following true/false questions, which cover all parts of this session.

Self-assessment question 7.4

1. In marginal costing and cost–volume–profit analysis, contribution per unit is the difference between the sales price and the direct costs for each unit. True/false

(continued on next page)

Self-assessment question 7.4 (continued)

2   Fixed costs are those costs that don't change with output volumes. True/false
3   One of the main limitations of contribution analysis is the 'limiting factor'. True/false
4   Break-even volumes can be calculated by dividing fixed costs by the variable cost per unit. True/false
5   A weakness in marginal costing and contribution analysis is the need to assume that variable costs per unit stay the same, regardless of volume. True/false

Feedback on page 109

Revision question

Now try the revision question for this session on page 346.

Summary

This session began by considering costs from the perspective of how they have traditionally been reported. We then looked at more recent developments that have reflected the changing economy and the emphasis away from manufacturing activity.

We also explored the way in which costs can be broken down into fixed and variable categories as the basis of making a number of key business decisions. This approach has flaws and limitations, though, and these were reviewed towards the end of the session.

Suggested further reading

Drury, C (2005) *Management Accounting for Business*, 3rd edition, chapters 2, 3 and 4. London: Thomson.

Feedback on learning activities and self-assessment questions

Feedback on learning activity 7.1

A direct cost that would also be fixed would be production overheads. Examples of indirect costs that would be variable include distribution expenses and sales commissions.

The traditional, direct v indirect layout is useful in terms of seeing how much the product physically costs to make, and thus what the gross margin is – i.e. the profit before indirect expenses are taken into account.

The fixed and variable costing layout helps the business make decisions about what to do, and about how sensitive the business is to sales prices and volumes.

While direct costs tend to be variable, and indirect costs tend to be fixed, there will, in practice, be circumstances when this is not the case.

Distribution costs is a good example of something that is indirect, but which is also often a variable cost.

Feedback on self-assessment question 7.1

Contribution per unit = £6 − £3.50 = £2.50

Break even volume = £7,500/£2.50 = 3,000 crates

Required profit volume = £12,5000/£2.50 = 5,000 crates

At £6.50, the contribution per unit becomes £3, as variable costs will remain at £3.50/crate.

Break even volume = £7,500/£3 = 2,500 crates

Required profit volume = £12,500/£3 = 4167 crates

Feedback on learning activity 7.2

If all the stores are making a profit at the store level, then they are all making a contribution to the head office overheads and the overall profitability of the business. Closing loss making stores down would wipe out that contribution, and leave a smaller number of stores having to pick up a proportionately larger amount of the central overheads.

Unless the closure of individual stores could somehow bring with it a compensating reduction in central costs (unlikely) it would be better to retain the stores as they are making a positive contribution to overall profitability.

Feedback on self-assessment question 7.2

Assuming no alternative use for the released capacity, we need to look at the costs that would be saved by using an external supplier. These are the only costs that are relevant to this decision.

Costs that would be saved are shown in table 7.12.

Table 7.12

Direct materials	60,000
Direct labour	50,000
Variable manufacturing costs (power, utilities etc)	5,000
Fixed manufacturing overhead	10,000
Total	125,000

The overhead costs – manufacturing and general – would, apart from the quoted £10,000 saving on the manufacturing side, both still be incurred, as there is no alternative use for the capacity and therefore other parts of the business would have to absorb them.

£125,000 per annum equates to £25 per unit. This means that the £30 quoted price should not be accepted, and the price would need to be below £25 before it becomes economical to outsource this supply.

Finance for Purchasers

Feedback on learning activity 7.3

Clearly, all organisations are different, but common limiting factor are likely to include:

- production capacity
- staff skills
- finance
- sales volumes
- regulatory constraints.

Feedback on self-assessment question 7.3

The answer is D

First we need to work out the contribution per unit for both products (table 7.17).

Table 7.17

	X	Y
Contribution per unit	£8	£10

Then we need to divide the contribution figures by the amount of the limited resource that will be used, giving us a contribution per unit of limited resource (table 7.18).

Table 7.18

	X	Y
Contribution per hour	£4	£2.50

This means that X ranks higher than Y.

Satisfying demand for X, the company should make 800 units, using 1,600 hours of skilled labour.

The remaining 400 hours can be utilised to make 100 units of product Y.

Feedback on learning activity 7.4

We are going to look at some of these issues in the next section. The three main difficulties that are associated with contribution analysis link in with the three prompts provided in the question.

The fixed v variable cost split is an artificial one, as most costs to some extent fall between the two behaviours. As far as price is concerned, all the examples worked with so far have assumed a constant price, even at different levels of activity and this might not be realistic. Similarly, the examples have described situations where only one product is made, or else where the product mix does not change. Again, this raises questions of practical reality.

Feedback on self-assessment question 7.4

1 This is false. Contribution is the difference (in this context) between the sales price and the variable cost per unit. Variable cost and direct cost might in some cases be the same, but not necessarily so.
2 True.
3 False. The limiting factor describes some resource constraint that can have an impact on the results of contribution analysis, but which isn't in itself a limitation of the process.
4 False. Fixed costs are divided by the contribution per unit.
5 True.

Finance for Purchasers

7

Study session 8
Pricing strategies

You can sell anything as long as the price is right. But will it make a profit?

Introduction

Pricing is a key issue for purchasers, who need to have an understanding of what prices they are being asked to pay, and how those prices might have been determined.

This session will look at different approaches to pricing, including the question of whether pricing should be driven primarily by the cost of a product or service ('cost-plus' pricing) or whether it should primarily be influenced by market factors.

The session will also draw the distinction between pricing for an external market, and pricing transactions between two parts of the same organisation ('transfer pricing').

Session learning objectives

After completing this session you should be able to:

8.1 Explain the use of 'market price' as a pricing strategy, and describe the circumstances in which it is appropriate.
8.2 Explain the use of costing as a pricing strategy, and describe the circumstances in which it is appropriate.
8.3 Explain the concept of transfer pricing, and the circumstances in which it is applied.

Unit content coverage

This study session covers the following topics from the official CIPS unit content document:

Learning objective

2.3 Determine alternative pricing strategies and assess their impact upon transfer pricing within an organisation.
- Market price
- Total cost
- Transfer pricing
- Variable cost
- Negotiated price

111

Finance for Purchasers

Prior knowledge

Study sessions 1 to 7.

Timing

You should set aside about 6 hours to read and complete this session, including learning activities, self-assessment questions, the suggested further reading (if any) from the essential textbook for this unit and the revision question.

8.1 Market pricing

One important distinction that we need to make at an early stage is the one between external and internal pricing. External pricing concerns the price charged for goods or services that are being sold to customers outside the organisation in question. However, in larger organisations, especially where there is a degree of vertical integration, the issue of internal pricing arises – that is, at what price should goods or services be sold to other parts of the same organisation, for example other divisions or other subsidiary companies. Internal pricing is often referred to as transfer pricing, and will be looked at later in this session.

Where a product or a service is being sold in a very competitive market, there are likely to be many similar products on offer. If, additionally, demand for the product or service is elastic – i.e. if the price goes down by a certain percentage, sales volumes will rise by an even bigger percentage – then it will be difficult for sellers to be able to choose what prices to charge. They will be at the mercy of the market, and will have to price their products on the basis of what the market will bear.

It then follows that the cost of producing the goods or providing the service must be kept lower than the market price, so careful attention will have to be paid to minimising and controlling costs.

What we mean by 'the market', though, is a complex area. The following factors, which are to an extent inter-related, all need to be taken into account when determining an appropriate market price:

- the competitiveness of the market
- strategic considerations
- the price elasticity of demand for the product or service
- the product life cycle.

Issues that drive the competitiveness of the market can usefully be considered with reference to the work of Michael Porter, the American business writer. To summarise one of his most well-known analytical tools, there are five forces which drive competition in business:

- existing rivalry between firms
- the threat of new entrants to the market

8 Pricing strategies

- the threat of substitute products (or services)
- the bargaining power of suppliers and
- the bargaining power of buyers.

While these ideas are not just about pricing, certain elements highlight factors that are going to drive the market price for any product or service.

The relative power of buyers and suppliers is key, and it is likely to be the biggest single influence on the price of a product. There has been a lot of debate recently, for example, about the amount of power the major supermarket chains have in the UK, and how suppliers of some types of product – for example farmers supplying meat – are unable to achieve a fair price. Yet other suppliers may have more leverage – for example the suppliers of very well-known branded products which customers expect to see on the shelves.

Supplier power will be strongest where there are only a few suppliers. It will also be strong where it is difficult, or expensive, for a buyer to switch suppliers.

Buyer power will be at its strongest where there is little differentiation over the product, where there are many different suppliers and switching between them, or to another product, is not costly.

The 'threat of substitutes' aspect also has clear links to pricing. If there is an obvious substitute for a particular product, then the ability to increase prices will be limited. This links to the price elasticity of demand.

The price elasticity of demand for the product or service is an economics concept that measures the extent to which a change in price will impact on the demand for the product. The actual calculation is:

$$\text{Price elasticity of demand} = \frac{\% \text{ change in demand}}{\% \text{ change in price}}$$

If demand for a product changes by a larger percentage than the change in price, then that product is said to be price-elastic. This is more likely to be the case where there are substitutes for the product or else where customers do not value the product particularly highly.

It follows, then, that where there are no real substitutes, or where the customer places a high value on a product or service, demand will be price-*inelastic*. In such circumstances there is likely to be more scope for achieving price increases that also improve profitability.

Strategic considerations reflect the way in which an organisation is planning to develop its business. If, for example, a company is wanting to increase its market share it may well use pricing strategy to help it achieve its goals. Thus, prices may be set at a deliberately low and loss-making level to build up sales volume and perhaps to put pressure on rivals, with a view at a later stage to raising prices to a more economic level.

The product life cycle describes the stages a product (or a service) will typically go through during its life. It charts sales volume against time.

Figure 8.1: Product life cycle

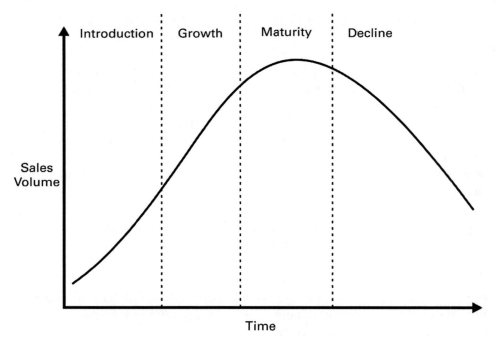

All products should go through the different phases in the cycle, though the time axis is not quantified in any way. As far as pricing is concerned, though, different stages of the cycle might prompt different attitudes to pricing.

There are, though, no rules about what the policy should be at any particular stage in the cycle. The introductory stage could suggest low pricing to encourage the trying out of a product – but by contrast we often see prices that are very high when a product is first introduced. This has recently applied to the launches of new electronic goods. Compare, for example, the price of a DVD recorder today compared with what it was at launch just a few years ago.

It is often the case, though, that a product in maturity is likely to be priced at a level that maximises short-term profitability.

A related pricing approach is price skimming. This approach involves taking advantages of situations where the market is relatively price-insensitive – for example where there is some novelty value to be had (and one could cite the example of the DVD recorder again – when they were first launched people were prepared to pay a high price as the product was completely new).

Penetration pricing involves selling products or services at a low price to build up market share. An aggressive penetration policy can sometimes lead to a price war, leaving all players in the market selling their goods at a loss. The UK newspaper market has only quite recently emerged from such a situation.

8 Pricing strategies

Learning activity 8.1

Consider a product or service that you are familiar with, and for which you are aware of the price.

- Where would you place that product in the 'product life cycle' as illustrated above?
- To what extent is the price of the product/service affected by its stage in the life cycle?
- To what extent is the price influenced by any of Porter's five forces?

Feedback on page 121

Now attempt self-assessment question 8.1 below.

Self-assessment question 8.1

1   If the price of a product increases by 10%, leading to a drop in sales of 20%, is demand for that product said to be (a) price elastic or (b) price inelastic?
2   What are the four stages of the product life cycle?
3   What is the typical time scale for each of the five stages?

Feedback on page 121

8.2   Cost-plus pricing

Cost base pricing

The main alternative approach to market-based pricing is to consider the cost of the product or service, and make that the basis upon which the price is established. There are, though, a number of different approaches that can be taken, all falling within the idea of cost base pricing.

Learning activity 8.2

Think of something you have paid for recently. It could be work related, or something you use on a personal basis.

- How do you think the price for the product/service is determined?
- What are the main market forces that determine the price?
- How does the price compare with what you estimate it might cost to make the product or provide the service?

Feedback on page 121

Finance for Purchasers

From your studying of study session 7, you will recall different ways of looking at costs, and different ways of measuring and classifying the costs of a product or service. In all cases, a business will decide the particular cost base it is using, and then may add on a suitable 'mark up' as a means of recovering the cost and also providing a profit element.

Among the costs bases that can be used are :

- *Total cost:* this includes all the costs, both direct and indirect, of the product or service being sold. this figure may exclude certain higher level overhead costs.
- *Production cost:* This includes all the costs incurred in producing the goods or services being sold.
- *Variable cost:* this just takes account of the variable costs involved. As such, the cost base will be lower than for the other two examples above, and so the percentage mark-up may be correspondingly higher so as to cover, or at least contribute to, the fixed costs involved.

Example:

A company has a cost base for a product as follows shown in figure 8.1.

Table 8.1

Direct variable costs	100
Direct fixed costs	50
Total direct costs	150
Indirect costs	70
Total cost	220

If the pricing approach is total cost plus 20% mark-up, the price will be 220 × 1.2 = £264

If the pricing approach is production cost + 75% (and we assume the direct costs are production costs) then the price will be 150 × 1.75 = £262.50

If the pricing approach is based on variable cost plus 160% mark-up, then the price will be 100 × 2.6 = £260

In practice it is unlikely that cost-plus pricing approaches will be rigidly adhered to. Management will rarely price products and services without reference to a range of other factors, including their knowledge of the market environment. Cost-plus pricing does, however, provide a target price that in theory should generate revenue sufficient to cover the selected cost base.

Another important consideration is the size of the 'mark-up'. While a company may have a target mark-up in place, the actual mark-up applied will have to take heed of the various market-based factors outlined in the previous session. It is not a question of using either a market-based or a cost-based approach. The market for a product and the cost of producing it will both have a part to play.

The extent to which one method outweighs the other will depend on the circumstances. When launching a product, for example, the marketing

8 Pricing strategies

department might have a view as to what the price should be. If the product is then costed, and the cost exceeds marketing's idea of the price, then the company will have to rethink – either looking for ways to reduce the costs, or perhaps at ways of enhance the product's image.

'Mark-up' v margin

Most cost-based pricing approaches involve establishing a particular cost base, and then adding a suitable mark-up. For example, if the total cost of a product was £80, and a 20% mark-up was to be applied, the selling price would be as shown in table 8.2.

Table 8.2

Cost	£80
25% mark-up	£20
Selling price	£100

This is different to the situation where the approach is to make a certain profit margin. If the required profit margin is 25%, the company is seeking a 25% return on its sales price. The calculation then would be:

Cost: £80

Needs to be 75% of the selling price.

So ... £80 × 100/75 = £106.67

Limitations

Cost-plus pricing has a number of limitations. These include:

- It ignores demand.
- It doesn't guarantee that revenues will exceed costs.
- It makes assumptions about sales volume before sales have been made.

However, cost-plus pricing is a widely used process. It is particularly relevant where a company has a large number of products, or where particular products are not significant influences on an organisation's overall profitability.

Activity-based pricing

As outlined in the previous session, traditional costing methods are to an extent being superseded by other techniques such as activity based costing (ABC). It therefore follows that the cost-based pricing models described above can be refined to incorporate different and more relevant approaches to the way products and services are costed.

Cost-plus pricing can also be looked at from a different perspective when launching a new product. A company may first determine what price the customer would be prepared to pay for the product. It would then deduct from the price the required profit margin, arriving at a target cost. The target cost would then be compared to estimates of the actual cost, and if it is lower than the actual cost, the company would have to explore

117

Finance for Purchasers

ways of reducing elements of the cost estimate. This approach is known as **target costing**, and is an approach we will look at in more detail in study session 10.

Self-assessment question 8.2

The cost per unit of a product manufactured by Company x is shown in table 8.3.

Table 8.3

Direct material	£24
Direct labour	£34
Variable overheads	£14
Share of fixed costs	£24
Total cost	£96

Company x uses variable cost-plus pricing.

If Company x seeks a 40% margin on sales, what is the selling price of the product?

1 £100.80
2 £120.00
3 £134.40
4 £160.00

Feedback on page 122

8.3 Transfer pricing

Transfer pricing is concerned with the way in which an organisation arranges **internal** pricing between different business units or divisions. It can be used for a number of different purposes.

One key aspect is taxation. For a multinational company, transfer prices might be set in a way that ensures that relatively high profits are made in parts of the world where taxation rates are lower, and vice versa. Although a fair price might be being charged, the tax authorities cannot be sure that this is the case and so will take steps to eliminate, as far as possible, manipulation of transfer prices as a tax avoidance strategy.

There are many examples of transfer pricing abuse, from the plastic buckets that cost nearly £500 and the £4,000 biro at the expensive end, through to the bargain prefabricated buildings that were allegedly transfer priced at less than £1 each.

Most larger economies now have rules in place requiring that taxable profits are not understated by the use of transfer prices. However, proving that manipulation has taken place can be difficult, and involves determining what the price would have been if the parties were unrelated – often termed the 'arm's length' price.

8 Pricing strategies

But it is not just about taxation and about moving profits from one division to another. Transfer pricing is also a useful tool for management, in that it can help them:

- measure (divisional) performance
- motivate divisional managers
- ensure divisional autonomy.

As with the pricing of external goods and services, there are a number of ways in which the actual transfer price can be determined:

- *At market price:* this would be most applicable where there are very similar (or identical) goods available in the external market.
- *At adjusted market price*: where it is necessary to reduce the true market price in order to encourage internal trading.
- Marginal cost transfer price.
- Full cost transfer price.
- Cost plus mark-up transfer price.
- Negotiated transfer price. This can be a very successful approach especially in circumstances where the desire is for genuine divisional autonomy.

An important issue with transfer pricing is the potential difficulties it can create. Sometimes the objectives of transfer pricing can cause conflict.

For example, if a company is looking for genuine divisional autonomy, as suggested above, it should allow a division to source its supplies externally as well as internally. This, though, might mean another division losing sales and/or not operating at full capacity.

Similarly, if a division can sell its products into an external market at a market price but is required first to sell internally at a cost-based price, then transfer pricing as a measure of performance might be compromised.

Learning activity 8.3

The following is extracted from an article that appeared in the *Financial Times* in November 2005. Read through the article, and then answer the questions that follow.

> Nearly two-thirds of companies have been challenged over the tax treatment of internal transactions in the past three years, according to a poll of 476 companies in 22 countries by Ernst & Young, the professional services group. More than 40 per cent of these audits resulted in adjustments by the tax authorities.
>
> The findings underline the growing tension between tax authorities and multinationals over 'transfer pricing', the pricing of cross-border transactions between subsidiaries, which accounts for more than half of world trade. Many tax authorities believe multinationals use transfer pricing to avoid taxation by shifting profits to low-tax jurisdictions.

(continued on next page)

Finance for Purchasers

Learning activity 8.3 *(continued)*

Globalisation has made transfer pricing planning more important as companies' supply chains have become more complex, the report said. 'As investment becomes increasingly mobile and multinational companies expand their global supply chains, it is clear that competition for investment and taxes is driving more legislation and enforcement by revenue authorities.'

The report highlighted the scope for multinationals to use transfer pricing to increase profits, with 29 per cent of respondents saying they used transfer pricing strategies in place of other tax planning strategies. 'Transfer pricing is increasingly perceived as less of a compliance issue and more of a planning issue that contributes values,' the report said.

Its importance is reflected in a trend for the tax department to become involved in new projects at an early stage.

Four out of five US companies now involve the tax function in the 'concept or initiation phase', compared with 40 per cent five years ago.

Describe how multinational companies might use transfer pricing policies as a means of improving profits.

How might transfer pricing impact on the planning of a major project or programme?

Feedback on page 122

Now attempt self-assessment question 8.3 below.

Self-assessment question 8.3

What is likely to be the main determinant of pricing of the following:

- electricity
- legal fees
- the building of a new hospital
- the launch of a new newspaper?

Feedback on page 122

Revision question

Now try the revision question for this session on page 346.

Summary

This session has looked at pricing from three main perspectives. First, we considered the fact that organisations selling established products will usually have to price in line with what the market can bear. Second, we looked at the need to make a profit and that therefore pricing will be influenced by how much it costs to make a product or deliver a service.

Finally, we briefly outlined the particular issues that prevail when prices need to be determined for goods or services being transferred from one part of an organisation to another.

Suggested further reading

Drury, C (2005) *Management Accounting for Business*, 3rd edition, chapter 4. London: Thomson.

Feedback on learning activities and self-assessment questions

Feedback on learning activity 8.1

The product life cycle can be applied at different levels – to the motor car, for example, as a mature generic product, but also to a particular model of car.

An example that one might use for this activity, then, is a new model of car. At introduction special offer pricing to get attention and get sales going, if successful price firms during maturity, rival brings out similar model creating sharper price competition and lower price to maintain share. Then time for a new model, so stock of current model needs to be shifted leading to drop in price.

A daily UK newspaper would be another good example. Having been a mature product for many years, the traditional newspaper is now seen as being in decline. The industry has been affected by Porter's five forces. Supplier power was the dominant influence towards the end of the last century – with very active unions, especially on the printing side, controlling working practices and keeping costs up. After some major reshaping, the industry became less reliant on this labour – but now faces huge pressure from the threat of a substitute product – news and comment freely available on the internet.

Feedback on self-assessment question 8.1

1 This would be price-elastic – as demand for the product has changed by a larger percentage than the change in price
2 Introduction, growth, maturity and decline. Some models include additional stages, but these are the four main elements of the mode.
3 There are no 'typical' timescales. It depends on the product – and, indeed, whether how broadly we define products. There will be different product life cycles for laptops compared to ultraportable notebooks as there will be for an individual notebook brand such as the Apple Macbook.

Feedback on learning activity 8.2

It is likely that, whatever the product or service you are analysing, the price is at least in part determined by market forces, as discussed in the first part of this session. That is because, whatever the cost, a firm can only sell a product at a price people are willing to pay.

Finance for Purchasers

If you have chosen a commodity type of product (for example electricity) the price is wholly market determined. For that reason, many electricity producers had major financial problems a few years ago when prices were low. In more recent times, the market price has risen to a point where producers can sell it for a lot more than it cost to produce.

If you have chosen a one-off service – for example you might have had some home improvements carried out. It is likely that the price you paid will be based on the cost of providing the work plus a suitable mark-up for the supplier. While there will be a market rate for builders, every job they do will be different.

In terms of trying to estimate how much the product or service cost, this might be quite difficult. And you may have thought about cost in different ways, including aspects that were looked at in study session 7. When relating price to cost, should we be looking at the total cost (i.e. including all overheads) or should we just be interested in the variable costs – the additional costs incurred in producing one extra unit?

Feedback on self-assessment question 8.2

The answer is 1.

The marginal cost of the product will be 24 + 34 + 14 = 72

And we are looking for a 40% mark-up on the variable costs, so the price will be:

72 × 1.4 = 100.80.

Feedback on learning activity 8.3

There is potential for transfer pricing to be used as a means of improving profits whenever subsidiaries of the same group trade with each other – especially when they are based in geographically different tax regimes. By selling to Company B at a high price, Company A would report higher profits and (assuming it is located in lower tax environment) make a tax saving for the group. Company B, meanwhile, assuming it to be located in a higher tax environment, would report lower taxable profits.

A lot has been done in recent years to eliminate such obvious abuse. But determining what the right price is can, as we have seen, be difficult and therefore transfer pricing can still be used as a means of improving profits at the margin.

Given that there is still scope to reduce taxes by giving careful consideration to where activities take place and how transfer pricing should be managed, planning a major project will have to take these issues into account.

Feedback on self-assessment question 8.3

- Electricity: market-based pricing. Electricity is a commodity, traded as such, producers and customers are at the whim of the market (which, in the UK, has recently been reformed to eliminate some perceived exploitation of the market). The product is necessary, with no obvious short-term substitute, and price inelastic.

- Legal fees: probably cost-based pricing, no two jobs are identical (although something like conveyancing may have more of a 'market' price). Costs determined by hours worked, and level and rates of people doing the work.
- The building of a new hospital: total cost plus – a one-off long-term project.
- The launch of a new newspaper: market-influenced, price-elastic (recent example of the launch of *The Sportsman*, generally viewed as overpriced at £1), strategic pricing at outset to gain exposure to readers?

Finance for Purchasers

Study session 9
Different types of expenditure

Introduction

In this session, unlike Keith Davis, we will look at how we can plan, control and manage capital projects in particular, but also recognise that some 'projects' and/or work will be classified/coded as revenue (also referred to as Opex, an abbreviation for operating expenditure). This area of procurement is often regarded as a specialist area of expertise, where knowledge of the sector in which the procurement specialist is working in is of great advantage. This applies usually, but not exclusively, to the areas of construction and property development, IT and company-specific equipment, eg pharmaceuticals, oil and gas, etc.

'We didn't actually overspend our budget. The Health Commission allocation simply fell short of our expenditure.'
Keith Davis (American Executive, Chairman of Wollongong Hospital)

Session learning objectives

After completing this session you should be able to:

9.1 Describe the tools and techniques required to facilitate capital spend.
9.2 Distinguish between Capex and Opex, and describe how the two can be used, and mixed appropriately, to suit the business case.
9.3 Summarise how public expenditure can be used to promote project development.

Unit content coverage

This study session covers the following topics from the official CIPS unit content document:

Learning objective

3.1 Analyse the use of the different types of expenditure.
   • Capital expenditure (Capex)
   • Operational expenditure (Opex)
   • Public sector expenditure

Prior knowledge

Study sessions 1 to 8 and 17 especially study sessions 4 and 17.

Resources

Obtain a breakdown of a construction project, together with all the design and regulatory fees, to ensure you have the total cost of acquisition available.

Also obtain either a building facilities management budget or a whole life costing model for a high-value piece of equipment. This will be essential in identifying the cost breakdown components and how they are evaluated and expressed in financial terms. If internal project data is not available it is suggested that a UK government reported project be used.

Timing

You should set aside about 3 hours to read and complete this session, including learning activities, self-assessment questions, the suggested further reading (if any) from the essential textbook for this unit and the revision question.

9.1   The principal drivers of capital projects

Most capital projects are a huge commitment by the company and represent a significant investment in the future and as such need to be planned and executed in a structured and highly organised method. For the purposes of this exercise we will consider the construction of a new manufacturing plant overseas and the professionals involved to explore the many layers and aspects of the project that need to be considered. It may equally apply to an individual/single capital purchase, eg a piece of equipment. Therefore, at the end of this study session you should be able to apply the logic to any capital project.

As this is an extremely complex area of procurement we can only begin to introduce the subject here rather than deal with it in any form of detail. It has also been the subject of many landmark reports by Sir Michael Latham. One such report entitled *Constructing the Team* set the UK government and construction industry agenda. It was based on the simple concept that through teamwork the construction industry could delight its customers. In short, the construction industry was 'ineffective', 'adversarial', 'fragmented', 'incapable of delivering for its customers' and 'lacking respect for its employees'. The Latham report set the agenda for reform and gave the industry targets. From this a raft of initiatives flowed. The report led to the establishment of the Construction Industry Board to oversee reform; subsequent initiatives were the Egan report in 1998 *Rethinking Construction*; the Construction Best Practice Programme, the Movement for Innovation and Constructing Excellence. *Rethinking Construction* led to the continued shift in construction practices. In it Sir John Egan stated: 'We have identified five key drivers of change which need to set the agenda for the construction industry at large: committed leadership, a focus on the customer, integrated processes and teams, a quality driven agenda and commitment to people'.

We will begin by considering what the drivers and constraints might be in the project described above;

- availability of land
- planning permissions
- environmental impact

9 Different types of expenditure

- regulatory framework:
  - building
  - operating
  - noise
  - fire and rescue
- political stability
- transfer pricing of products
- logistics and supply chain
- importation of equipment
- customs
- language
- applicable law and contact(s)
- cultural differences of approach/working
- local practices
- health and safety
- availability of workforce
- design and engineering capability
- testing and inspection
- quality control
- inflation and fiscal constraints
- standardisation v purpose built
- taxation treatment
- grants and subsidies.

All of these issues will have a bearing on the final investment decision and will affect the viability of a project.

Having identified the major drivers that will influence the project we must now turn our attention to the tools and methods by which we will begin evaluate these factors in an ordered and structured way. It is also critical that the method of evaluation is an accepted and trusted one (that is, independent, objective, with clear governance and controls in place, and by qualified professionals) that is capable of being benchmarked against comparable projects or investments.

In evaluating projects or individual capital purchases, the principal tools used will be reflected typically in a business case either within the body of the business case or within the appendices (of the business case).

1. The **accounting rate of return (ARR)**: using the known factors of annual average profit and the average/actual investment through calculation you will be able to deduce the ARR for the project. The higher the percentage, the better the project business case is.
2. The **return on capital employed (ROCE)** is a more reflective tool and can also be used to compare projects within the company and against its competitors. Also, ROCE is used more widely to measure a whole business and not just a project.
3. The **payback period (PP)** is the length of time it takes for an initial investment to be repaid out of the net cash inflows from a project.
4. A method is needed to evaluate and consider all the project costs, not just those of, say, the construction project one, which allows for the timing of both the costs and the benefits. This is achieved through the **net present value (NPV)** method.

Finance for Purchasers

5   The **internal rate of return (IRR)** of a particular investment is the discount rate that, when applied to its future cash flows, will make them equal to the initial investment itself. This method is closely related to that of the NPV method above.

ARR, PP, NPV and IRR are also dealt with in study session 17.

It should also be remembered that all projects should be capable of being audited at any point in the project life cycle and not just at the end.

An audit primarily provides an independent and objective opinion to the Project Owner or sponsor on risk management, control and governance, by measuring and evaluating their effectiveness in achieving the organisation's agreed objectives. In addition, the audit's findings and recommendations are beneficial to line management in the audited areas. These are primarily risk management, control and governance (comprising of the policies, procedures and operations) established to ensure the achievement of objectives, the appropriate assessment of risk, the reliability of internal and external reporting and accountability processes, compliance with applicable laws and regulations, and compliance with the behavioural and ethical standards set for the organisation.

There are four main principles that should be observed during an audit;

1   integrity
2   objectivity (i.e. no opinions expressed only factual statements)
3   competency of the staff involved
4   confidentiality of the information and findings.

The audit team will usually comprise of a lead auditor, the audit team, project sponsor or their representative and specialists as determined by the nature of the audit being undertaken on an as required basis.

Learning activity 9.1

Select a capital project, for example a new manufacturing facility within your own organisation or a publicly available document (e.g. Carbon Trust technology accelerator costs: http://www.carbontrust.co.uk/technology/technologyaccelerator/costs.htm or LSC 16–19 Capital Fund Guidance: http://readingroom.lsc.gov.uk/lsc/2005/funding/streams/16-19-capital-fund-guidance-2006-07-onwards.pdf (Annex E)) and from this highlight what drivers and constraints might affect the project and at what point in the project phases are they influencing it. This should only consider the following headings:

- health and safety
- environmental
- legal and regulatory.

Feedback on page 136

9 Different types of expenditure

Now attempt self-assessment question 9.1 below.

Self-assessment question 9.1

Write a short paper (1,000–1,500 words)on the elements of a project and/or investment that a post-project audit might cover.

Your paper should:

- include a list with short descriptions some of the more common or *real-life* findings and recommendations that are made by the audit team
- state who should be part of that audit team too, by job function and title.

Feedback on page 137

9.2 Making the choice between Capex and Opex

It should be acknowledged that there are clear rules on what can and should be classified or coded as a capital or revenue item. However, there are a number of key decisions based upon various factors that will affect the amounts and/or value of each and what alternatives are open to companies when considering how to achieve a specific goal or objectives.

The considerations might cover the following:

- The need to acquire equipment immediately and therefore question of buying piece equipment on a long lead delivery is not practical and consequently hiring or leasing may be the only option. In this case the equipment would not be a capital item, depreciated over a number of years but an expense/revenue/Opex item.
- If there is a need to produce a new R&D facility for a new product/concept for a short-term period of, say, a few years, the company could either:
    - decide to build and hope to re-model the building at a later date and capitalise the costs (Capex)
    - lease or rent a building and expense the costs (Opex)
    - buy modular buildings and look to dispose of them at the end of the project (Capex).
- In upgrading the IT infrastructure of the company, including hardware and software, licences, and so forth, the company could choose from a number of approaches:
    - upgrade the software and memory capacity of current hardware only where required to 'keep things going' for another two years and expense the items (Opex)
    - replace hardware and software, irrespective of age or capacity, for a new operating platform and system, and capitalise the whole amount and write it down over, say, five years (Capex)

Finance for Purchasers

    – lease all the necessary equipment (Opex)
    – outsource the whole activity of both assets and resources (Opex).

In looking at the scenarios above the decisions will depend on the approach the company wishes to take from a strategic point of view, all of which will be influenced by both internal and external factors, such as:

- cash on deposit
- cash flow
- market sector
- product life and turn around
- risk profile.

Some of the more common decisions facing project teams will be those related to a simple relationship between a high quality, low maintenance solution/equipment and a low capital cost option with a much higher ongoing maintenance and/or replacement cycle, for example:

1. a car costing £50,000 to buy that costs only £5 a year to maintain for 10 years will have a high capital cost and a low maintenance costs, whereas
2. a car costing £35,000 to buy that costs £2,000 a year to maintain for 10 years will have a low capital cost and high maintenance (or running) cost.

In this simple example you can see that the higher overall cost ignoring interest and other such factors will be (2), but it provides a better cash flow for the purchaser.

If this later concept is repeated many times over it is not inconceivable to change the initial capital requirements, in other words, to make it cheaper to build or procure by as much as 30–40%. When you consider that the business case evaluation looks at IRR or NPV, this will make a project/ investment that was marginal suddenly become an attractive proposition. Hence the need to understand more than just the financial appraisal elements contained in a business plan.

It is also conceivable that a company knowingly has a poor cash flow and limited borrowing facilities, but still has an imperative need to proceed with the project/investment. This may be due to timing issues, market forces, being currently un-competitive or other factors. As a result, the company may deliberately look to ways of avoiding spending capital as well as looking to re-finance the project/investment on completion through a sale and leaseback arrangement. Other options such as leasing vehicles may be available through commercial financing options. This is not irregular but does commit the company to a long-term debt not that dissimilar to the type of mortgage you might use to facilitate buying your own property. Equally, a simple example of a longer-term commitment might be that of the company signing a lease for a company car. While this will include the cost of planned maintenance and repair, it will not cover unplanned maintenance, or the employee leaving or moving into a new job role that no longer necessitates a company car. In short, this does not mitigate all the risks and may even generate some new ones.

9 Different types of expenditure

Learning activity 9.2

Using the example of a building project with the figures shown in table 9.1, recommend changes to the Capex/Opex mix to achieve the best IRR over three years.

Table 9.1

Project cost item	Option A		Option B		Student option	
	Capital	Revenue	Capital	Revenue	Capital	Revenue
Design fees	£310,000	Nil	£280,000	£30,000		
Regulatory fees	£28,000	Nil	£28,000	Nil		
Health and safety	£44,000	Nil	£44,000	Nil		
Legal fees	£56,000	Nil	£56,000	Nil		
Project management fees	£178,000	Nil	£178,000	Nil		
Site acquisition costs	£2,486,000	Nil	£2,486,000	Nil		
Infrastructure costs	£178,000	£8,000	£178,000	£8,000		
Superstructure costs	£2,224,000	£68,000	£2,224,000	£68,000		
Fit out costs	£1,088,000	£96,000	£1,088,000	£96,000		
External works	£174,000	£22,000	£174,000	£22,000		
Landscaping	£120,000	£32,000	Nil	£222,000		
Office equipment	£246,000	£42,000	£88,000	£240,000		
Manufacturing equipment	£1,888,000	£128,000	£960,000	£1,428,000		
Warehouse racking	£468,000	£46,000	£468,000	£46,000		
Expenses	Nil	£88,000	Nil	£88,000		

It is expected/anticipated that you will need to make assumptions based on different methods and approaches.

Feedback on page 137

Now attempt self-assessment question 9.2 below.

Self-assessment question 9.2

Draft a report of 1,000–1,500 words that summarises the key features and advantages/disadvantages of acquiring a specialised piece of bottle manufacturing equipment.

Assume the initial cost of the equipment will be £1.5 million, with an annual planned maintenance cost of £25,000 for first three years, £40,000 for the subsequent three years, a rebuild and automation upgrade in year 7 of £120,000 and annual maintenance of £45,000 in the final three years. You should also assume the equipment will be operating for 46 weeks of the year every year, except year 7, which will be 34 weeks only. The output of the machine will be 60,000 bottles per hour and there are 64 productive hours per week worked.

(continued on next page)

Finance for Purchasers

> **Self-assessment question 9.2** *(continued)*
>
> Calculate by either capital and annual expense or by payment to the supplier based on an agreed inflation-indexed unit cost per 1,000 items produced, with a minimum number of units guaranteed to the supplier.
>
> *Feedback on page 138*

9.3 Public facilities with private money

We will look at how public projects can be facilitated with either private funds or a mixture of private and public money to promote project development and deliver essential services such as the London Underground or local hospitals or schools.

Essentially there are two primary vehicles for doing this: **Private Finance Initiative (PFI)** and **Public Private Partnerships (PPP)**.

Firstly, there are very few differences, if any, between PFI and PPP. (These are so fine that they are not worth considering or are of negligible consequence.) The latter is in fact a better name for a method of procurement. A simple definition of a PFI/PPP project would be: 'A voluntary alliance entered into by public bodies, local authorities, or government departments (Ministry of Defence, MOD) and private companies, including consortiums specifically set up to deliver a public project or service.' Here are some of the key principles of PFI and PPP:

- Contracts are usually 25–30 years for the funding, design, building and operation of facilities.
- A **special purpose company (SPC)** is sometimes set up to contract with the awarding authority.
- Accommodation projects are well suited to this style of procurement. This includes the building or redevelopment of offices, schools and hospitals.
- The public sector in the vast majority of cases retain ownership of the asset at the end of the project term.
- Projects are heavily geared, with a typical finance structure being 90% debt, 9% bank equity and 1% contractor equity (although there are myriad different financing options).
- There are three key contracts, the project agreement between the client and a SPC, a building contract between the SPC and a building contractor, and a facilities management contract between the SPC and the facilities management contractor.

A typical PPP stage programme is set out in figure 9.2 below.

Figure 9.2: Typical PPP stage programme

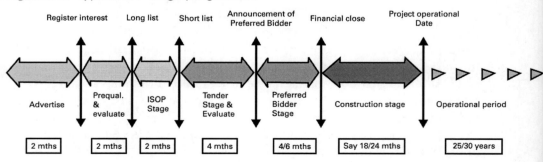

9 Different types of expenditure

There may also be a best and final offer (BAFO) stage prior to the selection of the preferred bidder.

It is easy to see from the above process how projects can take time to come to fruition. However, a well managed process should last between 12 and 16 months from public advertisement to contractual close, although this can depend upon the complexity of the project and time spent obtaining planning consents.

Appended below are the key roles and elements of the process that will be managed by one person but delivered by a cross-functional team consisting of many professional disciplines (e.g. accountants, lawyers, procurement, project management, chartered surveyors, chartered engineers, chartered builders, risk managers, health and safety, environmentalists, etc):

* client advisor
* developing operations proposals at the bidding stage
* costing of services
* life cycling
* managing the design process
* due diligence
* implementation
* contract delivery
* performance monitoring (client and supplier).

A host of official views and statistics are available via the UK HM Treasury website: HM Treasury PPP site: http://www.hm-treasury.gov.uk/documents/public_private_partnerships/ppp_links.cfm, which it is recommend you visit in order to answer your self-assessment questions.

The PPP Forum have also published a Code of Best Practice on the subject and should be seen as a good reference point, especially from a UK government point of view, as well as the UK government's watchdog, the NAO (National Audit Office).

It should be recognised that the PFI route is a more formal approach to take for the UK. The public sector contracts to purchase services on a long-term specified basis (as stated before, these contracts can be for 25–30 years and will often require contract drafting by specialist lawyers that will amount to many hundreds if not thousands of pages). The intent behind this approach is to take advantage of private sector expertise, which is incentivised by private sector finance at risk/reward for delivery. This will often include providing new and or substantially upgraded infrastructure that would otherwise take large sums of UK treasury money all at once (government cash flow in simple terms!), thereby reducing the number of public project/ schemes that could/would be carried in any one period of government. In return, the PFI contractor via the SPC will receive an agreed and usually fixed unitary charge for the duration of the contract.

Learning activity 9.3

Read the report *NAO Good Practice Briefing for PFI/PPP* and state what the six phases of a PFI project are according to the NAO. This report can

(continued on next page)

Finance for Purchasers

Learning activity 9.3 *(continued)*

be accessed at NAO Good Practice Briefing for PFI/PPP (PDF): http://www.nao.org.uk/Guidance/focus/focus_pfi_ppp.pdf.

Feedback on page 139

Now attempt self-assessment question 9.3 below.

Self-assessment question 9.3

Analyse the PPP Forum fact sheet dated 25 July 2006 (available through PPP Forum: http://www.pppforum.com/government) and suggest ways in which traditional procurement could be better represented or modified following the findings of the fact sheet published.

Feedback on page 139

Revision question

There is no revision question for this session.

Summary

This study session can only give an overview/insight into what is a very complex and highly sensitive area of procurement and finance for a business. Further study and/or training is recommended before entering the world of a practicing procurement specialist. However, this will hopefully whet the student's appetite for what can be a very challenging but rewarding area of procurement. However, to summarise the key learnings, they are:

- Most capital projects are a huge commitment by the company and represent a significant investment in the future and, as such, need to be planned and executed in a structured and highly organised method.
- In evaluating projects or individual capital purchases, the principal tools used will be reflected typically in a business case either within the body of the business case or within the appendices (of the business case).
- An audit primarily provides an independent and objective opinion to the project owner or sponsor on risk management, control and governance, by measuring and evaluating their effectiveness in achieving the organisation's agreed objectives.
- There are four main principles that should be observed during an audit;
  1 integrity
  2 objectivity (that is, no opinions expressed, only factual statements)
  3 competency of the staff involved
  4 confidentiality of the information and findings.
- It is highly likely that any business case will also look at a *sensitivity analysis.*
- The post project/investment audit is a critical step for ensuring benefits are delivered, lessons are learnt and that the process is improved for organisations over time.

9 Different types of expenditure

- Some of the more common decisions facing project teams will be that related to a simple relationship between a high quality low maintenance solution/equipment and a low capital cost option with a much higher ongoing maintenance and/or replacement cycle.
- A simple definition of a PFI/PPP project would be: 'A voluntary alliance entered into by public bodies, local authorities, or government departments (Ministry of Defence, MOD) and private companies, including consortiums specifically set up to deliver a public project or service.'
- The intent behind PFI/PPP as an approach to delivering public facilities is in essence to take advantage of private sector expertise, which is incentivised by private sector finance at risk/reward for delivery.

Suggested further reading

- Arnold, G (2002) _Corporate Financial Management_, 2nd edition. Harlow: FT/Prentice Hall
- Lumby, S and C Jones (1999) _Investment Appraisal and Financial Decisions_, 6th edition, chapters 3, 5 and 6. London: Chapman and Hall.
- McLaney, EJ (2002) _Business Finance: Theory and Practice_, 5th edition, chapters 4, 5 and 6. Harlow: FT/Prentice Hall.
- Pike, R and B Neale (1999) _Corporate Finance and Investment_, 3rd edition, chapters 5 and 7. Harlow: FT/Prentice Hall.
- Private Finance Initiative (PFI) via HM Treasury PPP site: http://www.hm-treasury.gov.uk/documents/public_private_partnerships/ppp_links.cfm

Guidance and support

- National Audit Office (NAO) Recommendations service: http://www.nao.org.uk/recommendation/
- Partnerships UK (PUK): http://www.partnershipsuk.org.uk/
- 4Ps: http://www.4ps.gov.uk/
- House of Commons 2001 Research paper: 'The Private Finance Initiative': http://www.parliament.uk/commons/lib/research/rp2001/rp01-117.pdf
- OJEC Links
- OJEC Tenders Electronic Daily Website: http://ted.europa.eu/Exec?Template=TED/homepage.htm&DataFlow=hRead.dfl&hpt=ALL&StatLang=EN
- Procurement Advice hosted by Office of Government Commerce: http://www.ogc.gov.uk/index.asp?id=35
- PPP Tender Documents hosted by Private Finance-i: http://www.privatefinance-i.com/

Government

- Financial Partnerships Unit, Scottish Executive: http://www.scotland.gov.uk/Topics/Government/Finance/18232/12255
- Private Finance Information Service, National Assembly for Wales: http://www.pfu.wales.gov.uk/
- Communities and Local Government: http://www.communities.gov.uk/
- Also: http://www.pppforum.com

- Downloads as available via www.cips.org: http://www.cips.org/. (Note that the CIPS website is frequently updated and new papers appear all the time as well as being updated.)

Feedback on learning activities and self-assessment questions

Feedback on learning activity 9.1

As you can appreciate there are a wide variety of scenarios and tools to be employed, but these all need to be relevant and set in context to each other within a business case. Equally it is highly likely that any business case will also look at a *sensitivity analysis* allowing the senior decision makers to understand what impact events will have if they change from the assumptions/forecasts and costs as stated within the business. It should also provide if possible what mitigating factors would be employed if that scenario becomes real.

The investment decision-making process should follow a clear 'gateway' process to ensure that the business is not exposed to undue risk or committed to a project/investment it can not afford or does not have the resources to adequately control. Typically the gates may look as shown in figure 9.1, and at each stage all three of the areas under consideration (health and safety, environmental, legal and regulatory) will be reviewed.

Figure 9.1: The investment gateway process

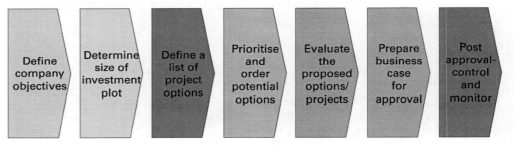

In essence there are really four main methods of appraisal from a financial perspective (pre-implementation), if we discount ROCE as a measurement tool for post-investment purposes. Generally speaking, the IRR and NPV methods tend to be the preferred and more commonly adopted methods within organisations.

Turning to the question of constraints and drivers, especially post implementation these might be one or all of the following, looking at the two aspects in turn.

Constraints:

- environmental impact assessment
- safety system review
- planning supervisors 'in life' review
- injunctions served by third parties
- orders issued by regulatory authorities/public bodies
- conditions associated with planning consents (buildings)
- accidents

9 Different types of expenditure

- enquiries – internal and public
- new legislation
- contamination (ground, air, water systems and so on)
- local residential areas adjacent to industrial/commercial premises
- local working hour restrictions – environmentally driven
- sites of scientific interest or natural habitats.

Drivers:

- company may be associated with either environmental or health and safety sector and therefore needs to be 'whiter than white' in its execution of a project on these areas
- board policy
- shareholder 'voice'
- public sentiment
- orders issued by regulatory authorities/public bodies
- conditions associated with planning consents (buildings)
- environmental impact assessment
- injunctions served by third parties
- project objectives.

One final important factor remains and that is of the post project/investment audit, a critical step for ensuring benefits are delivered, lessons are learnt and that the process is improved for organisations over time.

Feedback on self-assessment question 9.1

The paper should:

- evidence actual company audit extracts
- evidence published audits of either the public sector of the National Audit Office – NAO (UK) or other respected body from a recognised Government
- identify a logical approach to the audit and illustrate an audit plan
- make reference to ISO: 19011 and how to conduct your own audits

The key members of the audit should be:

- independent finance manager
- sponsors-nominated manager
- specialists as required; eg health and safety, environmental, legal
- production/operations technical engineer.

The paper should also identify an agreed methodology between all parties involved for the way the project/investment will be evaluated against its objectives and success criteria, eg how a Key Performance Indicator (KPI) might be calculated and from which source the data will be taken.

Feedback on learning activity 9.2

We can see that there will be a decision-making process to go through to determine the best way of approaching a project/investment to align with a specific organisation's circumstances. However, they are often governed/

Finance for Purchasers

influenced by factors beyond the boundaries of the project/investment itself or indeed the organisation as an entity.

Below is a suggested solution/option from the table presented, based on the lowest possible capital cost and assuming that some equipment and other elements can be leased/rented:

Table 9.2

Project cost item	Option A		Option B		Student option	
	Capital	Revenue	Capital	Revenue	Capital	Revenue
Design fees	£310,000	Nil	£280,000	£30,000	£280,000	£30,000
Regulatory fees	£28,000	Nil	£28,000	Nil	£28,000	Nil
Health and safety	£44,000	Nil	£44,000	Nil	£44,000	Nil
Legal fees	£56,000	Nil	£56,000	Nil	£56,000	Nil
Project management fees	£178,000	Nil	£178,000	Nil	£178,000	Nil
Site acquisition costs	£2,486,000	Nil	£2,486,000	Nil	Nil	*£3,850,000
Infrastructure costs	£178,000	£8,000	£178,000	£8,000	£178,000	£8,000
Superstructure costs	£2,224,000	£68,000	£2,224,000	£68,000	£2,224,000	£68,000
Fit out costs	£1,088,000	£96,000	£1,088,000	£96,000	£1,088,000	£96,000
External works	£174,000	£22,000	£174,000	£22,000	£174,000	£22,000
Landscaping	£120,000	£32,000	Nil	£222,000	Nil	£222,000
Office equipment	£246,000	£42,000	£88,000	£240,000	£88,000	£240,000
Manufacturing equipment	£1,888,000	£128,000	£960,000	£1,428,000	£960,000	£1,428,000
Warehouse racking	£468,000	£46,000	£468,000	£46,000	£468,000	£46,000
Expenses	Nil	£88,000	Nil	£88,000	Nil	£88,000
Total	£9,488,000	£530,000	£8,252,000	£2,248,000	£5,588,000	£6,098

* Annual rental charge of £154,000 × 25 years

Feedback on self-assessment question 9.2

An analytical approach is required, looking at the total costs over the life of the equipment or contract as well as discussing the advantages and disadvantages of the two principal routes to be evaluated.

Therefore looking at the costs over the life of the equipment:

Table 9.3

	Y1	Y2	Y3	Y4	Y5	Y6	Y7	Y8	Y9	Y10
Capital cost (£000): 1,500	150	150	150	150	150	150	150	150	150	150
Revenue cost (£000): 450	25	25	25	40	40	40	120	45	45	45
Production (1000/ year): 1,720,320	176,640	176,640	176,640	176,640	176,640	176,640	130,560	176,640	176,640	176,640
Unit cost/1,000 bottles: £1.13	£0.99	£0.99	£0.99	£1.08	£1.08	£1.08	£2.07	£1.10	£1.10	£1.10

As we can see, the cost per 1,000 bottles varies over the life of the machine and at certain periods would be difficult to handle with the end consumer in terms of price fluctuations from year to year if the real costs were applied. Therefore a 'smoothed' average of £1.13 would be acceptable (taking no account for borrowing of capital, interest, finance charges, inflation, and so on). However, if initial price to market needed to be the most competitive to gain first mover advantage, then the capital and expense route may be more attractive, with discounting in later years to offset the spike in year 7.

Finally it may be better, depending on the commercial price offered by the manufacturer, to place all the risk with him and to have a fixed or incremental price scale to ensure effective budgeting and risk transfer. However, if this route was adopted the business would have no assets as they would belong to the equipment manager and all the costs would be expensed, loosing the tax advantages of capital employed.

These are just some of the more obvious and simple factors, but it is likely in real life to be far more complex.

Feedback on learning activity 9.3

The six phases of a project according to the NAO on page 10 of the report are:

1 strategic analysis
2 tendering
3 contract completion
4 pre-operational implementation
5 early operational
6 mature operational.

Feedback on self-assessment question 9.3

The principal point to be argued here is that the PFI/PPP projects are four times better than traditional procurement! Is this valid? If so, what lessons could be transferred from PFI/PPP to traditional procurement methods?

In essence the forum is suggesting that traditional procurement merely looks at best to issue an ITT, negotiate the lowest price, place a contract and hope all goes well and, if it does not, look to some form of contractual redress. Clearly, in this situation, as the fact sheet asserts, 96% of projects are performing at least satisfactorily and 66% to a very good or good standard.

In essence the measures for improvement and enhanced procurement methods are covered in chapters 5 and 6 of HM Treasury's report *PFI: Strengthening Long-term Partnerships* (available by kind permission of Crown copyright via the website PFI: strengthening long-term partnerships: http://www.pppforum.com/documents/220306_longtermpartnerships.pdf). This also makes reference to the *Value for Money Assessment Guidance* (August 2004), which will be regularly updated and available from the website.

Finance for Purchasers

9

Study session 10
Evaluating project decision-making tools

Introduction

In this session we will look at how and where we can deploy some of the key decision-making tools to plan, control and manage capital projects in particular. This area of procurement is often regarded as a specialist area of expertise, with knowledge of the sector in which the procurement specialist is working being of great advantage. These tools and techniques can be adapted and applied equally to non-capital areas of procurement decision making as the need to ensure transferability of both skills and techniques is regarded as a higher cognitive skill for all procurement professionals.

'Making competent decisions takes more than a belief that you're right!'
Edward de Bono and Robert Heller, *Thinking Managers*

Session learning objectives

After completing this session you should be able to:

10.1 Explain 'whole life costing' and its function in the evaluation of capital projects.
10.2 Explain 'target costing' and its role in the assessment of research and development activity, and new product development.
10.3 Describe 'tear-down analysis' and its use regarding new product or service viability.
10.4 Summarise 'value management and value engineering' and how it can be used in capital project planning to understand different cost components and their relative importance.
10.5 Explain value for money (VFM) and its integration in the decision-making process.

Unit content coverage

This study session covers the following topics from the official CIPS unit content document:

Learning objective

5.3 Evaluate the most appropriate decision-making tools for projects across a variety of sectors.
  - Whole life costing
  - Target costing
  - Value engineering
  - Value for money (VFM)

Finance for Purchasers

Prior knowledge

Study sessions 1 to 9.

Resources

Obtain a copy of a completed or live business case and the latest or final project report, together with the milestone meeting details reviewing key aspects of the project. This should address the issues to be discussed in this study session. Equally you should obtain through your own organisation the guidelines for project and programme management, addressing the control and investment appraisal methodology. This may also be found in an organisation's change governance or investment appraisal guidelines.

Timing

You should set aside about 6 hours to read and complete this session, including learning activities, self-assessment questions, the suggested further reading (if any) from the essential textbook for this unit and the revision question.

10.1 Whole life costing

The description of **whole life costing (WLC)** is defined by BS ISO 15686 as: 'A method of project economic evaluation in which all costs arising, and benefits accrued from installing, owning, operating, maintaining, and ultimately disposing of a project are considered to be potentially important to that decision.'

However, there seems to be no consensus regarding the nomenclature to be used, with different UK bodies referring to it by other names and with other definitions! This is also true of the private sector, as well as there being a bias on the part of some parties as to the pure financial aspects of the methodology. In the USA 'life cycle costing' is used to mean whole life costing. Even the UK's OGC uses whole life costing and life cycle costing interchangeably – in the *Successful Delivery Toolkit* series the title of the document is *Life Cycle Costing*, yet its document *Achieving Excellence Guide No. 7* is entitled *Whole Life Costing*. The two mean the same thing as far as OGC is concerned.

WLC is a technique that quantifies financial values, quality levels, technical issues, and environmental considerations and service standards for assets, in particular buildings and equipment from inception and throughout the life of the asset. Principally, WLC can be characterised as a systematic approach, balancing capital with revenue costs to achieve an optimum solution over a whole life of the asset and factoring in the quality and service provision issues at the same time.

10 Evaluating project decision-making tools

A more detailed definition would state that WLC is the analysis of all relevant and identifiable financial cash flows, regarding the acquisition and use of an asset. As such it is important that we can test any aspect subject to analysis by the following key descriptions;

- Relevant: those costs directly attributed to the asset under review.
- Measurable: a method by which we can quantify it in some way.
- Assets: these can be whole buildings or a single small component.
- Acquisition: can be defined as the construction of a building or the purchase of a single component.
- Life: is defined as all costs involved in the use and function of the asset during its whole life including disposal.

WLC can be used at any stage of the procurement process, and can be implemented at the levels of facility, function, system and component. Both capital and revenue costs must be considered over the whole life of the asset in the form of annualised cash flows. This includes everything from initial design to end of life, including any disposal costs.

WLC is a tool to help in assessing the cost performance of an asset. More specifically, the decision-making process in selecting options that differ both in construction/manufacture and operational (lifetime) costs.

There is only one 'evaluation' criterion in whole life cost analysis – that the scheme with the lowest whole life cost is the preferred choice. This does not mean that the scheme with the lowest whole life cost *must* be implemented. The result of the WLC analysis is only one of the criteria imposed on the final selection of an option (see figure 10.1 below). The technical and environmental assessments, together with WLC analysis and client business input, will provide a single solution, which, although perhaps not optimum in any single assessment area, will be the best compromise between all of them.

The benefits of this process and approach can be summarised as follows:

- encourages communication and project definition
- cost of ownership and occupation are clarified
- total cost of ownership/occupation is optimised
- early assessment of risks
- promotes realistic budgeting
- encourages discussion and decisions about materials choices
- best value attained
- provides actual figures for future benchmarking.

In the context of property and construction development, whole life costing focuses on the role of the 'construction client', and emphasises the gains to be made on their behalf. However, whole life costing is a beneficial tool for organisations involved at all stages in the construction supply chain. This process also supports the need for cross-functional working and allows the procurement professional to take a pivotal role as facilitator.

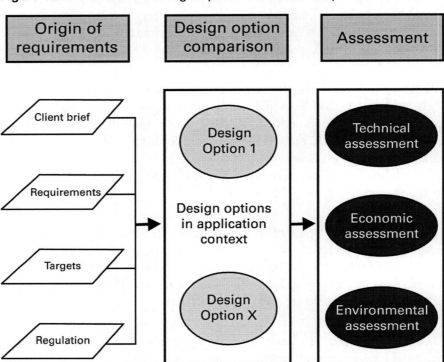

Figure 10.1: Whole life costing as part of the selection process

Next we must consider the 'when, what, how and who', and in the following example we have looked at the construction of a new facility as an example.

- *When:* at all important decision stages in procurement, construction and use of the property, eg: initial investment appraisal, feasibility study of alternatives, outline and detailed design, tender appraisal, assessment of variations, handover and post-occupancy evaluation.
- *What:* will vary according to acquisition by construction or by purchase/lease.
  Costs associated with the former include site costs, design, construction, fit-out and fees. Costs in use include management and maintenance charges and, finally, there are costs of disposal and deconstruction. Accuracy and thoroughness in recording decisions are vital to success. It is important to understand the sensitivity of the assessment to cost differentials over time as well as maintenance periods.
- *How:* there are many spreadsheet-based methods available to calculate whole life cost using discounted cash flows. Unfortunately they are not all the same and care needs to be taken in both selecting and comparing the different 'packages' that are available for use. In brief the Whole Life Costing Forum (WLCF) published methodology is:
  - To calculate WLC all cash flows, both positive (inflows) and negative (outflows) need to be identified for each year of the intended life of the asset. See the project as a cash flow.
  - The term 'asset' can mean a structure made up of multiple components or any individual component or series of components.
  - Cash flows are stated in actual cash terms, that is to say, all costs and incomes are at the levels expected in that year. There is no other allowance for inflation.

10 Evaluating project decision-making tools

- Asset life is the life of the asset required to function at acceptable levels.
- Day 1 of the cash flows commences on the first outflow or inflow. (Note when considering large, complex assets such as buildings some other WLC methodologies start Day 1 from the completion of construction adding the cost of construction as a single cost.)
- End of life costs are ignored on assessments with required lives longer than 10 years. (Note this is different from other methodologies and has been adopted to reduce risk and errors.)

The results of the cash flows can be analysed as:

- actual cash flows – the cash flows in each year
- total WLC – the addition of all the annual cash flows
- annualised WLC equivalent – the total WLC divided by the required life
- discounted cash flow – the discounting of the annual cash flows to produce a net present value (NPV) or discounted cash flow (DCF).
- The WLC can be assessed at any point in the construction process or at any point in the asset chain. WLC is more accurate when performance specification rather than product definition is used and the supplier or manufacturer.

- *Who:* this task can be carried out by many professionals from specialists, designers, finance, procurement and so on, providing the relevant training and experience is in place to both operate and interpret the results. Equally, as WLC is not an exact science, the skill and experience of the professional is key to ensuring good sound decision making each and every time.

Learning activity 10.1

Select a capital project with which you are familiar and identify a range of costs incurred at different stages in the projects life cycle. Ideally this would be in the range of 10–25 years.

Feedback on page 159

Now attempt self-assessment question 10.1 below.

Self-assessment question 10.1

Draft up a list that identifies the elements of a WLC model that are non-financial and how they could be evaluated, with one example for each.

Feedback on page 160

10.2 Target costing

Target costing was first introduced into the Western economies during 1970s from Japan, with some of the early and main adopters being Eastman Kodak, Honda, DaimlerChrysler, Caterpillar, the Boeing Company and Continental Tyres.

The main focus of target costing is in its application for new product development (NPD) and it can be described as a systematic approach towards aligning products designed and produced to meet a competitive pricing point at which the customer or end user is prepared and willing to pay. The approach is not that dissimilar to that of procurement category management in some ways, as you will see as we outline the principal steps and activates.

The principal steps to identify an NPD

1 Define the new product or service that has a viable and economic market into which it can enter. For example, this might be a new flavour of drink or a drink that has no sugar while all other current competitor products do have sugar.
2 Engage with current and prospective customer to ensure that what you are proposing is what they both need and see a place for in the current and future market. For example do not develop a new sugar-free apple drink first if this is the least popular flavour.
3 Establish the project boundaries in terms of quality, time to market, manufacturing capability, and so on. In short, ensure that what you might want to launch you can actually deliver and that it's not just a great idea.
4 Establish a database of all known facts and empirical data that will help shape and form the decision-making process. For example, you don't want to discover that you tried to deliver an apple sugar-free drink five years ago and couldn't stop the product from changing colour. We will look at the cost estimating group for this activity in more detail later in this section.
5 Form a cross-functional team to drive this NPD, complete with a project sponsor and team leader, with clear roles and responsibilities. As an example, there is no point in putting resources and effort into an NPD if the board won't give the product the go-ahead.
6 Having established what the product is, who will buy it and at what price, and so on, call the project team together to brainstorm and develop a series or workable options. For example, this might be a series of drink formulations and raw ingredients that might work.
7 Allocate tasks by team member, with clear output and requirements for the team to consider when they are reformed in an agreed or given time period. For example the food nutritionist might review the formulations and the procurement specialist may investigate the source of new or existing ingredients and supply parameters (cost, quality, availability, and so on).
8 Re-form the team to define an agreed or chosen formulation, sources of material, branding, and so forth that either fit the agreed scope for the NPD or require fine tuning to allow detailed development and product plan to be established. At this point we should acknowledge that there is normally a 'cost gap' to be closed and will require several iterations before being either suspended or concluded as a viable NPD.

Having got the NPD to the point of developing an NPD plan, remembering that only say 1 in 20 such projects will reach this point and

10 Evaluating project decision-making tools

fewer still will actually make it as new product or service, the detailed work must then begin, starting with:

The cost estimating group

Returning to step 4 in the process and particularly the cost estimating group. The role of this sub-group is to break the costs down into a whole series of cost targets for evaluation and costing. Normally this is a sub-group of the main cross-functional team, whose specific job it is to come up with the cost model and relate that back into tangible components or expenditure that the other members of the team can relate to. Therefore, if we take the example of a new sugar-free drink, the cost model would include:

- marketing costs
- sales costs
- distribution costs
- overhead allocation
- product support
- development costs
- operating/production costs:
  - equipment
  - training
  - systems
  - tooling
  - space requirements
  - storage
  - handling
  - health and safety
  - environmental
  - waste streams
- product costs:
  - secondary packaging
  - primary packaging
  - primary ingredients
  - flavours
  - stabilisers
  - artificial sweeteners
- profit margin.

This is not intended to be an exhaustive list but a simple example of how the cost estimating team needs to break down the target cost model and then populate it with empirical or new costs, where appropriate. This will enable the normal step of closing the cost gap;

Closing the cost gap

As we have stated earlier, the process of closing the cost gap is usually an iterative process. This will require the close coordination and collaboration of all departments, as we need to recognise that if we establish a new cost model and therefore the way forward for a new product, the organisation will have to deliver it.

This iterative process will involve many departments utilising new and existing approaches to deliver the product. Below are a few examples of

Finance for Purchasers

the types of activity that may have to be considered if the product is to be successful and make it to market.

- improved designs
- new materials
- new suppliers
- new supply chains
- new equipment tooling
- prototypes
- standardisation
- inventory reduction
- minimisation of bespoke elements.

The list is by no means exhaustive and will change and flex depending on the project or product needs.

Learning activity 10.2

Using the following data extract from a case study that identified the gap between target cost and projected cost, state what types of action would be appropriate in terms of bridging the gap for each objective.

Case study data:

- For all commercial equipment, the objectives must be to:
  - reduce complexity of supply
  - while delivering improved service to our customers and
  - providing greater control of commercial assets.
- Equipment supply goals must be to:
  - reduce total 'life costs' of commercial equipment
  - reduce overall level of commercial equipment capital expenditure
  - reduce value of equipment stockholding
  - reduce equipment losses and write off
  - improve equipment supply chain efficiency
  - reduce operational overheads
  - drive greater benefits from supplier partnerships.

Feedback on page 161

Now attempt self-assessment question 10.2 below.

Self-assessment question 10.2

Develop a target cost-estimating matrix such as table 10.2 for a product or service delivered by your own organisation and populate the following format to establish the whole cost and then go through an exercise to show

(continued on next page)

148

10 Evaluating project decision-making tools

Self-assessment question 10.2 *(continued)*

how you could reduce the cost to the customer or end user by 5%, while maintaining the current profit margin.

Table 10.2

Cost activity	Actual cost	Target cost	Method of delivery
Marketing costs			
Sales costs			
Distribution costs			
Overhead allocation			
Product support			
Development costs			
Operating/production costs:			
• Equipment			
• Training			
• Systems			
• Tooling			
• Space requirements			
• Storage			
• Handling			
• Health and Safety			
• Environmental			
• Waste streams			
Product costs:			
• Secondary packaging			
• Primary packaging			
• Primary ingredients			
• Secondary ingredients			
• Other 1			
• Other 2			
• Etc			
Profit margin			

Feedback on page 162

10.3 Value analysis – tear-down

This technique is firmly seated in the car manufacturing industry, where competitor products and/or components were dismantled or disassembled in a room and some form of dissection analysis performed on them. This method is reported to have been carried out by General Motors in the USA and is seen as the precursor to the formalisation of the technique of value analysis – tear-down (VA–TD).

A popular method rooted in this area of value analysis is reverse engineering, which ostensibly relates to starting with the finished products' performance and working back through to the concept stage of new product development (NPD). The process we are looking at should not be confused with the above as it is more complex, developed and formalised.

At this stage it is important that we look at the definition of VA–TD:

'VA–Tear-Down is a method of comparative analysis in which disassembled products, systems, components and data are visually compared; and their functions determined, analysed, and evaluated to improve the value adding characteristics of the project under study.'

We can further break this down by providing descriptions for each of the definition elements in the definition itself:

- *Comparative analysis:* Comparing two or more elements of a product or system having the same function.
- *Product:* the end item sold into the market.
- *System:* an active part of the product consisting of multiple components.
- *Component:* a single part or multiple pieces forming a single replaceable part.
- *Data:* elements of information that, when combined, form the basis for analysis.
- *Function:* a description of an intended action upon a defined object necessary to achieve a desired purpose.

The definition is intended to embrace the powers of observation, deduction and a broad range of value analysis techniques (to help understand problems and find improvement opportunities). It should also be noted that the formal process of VA–TD helped the process of reverse engineering, NPD, model additions, modifications and competitive analysis. For example, when looking at sports cars that look the same, perform similarly, and so on, it is by scrutinising the differences that it is possible to devise a new sports car that has the best of both and removes the worst of both! In the VA–TD process it is necessary for the team to determine the functional advantages of the product and the cost to perform them and therefore whether they add value (as determined by the end consumer).

Value analysis differs from other cost improvement techniques by questioning, defining and analysing the functions of components, rather than determining how a part could be made better or cheaper. Remembering that VA–TD is a comparative analysis tool it is possible to focus on a particular area and objective referred to as a *theme*, or *an issue of concern*. The structure of how this is organised is shown in figure 10.4.

Figure 10.4: VA–TD structure

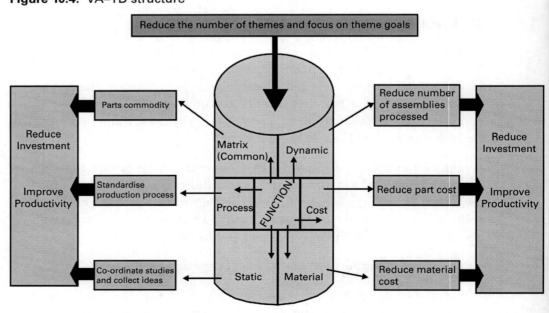

Next we must look at the procedures that need be followed, which mirror the six types of activity or process shown in figure 10.4. These can then be arranged sequentially, with the first five being referred to as analytical steps and the final step being referred to as a display step, as set out below:

1 dynamic tear-down
2 cost tear-down
3 material tear-down
4 matrix tear-down
5 process tear-down
6 static tear-down.

Before we look at each of these steps in outline, we should remember that the whole process is aimed at value, which from LD Miles' work (see section 10.4 below) is the simple formula applied to all of this:

- Value = Function/Cost

Equally, the key to successful VA–TD is the **job plan**, which is the structured five-step approach to value analysis developed by LD Miles but which also applies to VA–TD. In short, this can be summarised as follows:

- *Information:* the evaluation of all available information relative to the VA theme or project, which is then translated into the functional terms necessary to carry out the process.
- *Speculation:* the process of generating a large quantity of ideas (not solutions) that tackle the unique and creative ways to achieve the defined functions that relate to the theme or problem.
- *Planning (or analysis):* evaluation of the ideas generated, using weighted guidelines, performance and other requirements to distil out the best ideas.
- *Execution (or evaluation):* grouping the selected ideas into proposal scenarios and the evaluation of those scenarios in terms of financial, risk and implementation.
- *Reporting (or presenting):* preparation and presentation of the team proposals to a management board of key stakeholders, including seeking approval to implement the recommended changes.

Turning to the six steps in the VA-TD process, we will look at each in turn and provide a simple explanation of what each type of process is focused upon.

- *Dynamic:* this applies the principle of comparative analysis the process of assembly. The term 'dynamic' refers to all the design features that contribute to the time and cost of assembling the product in production. Some of these features include hand selecting parts to avoid tolerance build-up, the need for adjustment during assembly, the number of parts needed to perform a function, and the need for special assembly tools.
  In dynamic tear-down, following disassembly, the products are re-assembled as intended by the original equipment manufacturer (OEM). The sequence and the time taken are record in the simulated OEMs production procedure. The sequence and time are then compared and the function of each part is determined to assess its contribution to the value of the product.
- *Cost:* a method by which the costs of competitors' products are compared with those of comparable products. Because this step is solely concerned with costs, all cost-related information must be

included in the analysis. Information collected includes component cost comparison, assembly time translated into cost, and the results of other tear-down steps.

The primary objective is to assess the total cost of the product to market, less any general overheads, which may be more difficult to assess for competitors, However, we have read earlier how we can extract this from annual reports and the like. The purpose of the exercise is not to collect and compare the total costs of products but to obtain information for improving functionality, features and attributes, thereby enhancing their value as defined by the end customer. Evaluating competitive advantages through analysis, and isolating cost reduction factors through such analysis, achieve this.

- *Material:* with the growing concern for environmental issues and sustainability, a focus on material types and usage is key. Material tear-down can be classified into two types, depending on objectives; Comparison of materials, surface treatment, etc and analysis of material scrap/wastage rate. Both types of approach offer significant opportunities to reduce cost and improve product value. For example the costs of surface treatment to vehicles may vary in cost greatly but could alter significantly performance, whole life cost issues due to degradation and corrosion, etc. This type of experience and/or reputation could impact customer perception and potential future sales and brand reputation.

- *Matrix:* the types of tear-down analysis discussed so far relate to the comparison of products of the investigating company and its competitors. This type of analysis looks at its own product line for differences. In matrix tear-down the focus is to find where common parts across different products can be used to reduce variations and part numbers. This in turn will reduce inventory and investment costs as well as improving cash flow. Furthermore, this exercise will identify the base parts of an organisation, in other words, those that can be shared and therefore help inform future NPD.

- *Process:* this is similar to matrix tear-down in comparative product analysis, except that the emphasis is on process. Many similar parts or products are manufactured using similar processes. The process tear-down procedures compare and analyse the details of all these processes, from initial to final process. The objective is to integrate similar processes, modifying each process to deal with the production of different products on the same production line and improving line effectiveness overall. This means manufacturers can produce low-volume parts at a competitive cost.

  As discussed earlier, an effective way to achieve product improvement is to first develop as many common parts as possible. The remaining unique parts are then analysed using process tear-down to determine which of those parts can share the same production line.

- *Static:* there are two major steps to static tear-down. In the first step, the selected products, parts or materials subjected to dynamic tear-down (both investigating and competitor manufacturer organisations) are displayed in their disassembled form as component parts. The team then reviews and decides how to analyse each part.

  In the second step, the ideas that were suggested as a result of competitive analysis are used to form product strategies. Seeking

10 Evaluating project decision-making tools

improvement suggestions may also be done in the first step. However, it can be carried out more effectively as a second step, especially if they are presented with the relevant information and data in the second step. By displaying these ideas in this way it will enable the team to create new ideas and combinations as well removing duplicate ideas or options.

Learning activity 10.3

Carry out research using Yoshihiko and Kaufman (2005) and the key headings of the summary starting on page 181.

Feedback on page 163

Now attempt self-assessment question 10.3 below.

Self-assessment question 10.3

Note down in the correct order the sequence of steps that should be completed as part of static tear-down analysis.

Feedback on page 163

10.4 Value management and value engineering

We will focus exclusively on capital projects in the construction sector (although it is applied to other sectors). It should be recognised that value engineering and value management both evolved from methods first developed to look at the concept of value and functional approach. Lawrence D Miles pioneered this while he was employed at General Electric Company in the 1940s and 1950s. The technique developed was first called 'value analysis', a method of improving value in existing products. This technique was first used to identify and eliminate unnecessary costs. The value management approach has four main attributes or principles, which can be summarised below:

- management style:
  - emphasis on teamwork and communication,
  - a focus on what things do, rather than what they are (functional approach)
  - an atmosphere that encourages creativity and innovation
  - a focus on customer's requirements and
  - a requirement to evaluate options qualitatively to enable robust comparisons of options

Finance for Purchasers

- positive human dynamics
  - teamwork – encouraging people to work together towards a common solution
  - satisfaction – recognising and giving credit
  - communication – bringing people together by improving communication between them
  - fostering better common understanding and providing better group decision support
  - encouraging change – challenging the status quo and bring about beneficial change
  - ownership – the assumption of ownership of the outcomes of value management activities by those responsible for implementing them
- consideration of external and internal environment:
  - external conditions – taking account of pre-existing conditions external to the organisation over which managers may have little influence
  - internal conditions – within the organisation there will be existing conditions which managers may or may not be able to influence
  - degrees of freedom – the external and internal conditions will dictate the limits of potential outcomes and should be quantified
- Effective use of methods and tools:
  - means of achieving outcomes.

Value management is not simply a cost-cutting exercise, but identifies and eliminates the unnecessary cost (cost that does not contribute to a function) which is common in all construction projects. An example of this would be a boundary wall that was made of expensive materials and 2 metres high, but which only needed to keep sheep out from an adjacent field and could be constructed 1.5 metres high and of cheaper construction.

Value engineering is an exercise in which parties should engage in objective dialogue, not confrontation with an open mind receptive to new ideas, change and a willingness to cooperate with other team members assembled to assess the project. If approached correctly it will reduce or eliminate the factors that prevent good value projects from being realised. The factors that often prevent good value projects can be broadly categorised as follows:

- poor information
- lack of time
- insufficient resources
- unrealistic and unnecessary constraints
- poor communication
- lack of teamwork
- entrenched thinking and habits or attitudes
- politics.

For value engineering to be truly effective it must be carried out very early in the life of the project. Figure 10.5 shows how change and time have a direct impact on cost.

Figure 10.5: Change and time impact on cost

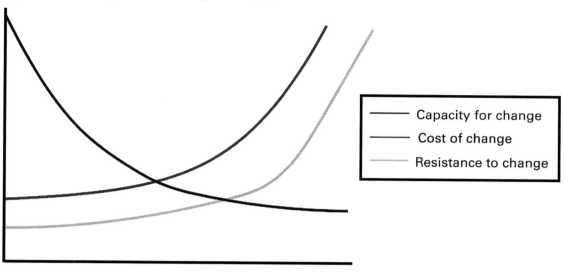

As we remarked earlier in the study session, the need to carry out value engineering early on is critical to its effectiveness and paradoxically, if carried out too late it could actually be destructive to the final cost and delivery of the project, see figure 10.6.

Figure 10.6: Cost versus project phases(time)

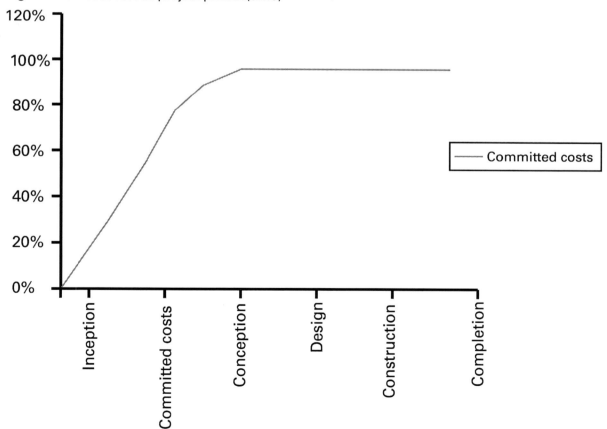

However, focusing on the positive aspects of value engineering we can see from the list below the benefits to a client or a design team are extremely attractive.

Finance for Purchasers

The benefits of value engineering to the client are:

- reduced building cost
- reduced waste
- improved satisfaction of needs
- improved concept
- improved processes
- improved solutions
- enhanced quality
- reduced time
- increased competitiveness
- high payback on study cost.

The benefits of value engineering to the design team are:

- efficient use of resources
- improved brief
- less conflict
- improved teamwork and communications
- options have been assessed objectively
- more focused design effort.

Learning activity 10.4

Give consideration to a well-known product (such as a car) in terms of different attributes that could/would are included in a value engineering analysis.

Feedback on page 164

Now attempt self-assessment question 10.4 below.

Self-assessment question 10.4

Identify at least six types of product or service, of which half would and half would not be suitable for value engineering or value management and give a brief rationale as to why you have chosen the product or service.

Feedback on page 164

10.5 Value for money (VFM)

Value for money (VFM) is the term used to assess whether or not an organisation has obtained the maximum benefit from the goods and services it acquires and/or provides, within the resources available to it. It not only

10 Evaluating project decision-making tools

measures the cost of goods and services, but also takes into account the mix of quality, cost, resource use, fitness for purpose, timeliness and convenience to judge whether or not, when taken together, they constitute good value.

Achieving VFM may be described in terms of the 'three Es' – economy, efficiency and effectiveness.

- Economy – Doing less with fewer resources (making savings).
- Efficiency – Doing the same as before, but with fewer resources (money, staff, space).
- Effectiveness – Doing more than before with the same, or less, resources.

The policy for pursuing VFM lies with all staff, and not just those with purchasing and financial duties.

The following aims could be set as an organisation's commitment to achieving VFM:

1 To integrate VFM principles within the organisation's existing management, planning, review and decision-making processes, particularly with regard to projects or activities with significant financial implications.
2 To adopt recognised good practice where appropriate.
3 To undertake or commission VFM studies into areas of activity identified as worthy of review.
4 To benchmark the organisation's activities against other similar activities and organisations where this is considered useful.
5 To respond to opportunities to enhance the economy, efficiency and effectiveness of the organisation's activities.
6 To demonstrate actively, to both internal and external observers, that the achievement of VFM is sought in all activities taken.
7 To ensure that all staff recognise their continuing obligation to seek VFM as part of their routine activities.

Integration of VFM principles into decision making

VFM must be a routine part of the decision-making process at all levels of management throughout the organisation. This is particularly important in planning or reviewing activities with significant financial implications. Larger organisations will set up a VFM committee, and this committee will seek assurance that VFM considerations are being given due weight in key areas of expenditure and will raise any concerns with the appropriate decision-making bodies.

As part of this integration of VFM into routine decision making, divisions and departments will be asked to submit a report on the application of VFM principles, detailing measures to improve economy, efficiency and effectiveness, and quantifying any financial benefits. Reports should draw attention both to existing activities that demonstrate continuing VFM, and to new opportunities for improving VFM. The VFM committee will need to be satisfied that VFM issues are being adequately addressed, and that all major areas of expenditure, including staff costs, are being properly scrutinised.

Divisions and departments of an organisation are well placed to identify opportunities for achieving greater VFM within their areas of responsibility. They will know what measures are likely to be effective, having regard to their particular circumstances and needs, and how to enlist the support and co-operation of staff.

Procurement

A major element in the commitment to achieving VFM is the drive to obtain goods and services that provide the best quality at the best price. This is primarily the responsibility of the purchasing department, whose mission is 'to fully support corporate strategies by delivering continuous improvement in value for money, based on whole life cost and quality, and to enhance the competitiveness of all key suppliers through the development of world class professional procurement systems and practices'.

Revision question

There is no revision question for this session.

Summary

In summary the four tools, techniques and methodologies above share a common theme of team collaboration, a disciplined approach and need to establish good planning and communication. Equally they all have applications across a broad spectrum of procurement activity, from direct to indirect goods and services.

Suggested further reading

- Association of Chartered Certified Accountants (ACCA) (2001) *Full cost accounting: an agenda for action*. London: ACCA. ISBN: 1 85908 352 8
- Edwards, S, E Bartlett and I Dickie (2000) *Whole life costing and life-cycle assessment for sustainable building design*. Watford: BRE Press.
- Horngren, CT, SM Datar and G Foster (2005) *Cost Accounting: A Managerial Emphasis*, 12th edition. Harlow: Prentice Hall.
- Innes, J (ed) (2004) *Handbook of Management Accounting*. London: Thomson/Gee with CIMA.
- Seal, W (2005) *Management Accounting*. McGraw Hill.
- Yoshihiko, S, and J Kaufman (2005) *Value Analysis – Tear Down*, 1st edition. New York: Industrial Press
- BS ISO 15686 and BS EN 60300.
- H M Treasury Green Book
- Office of Government Commerce (OGC) Procurement Guide 07
- CIPS –Whole Life Costing guide (pdf)
- Whole Life Cost Forum (M4i) – Movement for Innovation

Feedback on learning activities and self-assessment questions

Feedback on learning activity 10.1

Whole life costing can contribute significantly to the achievement of the financial and non-financial business objectives of many organisations. This is especially relevant in terms of customer service, internal business processes, and financial performance. Furthermore, the process is fundamental in decision making across all industry sectors to ensure that not just monetary values are evaluated but placed alongside the non-financial elements of asset acquisition.

The UK government has taken a decision to make all (except PFI and PPP – refer to previous section 9.3) construction procurement awards on the basis of whole life costs – HM Treasury guidance stipulates this specifically. However, Private Finance Initiative (PFI) and Public Private Partnerships (PPP) contracting need to evaluate the long-term risks, maintenance and operation of assets and therefore makes whole life costing a logical requirement for all parties concerned.

While whole life costing is a fairly simple and well-understood mathematical process it is a difficult concept for many to grasp, requiring a significant change of focus, and the difficulty of implementing it adequately, and the wider risks to business should not be underestimated.

The objective of WLC analysis, together with the quality, service, technical, environmental, and other evaluations is to provide the decision maker with sufficient information on which to base a reasoned judgement. *Critically none of the evaluations are designed to make the decision.* Figure 10.2 shows a typical cost/time diagram.

Figure 10.2: Cost/time diagram

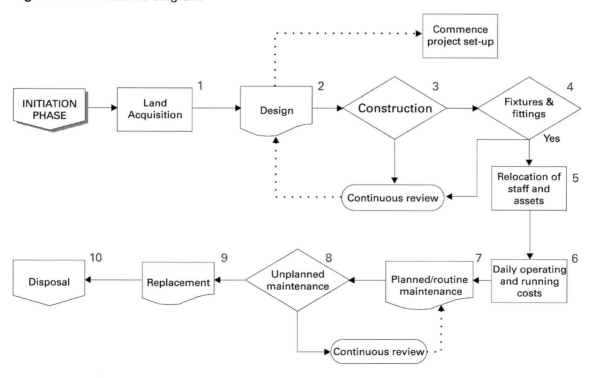

The above example looks at the typical phases and stages in a construction project. However, the logic equally applies to a single acquisition such as a piece of machinery/equipment.

This can be further subdivided and cross-referenced to other areas of study in this session to business case preparation, reporting, risk analysis, and so on, as follows:

Figure 10.3: Cost/time diagram

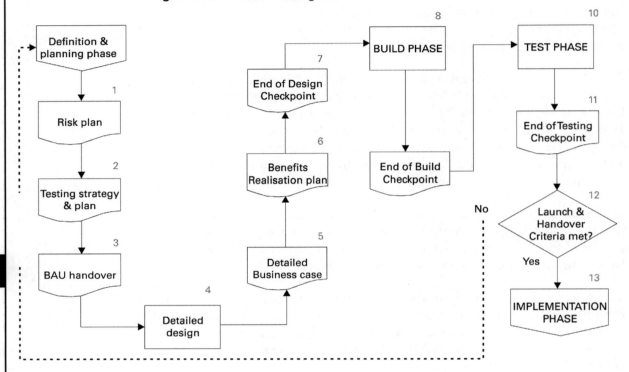

Feedback on self-assessment question 10.1

Essentially this should cover the headings of:

- Business needs/objectives – example: increase customer satisfaction via the customer feedback surveys by a total of 5% over the year from the current base position of 86%.
- Quality – example: measured compliance with a recognised annual quality audit against ISO 9001, either a specific score/rating or simple continued accreditation against the standard.
- Safety – example: BS safety checks on all equipment shall have a pass rate above 98.5% as a whole over the year.
- Environmental – example: successful completion of an environmental impact assessment with no high risk and a maximum of three medium risk areas.
- Technical – example: all SOPs (standard operating procedures) for all manufactured goods shall be reviewed and put online by the year end.
- CSR – example: identify top 20 suppliers (or those that combined account for 80% of the companies spend) and evaluate on-site the five key areas of:
    - working conditions
    - labour policy

10 Evaluating project decision-making tools

- healthcare in the workplace
- safety systems and policies
- minimum/maximum working hours policy and enforcement.

Feedback on learning activity 10.2

A salient point to recognise is that the value of products delivered by an organisation supply chain may range from, say, 40–80% of the whole product cost. In essence this emphasises the critical role that procurement professionals have to play in this type of 'up front' activity for an organisation. This is perhaps best illustrated by those companies who find themselves in a position where they have a product on the market, which may be very successful, but which is wholly reliant upon a sole supplier. This may be further complicated if there is no strong relationship with the supplier, the supply is erratic; they hold no patents or warranties, and so forth.

Most companies who have used the target costing approach on many occasions and intend to continue using the methodology go on to develop their own tools and systems to do this internally.

Remembering that the exercise is looking at a small section of the target cost model, we can reproduce it to look like table 10.1 as an example.

Table 10.1

Action plan	Target cost/value	Current cost/value	Gap	Actions required
Reduce complexity of supply	2,500 suppliers	10,000 suppliers	7,500 supply base reduction	Ensure all top tier supply commodities and service have no more than two providers
Improved service to our customers	93.5%	88.5%	5% improvement	Provide additional training to all customer facing staff in key improvement areas identified
Greater control of commercial assets	Assets on finance system £25.6 million versus £25.3 million on asset register	Assets on finance system £25.6 million versus £24.3 million on asset register	Improvement of £1 million of assets on register	Carry out asset base stock take in Q2 and cross-check against current asset register and put corrective process in place to prevent re-occurrence
Reduce total 'life costs' of commercial equipment	Operational budget reduced by £150,000	Operational budget £4.5 million	3% improvement in operational costs	Review older equipment and high maintenance equipment and reprioritise disposal and replacement in conjunction with new capital programme

(continued on next page)

Finance for Purchasers

Table 10.1 *(continued)*

Action plan	Target cost/value	Current cost/value	Gap	Actions required
Reduce overall level of commercial equipment capital expenditure	Reduce the capital budget by £1.2 million	Current capital budget £24 million	5% reduction in capital spend	Critically review all capital spend and deselect all low IRR projects to achieve target
Reduce value of equipment stockholding	Reduce current stock holding by £300,000	Current equipment stock holding value £15 million	2% reduction in stock holding	Remove or reduce slow moving stocks and duplicate stock holding and set up JIT project to target key/priority areas
Reduce equipment losses and write off	Reduce write off by £150,000 per annum	Current write off value per annum £3 million	5% reduction in write-offs	Improve quality performance monitoring plan at an operational level and ensure key stakeholders are specifically targeted and bonus based on compliance
Improve equipment supply chain efficiency	Order fulfilment time 36 days	Current order fulfilment time 42 days	6 day order fulfilment improvement	Critically review all long lead items and either work with existing suppliers or instigate new supply base to meet new targets
Reduce operational overheads	Reduce overheads by £450,000	Current operational overheads £27 million	2% reduction in overheads	Look at key overhead spend areas and working with departmental heads agree changes
Drive greater benefits from supplier partnerships	% NPD projects from supply base	Three NPD ideas from current supply base	Two additional NPD projects per year	Revitalise the need for innovation from the top tier suppliers, where typically NPD will be derived from targeting and providing bonus to key stakeholders who own the relationships

Feedback on self-assessment question 10.2

A sample answer is shown in table 10.3.

Table 10.3

Cost activity	Actual cost	Target cost	Method of delivery
Marketing costs	£3 million	£2.7 million	Reduce print costs
Sales costs	£4.5 million	£4.2 million	Reduce staff costs
Distribution costs	£2.1 million	£2.1 million	No action
Overhead allocation	£3.6 million	£3.6 million	No action
Product support	£650,000	£600,000	Reduce staff costs

(continued on next page)

Table 10.3 *(continued)*

Cost activity	Actual cost	Target cost	Method of delivery
Development costs	£450,000	£550,000	Increase product development staff and on costs
Operating/production costs: • Equipment • Training • Systems • Tooling • Space requirements • Storage • Handling • Health and Safety • Environmental • Waste streams	£4.8 million	£4.5 million	Reduce re-tooling costs through standardisation of product range in conjunction with the development department
Product costs: • Secondary packaging • Primary packaging • Primary ingredients • Secondary ingredients • Other 1 • Other 2 • Etc	£5.8 million	£5.3 million	Re-focus work on primary 12 categories with a view to overseas sourcing of packaging products, PET, Aluminium, etc
Profit margin	£2.9 million	£4.35	Net result of better management

Feedback on learning activity 10.3

The key headings are as follows:

- Create a model case for success
- Establish a level of competency
- Organisation
- Understanding by the top management
- Facilities
- Standardisation of operations
- Establishing the plan and setting the targets
- Value analysis.

Feedback on self-assessment question 10.3

These should be arranged sequentially as follows:

- plan event
- collect information
- select team
- collect parts/products to be analysed
- carry out preliminary investigation
- review static tear-down procedure
- conduct other/recommend other tear-down analysis
- develop the displays
- generate and collect ideas/options
- examine and review ideas/options

Finance for Purchasers

- develop follow up action plan
- presentation (optional).

Feedback on learning activity 10.4

It should be recognised that this methodology is now well established and has a role to apply with many other tools, such as whole life costing and expressing items in accounting terms such as NPV.

The example we will use here is the car dashboard, which in one manufacturer's car is made up of 263 individual components or component assemblies.

The considerations here are:

- Source of materials: can we source them cheaper while retaining the same function and design intent?
- Can we reduce the number of components to minimise 'build time'?
- Can we look at building the dashboard away from the production line and therefore optimise the speed of the line?
- Can we look at putting all the wiring looms together to achieve a 'plug a connector' arrangement, thereby minimising build time at the plant, even though product cost may be higher?
- Can we combine the instrument functions to optimise the number of dials?
- Can we replace some of the key materials with different materials without loosing function and design attributes?
- Can we minimise waste and packaging?
- Can we look at a 'through the wall' operation to reduce transport costs?

Feedback on self-assessment question 10.4

This list should include items such as:

Suitable areas:

- Brand images (that is, removing key images or colours): the rationale for this would be that by having fewer colours involved all future printing and artwork design costs will be reduced as a consequence of reduced complexity and set-up. This will apply to the physical production stages where branding occurs on the goods sold.
- Changing the formula for a household drink or food: the rationale for this would be that by reducing dependence on costly ingredients the product would cost less to produce while maintaining the same retail price point
- Software: the rationale for this would be to standardise all software versions and have software packages that already have a common/ generic interface thereby obviating costly development and bespoke software costs.

Non-suitable areas:

- Services that are not price-sensitive, such as a premier banking service: the rationale for this would be that is service that is key, not cost.

10 Evaluating project decision-making tools

- Organic foods: the rationale for this would be you are selling the organic product, not a mass-produced commodity, and therefore quality is the issue not cost.
- Medical active ingredients (it takes 10 years to develop a new one!): the rationale for this would be the prohibitive cost to develop a new formulation.

Finance for Purchasers

10

Study session 11
Sources of finance

Introduction

'Neither a borrower nor a lender be.'
Hamlet

All businesses need finance – both long-term and short-term – in order to operate.

This session will look at how businesses, and other organisations, are financed. We will look first at internal sources of finance – where businesses are able to generate their own funding. We will then turn to the main external sources of finance – where the business raises funding from external sources such as shareholders or lenders.

We will also draw a distinction between money borrowed on a long-term basis, known as 'debt', and long-term capital provided by shareholders, which is known as 'equity'. The relative merits of debt and equity will be introduced in this session, and developed further when we consider risk evaluation in study session 20.

Finally we shall look at public sector borrowing.

Session learning objectives

After completing this session you should be able to:

11.1 Describe internal sources of finance.
11.2 Describe external sources of finance (equity).
11.3 Describe external sources of finance (non-equity).
11.4 Explain public borrowing for the public sector (Bank of England and HM Treasury).

Unit content coverage

This study session covers the following topics from the official CIPS unit content document:

Learning objective

3.2 Evaluate and select a range of sources of finance to assessing funds for capital acquisitions and projects.
   - Retained profit
   - Controlling working capital
   - Sale of assets
   - Factoring
   - Overdrafts
   - Grants

Finance for Purchasers

- Venture capital
- Debentures
- Share issues
- Bank loans – medium or long term
- Leasing
- PPP/PFI
- Public borrowing for public sector (Bank of England and HM Treasury)

Prior knowledge

Study sessions 1 to 10, especially study session 5.

Timing

You should set aside about 7 hours to read and complete this session, including learning activities, self-assessment questions, the suggested further reading (if any) from the essential textbook for this unit and the revision question.

11.1 Internal sources of finance

Internal finance describes any finance that is generated from within the organisation's own resources.

The most important source of internal finance is retained profit. As we saw from earlier sessions, companies that make a profit can either distribute it in the form of a dividend, or retain it in the business – or, more likely, do a bit of both.

Retaining profit in the business then reduces the need to go outside and try to raise new external finance.

Sale of assets

Fixed assets can be sold as a means of raising finance. If the company has no use for the assets then converting them into cash to be used for other purposes is a useful and straightforward source of internal finance.

Learning activity 11.1

Refer back to the financial statements reviewed in learning activity 5.1. The company was UK Enterprise Plc, and we looked at their profit and loss account, balance sheet and cash flow statement for illustrative purposes.

What different source of finance is this company using?

How would you categorise the different elements of financing, in terms of whether they are internal or external?

(continued on next page)

11 Sources of finance

> **Learning activity 11.1** *(continued)*
>
> How would you categorise the different elements of finance in terms of whether they are short-term or long-term?
>
> (NB: It may be useful to refer to both the balance sheet and the cash flow statement when considering these questions.)
>
> *Feedback on page 186*

One way of generating finance from internal sources is by improved working capital management.

There are various definitions of working capital, but it essentially describes all the shorter-term assets and liabilities that a business has at any one time.

Generating finance internally will therefore involve managing these assets and liabilities in such a way that they free up cash at the earliest opportunity, and require the minimum amount of cash input at any time – without compromising the overall business operation.

It might be useful to first consider a diagram of what is known as the 'working capital cycle', and then look at individual elements of it (see figure 11.1).

Figure 11.1: The working capital cycle

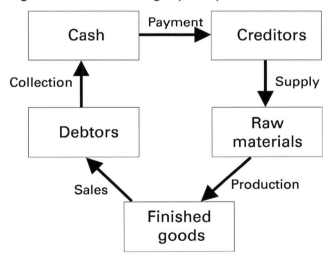

Money is constantly moving through any business. It will do so at different speeds, dependent on the nature of the business, and similarly the type of business will determine the number of different stages. The above illustration is for a traditional manufacturing business.

For a manufacturing business, a lot must happen before the cash from trading is received. A company has to:

- buy materials
- process them
- despatch the goods
- send out an invoice
- wait for payment.

Finance for Purchasers

There might therefore be a long period between the payment to trade creditors for the raw materials and the receipt of cash from the debtors. During this period money is tied up in working capital.

If we look at different stages in turn, we can see that management action can help free up finance – at no additional cost.

Managing stock

First, we should consider stock. Stock management involves a balancing act between on the one hand having enough of it to run the business properly and keep customers happy, and on the other hand not holding too much (as it ties up cash that could be used elsewhere).

Holding too much stock could lead to:

- higher finance charges, for example interest on overdraft use
- higher storage/insurance costs
- reduced liquidity – cash is tied up that could be used elsewhere
- wastage through obsolescence/deterioration

However, holding insufficient stock has its own dangers too:

- potential lost production
- higher replacement costs
- lost sales
- poor reputation.

Thus finance can be raised if stock levels can, on average, be reduced. But care needs to be taken to ensure that raising finance in this way does not harm the business in other ways.

Managing debtors

A company's credit policy is part of its overall marketing package and offering generous credit terms might be what it takes to make a sale. As with stock, though, this involves a trade-off between risk and return. The risk of extending credit is that the customer may pay either late or not at all. The return comes from the additional sales that are made by attracting more customers through flexible credit terms.

As with stock, the lower the amount of outstanding debtors, the more cash is available to run the business. Keeping debtor levels low is therefore another way in which working capital management can be a source of internal finance.

Debtor levels can be reduced by:

- using factoring or invoice discounting (which we will cover in section 11.2)
- carefully vetting and monitoring credit customers
- applying a strict credit policy with credit limits
- chasing up outstanding invoices

- offering cash discounts (but beware of customers who pay late but still take the discount).

Charging interest on late debts may also be an option – but not always one that companies are willing to pursue.

Bad debts represent an extra risk in extending credit. This is particularly so for businesses that have relatively high variable costs as they will have paid out more (in materials, labour and so on) to achieve the sale than will higher-margin businesses.

Managing creditors

Creditors provide a counter-balance to having large amounts of funds tied up in stock and debtors, and represent an opportunity of gaining additional finance at no cost. There is, again, a balance to be had. Taking extended credit is good for cash flow, but the risk is that it can be bad for a business's relationships and reputation.

Ways in which creditors can be managed more effectively include:

- negotiating better terms
- building up a good credit record
- making use of discounts.

There are three ratios that are commonly used to measure working capital management. They will be looked at in more detail when we look at the question of risk in study session 19, but are worth also bringing into play here. The ratios all involve taking one element of working capital as measured in the balance sheet – that is, stock, debtors and creditors – and looking at it in relation to a linked profit and loss account figure. The ratios are:

Stock days: (average stock × 365)/cost of sales

Debtor days: (trade debtors × 365)/turnover

Creditor days: (trade creditors × 365)/purchases or cost of sales

Multiplying the ratio by 365 allows us to express the measure as a number of days – so, respectively, these ratios will tell us how long it takes the business to sell goods, get paid by customers and pay suppliers.

These resultant figures will differ from company to company and from industry to industry. Clearly, stock turnover at a car showroom is likely to be a lot slower than for a greengrocer, but faster than, say, an aircraft manufacturer. What is more important is the trend that exists and the need, whatever the company, to keep the figure as low as possible.

The same applies to debtor days. In the UK the time it takes organisations to get paid on average can be surprisingly long – often, for smaller businesses, in excess of 60 days. The extent to which this is good or bad, however, and the ease with which the figure can be reduced will depend

Finance for Purchasers

on the credit terms being offered and what is considered the 'norm' in any particular industry.

To generate the maximum amount of internal finance through working capital management, a business needs to turn stock over and get paid as quickly as possible, but then to extract as much time from suppliers as it can.

Self-assessment question 11.1

Financial data for two food companies is shown in table 11.1. One is a cheese manufacturer, the other makes crisps.

Table 11.1

	Cheeseco (£)	Crispco (£)
Annual sales	36.6m	32.7m
Annual cost of sales	21.6m	22.2m
Annual materials purchases	12.8m	15.1m
Average product stock	6.5m	2.9m
Average trade debtors	4.1m	2.5m
Average trade creditors	2.4m	2.6m

Complete table 11.2 to work out approximately how quickly each company is:

- turning over their stock
- getting paid by customers
- paying their suppliers.

Table 11.2

		Cheeseco	Crispco
Stock days	(average stock × 365)/cost of sales		
Debtor days	(trade debtors × 365)/annual sales		
Creditor days	(trade creditors × 365)/annual sales		

Assuming an effective interest rate of 10%, work out the working capital management financing cost or benefit of the following:

- a 10-day improvement in the collection period?
- a 10-day deterioration in stock turnover?

What are the advantages, disadvantages and risks involved in both cases?

Feedback on page 186

11.2 External sources of finance – non-equity

We are now going to turn our attention to external sources of finance. One way of distinguishing external finance from internal finance is to recognise that it requires the agreement of someone outside the directors and managers of the business.

In most cases the 'someone' will either be a lender of capital, for example a bank, or it will be an existing or potential shareholder. Money raised from shareholders is known as 'equity', and will be covered in section 11.3. All other external finance is known as non-equity finance, and will generally involve borrowing in some shape or form. Money borrowed on a long-term basis is often referred to as 'debt'.

It is important to note that the distinction between what is equity and what is debt can sometimes be a little blurred, with certain more complex types of financing involving elements of both equity and debt. This issue has recently been the subject of much debate, with the accounting treatment of such finance being different under IFRS than it was under UK GAAP.

For the time being, though, we should focus on the more straightforward types of non-equity finance, and a useful starting point is to consider whether the finance is of a long-term nature, or short-term (see figure 11.2).

Figure 11.2

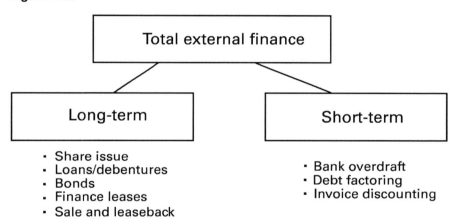

As is suggested by figure 11.2, there a number of different types of external non-equity finance available to companies. The choice is strongly influenced by what the finance is to be used for and, importantly, whether this use is longer or shorter term.

It is also worth noting that, of the external sources of finance listed above, only the 'share issue' is equity finance – the rest are all non-equity and we will therefore be looking at them in this section.

The idea that long-term finance should be used for long-term projects, and that short-term needs should be met by short-term financing, is a fundamental element of this session. However, in reality many organisations will have some assets that are technically short-term in nature, but are being utilised on a permanent basis. For example, a minimum stock level is likely always to exist, as is a certain level of debtors. The funding of such 'permanent' short-term assets may in practice be financed on a long-term basis, for example with a long-term loan – a situation that figure 11.3 should illustrate.

Figure 11.3

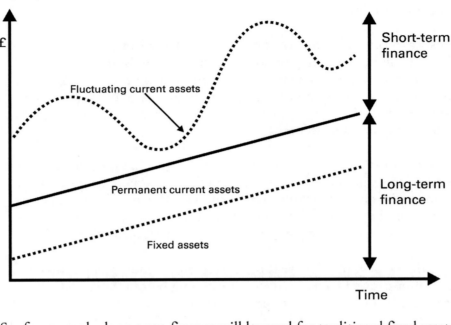

So, for example, long-term finance will be used for traditional fixed assets like computers, cars and machinery, but it might also be used for financing current assets to the extent that they are permanently in place (such as a core level of stockholding). Short-term finance would then be used to cover additional short-term asset requirements that arise from fluctuations in trade and seasonal variations.

Learning activity 11.2

Access a company's annual report and accounts and identify the sources of external non-equity finance currently in place.

Of the eight sources of non-equity finance referred to in figure 11.2 above, how many appear to be being used by the company in question?

What information can you glean about the cost of finance, and the extent to which the financing has changed in the course of the most recent financial year?

NB: Most listed companies make their annual report and accounts freely available on their websites – usually in the section headed 'Investor Relations' or similar.

Feedback on page 187

Long-term

Long-term loans

Many businesses make use of long-term loan finance. They will borrow money, typically from a bank, and agree to a set of terms and conditions

11 Sources of finance

that determine the interest rate, the capital repayment schedule and any security that is to be used to support the loan.

The security element is there to protect the lender in case the borrowing company defaults on the payment of interest or capital. The security will typically take either the form of a fixed charge on particular assets (eg some land) owned by the company, or what is known as a 'floating charge' which includes a range of assets which change over time – for example a floating charge may include debtors and stock holdings – both of which are constantly moving assets.

Included in the terms of many long-term loans are 'loan covenants'. These require the business to carry out certain actions, or meet certain criteria, for the loan to remain in place. For example, loan covenants might set out the requirement that assets pledged as security are properly insured, or that overall debt does not exceed a certain level.

The most common type of loan is a 'term loan', where a company borrows money for an agreed length of time. The time period should have some link to the use of the loan. If, for example, the loan is being used to invest in new land and buildings, the repayment period may be relatively lengthy. Also agreed would be the rate of interest, which might be fixed or variable. If variable, the interest rate is likely to be linked to an agreed benchmark such as the bank's base rate or LIBOR – the London Interbank Offered Rate, which is the interest rate at which banks borrow funds from each other.

Thus, the interest rate on a loan to one company might be at LIBOR (or Base rate) + 1.5%, but to a more risky business the terms might be LIBOR + 3%.

Debentures

Debentures are similar to long-term loans, although they have some additional features. Firstly, they are usually secured against some or all of the borrowing company's assets. Secondly, they are issued in units, which can subsequently be traded.

The term 'debenture' is often associated with sports stadia such as Wimbledon, Twickenham and the new Arsenal stadium. The original debenture holders will have lent money to the sporting organisation in question, typically to help fund the construction or development of a stadium. The debentures can subsequently be traded, and one important aspect which is likely to enhance their trading value is the fact that debenture holders are likely to have priority access to tickets and/or boxes.

Bonds

Bonds represent an extremely significant form of long-term finance, but they are largely restricted to very large companies only. Bonds are issued by large companies and other organisations around the world. A bond is simply a promise to repay an amount of money at some future point in time, and to pay an agreed amount of interest to the bondholder in the intervening period.

Most bonds are actively traded, so that the original lender can sell their bonds to another party. The price at which the bonds are issued, and subsequently traded, will be influenced by:

- the prevailing interest rates at the time, and
- the degree of perceived risk associated with the bond issuer at any point in time.

If interest rates rise, or are expected to rise, the price of bonds tends to fall. And if the financial status of the organisation that issued the bond deteriorates, then the price of its bonds will fall accordingly.

Companies that issue bonds internationally will have official credit ratings. Ratings agencies, the best known of which is Standard & Poor's, look at corporate bonds and give their opinion as to how risky they are. The ratings may range from AAA for the most secure bonds down to no rating at all for the most risky.

As an example, table 11.4 summarises some sterling corporate bond issues at August 2006 prices (when the UK base rate was 4.75%).

Table 11.4

Company	Interest	Maturity	Price (£)	GRY*	Moodys	S&P
Daimler	7.5%	2006	101.00	4.85%	A3	BBB
Tesco	7.5%	2007	102.45	4.94%	A1	A+
Boots	5.5%	2009	100.20	5.34%	Baa1	BBB+
Halifax	9.375%	2021	140.85	5.25%	AA3	AA-

*GRY = Gross Redemption Yield. This represents the total annual return with the current price factored in. Bonds are redeemed at £100.

The price of bonds is influenced by three main factors:

- the annual interest being paid (the 'coupon')
- the credit rating of the issuer
- the time left until maturity.

Corporate bonds with lower ratings are sometimes known as 'junk bonds' or 'high-yield bonds'. The lower the rating, the lower the price and therefore the higher the yield. The yield, though, is based on the premise that the company will pay the annual coupon. If the company is under financial pressure, there is the risk that payment will not be forthcoming. A recent example concerned General Motors of the US, whose credit rating was downgraded to the extent that the company's bonds endured a significant price fall.

Finance leases

When acquiring new machinery or equipment, a company may choose to buy it outright. Alternatively, as we have seen, it may decide to fund the purchase with a loan over an appropriate term. A third option is to lease the asset.

Leasing an asset is, technically, renting it for a period of time from a leasing company. The main benefit of this is that it eases cash flow. Instead of paying at the outset. A leasing arrangement will involve regular payments spread over the life of the asset.

The result is much the same as if a loan with regular repayments had been taken out. A key difference is that legal ownership of the asset remains with the leasing company (often an arm of a bank). However, as discussed in study session 4, the accounting treatment requires that the item being leased is treated as an asset in the lessee's books, with a corresponding liability to reflect that effectively this is borrowing by another name.

Sale and leaseback

When considering internal sources of finance, the sale of fixed assets was highlighted as a straightforward source of finance, assuming that the company had no further use for the asset in question.

Using the sale of assets in a different – and external – way, a company can utilise what are known as 'sale and leaseback' arrangements. Here an asset is sold – quite often it is likely to be business premises of one sort or another – to a financial institution, who then lease it back to its original owners.

Thus the company can continue to use the asset as before, but has raised what is often a significant amount of finance which can be put to more productive use. For example Tesco and Sainsbury's, major UK retailers, have both recently announced sale and leaseback plans for some of their stores. In Tesco's case, the five-year sale and leaseback programme expected to raise as much as £5 billion.

Short-term external finance

Overdraft

An overdraft is a short-term lending facility provided by banks. It is ideally suited as a means of financing a short-term need – for example to finance the purchase of materials for a large order, or to help a seasonal business through a quiet period.

The process usually involves the bank granting an overdraft facility with an agreed limit and at an agreed rate of interest. The interest rate is likely to be variable, and linked to the bank's base rate (for example, base rate + 3%).

Overdrafts are very flexible, and reasonably cheap in that the bank only charges interest on the amount of overdraft being utilised, not on the amount of the facility.

The main drawback from the borrower's standpoint is that overdrafts are repayable on demand.

Factoring

Factoring is a flexible source of finance where a factoring company (usually part of a bank) agrees to immediately advance to a business a certain percentage (usually 70–85%) of sales invoices. Factoring is generally a way of raising finance for the small and medium sized companies.

How factoring works

There are three parties in the factoring process:

1. The 'client business', the company selling goods and/or services to a credit customer. The client business uses a factoring company to finance this process.
2. The 'credit customer', to whom the goods and/or services are sold on credit by the client business.
3. The 'factoring company' (factor), usually part of a bank.

There are six stages in the factoring process:

1. The client business supplies goods and/or services on credit to the credit customer.
2. The client business raises and sends an invoice to the credit customer, requesting that settlement is made directly to the factor.
3. The client business sends a copy of the invoice to the factor.
4. The factor then pays the client business 70–85% of invoice value, less fees.
5. The credit customer settles the invoice by paying the amount due to the factor.
6. The factor then pays to the client business the balance due on the invoice (30–15%), less discount charges.

In the factoring process, the client business sells its credit invoices to the factor, and at the same time the factor then takes on the responsibility for collecting the amounts due from the credit customers. It is this management of the client business' sales ledger that generates the administration charge (between 0.5–1.5%) charged by the factor. The client business has these additional charges to pay to the factor, but gains benefit by saving costs by not having an in-house credit management department to collect its sales ledger debts when they fall due.

Figure 11.4

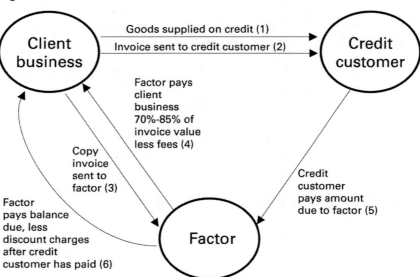

Factoring is a fast-growing source of finance, and has a number of variations, but is mainly used by small and medium-sized companies, trading from business to business, that sell goods or services on credit, and seek help in financing that process.

One of the benefits of this form of finance is that the factoring company take on the responsibility for collecting the amounts due on sales invoices from your organisation's customers.

A possible downside to the factor collecting these debts is that the factor may be more professional in its collection activity, and this could 'upset' the relationship between the client business and the credit customer.

There are two main costs in factoring, and these are:

- administration charges – the fee charged by the factor to the client business for the administration of the sales ledger, expressed as a percentage of the invoice value (0.5–1.5%).
- discount charge (not interest) – this is the cost of money advanced against sales ledger invoices, and works like interest in that it is charged at a percentage above bank base rate.

There are two main types of factoring, recourse factoring and non-recourse factoring.

Recourse factoring means that if the credit customer fails to pay its invoices after a set time period, the factor will require any funding already provided against that invoice to be repaid by the client business, normally recovered from later invoices.

Non-recourse factoring means that the factor provides bad debt protection. This is normally based on limits set by the factor per customer, dependent on the creditworthiness of the customer. Charges for this type of factoring will normally be higher than recourse factoring.

Should the client business go into liquidation, the factoring company has title to the sales ledger invoices, and would continue to collect on these invoices until such time as their debt has been settled – remember the factoring company bought the invoices at the commencement of the factoring process.

Invoice discounting

Invoice discounting is a variation on the factoring theme. The outsourcing of the sales ledger is an integral part of factoring, but this need not be so in order to release immediate cash on sales ledger invoices.

Invoice discounting is a confidential facility for financing the sales ledger invoices – the credit customer is unaware that their invoices have been sold to an invoice discounting company (usually part of a bank), and they settle the invoices directly to the client business.

The criteria for obtaining an invoice discounting facility are higher than for factoring and the supplier of the facility will be influenced by several factors:

1 The quality and quantity of customers with particular attention to spread.

Finance for Purchasers

2 The supplier should be able to demonstrate good credit control procedures, with debts being collected in a timely manner.
3 A good computerised sales ledger system should be in place, and always kept up to date.
4 The business should be able to demonstrate that it is trading profitably, and has a tangible net worth.

There are six stages in the invoice discounting process:

1 The client business supplies goods and/or services on credit to the credit customer.
2 The client business raises and sends an invoice to the credit customer.
3 The client business sends a copy of the invoice to the invoice discount company (IDC).
4 The IDC then pays the client business up to 90% of the invoice value.
5 The credit customers settle the invoices by paying the client business, which pays the settlements into a client account at the IDC.
6 The IDC then pays to the client business the balance due on the invoices, after clearance of the client business' cheques, less fees and charges.

Invoice discounting is cheaper than factoring because the administration charges (fees) deducted from the initial payment by the IDC are less that the fees deducted by a factoring company, due mainly to the fact that the IDC does not run the credit management department. The reduction in fees is counteracted by the additional costs involved in running an in-house credit management department. Benefits of an in-house department are that good customer relations cannot be disturbed by any third party.

Self-assessment question 11.2

For the following business activities, identify the sources of finance that would be appropriate. (Note: more than one source of finance may be appropriate in each case.)

The building of a new football stadium

The purchase of raw materials for an electronics manufacturing process.

An airline acquiring new aeroplanes.

Investing in new IT hardware.

Financing the delay in getting paid by customers

Feedback on page 187

11.3 External sources of finance – equity

Ordinary share capital

Ordinary share capital represents the money raised by issuing ordinary shares. All companies have an 'authorised share capital' (the amount of money they are allowed to raise by issuing shares) and an 'issued share capital' (the amount of money they have raised by issuing shares).

Ordinary shareholders have a vote (usually one vote per share held). They will also receive dividends, when paid, in proportion to their shareholding.

There is no fixed rate of dividends, and payment of a dividend requires there to be sufficient 'distributable reserves' – which effectively means that dividends can only be paid out of profits that have already been made.

A benefit to the company of having share capital is that the dividend is discretionary. This means that, even if profits are being made, there is no requirement for any all or any of this to be paid out to ordinary shareholders. This can be very useful for a growing business that needs finance to help the growth develop, and it links directly to the idea, discussed earlier in this session, of internal finance.

A company that, until, a couple of years ago, had never paid a dividend was Microsoft. The company grew rapidly from its inception in the 1970s, and to help finance that growth all profits were – until recently – retained in the business. By contrast, a business in a very mature industry where there is little scope for dramatic growth – a utility for example – is likely to pay out the bulk of its profits as a dividend.

Ordinary shareholders face high risks. In the event of the company failing, they will be at the back of the queue – well behind other interested parties such as banks, trade creditors and preference shareholders – when it comes to distributing any remaining assets.

However, an ordinary shareholder's liability is limited to the amount they have invested (or agreed to invest). Hence the term 'limited' company.

Rights issues

If a company wishes to raise additional ordinary share capital it often has a 'rights issue'. This will involve existing shareholders being offered (i.e. they have the 'rights' to) new shares in proportion to the number of shares they already hold. They might, for example, be offered two new shares for every three they already hold – and the new shares would be priced at a discount to the prevailing pre-rights price in order to make them attractive.

Preference share capital

Preference shares are another form of equity finance. They differ to ordinary shares in the following ways:

- They do not usually have voting rights.
- There is normally a fixed dividend.
- The dividend takes preference over the ordinary dividend.
- In the event of business failure, preference shares rank more highly than ordinary shares.

Venture capital and development capital

One source of finance that a young, small but growing company might seek is venture capital. This involves shares being issued to a venture capital

Finance for Purchasers

company (often the arm of a major financial institution). The venture capital company will, in exchange for the shares, put money into the business to help it grow. They may also take some active part in the running of the business.

The hope – from the perspective of the venture capitalist – is that the business does grow and that the shares can later be sold at a profit – either by finding a new buyer or by floating the company on a stock market. A venture capital firm will have a portfolio of investments. It is a risky business, and a proportion of investments – perhaps as high as 20% – is likely to fail completely.

Development capital involves a very similar approach, although it will usually apply at a later stage in the development of the business.

Business angels are wealthy individuals who work in a similar but often less formal way to venture capitalists. They tend to focus on the extremely small end of the market – and it can be a long time before an exit route – being able to sell the investment at a profit – can appear.

Learning activity 11.3

Body Shop International was recently sold to the international cosmetics group L'Oréal for £652 million. Body Shop had begun life in the mid-1970s. To fund her second shop in Sussex, Anita Roddick – the company's founder – sold a half share in the business to Ian McGlinn, a local garage owner.

Mr McGlinn still held a 21% at the time of the sale to L'Oreal, giving him a £137m return on his £5,000 investment.

Why might Ms Roddick regret not being able to borrow from the bank the £5,000 she needed in 1976? What, at the time, might have led her to sell half the shares in the business for £5,000?

Feedback on page 187

Now answer these self-assessment question 11.3 below.

Self-assessment question 11.3

1 Venture capital companies invest in a company with a view to selling that investment at some future stage: True/false?
2 Authorised share capital describes the amount of money that has been raised by issuing shares: True/false?
3 Preference shareholders have priority over all other interested parties in the event of business failure: True/false?

(continued on next page)

11 Sources of finance

Self-assessment question 11.3 (continued)

4   The equity of a company will include finance that has been raised both internally and externally: True/false?

Feedback on page 188

11.4 Public sector sources of finance

So far in this session we have considered the various sources of finance available in the private sector. Public sector organisations also need finance, and the main sources here are:

- borrowing
- taxation
- grants
- finance from the Private Finance Initiative (PFI) and from Public Private Partnerships (PPP).

Central government raises substantial amounts of money through borrowing. It does this through activities such as issuing bonds and offering savings products through its National Savings and Investments agency.

Bonds issued by the UK government are known as 'Treasury stock' or 'gilts'. They work in similar fashion to corporate bonds, in that they will usually have a coupon (that is to say, a fixed amount of interest that they will pay) and a maturity date. Issuing these bonds allows the government to raise cash in line with its needs. Investors in UK government stock will be attracted by the security of the investment, and government stock is actively traded with prices being largely influenced by views on current and future interest rates.

Learning activity 11.4

Table 11.5 shows a selection of UK government stock prices. The table shows four different issues. The four columns show:

- the stock, coupon and maturity date
- the latest price (per £100 of stock)
- the redemption yield (which shows the cash return a buyer at the latest price would get if they held the stock to maturity)
- the amount raised by the particular stock issue.

Table 11.5

	Price	Redemption yield	Amount (£ billion)
Treasury 4.5% 2007	101.18	4.62%	12.07
Treasury 4.75% 2010	99.77	4.81%	12.77
Treasury 8% 2013	119.57	4.77%	6.49
Treasury 5% 2025	105.61	4.55%	16.19

The Bank of England official interest rate at the time of this data was 4.5%.

(continued on next page)

183

Finance for Purchasers

> **Learning activity 11.4** *(continued)*
>
> Why is the price of the 2013 stock so much higher than the 2010 stock?
>
> The coupon payable on the 2010 stock is 4.75%, and on the 2025 stock it is 5%. Why are the prices of these two stock not more closely aligned?
>
> What would stop the government simply issuing as much stock as it wants, in order to finance everything it would like to do?
>
> Why might a private investor buy government stock when:
>
> 1 they could get a slightly better yield on an internet deposit account with a major UK bank and
> 2 they could get a higher yield by investing in a corporate bond issued by one of the UK's major retailers?
>
> *Feedback on page 188*

Most other public sector organisations can also borrow from the financial markets, for example by issuing bonds. They are often able to do so at relatively low rates of interest, as investors tend to regard such investments as relatively safe.

Public sector activity is also funded by taxation receipts, which we looked at in study session 2.

Grants are available for some public sector bodies. Local authorities are, for example, partly funded via European Union grants.

Public Private Partnerships and the Private Finance Initiative

Both these types of funding stem from recent UK government initiatives to introduce private sector ownership and expertise into the public sector.

The term 'Public Private Partnerships (PPP)' describes any private sector involvement in public services. The Private Finance Initiative (PFI) is one very significant such example.

The PFI essentially involves the public sector entering into a long-term contract to purchase services from the private sector.

Under a typical PFI scheme, a capital project such as a school or hospital will be designed, constructed, financed and managed by a private sector organisation – often a consortium involving a number of different companies. The consortium might, for example, include a bank as well as the various contractors involved in the project.

These consortia are sometimes known as Special Purpose Vehicles (SPVs). The SPV will raise its own debt and equity finance and deliver the required assets and services to the public sector against a range of targets and performance objectives – in exchange for payment.

This links directly to public sector finance because one of the key benefits of PFI for the government is that it avoids any direct financing requirement

11 Sources of finance

– this is done by the private sector SPV. This enables public sector infrastructure projects to be undertaken without it impacting on the government's borrowing position, or necessitating tax rises.

The government's borrowing position as a whole is known as the National Debt – the total amount of borrowing accumulated by the government that is still outstanding. It is directly linked to the Public Sector Net Cash Requirement, which is the annual amount of money the government needs to make ends meet, once tax receipts and government expenditure have been taken into account. Each year the National Debt will rise by the amount of the PSNCR, and fall by the amount of debt that is paid off.

Other benefits include the potential for a PFI to provide better value for money, as well as the transfer of a number of risks, which would ordinarily be borne by the government, to the private sector. Risks transferred include:

- design risk
- construction risk
- operating risk
- demand risk
- residual value risk
- obsolescence risk.

The PFI has, however, had a controversial history thus far. Critics question the extent to which some of the above risks are genuinely transferred to the private sector. They also point out that government can raise finance more cheaply than the private sector, and suggest that paying for projects in this way and over a longer period of time ends up being more expensive.

Self-assessment question 11.4

What impact will the following have on the National Debt?

- The issue of new Treasury stock.
- The repayment of a bond by a local authority.
- The signing of a new PFI to build and manage prisons.
- An increase in the rate of VAT.

Feedback on page 188

Revision question

Now try the revision question for this session on page 346.

Summary

This session has looked at different sources of finance – distinguishing between external and internal finance, and between longer- and shorter-term finance. Having finance that is appropriate to the need is vital for any organisation, as is matching the term of the finance to its likely use.

Finance for Purchasers

Feedback on learning activities and self-assessment questions

Feedback on learning activity 11.1

There are four main sources of finance evident from this data:

- loans (under long-term liabilities)
- overdraft (under creditors due in less than 1 year)
- share capital (and share premium) representing amounts raised by issuing shares
- retained profits (also known as revenue reserves).

The first three sources of finance – loans, overdraft and share capital (+ premium) are external. The loans and the overdraft have been borrowed from an external source – probably a bank – while the share capital and share premium have been raised from shareholders following share issue. (The 'premium' part occurs when shares are issued at more than their nominal value. If what are nominally 50p shares are issued at 60p, then there would be a 10p premium per share.)

The only internal source of finance that is clearly evident is the retained profit.

Only one element of the above would be considered short-term in nature – the overdraft. The rest are all long-term sources of finance.

Feedback on self-assessment question 11.1

Table 11.3

		Cheeseco	Crispco
Stock days	(average stock × 365)/cost of sales	109 days	47 days
Debtor days	(average stock × 365)/cost of sales	41 days	28 days
Creditor days	(trade creditors × 365)/purchases or cost of sales	68 days	63 days

10-day improvement in the collection period

In the case of Cheeseco, debtor days have improved by approximately one-quarter (from 41 to 31 days). Average debtors would therefore fall by one-quarter also, to approximately £3 million. The saving would therefore be 10% of the £1m reduction in average debtors – about £100,000 over one year.

With Crispco, the improvement is over 35%. Their average debtors figure would therefore fall by about £875,000, so the saving would be 10% of that figure or £87,500.

The advantage of the improvement in the collection period is the immediate and ongoing financial benefit. The potential disadvantage – and risk – concerns the possible alienation of customers who might seek out an alternative supplier. This might also impact on the company's reputation in terms also of gaining new customers.

11 Sources of finance

10-day deterioration in stock turnover

This will require cash to be tied up in stock for a longer period. Cash tied up in stock earns no interest – and this will be the cost the company incurs.

Quantifying this, in the case of Cheeseco the percentage increase in the average stock figure would be just over 9% (10/109) – that is, the stock figure would rise from £6.5 million to £7.1 million. The cost of financing this would therefore be 10% × £600,000 = £60,000.

A similar cost would apply to Crispco. Their stock would on average rise by over 21%, taking it from £2.9 million to £3.5 million, an increase of £600,000 which would cost £60,000 per year to finance.

There is little advantage to be had from a slowing of stock turnover, other than perhaps a reduction in the risk of running out of stock. The main disadvantage is financial – cash is tied up unnecessarily – and the main potential risk is that stock becomes outdated or obsolescent.

Feedback on learning activity 11.2

The best initial source of information within an annual report is the balance sheet. Here you should be able to identify either directly, or via reference to notes to the accounts, some essential information about share capital, retained profits, long-term loans and bonds, and shorter-term financing such as overdrafts and the use of factoring services.

The notes should provide more detailed information, especially in relation to longer-term borrowing where interest rates and maturity dates can be identified.

Feedback on self-assessment question 11.2

The building of a new football stadium – long-term loan, bond, debentures, share issue.

The purchase of raw materials for an electronics manufacturing process – overdraft.

An airline acquiring new aeroplanes – long-term loan, finance lease.

Investing in new IT hardware – lease, loan.

Financing the delay in getting paid by customers – credit factoring, invoice discounting.

Feedback on learning activity 11.3

Ms Roddick might have no regrets at all, but the decision appears to have cost her a substantial amount of money.

Bank finance would have involved interest payments on a £5,000 loan, and repayment at some future stage, but if a loan was not forthcoming, equity finance may well have been the only possible alternative.

Even if loan finance was available, the need to pay interest, and to repay the amount borrowed, might have stretched the business. By getting in an equity investor, the running costs of the business would not have been affected and this may have helped the business grow more quickly.

Mr McGlinn, by buying ordinary shares in the business, took on a significant risk and faced the potential loss of the entire £5,000, as is often the case for those investing in very small enterprises. While most 'business angels' take on a portfolio of investments, it was in fact Mr McGlinn's only investment.

Feedback on self-assessment question 11.3

1 True: this is how they make their money.
2 False: it describes how much it can issue.
3 False: they only have priority over ordinary shareholders.
4 True: retained profit (internal finance) is included in the equity.

Feedback on learning activity 11.4

The price of the 2013 stock is much higher than the 2010 stock because the coupon is higher – 8% as opposed to 4.75%. Investors will pay more for a stock that pays an annual 8p per pound than it will for one that pays 4.75p.

The prices of the 2010 and 2025 stocks are not more closely aligned partly because, at the time, there had been significant demand for longer-dated stock as a result of pension funds looking to secure fixed income investments to better cover their medium- and longer-term liabilities.

The government cannot simply issue as much stock as it wants. First, the government has a stated commitment to keeping public debt below 40% of GDP 'over the economic cycle', although there has been debate about what the 'economic cycle' actually means. Second, and perhaps more importantly, government can only issue stock for which there is a demand. Issuing more and more debt in this way would therefore become increasingly expensive.

A private investor will consider the return on investment, but will also reflect on the risk factor. A deposit account with a UK bank might be extremely low risk, but a government bond might be deemed to be risk free. A bank, therefore, tends to offer a slightly better rate of interest.

Investing in a retailer's corporate bond is will similarly be higher risk than government stock – and therefore must offer a better return.

Feedback on self-assessment question 11.4

- The issue of new Treasury stock will increase the National Debt.
- The repayment of a bond by a local authority will reduce the National Debt.
- The signing of a new PFI to build and manage prisons will have no impact on the National Debt.

- An increase in the rate of VAT might, indirectly, reduce the National Debt if it results in an increase in tax revenues and therefore a reduction in the amount the government has to borrow.

Finance for Purchasers

11

Study session 12
Developing and managing budgets

Annual budgets are a key feature of most organisations' planning and control processes. Are they useful, and is there an alternative?

Introduction

Most organisations use budgets to some degree as part of their planning process. This session will look at issues concerning how budgets are put together, and also, perhaps more importantly, how they are used. Budgeting is a management tool, and its success often depends on the way in which it is used from a managerial point of view.

How useful budgets are is a topical question. They can use up a lot of resources, and unless the benefits outweigh the cost of those resources, the usefulness of budgeting can legitimately be challenged. This session will therefore summarise some alternative approaches to what might be termed 'traditional budgeting'.

Session learning objectives

After completing this session you should be able to:

12.1 Recognise the importance of setting and controlling budgets to achieve performance targets.
12.2 Create and present a budget to support a business plan.
12.3 Describe the benefits and limitations of using budgets.

Unit content coverage

This study session covers the following topics from the official CIPS unit content document:

Learning objective

4.1 Explain how to develop and manage budgets to achieve target performance.
 • The importance of setting and controlling budgets to achieve performance targets
 • The importance of setting a realistic budget
 • Financial objectives
 • Motivational objectives
 • SMART objectives
 • How to create and present a budget to support a business plan
 • The importance of financial forecasting

Prior knowledge

Study sessions 1 to 11.

Resources

Timing

You should set aside about 4 hours to read and complete this session, including learning activities, self-assessment questions, the suggested further reading (if any) from the essential textbook for this unit and the revision question.

12.1 Setting and controlling budgets to achieve performance targets

All organisations need to plan. They need to plan over the longer term, typically around 5 to 10 years, but also over the shorter term, typically up to a year.

Longer-term business plans are often referred to as **corporate plans**, and they tend to consider how an organisation is to achieve its longer-term objectives. Such plans will be more strategic in nature, addressing factors such as market position, strengths and weaknesses, and the opportunities and threats that it faces (referred to as a SWOT analysis).

Corporate plans will also consider the direction the organisation is to take – for example should it adopt a strategy of consolidation, diversification, new product development or new market development?

They will also address **macro-environmental factors**, such as the state of the economy, demographic trends, changes in society and its attitudes, potential changes in the law and the likely make-up and approach of government. In other words, what is going on in the wider world that is likely to have an impact on the organisation – and what will be done to deal with it.

Once a corporate plan has been formulated, shorter term operating plans need to be devised to ensure that the broader plan can be achieved. The crucial factor is that budgets represent one element of the overall internal planning and control of an organisation. Management will formulate long- and medium-term strategic plans for the business, and these will be refined into shorter term operating plans. This is illustrated in figure 12.1. Short-term operating plans – or 'budgets' – are part of the process of implementing the longer term plans. Both the long and the short-term plans need to be moving in the same direction and trying to achieve the same overall objectives.

Figure 12.1

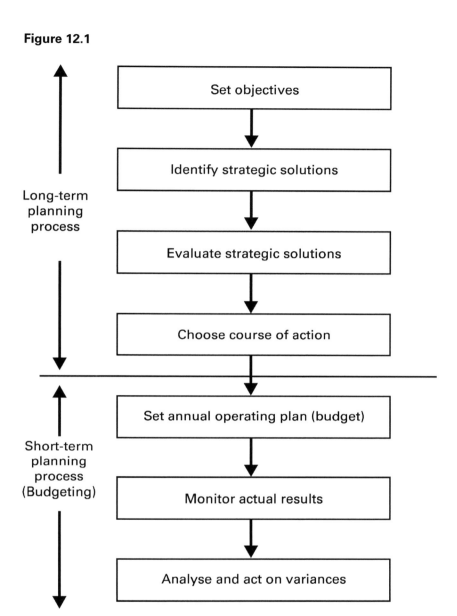

Budgets are the main example of short-term operating plans. They usually have a timeframe of one year and are very often financial in nature – although an organisation can also budget for other resources such as people or materials.

Budgets may be prepared for any part of an organisation, for example business units, departments and cost centres. They will be consolidated into an overall organisational plan – sometimes referred to as the 'master budget' (see figure 12.2).

Figure 12.2

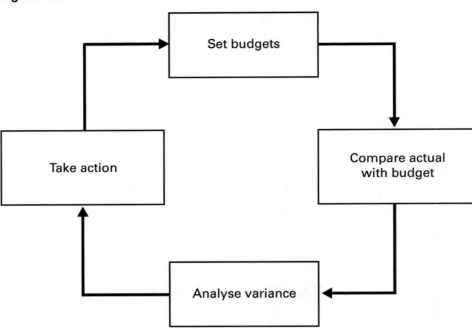

Actual performance against these plans can then be monitored to check progress and in the light of these results corrective action can be taken or the plans can be revised. This is a vital part of the budgeting process, known as 'budgetary control, and discussed in more detail later in this session.

All plans must allow for the possibility of revision. Circumstances and conditions change and management must be able to respond and adapt or amend its plans in the light of these changes. Even if it changes dramatically, the original plan is still useful. Without planning, an organisation will have no direction, and nothing against which to monitor its progress – and getting plans and forecasts wrong can be, in itself, a useful learning exercise and makes those involved more aware of the environment in which they are planning.

So, **budgetary control** is the process of monitoring actual results against those planned or budgeted, and of investigating any significant variances. Such variances may indicate a failure to adhere to the plan, or the failure of the plan itself – but in either case some corrective action is likely to be necessary.

Learning activity 12.1

Speak to a budget holder in your own organisation. Ask them to describe the way that budgetary control is carried out in the organisation. What happens at the different stages of the budgetary control cycle (as illustrated above)? How are the budgets set? How are variances reported? What does the budget variance review process involve?

Feedback on page 203

12 Developing and managing budgets

Budgets will be prepared for all the main areas of activity within an organisation, including service departments and items of investment. They would typically include sales, production, overheads, cash and capital expenditure.

Budgeting is part of a concept known as **responsibility accounting** – it identifies plans and actual performance against the people responsible. As a result, it is necessary to group the organisation into responsibility centres, often called **budget centres**. Budget centres may comprise a single cost centre or a number of cost centres – or indeed profit centres if income as well as costs are being budgeted.

Budget centres will include items over which the appropriate managers have control and these are known as **controllable items**. A budget centre may also include items over which the local managers have no control – **non-controllable items**.

The budgetary control: cycle is a key element of effective budgeting. Once budgets have been set they must be *used*. That will involve the system producing data that compares what was forecast to what actually has happened. It also means the budget holder identifying *why* any significant variance has occurred. Proper identification of the root cause of the variance will enable appropriate corrective action to be taken and should ensure future year forecasts to be more accurate.

Self-assessment question 12.1

Are the following statements true or false?

1   Budgets are set at the beginning of the financial year, and represent a fixed benchmark against which the year's performance is monitored.
2   The terms 'budget' and 'corporate plan' describe the same thing, and are interchangeable.
3   Budgetary control is an ongoing process that measures performance against budget and involves taking appropriate action to deal with differences between the two.

Feedback on page 203

12.2 Creating and presenting a budget to support a business plan

As a purchaser, you may have some involvement in the setting of your own organisation's budget. You may therefore have some experience of the need for budgets to meet the needs of the organisation in a number of different ways, and that in practice there will be elements of compromise involved in putting budgets together.

Budgets should support the organisation's objectives. This includes the idea, already discussed, of budgets being set in line with the longer-term objectives as outlined in a corporate or strategic plan. But there may be particular objectives that might be measured more specifically – for example, the financial return the organisation is aiming to achieve.

Budgets should be realistic. Figures in budgets should be primarily about what is expected to happen. The sales budget should be about realistic expectations based on economic reality, rather than a challenging target for the sales force. Budgets should not be about setting unachievable targets, but equally not about setting soft targets that don't adequately stretch resources.

One important aspect of this is known as the **limiting factor**, or **principal budget factor**. This is an important concept that needs to be understood whenever budgets are being set. There will always be one element of the budget that will constrain everything else.

The limiting factor might be sales volumes – there is no point in budgeting to produce 50,000 units of a product if the company can only sell 30,000 units. But equally it might be production capacity – if the factory's maximum output is 25,000 units then budgeting for 30,000 unit sales, even if achievable, is pointless.

The limiting factor might also involve elements such as available skilled labour or components.

Budgets need to be internally consistent. For any large organisation, a range of different budgets will have to be prepared and agreed. There therefore needs to be good internal communication about the activities of various departments and divisions, especially in terms of the potential knock-on effects of any unusual activity they may be planning.

There also needs to be a consistent and probably formalised approach to factors that will impact on all budgets. For example, budgets may well build in the likely impact of inflation, or factor in foreign exchange rates. There needs therefore to be an organisation-wide view of what inflation and exchange rates are expected to be so that figures can be drawn up on a consistent basis – these are sometimes referred to as **budget assumptions**.

A simple acronym commonly used in the context of budgeting and objective setting, and which links directly to some of the above points, is **SMART**:

- **S**pecific: objectives should clearly specify what they are intended to achieve.
- **M**easurable: you should be able to measure whether objectives are being met or not.
- **A**chievable: are the objectives achievable and attainable?
- **R**ealistic: are the objectives achievable given the resources available?
- **T**ime: objectives should be set within agreed, and achievable, time constraints.

The budgeting process usually begins well in advance of the budget period. Sometimes this could be as much as six months in advance, but the further away from the actual period the more difficult it is to make an accurate forecast. Senior management must first set key objectives – as outlined at the start of this session – and these must be communicated throughout the organisation.

Budgets can then be prepared for individual parts of the organisation, sometimes referred to as 'budget centres'. A process of review, revision and resubmission can then take place. The way in which this process works, and whether it is driven from the top or initiated at the budget centre level, will differ depending on the organisation – the terms 'top down' and 'bottom up' budgeting describe different approaches, but ultimately budgets will be submitted to senior management for consideration and (eventual) approval. The process can involve several resubmissions before agreement is reached.

A budget where the final figures are agreed and set, and where these figures will remain in force for the period, is known as a **fixed budget**. Where volumes of output or turnover are difficult to forecast, a **flexible budget** may be more appropriate. A flexible budget involves changing the budget during the budget period to reflect changing circumstances.

This is particularly appropriate where major costs are driven by volumes of activity (in other words, where many costs are variable rather than fixed). In such cases a wrongly forecast sales figure would have a major impact on the rest of the budget, and make it unworkable. For this reason, production-related budgets often have flexible elements.

All budgets should be prepared by managers taking time to consider their objectives, the resources at their disposal and the most effective way of using the resources to achieve these objectives. The are two main **approaches** to drawing up a budget. They are **cost-plus (or 'incremental') budgeting**, which involves taking last year's figures and adding on an element for rising prices/costs, and **zero-based budgeting (ZBB)**, which requires all budget items to be justified in terms of cost/benefit before being included in the budget.

Cost-plus budgeting, because of its simplicity and ease of application, is popular. It may, however, be a flawed approach and any inherent budget inefficiencies will be carried forward, and compounded, from one period to the next.

Zero-based budgeting might therefore seem a more useful approach, and in theory it is. The problem is that to carry it out properly requires substantial extra time and effort, which may not always be worthwhile.

Learning activity 12.2

Arrange a meeting with someone in your organisation who has direct involvement in the overall budgeting process.

Establish how budgets are put together in your own organisation, and consider some of the issues raised in this session so far:

- What organisation-wide budget assumptions exist?
- What limiting factors are there?
- How is forecasting carried out?
- To what extent are 'incremental budgeting' and 'zero-based budgeting' techniques used?

Feedback on page 203

Budgets are usually set and managed in terms of income and expenditure, and therefore are directly linked to forecast profit. Profit, as we know from earlier sessions in this course, is not the same as cash flow, and organisations

Finance for Purchasers

need additionally to be able to forecast movements in cash flow. This enables them to predict their future cash position and know, for example, if and when they may need overdraft facilities or if and when they may have surplus cash that needs to be invested.

The tool for predicting cash flow is the **cash flow forecast** (sometimes known as the 'cash budget'). This involves making forecasts of what cash movements are going to occur over, normally, the next 12 months.

There are therefore key differences between a cash flow forecast and an income and expenditure budget. A cash flow forecast will include:

- cash to be used for capital expenditure
- cash coming in from new loans and share issues
- cash to be used to repay loans
- cash to be paid to suppliers (when it is paid)
- cash to be received from customers (when it is paid).

A cash flow forecast will be set out in a way that suits the management of the organisation using it, but would typically look something like table 12.1.

Table 12.1

	Jan	Feb	Mar	Apr	May	Jun
Receipts:						
Cash from customers	X	X	X	X	X	X
Fixed asset sales	X	X	X	X	X	X
New loan / share issue	X	X	X	X	X	X
Total receipts (a)	X	X	X	X	X	X
Payments:						
Cash to suppliers	X	X	X	X	X	X
Overhead expenses	X	X	X	X	X	X
Fixed asset purchases	X	X	X	X	X	X
Loan repayments etc	X	X	X	X	X	X
Total payments (b)	X	X	X	X	X	X
Net cash flow (a-b)	X	X	X	X	X	X
Opening cash balance	X	X	X	X	X	X
Closing cash balance	X	X	X	X	X	X

An income and expenditure budget will, by contrast:

- show depreciation (but not the amount spent on capital items)
- exclude movements of capital, such as loan repayments and share issues
- reflect expenditure and income when they are incurred and earned, rather than when they are paid.

Self-assessment question 12.2

The following information relates to Company X, a wholesale trading company:

On 1 January, the cash at bank is expected to be £35,000.

The stock position will be £25,000 at 1 January, and £17,000 at the end of June.

(continued on next page)

12 Developing and managing budgets

Self-assessment question 12.2 *(continued)*

Customers pay for the goods that they buy: 50% at the end of the month following the month of sale, 50% at the end of the second month following sale.

The company pays its suppliers at the end of the month following its purchase of goods.

Budgeted sales and purchases are as shown in table 12.2.

Table 12.2

	Sales	Purchases
	£	£
November	40,000	20,000
December	50,000	24,000
January	50,000	44,000
February	54,000	38,000
March	60,000	36,000
April	64,000	38,000
May	64,000	38,000
June	64,000	38,000

Other information:

General expenses, including salaries, of £12,000 are incurred and paid for each month.

Depreciation of the company's existing assets for the forthcoming year (Jan–Dec) will be £36,000 (in other words, £3,000 per month).

A computer system costing £80,000 is to be acquired and paid for at the end of March. It will be depreciated on a straight line basis over a 4-year period, with no residual value. This depreciation is in addition to the annual £36,000 referred to above.

1. Prepare a cash flow forecast for the six months January to June by completing table 12.3.

Table 12.3

	Jan	Feb	Mar	Apr	May	Jun
Receipts:						
Total receipts						
Payments:						
Total payments						
Net receipts / payments						
Opening cash balance						
Closing cash balance						

2. Calculate what the budgeted profit will be over the same period (a month-by-month calculation is not required).

Feedback on page 204

12.3 The benefits and limitations of using budgets

There has been a considerable amount of debate in recent years about the practical value of traditional budgeting processes in a rapidly changing business environment.

For budgeting to be **successful**, certain conditions need to exist:

- There needs to be senior management involvement and commitment.
- Longer term corporate objectives must be clear (the budgets will link in with these, as discussed earlier).
- Budget holders should understand what is expected of them, and what their responsibilities are.
- Budget holders should be involved in the budget-setting process, and not simply handed a budget that has been agreed on their behalf.
- Systems must be effective in supporting the budgeting process.
- Budgets must be flexible enough to allow for revision or amendment where necessary.

Where a proper system of budgeting and budgetary control exists, a number of **advantages** will arise:

- Managers will be forced to plan and to think ahead.
- Operating plans will be communicated throughout the organisation.
- There will be coordination of actions and effort throughout the company.
- Staff (ie budget holders) should be motivated.
- Management's performance and adherence to plans can be controlled.
- Managers can act quickly when things go wrong.
- Managers can detect changing circumstances early and take corrective action.

Problems and difficulties can arise in budgeting:

- Managers may become over-reliant on budgets as a performance measurement tool.
- Budget holders may not understand what is expected of them.
- Managers may tend to focus on their own local needs – if they are measured against local budget performance rather than those of the whole company. This can lead to what is known as 'dysfunctional' behaviour – where decisions are not made in a way that benefits the organisation as whole.
- Budgets may be inaccurate.
- Budgets may be abused through the inappropriate inclusion of 'contingencies' and 'fat'.
- Conflict may arise where different parts of the company are competing for limited resources.
- Budgeting data may be late, inaccurate or incomprehensible.

With some of these problems in mind, a lot of thought has gone into considering other means of measuring performance and managing resources that are both more cost-effective and practically useful.

12 Developing and managing budgets

Learning activity 12.3

We are about to consider alternatives to traditional budgeting processes. Before doing so, it might be useful to think about why alternatives might be necessary, and what they might involve.

If an organisation were to do away with the traditional process of drawing up a budget at the start of the financial year:

- what circumstances might have prompted the change, and
- how might it still be able to measure performance in a useful way?

Feedback on page 204

Traditional budgeting processes have been in existence for many years. The increasingly competitive environment in which organisations are operating has led some to call for a more flexible and dynamic approach. Shorter product life cycles, technological developments, less certainty and the pace of change have meant that budgeting – with its focus on past activity and the idea that the future is predictable – has been under the spotlight. Is it still useful? Is it worth the money and effort that goes into it? Are there more useful alternatives?

The weaknesses of traditional budgeting have led to a movement for change, which has become known as 'Beyond Budgeting'. This highlights the weaknesses of traditional budgeting, which include:

- Budgets add little value.
- Budgets take up too much management time.
- Reliance on agreed budgets can have a negative impact on management behaviour.
- Budgets are often the result of internal bargaining, rather than any more rational allocation of resources.
- Budgets can constrain innovative behaviour and the ability to respond to a changing environment.
- The focus of budgets is too internal.

One way of dealing with some of these issues is to have 'rolling' budgets. This would involve, for example, the drawing up of a new 12-month budget every month – i.e. there is always a budget that projects 12 months forward, and it also takes account of recent changes and developments in the underlying business environment.

Another key element of an alternative approach is to devolve a greater degree of responsibility to operational managers in an organisation, and, rather than constraining their available resources, setting them key performance ratios as targets. In other words, instead of being allocated a specific monetary target (such as a profit figure) they are given a relative target (such as percentage return on capital employed).

Finance for Purchasers

An indirectly related approach is the 'Balanced Scorecard'. This is a technique used by an increasingly large number of organisations, that measures performance against a range of indicators (often referred to as 'key performance indicators' or KPIs). The point about the Balanced Scorecard is that the indicators are more wide ranging than the more traditional emphasis on financial measures.

Thus, performance might be measured against the following four headings shown in table 12.8.

Table 12.8

Financial	Customer	Business process	Learning and innovation
Return on capital	Customer satisfaction	Wastage %	Staff turnover rates
Sales growth	Market share	Changeover costs	£ training spend
Capital gearing	Telephone response times		R&D spend

Cash flow forecasts and budgeting have been discussed earlier in this study session. They both are important management tools in the successful running of a business, and both come under the banner of financial forecasting. They both interact with each other, and it is difficult to accurately produce one without the other.

A sole trader should produce his budgets and cash flow forecasts, to identify how the future of his business will turn out in the following months and years. In the same way, multinational conglomerates will also be producing cash flow forecasts and budgets, to enable not only their short-term future to be planned out, but possibly also 5 year plans, or even longer with some types of organisation.

Financial forecasting is therefore essential to a well-run and managed business, however small or large, and the accuracy of this forecasting will identify any future pitfalls that might occur, and also give an indication to future profitability and possible expansion.

Regular comparisons of actuals to the forecasts will enable any variances to be identified at an early stage, and allow for adjustments to be made quickly.

Self-assessment question 12.3

List the pros and cons of traditional budgeting.

Feedback on page 205

Revision question

Now try the revision question for this session on page 347.

Summary

In this session, we have looked at the how budgets are put together, and how they are used as a managerial tool. We have considered different approaches to budget preparation, and looked at the budgetary control cycle that many organisations use as an essential part of budget management. We also examined the role and purpose of cash flow forecasting.

We then addressed the idea that traditional budgeting processes may not always be worth the resources used to support and maintain them, giving rise to the development of some alternative approaches.

Suggested further reading

Drury C (2005) *Management Accounting for Business,* 3rd edition, chapter 10. London: Thomson.

Feedback on learning activities and self-assessment questions

Feedback on learning activity 12.1

Most organisations will utilise a budgetary control process. The model, as illustrated, is very simple but in practice something very similar is likely to take place. The extent to which organisations properly go through all stages of the cycle may vary – with the variance analysis stage being key. Organisations will have different approaches to the way this is done – some more formal and rigorous than others.

Feedback on self-assessment question 12.1

1 This statement may be true for certain organisations, but not always so. Sometimes budgets do remain fixed through the year, and that can be a sensible approach where, for example, the majority of items are fairly predictable in nature. A purchasing department's budget might be a case in point.

However, a budget that involves production costs might be more sensitive to changes in output or sales, as many of the costs are likely to be variable in nature – and a change in volume of activity will trigger a change in many costs. Flexible budgeting would be more appropriate in such cases.

2 This is false. The term 'budget' usually refers to shorter term operational plans, with a typical time horizon of one year. Corporate plans, by contrast, typically have a timescale of around five years.

3 This is true.

Feedback on learning activity 12.2

Different organisations will have different approaches, but in terms of the individual areas above there should be information available that relates to the four areas asked about.

Finance for Purchasers

As far as 'incremental' v 'zero-based' is concerned, it is likely that most organisations will incorporate elements of both.

It is unlikely that previous activity, where it exists, is ignored and so an element of 'incremental' is bound to exist in many budgets. Also, given that 'zero-based' budgeting is very demanding of resources, it is rarely used across a whole organisation on an annual basis. However, it may be practised periodically (i.e. not every year) and/or on an individual business unit/department basis (e.g. just parts of the organisation in any one year.

Feedback on self-assessment question 12.2

Table 12.4

	Jan	Feb	Mar	Apr	May	Jun	Total
Receipts:							
Receipts from debtors	45,000	50,000	52,000	57,000	61,000	64,000	329,000
Total receipts	45,000	50,000	52,000	57,000	61,000	64,000	329,000
Payments:							
Suppliers	24,000	44,000	38,000	36,000	38,000	38,000	218,000
General expenses	12,000	12,000	12,000	12,000	12,000	12,000	72,000
Computer system			80,000				80,000
Total payments	36,000	56,000	130,000	48,000	50,000	50,000	370,000
Net receipts / payments	9,000	(6,000)	(78,000)	9,000	11,000	14,000	(41,000)
Opening cash balance	35,000	44,000	38,000	(40,000)	(31,000)	(20,000)	35,000
Closing cash balance	44,000	38,000	(40,000)	(31,000)	(20,000)	(6,000)	(6,000)

Table 12.5 Profit calculation

	£
Sales in the period	356,000
Less:	
Cost of goods sold*	240,000
Depreciation**	28,000
General expenses	72,000
Profit	16,000

Table 12.6 *Cost of goods sold calculation

Opening stock (at 1 Jan)	£25,000
plus purchases (Jan–Jun)	£232,000
less closing stock (end Jun)	£17,000
= cost of goods sold	£240,000

Table 12.7 **Depreciation calculation

Original depreciation £36,000 × 0.5 =	£18,000
Computer depreciation (£80,000 / 4) × 0.5 =	£10,000
	£28,000

Feedback on learning activity 12.3

As we are about to consider, the decision to replace traditional budgeting is likely to have been prompted by a belief that traditional budgeting utilises a lot of resources, and might not always create benefits that outweigh the cost of those resources. There might also be a belief that traditional budgeting can be (among other things) very internally focussed, very constraining, artificially bound by the concept of a financial year and a cause of behaviour that is not always to the benefit of the organisation as a whole.

Identifying alternative approaches can be more difficult, but ideas might centre around the idea of using relative performance measures (such as financial ratios) rather than finite monetary amount, and restating the budget at more frequent intervals than the traditional annual round.

Feedback on self-assessment question 12.3

Pros:

- It forces planning.
- It acts as a control mechanism.
- It can highlight problem areas and enable them to be tackled.
- It gives people responsibility and might motivate.
- It involves communication and co-ordination across different parts of the organisation.
- It aids performance measurement.

Cons:

- It can be too rigid.
- It can cause dysfunctional behaviour (taking action to meet a local budget, at the expense of the overall organisational good).
- It can constrain innovative ideas and behaviour.
- It can be abused (setting soft targets, using inappropriate contingencies, spending money simply because it is in the budget).

Finance for Purchasers

Study session 13
Assessing resource requirements

Introduction

This study session will introduce you to areas that span the border between finance and HR in assessing the business needs in terms of human capital. This activity is principally seated in business planning but lasts for the life of the project, the investment, the employee, the business and so on.

As we will discover salary and associated benefits costs are one, if not the highest, overhead category of most companies. It is therefore essential that the procurement professional can not only manage people, but also ensure that the organisation gets value for money in deploying those resources.

Because it is so difficult to measure human capital, it remains the most valuable asset not to appear on the balance sheet!

Session learning objectives

After completing this session you should be able to:

13.1 Assess resource requirements in terms of cost benefit to deliver a project within the optimal time frame.
13.2 Assess and allocate people resources against a range of criteria.
13.3 Assess financial requirements.

Unit content coverage

This study session covers the following topics from the official CIPS unit content document:

Learning objective

4.2 Analyse resource requirements and their application in purchasing activities.
   - Time
   - People
   - Money
   - Quality

Prior knowledge

Study sessions 1 to 12 and 17, especially study sessions 4, 9 and 15. Also Leading and Influencing in Purchasing, study sessions 09, 13, and 17.

Resources

You will need access to a project plan and internet access to complete this session.

Timing

You should set aside about 4 hours to read and complete this session, including learning activities, self-assessment questions, the suggested further reading (if any) from the essential textbook for this unit and the revision question.

13.1 How to identify the tasks or projects (business needs) that will provide the best use of human capital (people)

We will look to re-use and build upon the material presented in study session 3 Leading and Influencing in Purchasing. To refresh your memory, table 13.1 reflects upon the way we should identify the individual tasks that need to be done.

Table 13.1 An implementation plan for individual tasks

What is being done?	**Why** is it being done?	**What else** is being done?
Who is doing it?	**Why** are they doing it?	**Who else** could do it?
When are they doing it?	**Why** then?	**When else** could it be done?
Where is it being done?	**Why** there?	**Where else** could it be done?
How is it being done?	**Why** that way?	**How else** could it be done?

To make this even simpler we can redefine this as the planning phase or process, which would look like figure 13.1.

Figure 13.1

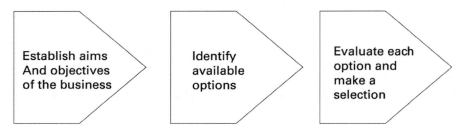

If we then break this down in terms of each block of activity, we can consider each aspect in turn.

Establish the aims and the objectives of the business. This will be derived from three primary sources (see below) that have defined specific tasks, activities and projects that will require resources allocating to them. The primary sources can be considered as:

1   From the company's objectives a set of tasks defined directly from the board or senior management – for instance, business actions (sell more

of X product), defined investments (acquire a new business or plant) or projects/programmes (new equipment for factory Y).

2. Functional directors or business heads – interpretation of the company's objectives as they translate into high-level actions for the area under the control of the functional director or business head, for instance, sales and marketing need a new advertising campaign to sell more of product X and have a budget £5 million to deliver £25 million of additional sales.

3. The purchasing function itself will identify projects or tasks, for instance the supply chain for product X will only currently support £15 million worth of sales and needs to enhance the supply chain to meet the new sales targets.

In assessing the existing and new requirements defined by the business, the procurement professional needs to assess all these needs in terms of human capital to deliver the total plan. In doing this he/she will certainly ask all the questions posed in table 13.1, but will ultimately have to balance the 'triangle of finite resources' (see figure 13.2).

Figure 13.2: Triangle of finite resources

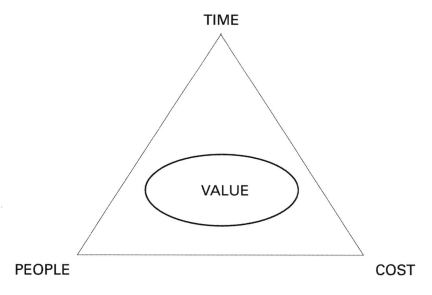

As you can see, the optimum balance will create value for the organisation. However, any imbalance in any one of the finite resources will destroy value and create tension in the organisation.

Inevitably when the procurement professional assesses the whole of the activities and projects list for the organisation, there will invariably be more to do than there are resources.

We will look at the assessment and allocation of resources in the next section. Before we can assess, allocate and match the resources against the identified and final list of tasks or projects we must conclude this section by looking at the selection and prioritisation process. This was covered in part in Leading and Influencing in Purchasing (study session 17 section 3), and will now be discussed in further detail below.

Finance for Purchasers

In much the same way as we would look to develop a risk register (see section 15.2), we must have the discipline to categorise all the activities and project tasks in a log (see table 13.2) and individually assess them against the following key criteria to create an objective unbiased list, based on the value they will deliver to the organisation. Depending on the type and profile of organisation, the key criteria might look like the following;

- *Legal/regulatory:* There may be new legislation that requires existing equipment or facilities to be upgraded, for example the Disability Discrimination Act (DDA) require places of work, public access, and so forth to upgrade premises to provide, amongst other things access for wheelchair bound people to again access easily and freely to their premises/place of work.
- *Environmental:* The board of directors may have made the commitment to shareholders to recycle 85% of all waste from production processes.
- *Health and safety:* In response to the 'duty of care' responsibilities placed on all directors and officers of a company to ensure that all staff are legally qualified to drive, have current licences, and so on. They have agreed to embark upon a safety programme looking at driving skills and standards.
- *Sales:* To deliver the stated growth plan of the business it will need to grow its share of the market in new and established sectors.
- *Marketing:* Developing the brand awareness in an expanding population segment, eg over 65 years of age.
- *Customer service:* Improve customer service through increased client contact in an effort to retain existing business as opposed to have to win new business.
- *Quality:* Improve quality standards of all/part of the product portfolio to compete with cheaper lower cost base countries taking market share.
- *Cost:* Reducing the overall indirect cost base to bring the company inline with benchmark competitors in the same sector.
- *Supply chain risk:* Reduce vulnerable niche suppliers or services to remove dependencies and create competition.
- *Innovation:* Develop a more robust R&D pipeline with a greater number of new products or services to replace an ageing portfolio.

The above list is by no means exhaustive and will depend on the organisation's objectives and business needs. The above criteria will then be ranked and weighted, based upon the stated priorities of the organisation, with the usual default that any legal or regulatory requirements will always be a high priority as they are mandated by law. For example, if sales are the most important activity to deliver according to the company's stated objectives then it will be weighted 10 (maximum possible 10 and lowest possible 1). On the other hand, if environmental issues are not a concern at all then they would be weighted 1, 2 or 3, and so on.

Accordingly, the above criteria will inform the 'headings' we referred to earlier that would appear in table 13.2. You will see that we have identified (in bold) the top 10 projects based on the weightings and (value) score. For example, the value score may reflect the level of benefit it will deliver to the company, how closely aligned is it to the strategic objectives, and so on. Again, this will be scored from 1 to 10 depending on how much value it is assessed of delivering to the organisation.

13 Assessing resource requirements

Table 13.2 Company tasks and projects list

Task:	Project/ activity	Business area	Weighting (1–10)	Value score (1–10)	Overall score (max 100)	Comments
1	Activity 1	Sales	6	2	12	
2	Activity 2	Environmental	4	5	20	
3	etc	**Marketing**	**9**	**8**	**72**	
4		**Legal**	**10**	**8**	**80**	
5		**Health and Safety**	**10**	**8**	**80**	
6		Legal	10	3	30	
7		Sales	6	2	12	
8		**Sales**	**6**	**9**	**54**	
9		**Customer service**	**8**	**7**	**56**	
10		Quality	5	4	20	
11		**Quality**	**5**	**7**	**35**	
12		**Supply chain**	**7**	**9**	**63**	
13		**Supply chain**	**7**	**8**	**56**	
14		Marketing	9	1	9	
15		**Cost**	**10**	**7**	**70**	
16		Innovation	1	9	9	
17		**Cost**	**10**	**9**	**90**	
18		Cost	10	2	20	
19		Cost	10	1	10	

In this example the organisation has selected 50% of the projects to allocate time, money and resources to, based upon the value criteria adopted above (that is, weighting × value score). This is only one way of prioritising the projects and activities. Other methods and 'cut off' points (greater or lesser than 50%) will depend on the organisation's capacity to support them in terms of funding (cost), the time available to achieve the stated benefits and the resources available to the organisation. The next task for the procurement professional will be to look at allocating the right resources to the tasks and projects the organisation has agreed to support. For example, against the profile of the projects and activities, do the procurement team in-house have the requisite skills, experience, time and diversity of resources to handle the proposed plan?

Learning activity 13.1

Using table 13.2 as a template, insert a selection of 19 company activities (your own or a published set) and develop or transfer the weightings (which have clear rational for the stated company/business) for all the above business area criteria. Then draw up a shortlist of 80% of the top projects or tasks to take forward self-assessment question 13.1 below, where you will match resources to tasks/projects.

Feedback on page 219

Now attempt self-assessment question 13.1 below.

Finance for Purchasers

Self-assessment question 13.1

Draft a memo to accompany the final list of selected projects and activities (80% of the original list of 19 produced in learning activity 13.1 above) and make recommendations as to how this list of projects/tasks should be approached.

Furthermore, can the tasks or projects be 'smoothed' to balance the phases? Give some reasons why this may be required.

Feedback on page 219

13.2 Categorising people and matching them to the business needs to deliver optimum value

Having established the business needs (the prioritised set of projects and tasks), we now need to set about the task of matching those demands against the resources we have within the organisation, and identifying any gaps there may be, under or over. This will be best achieved by defining the skills needed to best deliver the identified tasks and projects and then map them against the resources that are available within the organisation. We will deal with gaps, dependencies, risks and assumptions later in this session.

By selecting the final list of tasks and re-defining them we can begin to *profile the skills* needed. This might look something like the matrix in figure 13.3.

Figure 13.3: Project/activity categorisation matrix

Task	Project/activity (name + description)	Business area	Direct /indirect	UK	R of W	Skill grade	X F T	Overall score (max 100)	Comments
17	Ripon	Cost	D		X	MM	X	90	
4	Wetherby	Legal	I	X		S		80	
5	Leeds	Health and safety	D		X	J	X	80	
3	Harrogate	Marketing	I		X	S	X	72	
15	Knaresborough	Cost	I		X	MM	X	70	
12	Wakefield	Supply chain	D		X	MM	X	63	To be put in phase 1 due to dependency on project Leeds
9	Skipton	Customer service	I	X		S	X	56	
13	Bradford	Supply chain	D		X	MM	X	56	
8	York	Sales	D		X	S		54	
11	Ilkley	Quality	D	X		J	X	35	

Key:

Phase 1	
Phase 2	
Phase 3	
R of W	Rest of the World
UK	United Kingdom
Grade	Senior (S), Middle Manager (MM), Junior (J)
XFT	Cross-functional team required
L	Languages required: Fr, It, Sp,

From the simple example above, in table 13.4 we elaborate how a fixed organisation structure will present both its challenges and opportunities.

Table 13.4

Challenges	Opportunities
Indirect/direct category experience	Experience in a new category
Senior/Middle Manager/Junior mix wrong	Promotion
Insufficient support resources	Use of cross-functional team
Extensive travel needed	Travel opportunity
Interim/consultants needed	Learning and development
Insufficient experience	Development opportunity
Wrong skill base	Training
Too few resources	Stretch target + bonus

Among all this we must learn to develop the skills that allow us to grow, develop and retain good people while meeting the challenges of the business. In collaboration with our HR colleagues we must learn to identify the following key areas in order to develop and maintain a high performing and motivated workforce through the following actions:

- training
- development

Finance for Purchasers

- career progression
- succession planning
- mentoring
- high-performer schemes
- job transfer schemes
- good working environment
- diversity in the job role
- reward and recognition schemes
- sponsorship (especially graduates)
- good leadership.

We must also deal with the unplanned aspects that go with the territory of those who resign, retirement, go on maternity leave, go on long-term sick leave, and so on. Because of the complexities of this area we do not have time to explore them in this session, but must be fully aware of them.

Having looked at all the variables, we must eventually make a decision based upon the facts before us and exercise good judgement in selecting the right people for the tasks and projects that are to be completed. Having done all this there are still no guarantees that we have 'got it right' and we must be receptive and flexible to making changes that best fit the needs of the business and the people who work for the organisation.

Finally, we must remember that people in financial terms can be either be classified as Capex or Opex depending on whether they are working on an investment that will ultimately be capitalised as an asset to the business, or whether they are working on a company-wide initiative as an overhead and therefore will be classified as Opex.

Learning activity 13.2

Review the people resources used on a project that you are familiar with, either from your own organisation or recent research and compare how were they selected in relation to the criteria considered in figure 13.3, using a matrix table.

Determine what skills they have, what would happen if they left and whether they are employees or interim/consultant staff.

Feedback on page 220

Now attempt self-assessment question 13.2 below.

Self-assessment question 13.2

Can we classify people costs as capital items in the following scenarios? Answer true or false.

1   The project manager on a multi-million pound new factory building being built for an organisation.

(continued on next page)

13 Assessing resource requirements

> **Self-assessment question 13.2** *(continued)*
>
> 2 The project procurement manager engaged full-time on the above project?
>
> 3 Part-time internal resources deployed on the above project, for the life of the project, costing the organisation in excess of £100,000.
>
> 4 External health and safety consultants who visit the site once a month and will charge an estimated £20,000 over the life of the project.
>
> *Feedback on page 222*

13.3 Project costing and cash flow forecasting of people resources

Remember that cash flow is the lifeblood of an organisation.

As we have seen in study sessions 4 and 9, the need to classify costs as capital or revenue is critical to the way the company's performance is measured and how capital assets are then depreciated/appreciated over a period of time, depending on whether it is equipment (depreciation) or land and buildings (appreciation). This classification will also affect the way cash flow is calculated within an organisation.

The process begins by identifying the project schedule (the planning process) for each and every project or activity the organisation has committed to fund or invest in. For example, project Ripon in figure 13.3, as well as all the other projects listed, will all need to be evaluated on its own merits. Against this project schedule an estimate is made of the time commitment/involvement for the procurement resource (and type). All these resource profiles and costs are then aggregated in a schedule to produce the base costs (refer to the exercise in section 15.1), in addition to which we must now add an estimate for all the associated costs, for example:

- travel
- accommodation
- subsistence
- training
- development
- equipment.

Once the resource (and associated) cost for each project – which may include more than one person, part-time resources, external resources, support staff and potentially the overhead of the function (director, administration staff, support and research staff, and so on) – has been calculated, this is then presented to the project owner for incorporation into the project budget. At this point we will also need to address the question of when, where and how these resources will be deployed in relation to the project plan or schedule. As you have seen from study sessions 4 and 9 there are four principal components to forecasting cash flows: sales (inflow); costs and purchases (outflow); adjustment of assets, issue or redemption of shares (outflow); and taxes and dividends (outflows). From this simple set of rules a cash flow statement can be prepared.

Our task is to concentrate on developing and refining as accurately as possible, in this instance the outflow of cash, owing to resource and associated costs with a project or activity. Normally these are broken down by monthly amounts in which the cost or expense occurs. Accordingly the cash flow statement might look something like table 13.6.

Table 13.6 Cash flow statement for project costs

Activity	Jan	Feb	Mar	Apr	May	Jun	Jul	Aug	Sep	Oct	Nov	Dec	Annual total
Senior manager													
Middle manager													
Junior manager													
Research assistant													
Admin and O/H													
Travel													
Accommodation													
Training													
Expenses/misc													
External resources													
Total													

We need to remember that this is a forecast and not the actual costs, and therefore once agreed we will need to ensure that we track the actual costs against the forecast costs. This is usually done monthly to accord with the baseline that has been agreed. It should be acknowledged that it is normal to expect actual costs to vary both up and down in relation to the forecast, so we must always communicate this factually and quickly (as it occurs). Equally, as the budget owner, if actual costs do exceed forecast costs we will need to take action. Firstly we need to understand why a variance has occurred and secondly what actions can we take to correct the over spend. Some of the questions/actions might include:

- Can we use fewer resources?
- Are we travelling too often (use video conferences, and so forth)?
- Can more junior staff carry out the work?
- Could external/internal resources do it more effectively?
- Is cheaper accommodation available, and so on?
- Is the project/activity ahead of schedule and therefore justified?
- Is the project different to the original scope?

A final point we should consider is the procedure of *sensitivity analysis*, especially as we are dealing with a projected resource cost and not an actual one. For example, we might want to consider what the impact of the project over- or under-running by a month may be on the overall budget and cash flow for the project. Another approach may be to carry out a scenario analysis, not uncommon on projects, where we might look at, for example:

- an optimistic view of future events
- a pessimistic view of events (or worst-case scenario)
- a most likely view of events.

This will inform the decision-making process, usually at the point the business case is being considered so that management can take a view based

13 Assessing resource requirements

on experience or level of project difficulty. Equally, the board of directors may consider the project team too over/under-optimistic about future events and want to be able to sanity check this with their own views, but on an informed basis.

Learning activity 13.3

Populate table 13.6 using the following assumptions and data about project Ripon:

- senior manager costs £64,000 per year
- middle manager costs £48,000 per year
- junior manager costs £31,000 per year
- research assistant costs £24,000 per year
- admin and overheads are fixed at £3,600 per person per year
- accommodation is £120 per night
- travel is £2,400 per visit.

The senior manager spends one week per month of his time associated with the project and makes three visits per year of one week duration. The middle manager is allocated full-time to the project and makes trips once every six weeks to return home for a long weekend of four days and is given an inconvenience allowance for the project of £16,000 per annum. The junior manager supports the project from the office and it takes 25% of her time. The research assistant spends 15% of his time allocated to the project. The procurement director makes only one visit to the project in the second month.

Training is organised twice a year for all staff, except admin staff, in March and September, and costs £3,400 per head all inclusive of training and venue costs. Generally expenses for each member of staff are aggregated at £75 per week/per person.

Calculate the annual budget for the project and the cash flow forecast.

Assume that all on costs are included in the salaries and that no bonuses are to be included other than stated and that salaries and costs are straight-line costing.

No other miscellaneous costs have been detailed, but you may make and state your assumptions in calculating the cash flow and annual budget.

Make no allowances for holidays or bank holidays and round to the nearest whole pound.

Feedback on page 222

Now attempt self-assessment question 13.3 below.

Finance for Purchasers

Self-assessment question 13.3

Following on from learning activity 13.3 above, carry out a scenario analysis looking at the best case scenario that projects the following events:

1   The project completes two months earlier than scheduled.
2   The last two months of the middle manager's time can be spend back at his normal office, with no other staff visits.
3   Research is concluded in the half the estimated time.
4   The September training event is postponed/cancelled to the end of the year.

What will the overall cost saving be to the project?

Feedback on page 223

Revision question

There is no revision question for this session.

Summary

In summary it can be seen the procurement specialist must also be familiar with:

- planning
- scheduling
- evaluation techniques
- cash flow forecasting.

These are the minimum requirements for a departmental head.

Suggested further reading

- Association for Project Management (2006) *APM Body of Knowledge*, 5th edition. High Wycombe: APM Group.
- Atrill, P (2005) *Financial Management for Decision Makers*, 4th edition. Harlow: FT/Prentice Hall.
- Bower, JL, and CG Gilbert (2005) *From Resource Allocation to Strategy*. Oxford: Oxford University Press.
- BPP (2002), *AAT Assessment Kit*, 8th edition, Units 8 and 9, Managing Costs And Allocating Resources, BPP Publishing Limited.
- Devaux, SA (1999) *Total Project Control: a manager's guide to integrated project planning, measurement and tracking*. New York, Chichester: Wiley.
- Franco, G (2006) *Leading and Influencing in Purchasing*. Stamford: CIPS. Study sessions 9, 13, and 17.

13 Assessing resource requirements

- Pennypacker, JS, and LD Dye (2002) *Managing Multiple Projects: Planning, Scheduling and Allocating Resources for Competitive Advantage.* New York: Marcel Dekker.
- Schwindt, C (2005) *Resource Allocation in Project Management.* New York: Springer.

Feedback on learning activities and self-assessment questions

Feedback on learning activity 13.1

Fictional projects or activities are acceptable as opposed to real world examples. Table 13.3 takes a pharmaceutical company as an example, and examines how it might weight the priorities it has as a business.

Table 13.3

Task	Project/ activity	Business area	Weighting (1–10)	Value score (1–10)	Overall score (max. 100)	Comments
1	Activity 1	Sales	9	2	18	
2	Activity 2	Environmental	8	5	40	
3	Etc	Marketing	6	8	48	
4		**Legal**	**10**	**8**	**80**	
5		**Health and safety**	**10**	**8**	**80**	
6		Legal	10	3	30	
7		Sales	9	2	18	
8		**Sales**	**9**	**9**	**81**	
9		**Customer service**	**7**	**7**	**49**	
10		Quality	10	4	40	
11		**Quality**	**10**	**7**	**70**	
12		**Supply chain**	**8**	**9**	**72**	
13		**Supply chain**	**8**	**8**	**64**	
14		Marketing	6	1	6	
15		**Cost**	**8**	**7**	**56**	
16		**Innovation**	**10**	**9**	**90**	
17		**Cost**	**8**	**9**	**72**	
18		Cost	8	2	16	
19		Cost	8	1	10	

These ratings are based on the fact that product quality is paramount to a drug company, as it has to have validated processes that ensure the product is 100% correct all of the time. Equally, innovation is the key to the next 'blockbuster' drug. Cost is less critical, as its profits will follow from strong sales and direct, focused marketing to the medical community in the main, without the need for mass media to promote the brand per se.

Feedback on self-assessment question 13.1

The student should have identified a list of phases and stages within the 80%. To apply the same procedure to table 13.2 would result in the following prioritisations:

- Phase 1: tasks 17, 4, and 5
- Phase 2 : tasks 3, 12, 9, 13 and 8

Finance for Purchasers

- Phase 3: task 11 + any other tasks that can be effectively dealt with from the list, starting with task 6.

There may also be an overriding factor for task 6 in that it is a legal requirement and should be carried out anyway. The selection of tasks is based on the highest overall score projects are dealt with first, limited by the resource base of the organisation. In other words, you can't do everything all at once because of resource constraints, the scale of change an organisation can withstand at any one time, and so forth.

Also 'smoothing' the tasks to better fit with the resource base or constraints and is common in most organisations as factors such as:

- the physical number of key resources that can be deployed is a constraint
- ensuring adequate time for training and development
- project overruns
- unforeseen external factors requiring a re-balance of the portfolio
- new priorities being defined by the board.

Feedback on learning activity 13.2

This exercise should mirror [learning-a], adding a further column(s) that identifies the gaps and assesses the size of that gap.

Figure 13.4

Task	Project/activity (name + description)	Business area	Direct/indirect	UK	R of W	Skill grade	L	Overall score (max 100)	Avail-ability	Support staff	Business knowledge to specific area needed?	Comments
17	Ripon	Cost	D		X	MM	X	90	Q2	Analyst	No	Spanish (Sp) required
4	Wetherby	Legal	I	X		S		80	Q1	Lawyer	No	Independent project - could outsource
5	Leeds	Health and Safety	D		X	J	X	80	Q2	H&S expert + Lawyer	Yes	Linked to manufacturing area, critical to ongoing compliance and a top 3 product
3	Harrogate	Marketing	I		X	S	X	72	Q2	External Agency	Yes	Incumbent agency has held account for 12 years without review
15	Knaresborough	Cost	I		X	MM	X	70	Q2	Analyst	No	
12	Wakefield	Supply chain	D		X	MM	X	63	Q1	Research Assistant	Yes	To be put in phase 1 due to dependency on project Leeds
9	Skipton	Customer service	I	X		S	X	56	Q2	Admin support × 4	Yes	Most of the issues surround the current call centre operation off-site
13	Bradford	Supply chain	D		X	MM	X	56	Q2	Research Assistant	Yes	Highly complex – Far East sourcing issue via agent
8	York	Sales	D		X	S	X	54	Q3	No	Yes	Highly sensitive. Therefore XYZ person needs to handle due to relationship issues
11	Ilkley	Quality	D	X		J	X	35	Q4	QA technician	No	Narrowly avoided product recall – pull forward if possible

As you can see, not just objective but subjective assessments will come into play, which is where the 'soft skills' will be critical to delivering a successful solution.

Finance for Purchasers

Feedback on self-assessment question 13.2

As we can see from the abstract from study session 4, some broad rules apply (see table 13.5).

Table 13.5

	Revenue expenditure ('expense')	Capital expenditure
Definition	Spending on assets that are used up or 'consumed' within the financial year	Spending (acquiring or improving) on assets being used on a long-term basis
Examples	Buying materials	Buying equipment
	Hiring a car	Buying a car
	Maintaining a power station	Building a power station
Effect on financial statements	Included in P&L in the period incurred	Value of asset shown in balance sheet, at cost less depreciation to date. Depreciation of asset included in P&L. Also re-valuation upwards of assets such as land and buildings.
Potential impact on profit	Unless controlled, can have a direct bearing on profitability	Profits only impacted via depreciation – but investment is necessary for longer-term profitability.

The answers are therefore as follow:

1 True
2 True
3 False
4 True

Feedback on learning activity 13.3

The table should look something like table 13.7.

13 Assessing resource requirements

Table 13.7

Activity	Jan	Feb	Mar	Apr	May	Jun	Jul	Aug	Sep	Oct	Nov	Dec	Annual total
Senior manager	1,231	1,231	1,231	1,231	1,231	1,231	1,231	1,231	1,231	1,231	1,231	1,231	14,772
Middle manager	4,000	4,000	4,000	4,000	4,000	4,000	4,000	4,000	4,000	4,000	4,000	4,000	48,000
Junior manager	646	646	646	646	646	646	646	646	646	646	646	646	7,752
Research assistant	300	300	300	300	300	300	300	300	300	300	300	300	3,600
Admin and O/H	501	501	501	501	501	501	501	501	501	501	501	501	6,012
Travel	2,400	4,800	2,400	2,400	2,400	2,400	0	4,800	2,400	0	2,400	4,800	31,200
Accommodation	3,720	3,480	3,720	3,720	3,240	3,120	3,720	3,840	3,120	3,720	3,120	3,840	42,360
Training			5,675						5,675				11,350
Expenses/Misc	1,871	1,871	1,871	1,871	1,871	1,871	1,871	1,871	1,871	1,871	1,871	1,871	22,452
External resources	0	0	0	0	0	0	0	0	0	0	0	0	0
Total	14,669	16,829	20,344	14,669	14,189	14,069	12,269	17,189	19,744	12,269	14,069	17,189	187,498

Feedback on self-assessment question 13.3

The answer should be:

- Final 2 months saved: £17,189 + £14,069 = £31,258
- September and October travel and accommodation saved: £3,720 + £5,520 = £9,220

Finance for Purchasers

- Researcher cost halved £3,600/2 = £1,800 + £292.50 (apportioned expenses based at £75/week × 26 weeks × 15%) + £270 (apportioned overheads £3,600 per person per year × 50% × 15%) = £2,362.50
- Training cancelled/re-scheduled = £5,675
- Total saving = £48,515.50 (26% of the budget).

Study session 14
Communicating findings and recommendations

Introduction

This study session is designed to help you both deliver and construct key documents that you will need either to present or support in your role as a purchasing professional. It also covers to a certain extent the roles and responsibilities of the people involved. This study session will specifically focus on the 'communication' aspects of reporting financial and non-financial results and the tools and techniques necessary to ensure effective delivery as well as effective written and oral presentations. The whole process of communication is a key activity: no matter how good the news, if you can't communicate it you will not see the results!

'I feel that if a person has problems communicating the very least he can do is to shut up.'
Tom Lehrer

Session learning objectives

After completing this session you should be able to:

14.1 Communicate key data clearly, and illustrate it through graphical delivery where appropriate.
14.2 Construct and present a business case.

Unit content coverage

This study session covers the following topics from the official CIPS unit content document:

Learning objective

4.3 Communicate findings and recommendations effectively.
 • Target audience: finance professionals and other parts of the business
 • Budget presentation
 • Presenting the business case

Prior knowledge

Study sessions 1 to 13.

Resources

Obtain copies of business plans, reports and presentations made to senior bodies within your organisation or alternatively annual reports from publicly quoted companies or government departments.

Timing

You should set aside about 4 hours to read and complete this session, including learning activities, self-assessment questions, the suggested further

Finance for Purchasers

reading (if any) from the essential textbook for this unit and the revision question.

14.1 Effective presentation and communication of key data

One of the most important and central tasks as part of the procurement 'toolkit' is the ability to effectively communicate at all levels within an organisation in a variety of different ways: presentations, reports, groups, face to face, posters, emails, and so on. In the context of procurement and the financial aspects of the subject matter, it is more than likely that most presentations and communications will be of a business technical nature. This will mean that the presentation of critical data and information, including financial information, will be a common feature. As well as presenting honestly and accurately financial and non-financial data, we need to find clear, creative and engaging ways in which to do this.

It is important from the outset that we keep in mind the need to find creative and engaging ways to present and communicate the facts without losing sight of what the critical requirements are. For example:

- cost/benefit analysis and justification
- delivery of targets or investments
- terms of contract or supply
- financial references
- resource issues
- phasing and milestones
- assumptions
- risks and mitigation actions
- key performance measures
- timetable of events.

As you can see from the above, which is by no means an exhaustive list, the subject matter is and will be factual by its nature. However, some basic principles need to be observed throughout the whole of this section:

- Understand your target audience.
- Ensure you have a planned approach.
- Answer the fundamental questions:
  - What is the situation today?
  - Where do we want to be?
  - How are we going to get there?
- Make it clear and simple.
- Ensure what you deliver is aligned with company strategy and objectives.
- Demonstrate ownership.

Each and every presentation and form of communication must be carefully constructed to reach the target audience and deliver an effective message that will in turn deliver a required outcome or approval. In constructing any document or delivering any form of presentation, ensure you have critically reviewed the content, preferably as a group, and have honestly answered the 'all-important' questions from the recipients:

- What's in it for me? (the WIFM factor)
- Have we missed any key facts, unpalatable though they may be?

14 Communicating findings and recommendations

- Is it realistic and objective?
- Are quotes accurate and agreed with the recognised party?
- If there is an established process are you following it?
- Is the language and style unbiased and ethical?
- Avoid personal criticism or unnecessary contentious statements.

So whether you are communicating a business plan or even a change to the office layout, we all need to understand how to *communicate* and *present effectively*, whatever the subject matter. This section will look at the aspects and elements of communication and effective presentation as the two main core elements.

Starting with *communication* we need to be very clear what the message is, who we are delivering the message to and what is the best way to do this. This will vary from formal to informal, factual to motivational.

We look next at the steps that will need to be taken and the order in which you are likely to consider them, always remembering that no two communications and/or presentations should be the same, because there are so many variables to consider, as we can see below.

- What are the *stated strategies and objectives* of the target group or audience?
- Who are the intended *audience*, what do you know about them and what do you need to find out about them?
- *Don't assume* anything from the outset.
- Have a *plan* that provides all the steps for successful delivery of your communication or presentation.
  This plan should look at all the steps in the process;
    - timing
    - events
    - facts and data
    - key milestones
    - related events or activities
    - who to invite and why
    - when to invite them
    - how to invite them
    - sponsorship.
- Ensure key players and stakeholders can be engaged before you embark upon the task of engaging a wider audience.
- Do you need advice?
- Planning an event, if needed in terms of administration, and so on:
    - Do you need to send reminders or updates?
    - Clear sensitive issues before a major event.
    - Manage the content(s) so it isn't a marathon
    - Ensure you have time to critically evaluate your communication.
    - Develop sample answers to difficult questions.
- *Clarity and focus on what the material content of the communication will be* as well as what you must leave out (even if it took days to research, compile, write it). This is particularly true of reports and presentations, remembering that detail should be placed in the appendices of a report or as supplementary slides, held for reference only when questioned.
- Equally essential is to understand the *audience's knowledge base* and the likely level of interest in what you are going to communicate.

Finance for Purchasers

- Provide a *clear structure* of framework to your communication:
  - *Introduction:* Who you are, the topic and an outline of what is being communicated
  - *Aims and objectives:* What are the main points, and what do you want from the audience?
  - *Content body:* The main subject matter in a concise and clear style and in a language that the audience will respond to.
  - *Conclusions:* Reinforce the key messages, key facts and the action/ response you want – for instance, to approve a business case.
  - Give the opportunity for questions or responses.
- Decide upon the *language and style* you will use, as this will differ, in part depending on whether it is a written report, email, presentation, and so on.
- Try to *anticipate the audiences' reactions*, even if they are negative or difficult and make sure you have answers to those types of question or response.
- *Do not attempt to answer or respond to questions you really do not know the answer to*; get the facts and data and respond within a given time frame.
- Ensure that you *listen actively*, not hearing only what you want to hear.
- Ensure that if you make commitments that you live up to them or any trust you have will be lost with the individual or group(s).
- Make sure you *maintain people's interest* throughout, as delivering just pure facts and data alone will not be enough.
- Try to *build trust*.
- *Control* the whole communication process as far as reasonably practicable.
- *Confirm your understanding* of any responses, approvals, objections, and so on.
- *Maintain communication*, it isn't a one-off event.

Turning specifically to effective presentation, we must consider all of the points above and then look at these in the context of a 'public' situation and what some of the key aspects to consider are. It has to be said that there is no formula which, if applied, will ensure you have a successful presentation every time; even those most practised in public speaking do not achieve this. However, it is important that you develop your own style and follow a framework of rules that will at least enhance your chances of success.

The *framework of five rules* broadly encompasses the following;

1 The audience:
  - (a) Who they are
  - (b) Why they are here
  - (c) What they will get out of the presentation
  - (d) How many people there are
  - (e) Prior knowledge of the subject – don't tell them what they already know
  - (f) Get the audience's attention
  - (g) Keep control of the presentation event.
2 The content:
  - (a) Ensure you cover all the housekeeping rules at the beginning:

14 Communicating findings and recommendations

     (i)   health and safety (emergency exits, fire alarm procedure, and so on)

     (ii)   mobile phones off

     (iii) message board outside if needed

     (iv) toilets/cloakroom.

  (b) Keep it simple.

  (c) Ensure that any text, colour or background to slides are sized correctly, are easy on the eye and have graphics where appropriate (charts, graphs, pictures, and so on).

  (d) Only include what is necessary – be critical.

  (e) Time the presentation to the allotted time or slot.

  (f) Structure the content – introduction, middle, conclusion, and so on.

  (g) Ensure you use the 'news' approach; tell them what you're going to tell them (introduction); tell them (middle and content); tell them what you have told them (conclusion).

  (h) The main content should always be divided into logical 'bite-sized' pieces and displayed in summary format – no sentences unless they are quotes.

  (i) Don't waffle!

  (j) Allow time for questions.

3   The venue:

  (a) Ensure the venue is 'sized' according to the audience – not cramped, nor too few in a large hall, dark, poor acoustics, and so forth.

  (b) Ensure you visit the venue before you present if possible and use familiar equipment.

  (c) Have a back-up system or equipment ready before the day of the presentation.

  (d) Check everyone can see the presentation.

  (e) Don't block the presentation while speaking

4   The delivery:

  (a) Build a relationship with audience.

  (b) Practice your presentation in advance (and time it).

  (c) Remember tone of voice and body language can count for as much as two thirds of the message.

  (d) Do not use slang.

  (e) Smile. Don't look confused, anxious, bored or negative.

  (f) Be enthusiastic and 'sell' yourself and your ideas.

  (g) Adopt good body posture and whatever the occasion don't dress down.

  (h) Keep hands free from distraction objects – pens, paper, and so on.

  (i) Keep eye contact with your audience.

  (j) Speak clearly and normally – don't rush.

  (k) Don't just read the presentation, deliver it!

Finance for Purchasers

(l) Deal with questions:
- (i) ensure you have understood the question
- (ii) answer effectively
- (iii) don't waffle or guess
- (iv) if you don't know, say so and agree to come back with an answer within a given time frame
- (v) acknowledge differences of opinion politely
- (vi) be professional
- (vii) thank the audience.

5 And finally:
- (a) Ensure you know the topic inside out or you will be found out!
- (b) Get someone you know in the audience to give you objective feedback.
- (c) Get to the venue on time (don't be late).
- (d) Only use humour where appropriate.
- (e) Don't exaggerate or use jargon or acronyms (or at least explain them if you do).

And one final quote before we leave the subject:

'Great ideas need landing gear not just wings.'

CD Jackson

Learning activity 14.1

Taking the five framework rules of presenting above, place them in a matrix and weight them according to importance and then score yourself along with an impartial observer for your next three lectures or presentations, internally or externally. Develop a list of the top five things you most need to change about your own presentation(s) having observed accomplished and respected presenters.

Another way of looking at the art of presentation is to remember the eight Ps;

- Preparation – to avoid panic
- Perception of the audience's needs – to engage them
- Precise purpose – clear goal to achieve
- Powerful introduction – to grab their attention
- Prioritised topics – to ensure the most important message gets through
- Personal delivery – to keep them warm and engaged
- Pictures (graphs and similar) – speak a thousand words
- Persuasive conclusion – to end on a high.

Feedback on page 238

Now attempt self-assessment question 14.1 below.

Self-assessment question 14.1

Given the following data in the table 14.2, define what are the key points for consideration or discussion. Then re-present the data in a way that improves its ability to be communicated in a presentation (that is, not in its current table form).

Table 14.2

	Actual spend £	Number of suppliers	Number of transactions	Average value of transactions £	Average spend per supplier £
Overheads					
Cleaning equipment	132	1	1	132	132
Publications	500	1	1	132	500
Staff recruitment	3,950	1	1	132	3,950
Subscriptions	46,982	21	58	810	2,237
Hotels	58,473	2	45	1,299	29,237
Insurance	76,462	5	29	2,637	15,292
Pest control	80,072	6	117	684	13,345
Cash collection	104,807	2	29	3,614	52,404
Furniture	132,085	5	9	14,676	26,417
Corporate communications	158,484	12	49	3,234	13,207
College courses	196,136	8	91	2,155	24,517
Mail	198,014	9	916	216	22,002
Travel	215,667	5	54	3,994	43,133
Relocation	246,774	16	364	678	15,423
Research general	259,665	14	105	2,473	18,548
Clothing	334,124	22	2,173	154	15,187
Stationary/Office suppliers	485,285	45	2,766	175	10,784
Cleaning	574,796	53	678	848	10,845
Health care	608,100	8	120	5,068	76,013
IT training	638,048	10	155	4,116	63,805
Office equipment	685,653	32	818	838	21,427
Training	717,699	64	376	1,909	11,214
Training conferences	726,842	24	125	5,815	30,285
Parcel deliveries	799,928	19	1,737	461	42,101
Solicitor/Legal costs	826,900	34	438	1,888	24,321
Security	991,705	34	383	2,589	29,168
Catering	1,183,590	28	619	1,912	42,271
Consultancy	1,192,599	78	655	1,821	15,290
Telephone charges	1,523,177	28	1,813	840	54,399
Computer	2,628,152	72	1,031	2,549	36,502
Temporary labour	3,806,331	107	3,698	1,029	35,573
Total	**19,501,132**	**766**	**19,454**	**1,002**	**25,458**

Feedback on page 239

14.2 How to prepare and deliver a business case.

The dictionary definition is as follows: 'a business plan sets out the method for running a specific activity over a specific future period'. So with that in

Finance for Purchasers

mind we need to be very clear about the contents of a business plan from the outset as well as what belongs in the appendices to support it.

Learning activity 14.2

Find a business plan from your own organisation or one that is available from the internet or a study reference book and identify what is covered in the plan. Compare it with the putline given in this study session and then assess it in terms of its strengths and weaknesses.

Feedback on page 239

You should consider the following list to reflect the typical business plan content:

- contents
- key parties and contacts (and references)
- executive summary
- description of the business or activity
- market positioning and overall shape and size
- describe your strategy
- define your objectives
- explain your planned method (of approach)
- set out your financial projections
- review the risks and assumptions (as well as dependencies and opportunities)
- deliver a conclusion.

As we have stated before, the highly detailed and supporting aspects of the business plan should be placed in the appendices, which might incorporate the following:

- detailed processes
- definitions
- product/equipment specifications
- marketing information-visual or market analysis
- detailed financial analysis and projections
- biographies of key team members.

The business plan should be as succinct a document as possible to allow the reviewer, investor or senior stakeholder to quickly assimilate all the key facts and issues and make an informed decision without the need to further question or reference.

The plan owner should write the business plan, with contributions from the team(s), who will either deliver the plan or will be directly impacted by the plan. This is not always possible due to conflict of interest issues or HR-related issues. Some of the most effective tools and ways of doing this can be summarised as follows:

1   Use a previous business plan as a guide to content and structure.

14

232

14 Communicating findings and recommendations

2   Delegate specific sections to functional specialists, such as health and safety, environmental and financial.

3   Brainstorm the key areas.

4   Perform a SWOT (Strengths, Weaknesses, Opportunities and Threats) analysis.

5   Get benchmark data to inform your position.

6   Look at different scenarios to ensure your plan is viable even if things go wrong (as often they do).

7   Map the external factors that you can not fully control.

8   Use terminology, methodology and formats that are recognised or standard to the authorising or approving body.

Set out as figure 14.1 is just one example of a business plan template or model document that could be used. There are many other variations on this. Equally a standard template may be available in your own organisation to illustrate the structure and content needed to achieve the objective of obtaining funding or approval for your activity or business:

Figure 14.1: Example of business plan template

(Project/Programme Name)
Business Plan XXXXXX
Document information

Author:	
Version:	
Status:	
Date:	
COMPANY CONFIDENTIAL	

Version history

Version	Issue date	Author	Description of change

Distribution list

Other reference documents

Version	Document

Sign-off – authorisation to proceed

Position	Name	Date	Signature
Executive sponsor			
Accountable director			
Functional directors impacted by business plan			
Project director			
Programme manager			
Finance director			

Finance for Purchasers

PROJECT PROPOSAL

Project/programme name:	

1 PROJECT DETAILS

Executive sponsor	
Accountable director	
Accountable programme director	
Programme manager	
Specialists: *	

* as required- health and safety, environmental, HR, etc

Primary business driver (tick one only)					
Mandatory (legal/regulatory)	Cost reduction	Sales generation	Sales retention	Customer Service	Business risk

Functional areas impacted (tick all that apply)					
Sales/Marketing	Operations/ Manufacturing	Finance	HR/Legal	H&S/ Environmental	Purchasing

Activity category (tick one only)					
Programme	Major project	Mid-range Project	Small project	Advisory only

2 MANAGEMENT SUMMARY
(This should include a statement on the current situation.)
- A
- B
- C
- D
- E

3 OVERVIEW OF PROJECT/PROGRAMME

3.1 Current situation

3.2 Description

3.3 Business issues and rationale for project

3.4 Project/programme objectives

3.5 Options considered and why preferred alternative is preferred

3.6 Scope

3.7 Approach

3.8 Planned start and end dates

3.9 Key deliverables and milestones (with provisional timescales)

4 MARKET OVERVIEW and REVIEW
4.1   Current external market

4.2   Product/Service – market position

4.3   Current and future competition

4.4   Prospective customer base and why

4.5   Market knowledge/intelligence

5 FINANCIAL SUMMARY
5.1   Estimated costs

Estimated end-to-end total project costs – £000	2006	2007	2008	2009	2010
Development costs					
Capex (i.e. gross cost of Capex items)					
Incremental operating costs to end of year of implementation					
TOTAL					

Project budget required in current calendar year	[Insert year]
Strategic investment (SI)	£000
Business as usual (BAU)	£000
Other (please detail)	£000
TOTAL	£000

Funds required to reach first business case submission	
Date planned for first business case submission	[Insert date]
Type of business case submission	Detailed/Short Form
Strategic investment (SI)	£000
Business as usual (BAU)	£000
Other (please detail)	£000
TOTAL	£000

5.2   Estimated quantifiable financial benefits

Benefits – £000	2006	2007	2008	2009	2010
Cost savings					
Sales generation					
Sales retention					
Other (please detail)					
TOTAL					

5.3   Estimated other benefits
    Non-quantifiable financial benefits
    Quantifiable non-financial benefits
    Non-quantifiable non-financial benefits

Finance for Purchasers

6 RISKS AND ISSUES

6.1 Principal risks identified
- Project risks
- Operational risks
- H&S risks
- Environmental risks
- etc

6.2 Principal issues identified

6.3 Mitigating actions/plan

6.4 Any dependencies identified (this project on another, or another on this project)

6.5 Any assumptions upon which this project is reliant

6.6 Constraints – external/internal

6.7 External issues that can not be controlled by the project

6.8 Key personnel (required to deliver the project)

7 STAKEHOLDER CONSULTATION

Have you consulted…?

Board of Directors	Finance	HR	Business strategy unit	Purchasing
Risk management	Security	Legal	Operations	Sales
Marketing	Health and safety	Outside consultants (specify)	Facilities management	Environmental

Tick if consulted and support obtained (where required). Record name and dates of contact consulted.
Type 'N/A' if considered but not consulted due to non-applicability.
Type 'X' if consulted and not supportive. Record name of contact. Add commentary for reasoning, impact and proposed steps to address below.

8 CONCLUSIONS AND RECOMMENDATIONS
- X
- Y
- Z

APPENDICES
1.
2.
3.
4.
5.

14 Communicating findings and recommendations

You may also wish or need to add a section that defines the project's success criteria and how it will be measured.

Business cases that are intended for running and managing a business should be considered as live working documents and should be reviewed and updated regularly as change will be a certainty. Finally decide whether you could improve the language, style, graphics or the structure of the business plan for its intended audiences (remember there will be more than one). Above it should be ambitious, but truthful, credible, but inspiring.

Self-assessment question 14.2

Carry out a SWOT analysis on the business overheads detailed in learning activity 14.1 above for incorporation into a business case. You should assume that the business is heavily reliant on manufacturing excellence, new product innovation and defending products in established markets. You may make as many assumptions as you need to demonstrate your points, but they must be stated.

Feedback on page 240

Revision question

There is no revision question for this session.

Summary

Whether you are delivering a key piece of communication or constructing a business case, the checklist will look something like this:

- *Who are you?* Your background and track record of the main players. Stakeholders and investors particularly want to see a strong management team with a track record.
- *Where are you?* Company status; start-up or existing business? And the management structure and share allocations.
- *Where are you going?* Your goals, objectives and ambitions for your activity
- *Key financials:* You must know exactly your incomings and outgoings. Know how your industry measures success, and quote figures accordingly: for example, 'average spend per customer'.
- *What is it?* Describe your product or service in layman's terms.
- *Who wants it?* Where is the market for your products or services?
- *Why might they want it?* Does your product or service solve a problem or add value?
- *How many people are likely to want it?* Information on market size

237

Finance for Purchasers

- *How will you tell them about it?* Describe your marketing strategy, and pricing policy
- *And how do you provide it?* This is your 'operations' question. What are the costs of production or resources, how might they vary, and who are you reliant on (dependencies, risks, assumptions)?
- *Who else has it?* Analyse the competition. If there is none, why?
- *How are you different?* Better, faster, cheaper, niche provider?
- *What are the risks?* Be realistic without being pessimistic
- *What are the rewards?* 'What's in it for me'?, and explain how you arrived at your estimates and forecasts.

Suggested further reading

- Butterick, R (2005) *Project Workout: A Toolkit for Reaping the Rewards of all your Business Projects*, 3rd edition. Harlow: FT/Prentice Hall.
- Davies, A, and M Hobday (2005) *The Business of Projects*. Cambridge: Cambridge University Press.
- Graves, SB, and JL Ringuest (2002) *Models and Methods for Project Selection: Concepts From Management Science, Finance and Information Technology*. Berlin: Springer.
- HM Treasury (2003) *The Green Book: Appraisal and Evaluation in Central Government*. London: TSO.
- Stuteley, R (2002) *The Definitive Business Plan*, 2nd edition. Harlow: FT Prentice Hall.
- Business plan template (principally small businesses) is available via the NFEA website http://www.smallbusinessadvice.org.uk/busplan/bpdownloads.asp.
- Various papers and research publications on the topics in this session are also available from the CIPS website at http://www.cips.org.

Feedback on learning activities and self-assessment questions

Feedback on learning activity 14.1

Make a simple table with the headings:

1   framework rule
2   weighting (1–10) – focus on the things you don't do well!
3   score (yours and the impartial observer)
4   observations/comments.

Then prepare a summary list of realistic actions, shaped by what you have learnt and what they both you and the observer have observed. Remember: be honest with yourself.

Table 14.1 shows an example of how this might look.

14 Communicating findings and recommendations

Table 14.1

Presentation	Framework rule	Weighting	Score	Observations
Commercial committee	Audience	9		
	Content	6		
	Delivery	10		
	Venue	5		
	Final items	8		
Business case	Audience	9		
	Content	6		
	Delivery	10		
	Venue	5		
	Final items	8		
Project capital growth	Audience	9		
	Content	6		
	Delivery	10		
	Venue	5		
	Final items	8		
Team objectives for the new year	Audience	9		
	Content	6		
	Delivery	10		
	Venue	5		
	Final items	8		
Category plan to stakeholders	Audience	9		
	Content	6		
	Delivery	10		
	Venue	5		
	Final items	8		

Remember that your scores should improve each time you present and there will always be things you can't control. That's life!

Feedback on self-assessment question 14.1

It is expected that you will rank the spend by percentage and compare high and low spends in relation to the number of suppliers and areas for consolidation.

A pie chart, bar chart, graph or similar would be created to show how the spend is allocated, depending on the target audience (what level of detail and how succinct should it be to suit the target audience group). Therefore, you could look at this from the point of view of a board of directors, or a peer group of managers, or a group of technically/professionally qualified accountants and analysts, all of whom would require a different style and approach as well as content to the presentation.

Feedback on learning activity 14.2

The comparison should identify the formal elements of the business plan, eg:

* title
* stakeholders

Finance for Purchasers

- version control
- sign off
- all sections and sub-sections covered.

Construct a simple table with two headings – Strengths and Weaknesses – and fill in items, with a brief description of the rationale for your selection.

Feedback on self-assessment question 14.2

A sample answer might look like table 14.3.

Table 14.3

STRENGTHS	WEAKNESSES
Low overhead to sales ratio	Insufficient insurance coverage
Good investment in training	Healthcare provision too high
Strong cash flow	Training budget not under control
High staff morale	Telephone charges disproportional/high for the business
Good employee benefits package	
High investment in new technology	
OPPORUNITIES	THREATS
Reduce temporary labour costs	Insufficient communications
Reduce supply base in key areas (such as cleaning)	New market entrants
Office equipment rationalisation	Lower cost economies produce generic products
Innovate working practices to reduce relocations	Innovation not prioritised
Refresh the supply chain	Lack of investment in new products
Buy new concepts for manufacture	

Study session 15
Managing costs

Ever wanted to be a control freak? Well now's your chance!

Introduction

This study session is designed to help you navigate your way through the areas of finance and to a certain extent the roles and responsibilities of the programme/project manager that interact with procurement activities. This study session will specifically focus on the 'planning and control' aspects of finance and the tools and techniques necessary to ensure effective planning as well as cost control. The latter activity is often used in conjunction with forecasting and/or estimating to ensure that a total budget or plan is kept within budget as an overrun could put the project at risk, despite any contingency that may be held.

Session learning objectives

After completing this session you should be able to:

15.1 Assess control techniques used in project/programme cost management.
15.2 Use appropriate and reliable benchmarking data to evaluate key aspects of project/programme management.
15.3 Summarise key review stages in the cost management process.
15.4 Describe procurement spend authority levels.

Unit content coverage

This study session covers the following topics from the official CIPS unit content document:

Learning objective

4.4 Develop process and plans for managing costs.
- Estimating
- Controls
- Review stages
- Contingency planning
- Who should be involved
- Tools and techniques
- Procurement spend authorities

Prior knowledge

Study sessions 1 to 14 and 18.

Finance for Purchasers

Resources

Obtain the detailed project plans, budgets and monthly cost reports for a multi-million-pound/dollar project, together with the change control and/or variation order files. Also, obtain documentation for a benchmarking exercise and related data from a trusted source

Timing

You should set aside about 4 hours to read and complete this session, including learning activities, self-assessment questions, the suggested further reading (if any) from the essential textbook for this unit and the revision question.

15.1 Base estimates and change control for capital projects

With reference to capital projects and programmes, cost management involves the overall planning, co-ordination, control and reporting of all cost-related activities from 'cradle to grave', including start-up, operation and maintenance. It is the whole process of identifying all the costs associated with the investment, including but not limited to:

- informed decision making
- best value for money
- control of all costs
- scope change control
- ensuring objectives are delivered (not deviated from or diluted)
- realism versus estimates or forecasts
- risk management
- adequate and appropriate resources.

Other frequent recurring problems are associated with incomplete designs or specifications, inadequate design coordination, activity/workflow control and coordination, planning and building control issues (for construction projects), lengthy transition periods from implementation (especially where parallel running of new and old systems on IT-related projects), and so on. Having established the number of variables that do and can positively and adversely affect projects and programmes, we must now turn our attention to how we can create base estimates and manage and control projects from this point.

We must therefore consider what the primary components are that procurement professionals need to be aware of in engaging with capital projects:

1 scope definition
2 planning
3 estimating
4 forecasting
5 change control
6 contingency planning
7 risk management

8   the whole team
9   the supply chain.

Looking at each of these headings in turn:

Scope definition

This process must be carried out before all other activities as it effectively sets the framework to work within. Many projects and programmes have and will probably continue to be unsuccessful for the simple reason that the objectives and deliverables were either undefined or unclear at the outset.

In essence, it must define exactly what is to be delivered to whom and by when. How it must operate and what its overall cost is (capital and revenue – pre-, during and post-completion). The language of the scope definition document should be unambiguous and not open to interpretation. This document should be capable of being tested throughout the life of the project or programme to ensure that what is being delivered/implemented still holds true to the original intent and objectives as set out. The most important thing for any professional engaged on a project at any point where this does not exist is to shout, 'stop!'. There have been too many instances of great designers and engineers in the past busily working away clocking up time and cost to deliver a 'scheme' that does not meet with approval or meet the business needs.

Planning

This process begins once we have in place specifications, statement of requirement(s), high-level problem statements and business requirement specifications. Some of these may be ambiguous or unclear and the skill of the planner is to ensure that these issues are identified, documented and that a clear statement of needs or requirements is obtained before the plan is competed. It is also important that once a plan has been agreed that it is 'frozen' to ensure that a baseline position from which all and any changes can be tracked.

Usually a plan will be constructed at four levels: executive summary, business case, working and execution (fully detailed). The diagrammatic representation of the activities and/or tasks is particularly useful in establishing a clear means of communication across all disciplines. This will usually be in the form of a Gantt chart or schedule. These can be viewed by selecting one of the four series of Building Practice Guidelines: Typical Linear Responsibility Charts at Max Wideman Project Management: http://www.maxwideman.com/papers/index.htm). This subject is also addressed in CIPS Level 6 – Leading and Influencing in Purchasing study session 13.

In drawing up plans it is recommended that a formal structured planning framework and methodology is used, which is selected on the basis of the project or programme to be invested in, for instance, construction, IT or business transformation. A checklist of key considerations is also a useful tool too, and should comprise at least the following headings;

• Resources
• Decision points
• Legal issues

Finance for Purchasers

- Work tasks: infrastructure, equipment, etc
- Research
- Communications and PR
- Risk
- Inspections
- Importation
- Approvals: planning, etc
- Quality
- Environmental assessments, etc
- H&S issues
- Finance: cash flow, approvals, sign off, etc.

This is by no means an exhaustive list, but the items should reflect the type and nature of the investment.

Estimating

Estimating is usually concerned with predicting costs, resources and effort at an early stage within the investment process. It is closely allied to the planning phase and is used to assist in identifying the 'size' of the tasks and critical activities as well as any risks, assumptions or external factors that may affect the project. In short it will evaluate;

1   Products/services: size, values, quality, dependencies, and so on.
2   Processes: duration of activities, methods of working, constraints (legal, H&S, environmental, and so on).
3   Resources: individuals, disciplines, when, experience, and so on.

Estimates must consider many attributes, such as whole life costs (refer to study session 10), which by definition includes acquisition, operation, maintenance and disposal costs, displacement costs, best and worst case scenarios, stated assumptions (say on efficiency, product wastage in trials or old stock write-off) and transition periods (additional supervision, lower productivity, duplication of activity, and so on). We must also consider internal costs associated with the project too: consultancy fees, legal advice, public body fees and licences.

Estimates are initially produced as a *base estimate* and are subsequently changed to reflect risks and assumptions to calculate a consequential or relative cost base. As the risks and assumptions are documented it will allow the project team to reduce or remove these back to the base cost or replace them with a known or more accurate cost, such as a firm quotation from a supplier or service provider.

Typically all costs will be placed into what is called a **work breakdown structure (WBS)** so that areas of costs and associated costs can be quickly and readily identified and amended based on new or better information as the project progresses. This fits with the process of gateway reviews designed to ensure that the project is regularly and rigorously reviewed as a whole and only released to the next stage once it has satisfied the criteria of that review (see below). It is important to realise that the whole process of estimating should be an iterative one throughout the life of the project.

A WBS can be defined thus:

'A categorisation or hierarchical set of codes assigned to some activities and to products that will result from the project. It is used in developing a project plan. A WBS provides a single, consistent, and visible framework for reporting progress, for identifying status of planned and expended costs, and for controlling expenditures throughout the life of a project. A WBS is independent of time: it indicates what is to be done, not how, when, or by whom.'

Note that this is just one definition; there are others available.

Forecasting

Forecasting is the process of determining the final out-turn cost of the investment based on all the various inputs and factors. This will be a blend of the outputs of actual costs, estimates, plans and objectives, synthesised by management view to deliver a prediction of the final result or key milestone (usually) for the investment. It will usually be accompanied by a statement of its accuracy based upon the stage of the project or investment.

Change control

This process starts once the project/programme scope and/or business requirements have been defined and 'frozen' to create a baseline from which to measure or work. Without this discipline the project is unlikely to be successful in either delivering its stated objectives or delivering within the stated time and cost parameters set and agreed by the budget holder(s) or key stakeholder(s). Equally it will not satisfy the value for money test now being applied to many, if not all, projects in the UK public sector.

A recognised methodology such as 'Changefirst®' exists, as well as in company change governance frameworks, that clearly stipulate and define how change control should be effectively enforced on projects. These will all vary slightly in form or content but will have the same overall requirements and framework in broad terms. I have defined this framework of requirements as the **SOAPP** requirement (to keep things *clean*!):

- *Standards:* The way in which any change control method must be applied during the life of the project.
- *Organisation:* The business needs to have the relevant people across its organisation in place and qualified to evaluate and make decisions based upon a set criterion for and on behalf of the business.
- *Accountable:* Key roles such as stakeholders, budget holders and project managers need to have clear roles and responsibilities that make them accountable for their decisions and actions.
- *Processes:* A series of defined steps and actions that need to be followed upon notification of a request for change.
- *Principles:* This is the clear guidance on how the process of change should be managed on a without exception basis.

Within this formal framework there will be the need to ensure that delegated powers exist for minor changes, as a delayed decision will cost more than the change itself. Furthermore, there must exist the mechanisms and flexibility to deal with emergencies in accordance with a documented process with defined nominated budget owners. Changes will occur that are planned, unplanned, regulatory and safety requirements or simply proactive

Finance for Purchasers

changes to avoid future issues identified during a risk assessment or as part of an improvement to the intended plan (which will usually yield greater benefits as a consequence of the change). Consequently the framework must be capable of dealing with all these scenarios and in any combination.

Contingency planning

The level of contingency will be a direct function of the quality and accuracy of the initial requirements and/or project definition. From this and other factors such as the level of accuracy of the estimate, the range of estimating in terms of best- and worst-case scenarios, similar projects, skill and quality of the team preparing the estimates, and so on, we can derive a contingency level. A good plan will use the WBS to identify associated risks and contingencies as well as factors that are outside the control of the team (political, regulatory, environmental, and so on). As stated earlier, this will allow the project team to refine the estimate or business case proposal over time, allowing it to be maintained throughout the project life cycle. In conclusion, it can be seen that care should be taken not to adopt the rule of thumb that 10% of the whole project cost will cover everything, it needs to be more scientific than that.

From the detailed budget or cost plan that has been carefully created using a WBS, the team should create risk mitigation plans (see 'Risk management' below). These plans are notoriously difficult for software development projects by their nature, in that they are new product developments most of the time and therefore should be at the upper end of the scale of risk and therefore contingency. In some cases this may be as high as 40% of the estimated cost – a fact that should not be ignored in order to gain board approval using a lower level of contingency than necessary!

Risk management

A formal managed process that has its outputs integrated into the formal review stages of a project/investment or business case. In most cases the risks will be identified by all members of the team and will be placed in a risk register. Each risk should then be logged and classified with a:

- unique reference
- date: initial and updates
- who identified the risk
- description of the risk
- impact of the risk: high/medium/low
- dependencies (such as other associated tasks)
- mitigation measures (make the tasks independent)
- actions required, by the project engineer for instance
- evaluation and sign-off by the project sponsor or budget holder.

Good risk management will identify risks in advance of them occurring and allow the project team to respond proactively rather than reactively. As we can see from the risk register requirement above, a formal process owned by one person gives a central focus to the issue of risk as well as ownership of the required actions. Experience shows that:

- to avoid making a decision can be worse than making the wrong decision

- a continuous review of the project/investment with the wider team is necessary to flush out issues early and will result in a better project
- flexibility should be incorporated, in the design for example, to allow other factors/information to guide the decision-making process.
- you should engage with the supply chain (see below).
- it is necessary to transfer areas of controlled risk to other parties who are better placed to manage the risk, either by contract, specification or other means
- to carry out a trial or scaled-down version of a particular problem or issue away from the project (to determine the best approach, for instance how to avoid clashes between services within a building) will remove risk from the live project environment
- with IT/software functionality, rigorous integrity and stress testing is essential before it is applied to the live business environment
- changes in the market or client modifications or expectations do occur, for example a manufactured product or service may need to be modelled in its new form, or simulation techniques may be needed (Monte Carlo, and so forth) to show the effect of changes
- you shouldn't be afraid to request that the project stops if it's that major or catastrophic!
- to de-risk a new approach may mean that the project team has to revert to tried and tested methods rather than the proposed new or novel methods and processes.

A **Monte Carlo simulation** is a computerised technique that is the basis for probabilistic risk analysis, and which replicates real-life occurrences by mathematically modelling a projected event. Monte Carlo simulation uses predefined probability distributions of risk variables to perform random modelling over many 'simulations' or computer trials. (Please note that there is more than one definition available for this technique.)

In short, place the risk with the person/organisation that is most capable and able to mitigate and control that risk.

The whole team

In delivering a project or investment a 'whole team' approach is necessary to ensure that the correct input is delivered at the right time. Hence the necessity to engage with the supply chain, which is responsible for delivering many elements of goods and services that make up the whole project. Delivery of a project can be compared metaphorically to that of a great piece of music being delivered by an orchestra, while acknowledging that the soloists have their part to play but not all of the time!

In essence the key players will be:

- sponsor (the UK government departments define this as a Senior Responsible Officer, SRO)
- budget holder (if they are not the same person)
- client representative
- project/programme manager
- cross-functional team: business areas impacted by a project or change
- functional specialists: finance, environmental, health and safety, IT.

Finance for Purchasers

In support will be the estimating, forecasting and planning (project and business) functions.

The supply chain

It should go without saying that the supply chain should be engaged as early as possible, as it is likely that they could be responsible for delivering up to 80% or more of the project!

In most instances the resulting work from the areas and functions described above will lead to a formal business case, which is approved by the board or governing body of an organisation for delivery. This will lead into the area of project/programme management and benchmarking as part of the delivery of that business case or investment.

Learning activity 15.1

Define and develop a risk management matrix to control five appropriate aspects of a project or programme.

Feedback on page 257

Now attempt self-assessment question 15.1 below.

Self-assessment question 15.1

Answer the following questions describing contingency examples – and whether a contingency would be appropriate and why.

1   Could the client, if he/she wishes to increase the amount of marketing and publicity for the project during early construction, take this from contingency funds?
2   The project has discovered a new method of packaging its products that will cost £25,000 but deliver savings of £35,000 per year in reduced wastage and material costs. Could the additional capital be taken from contingency funds?
3   A new law will come into force six months before the project is due to be completed, requiring the fire alarm to be upgraded, but this is unbudgeted and unplanned for. Should this come from contingency funds or wait until the project is finished and carried out then?
4   During the early stages of a software upgrade it is realised by the project team that the current software is not compatible with the new version. The costs for development work, rectification and delay will take in excess of three times the current contingency, but will deliver a better solution than the business case and put the company one year ahead of its competitors. Should this be taken from the contingency fund under the current business case?

Feedback on page 259

15.2 Project/programme evaluation by benchmarking

Benchmarking is a management tool used to improve business performance and has been defined as 'the search for industry best practices which lead to superior performance'. The technique is not bound by the industry or sector in which the company operates but looks across all industries and sectors for similar processes, irrespective of whether the outputs from the comparable processes are different. This is even true for areas of business that are acknowledged as difficult to benchmark like IT.

Businesses that strive to be in the upper quartile of performance need to compare how well they are doing with others and where they can make improvements to get ahead and stay ahead of the competition. Estimates vary in terms of the cost benefit ratio of carrying out benchmarking, but a conservative estimate would put it between seven and twelve times that of the original investment, not allowing for DCF or other measures.

Benchmarking should also allow the organisation to identify which areas to target for improvement or which processes are weak and in need of improvement. Equally it will allow management to set targets for improvement by understanding the gap that exists between its own organisation and what best practice organisations are delivering. In essence the approach will progress as follows:

Level → Approach → Types → Methods → Techniques

Level

Generally speaking benchmarking will occur at three levels in an organisation:

1   *Strategic:* Those areas that affect the direction and plans in the longer term and by definition will not be a 'quick win'. For example, market share, organisational structure, and so on.
2   *Functional:* Across the departments of a business or a whole area of the business operation. For example, finance and procurement, the way they are organised and what they deliver in benefits, and so on, or the company overheads, supply chain and R&D activity.
3   *Operational:* Within individual areas or processes in an organisation. For example, how the distribution of finished products is handled across the business, purchase to pay system, specific raw material supply chain, and so on.

Approach

There are a number of different approaches to benchmarking but they can be broadly categorised as:

*   *Strategically led:* This is where the benchmarking study is linked to the company's strategy, objectives and therefore its ability to achieve them relative to the competition. This may be achieved by using Porter's Five Forces, PEST analysis, Critical Success Factors (CSFs), and so on.

Finance for Purchasers

These methods have been covered in other level 6 CIPS units, including 'Leading and Influencing in Purchasing'.

- *KPI:* The approach is exactly what it says in the title. What are the KPIs of the organisation, at what level they are set and how they are performing against them in comparison to the benchmark organisations? Identify by comparison the 'gaps' and a series of actions to close them.
- *Functional:* This relates to factors such as ratios. For example, employees per function to control spend in procurement, for instance £500 million spend and 25 employees versus a benchmark of £500 million spend and 18 employees. How is this done in the benchmark organisation and what categories of spend are controlled by each head in the benchmark organisation?
- *Customer-focused:* Understanding what is important to the customer and how they value it will lead to a movement in the way the organisation responds and organises itself to deliver goods and services to its customers. Holding workshops with key customers by segment and identifying weak areas or poor areas of performance for improvement, as well as how to measure customer satisfaction going forward.
- *Quantitative/Qualitative:* This is exactly what it states and can be applied to very precise targets in the organisation, especially where there are comparable benchmark examples available. Examples are graphs, charts and league tables or recognised 'best practice' by the sector.

Types

There are two primary types, as we mentioned in the introduction: first, within the sector the organisation operates, such as pharmaceuticals; and second, across a wide range of sectors, such as insurance, construction and banking.

Methods

1. Data sources that are in the public domain, such as databases, press releases, company reports and websites as well as conferences.
2. Purchased data sources provided by analysts as well as financial specialists such as Dunn & Bradstreet that will give credit ratings. However, these are fixed values and are not bespoke to the targets identified by the organisation.
3. Tailored research based on specific targets set by the organisation seeking to benchmark itself against set criteria that are not readily available or require interpretation from known or readily available sources, for example, purchased databases. This will be independently commissioned and may target one or more organisation for benchmarking depending on constraints and willingness of the benchmark organisations to participate.

Techniques

These will vary depending on the level of benchmarking, but might include:

- activity analysis
- profiling

- process reviews
- questionnaire
- best practice
- supplier intelligence
- reference models.

This should all be carried out according to the agreed code of conduct and will deliver most benefit if the activities are focused on areas of high value, high activity, high risk, and so forth. During the whole process, communication at all levels in the organisation is essential as well as the reasons why a process or operation needs to change and what the benefits are (change management is also covered elsewhere in the syllabus).

Finally, ensure that there is a benefits realisation plan arising from the benchmarking as the investment in benchmarking needs to yield improvement and payback to the organisation.

The APQC Process Classification Framework (PCF) is a non-profit-making US organisation that promotes the best practice in benchmarking, amongst other things and outlines its PCF as detailed in figure 15.1.

Figure 15.1: Process Classification Framework™

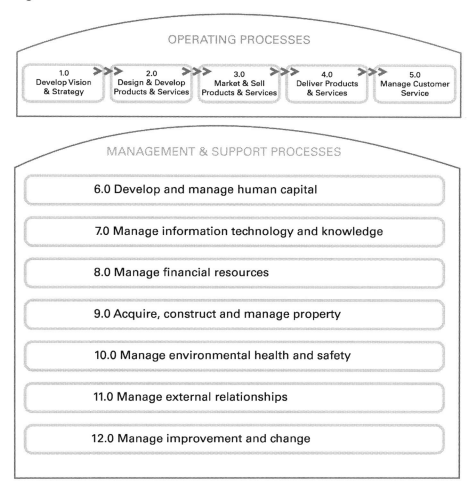

The PCF was developed by APQC and member companies as an open standard to facilitate improvement through process management and

Finance for Purchasers

benchmarking regardless of industry, size or geography. The PCF organises operating and management processes into 12 enterprise-level categories, including process groups, and over 1,500 processes and associated activities. The PCF and associated measures and benchmarking surveys are available for download and completion at no charge at APQC: http://www.apqc.org/OSBCdatabase.

Effective benchmarking requires common definitions and processes. Like a shared language, organisations need to make apples-to-apples comparisons to obtain accurate benchmarks and metrics. APQC's Process Classification Framework[SM] (PCF) is a taxonomy of cross-functional business processes intended to allow objective comparison of organisational performance within and among organisations.

APQC's PCF was developed in the early 1990s by APQC and a group of members from a number of industries and countries throughout the world. Originally envisioned as a tool to aid in performance improvement projects, the framework evolved into the broad taxonomy that it is today. With more than 10 years of use, the PCF has continued to evolve to meet the needs of organisations throughout the world.

The PCF now forms the foundation of the Open Standards Benchmarking Collaborative (OSBC). Organisations can participate in complimentary research projects to determine their performance against other organisations in terms of the processes described in the PCF. Furthermore, the PCF enables organisations to understand their inner workings from a horizontal process viewpoint rather than a vertical functional viewpoint. The PCF does not list all processes within a specific organisation, and every process listed in the framework is not present in every organisation.

The PCF is used by many organisations of varying sizes. Smaller organisations can easily leverage the breadth of the PCF to determine which processes need additional review or development. Larger organisations leverage the deep research that is organised along PCF guidelines to objectively aid in comparing performance to that of peers or against baselines during process improvement efforts. All organisations can benefit from the abundance of key performance indicators available in terms of the processes and process categories defined in the PCF.

Learning activity 15.2

Carry out research into benchmarking. Using a real-world benchmarking exercise (go to APQC: http://www.apqc.org/portal/apqc/site?path=/research/bmm/osbc/sc/index.html and open the 'access sample report' and the PCF download), answer the following questions.

Apply what you have read to the activity/project that you have been directed towards and state how you would apply a benchmarking exercise in your own supply chain given the exercise above;

1   Define the business concept and long-term vision.
2   Develop the strategy and concepts for new products and services.

(continued on next page)

15 Managing costs

Learning activity 15.2 *(continued)*

3   Plan for and acquire necessary resources (supply chain) – main tasks only.

Feedback on page 259

Now attempt self-assessment question 15.2 below.

Self-assessment question 15.2

Complete a list and brief description of the circumstances that need to be in place for successful benchmarking activities to be carried out.

Feedback on page 260

15.3 Key review stages

Project(s) or investment(s) governance should be subject to a number of defined key stage reviews to ensure that it is on track to deliver the objectives and benefits as set out in the original business case or investment plan. The stages will/should include all major decision points as part of a gateway process to ensure that the next level of cost, time and resources are not committed before the previous level has been delivered or satisfied such that the benefits defined are not compromised by the previous stage. Equally, no new risks or issues have come to light that need to be addressed or accounted for.

Before looking at the subject in depth, we will ask you to consider you learning objective upfront so that you can reflect on this while working through the study session itself.

Learning activity 15.3

Research and summarise a cost management review process that takes place in your own organisation or that of readily available source from the Internet. Also, what is the quality of the cost review process and what is critically missing/added?

Feedback on page 260

All key stage reviews need to be carried out by an independent and qualified body, either by seniority, experience or nomination. It also needs to be

Finance for Purchasers

recognised that there may be non-financial performance measures or benefits to be assessed or reviewed as part of the process, too. The review stages or gateways will be clearly identified at the outset and clearly communicated to all parties involved by the project or programme manager.

This process does not seek to replace the normal project reviews, cost reports, change control, risk management and so forth, but is a formal process defined as part of the governance of the project or programme as whole and will be applied to all projects/programmes or investments that meet certain criteria. We will define this later in the section. The key stage reviews will have definitive formats and measures to ensure comparability and consistency in measurement and evaluation of a project or investments performance.

In essence the review stage should adopt the following format:

1. Management summary
   - Purpose of review
   - Progress since last review
   - Planned progress to next review
   - Key risks and issues
   - Business case update
   - Decisions required at this review
2. Restate the objectives, benefits and changes of project
   - Business issue(s) to be resolved/opportunity to be taken
   - Rationale for this solution to the issue/opportunity
   - Benefits to the business
   - Project objectives restated
   - Note any changes in project objectives since commencement and reasons
3. Project history
   - Original timescales, deliverables and planned benefits
   - History (with dates) of key changes in timescales, deliverables and planned benefits since inception – and reasons for each change
4. Actions from the last review
   - Restate decisions made at the last review
   - Restate what was to have been achieved by now (from last review report)
   - Date current review originally planned (reasons for change if date not hit)
5. Achievements since the last review
   - Progress against plans
   - Checklist of achieved/not achieved against last review (reasons why not if not achieved)
   - Impacts on project not foreseen at last review (for example, new dependencies on other projects, difficulties in this project not foreseen and requiring action since last review)
   - Confirmation that this review has been reached within funding authorised for release at last review (if applicable)
6. Overall project status
   - Current Red/Amber/Green (RAG) status and reasons
   - What's going well? What is more difficult?

- Likelihood of hitting key upcoming milestones and ultimate project implementation/deliverables
- Project resources – adequate?
- Budget – sufficiency
- Deliverables planned – fit for purpose?
- Dependency on/relationship with any third-party suppliers
- Quality management
- Environmental management
- Health and Safety Management
- Regulatory compliance
- Stakeholder management
- Change management and communications
- Any other issues

7 Technical review
- Design review
- Engineering review
- IT development status
- Software development status
- Any significant changes in design/functionality
- Current (specific) issues
- Relationship with suppliers and/or service providers, if applicable

8 Change control
- Any change requests requiring agreement as part of this review, to enable progression to next review as planned

9 Risk review
- review of compliance with all group-mandated policies: operational, risk, IT, security, business continuity, H&S, environmental, CSR, and so on
- Review of critical risks, issues, dependencies and assumptions
- Decisions/support required to manage them so as not to prevent project completion/benefits realisation

10 Business case review
- Original planned total costs and benefits
- Current planned total costs and benefits – and reasons for variance
- Business case status –financial and non-financial measures
- Are the assumptions on which business case was built still valid?
- Benefits realisation – current status. Will all the factors needed to realise benefits be in place?
- Current year budget – on track?

11 Objectives and plans to next review
- What needs to happen between now and the next review
- What will need to be decided at the next review?
- What is the planned date of the next review?
- What is the funding requirement through to next review – cash flow (if applicable)?

12 Key decisions required at this review
- Go/No Go to next phase of work?
- Agreement needed to any key documentation (internal/external)?
- Decisions around change requests and risk register?
- Funds release authorised to next stage?

As you will have seen from study session 14, there are different methods of presenting this information.

Finance for Purchasers

> ### Self-assessment question 15.3
>
> Place in the correct order the contents of a benefits realisation plan and at what interval(s) will it normally be reviewed/published.
>
> *Feedback on page 261*

15.4 Procurement spend authority levels

Comment has been made earlier in this study session regarding capital projects, and one of the most important factors in the management of all costs involved is to ensure that expenditure projected and incurred has been correctly authorised according to the company authority levels.

All organisations should have spend authority levels, similar to the levels used in the authorisation and use of purchase orders. There will have been set spend levels within the purchasing department for the signing and authorisation of purchase orders, which will then be incorporated in the project management and purchase of goods and services.

All organisations will have different levels of authority, depending on the type of business involved, but suggested levels could be:

- Level 1 – low spend, up to say £1,000 – to be authorised by supervisor/team leader within purchasing department
- Level 2 – up to say £10,000 – to be authorised by purchasing manager
- Level 3 – up to say £100,000 – to have been processed and confirmed by purchasing manager, and then authorised by a director
- Level 4 – up to say £1,000,000 – as level 3, but two directors.

The above levels are only an example, and individual company levels will fall in line with their spend levels, type of business and company policy.

Study sessions 16 and 17 also deal with cost base and investment decision making, and spend authority levels should form part of the study for these sessions.

Revision question

There is no revision question for this session.

Summary

It can be seen that the control, monitoring and reporting of high-value capital projects needs to understood by all members of the cross-functional team that delivers the project or investment. Equally, the tools and techniques can be applied at all levels and stages of the project or investment.

It is not uncommon for very large investments in a company's portfolio to be reported upon in investor briefings annual reports and the like.

Suggested further reading

- Association for Project Management (2006) *APM Body of Knowledge*, 5th edition. High Wycombe: APM Group.
- CIMA (2001) *Benchmarking – Concept and Practice with Particular Reference to the Finance Function*, CIMA Publishing, ISBN: 1-85971-488-9
- HM Treasury Green Book Guide (Green Book online: http://.greenbook/hm-treasury.gov.uk).
- Lewis, JP (2006) *Project Planning, Scheduling and Control*, 4th revised edition. New York: McGraw Hill.
- Office of Government Commerce Successful Delivery Toolkit: OGC: http://www.ogc.gov.uk.
- Rad, PF (2001) *Project Estimating and Cost Management: management concepts*. Vienna: VA.
- Turner, JR, and SJ Simister (2000) *The Gower Handbook of Project Management*, 3rd edition. Aldershot: Gower.
- A wide variety of papers and case studies at Max Wideman Project Management: http://www.maxwideman.com/papers/index.htm

Feedback on learning activities and self-assessment questions

Feedback on learning activity 15.1

Your matrix should look something like table 15.1.

15

Table 15.1

Ref	Risk	Identifier	Date notified	Date updated	Areas impacted	Impact			Dependencies	Mitigation	Actions	Sign-off
						Cost	Time	Res's				
ABC1	IT	S. WARE	18/10/06	24/10/06	Finance Purchasing Manufacturing	H	M	M	New release of software, expected Feb 2007	Develop bespoke solution Temporary manual work around process	IT Head	
DCE2	legal	L. AWYER	15/10/06	24/10/06	Manufacturing	L	M	L	New import laws from non EU states	Seek clarification from HM Revenue & Customs	B. ARRISTER	
GHH3	Design	E.N GINEER	16/01/06	24/01/06	All	H	H	M	None	Carry out value engineering exercise on all offices to reduce shortfall in net office space versus business needs	P. MANAGER	
ETC												

Feedback on self-assessment question 15.1

1 No. This decision should be deferred to the latter stages of the project.
2 Yes. Benefits are built into the existing business case.
3 Yes this should come from contingency funds. Legal requirement.
4 No. The project should be stopped.

Feedback on learning activity 15.2

The student should follow the framework and logic as detailed in the main text and as laid out by the APQC, which, broadly summarised, is as shown in figure 15.1.

The response to the question should follow the recommendations shown in the downloaded version of the PCF, as stated. Therefore the responses should at least deliver the following process order for each of the three sub-questions:

1 Define the business concept and long-term vision:
  (a) Assess the external environment:
      (i) analyse and evaluate the competition
      (ii) identify economic trends
      (iii) identify political and regulatory issues
      (iv) assess new technology innovations
      (v) analyse demographics
      (vi) identify social and cultural changes
      (vii) identify ecological concerns.
  (b) Survey market and identify customer needs and wants:
      (i) conduct qualitative/quantitative analysis
      (ii) capture and assess customer needs.
  (c) Select relevant markets.
  (d) Perform internal analysis:
      (i) analyse organisational characteristics
      (ii) create baselines for current processes
      (iii) analyse systems and technology
      (iv) analyse financial positions
      (v) identify enterprise core competencies.
  (e) Establish strategic vision:
      (i) align stakeholders around the strategic vision
      (ii) communicate strategic vision to stakeholders.
2 Develop the strategy and concepts for new products and services:
  (a) Research customer and market needs.
  (b) Manage portfolio.
  (c) Plan and develop cost and quality targets.
  (d) Develop product life cycle and development timing and targets.
  (e) Research leading technology components and development requirements.
  (f) Integrate leading technology into product/service concept and components.
3 Plan for and acquire necessary resources (supply chain):
  (a) Manage demand for products and services.
  (b) Procure materials and services.
  (c) Produce/manufacture/deliver product.

(d) Deliver product service to customer.

(e) Manage logistics and warehousing.

Feedback on self-assessment question 15.2

The list should include:

- Sponsorship at a senior level in the organisation: are the board and key stakeholders engaged and supportive?
- Clear targets and objectives for the benchmarking: no ambiguities allowed and clearly defined process in place like the PCF.
- Definition and agreement of the approach and methods: for example, the PCF or its equivalent. This may already be established internally.
- Skilled resources to carry out the benchmarking: people that have demonstrable experience of this type of activity.
- Clearly defined 'gap' and action plan to close this: all the areas that need improvement are defined and clear set of tangible actions stated with owners and dates for delivery/completion of those actions.
- The use of the techniques listed above or other approved methods (EVA, accuracy or measures, predictability of out-turn, and so on): as stated before, a clear and communicated methodology at the outset, whatever you agree it should be.
- Best practice: simply the best method of approach known to the team and organisation.
- Benefits realisation plan: a plan that details from the actions, when completed what will the benefit in financial or other terms will accrue and how it will be measured.

Feedback on learning activity 15.3

Create a simple table that reflects what we have stated in the study session versus what your own organisation or example has in place, with a gap analysis in terms of what is additional and what is missing and your opinion on whether this is relevant and critical to the review process.

Some of the general issues that are missing from cost reviews can be summarised as follows:

- Key risks and issues – especially the mitigating actions.
- Decisions required at this review – perhaps you have told the key stakeholders what is happening, but this is your chance to get you want from them (you have got their attention).
- Note any changes in project objectives since commencement and reasons – it is critical to 'manage expectations' as sudden changes can provoke extreme and unwanted responses from senior management, due to this lack of information.
- Restate decisions made at the last review – remind people of what has already been agreed as this will avoid unnecessary and unproductive dialogue/time.
- Impacts on project not foreseen at last review (for example, new dependencies on other projects, or difficulties in this project not foreseen and requiring action since last review) – things may be obvious

to the project team but they need to be spelled out, as assumptions are often dangerous.

- Change management and communications – especially forthcoming communications. They need to hear from the project team first and be allowed to discuss the content and approach, before not after the event.
- What needs to happen between now and the next review – again, do the key stakeholders need to do or not do something to enhance the chances of project success?
- What will need to be decided at the next review – a clear statement of what is needed so that background and or research on a particular decision point can be carried out before the review, thereby making the review more engaging effective and efficient.

Feedback on self-assessment question 15.3

The benefits realisation plan should set out the following as ordered below:

- what the benefits are
- anticipated value of the benefits
- means by which the benefits will be achieved
- the process by which the benefits are identified, managed, tracked and realised
- timing of the benefits and assumptions/dependencies
- individual(s) responsible for the realisation and monitoring of each benefit/cost (benefit owner)
- links between benefits management and the business case
- confirmation from the relevant business areas of the respective benefits
- expected timing of benefits reviews and the post project benefits review.

A formal benefits realisation plan will be used to develop a quarterly review report. This pack will be distributed to the accountable sponsor and reviewed by the finance director or his nominee and will highlight variations from the original benefits sanctioned in the business case.

However, in terms of ongoing project management for the team and the key beneficiaries, it would be normal to provide a summary report format once a month to this group. This may be changed by all the stakeholders agreement to accord with the companies annual budget and/or end of year close to facilitate more accurate reporting externally or for audit purposes.

Finance for Purchasers

Study session 16
Managing the cost base of the purchasing function

Introduction

Hopefully at some point, if not already, you will be managing a team of procurement specialists and practitioners to deliver value for your organisation. In doing so, it is essential that you have your own house in order!

This study session will build upon other areas of expertise you will gain from this and other modules in managing resources and keeping good cost control, an essential part of which is ensuring that those that are part of your team have true *ownership* of the budgets and expenditure that they can directly influence and control in partnership with the departmental head. It is essential that a departmental head does not see managing the cost base of the purchasing function as a purely mechanical exercise too!

So you want to manage your team well? This session could help you make yours the best-run department in the organisation.

Session learning objectives

After completing this session you should be able to:

16.1 Define which budget 'lines' should be used generically, the apportionment methodology and how forecasting is critical in this context.
16.2 The use of empirical data and forecasting techniques.
16.3 Compare real documents or procedures from the workplace with given models or principles, noting the importance of delegation and clear lines of responsibility and ownership.

Unit content coverage

This study session covers the following topics from the official CIPS unit content document:

Learning objective

4.5 Develop a plan to manage the cost base of the purchasing function.
- The principles of cost management
- Planning
- Co-ordination
- Control
- Reporting
- Effective programme and project management.

Prior knowledge

Study sessions 1 to 18, especially study sessions 13, 15 and 18.

Resources

A copy of the internal overhead allocation and breakdown for your organisation, together with all the supporting guidelines for their use.

A copy the UK's National Audit Office (NAO) report on the BBC prepared in June 2006 and available online via BBC overheads review: http://www.bbcgovernors.co.uk/docs/reviews/vfm_overheadsreport.pdf.

Timing

You should set aside about 5 hours to read and complete this session, including learning activities, self-assessment questions, the suggested further reading (if any) from the essential textbook for this unit and the revision question.

16.1 The process of budgeting, apportionment and the need for forecasting

In this section we look at the background to purchasing function costs and illustrate the sensitivity of purchasing cost management to the 'bottom line'.

Generally speaking, the purchasing function is and will always be an overhead to the organisation and will need to demonstrate that it is adding value. There are exceptions to this such as specific project-based activity, which will be apportioned to the project and more than likely capitalised as part of that project. Accountable purchasing staff should consider the task of controlling the departmental overheads as a primary and integral part of their role. In this role we shall look at the three key components:

1 budgeting
2 apportionment
3 forecasting.

Pivotal to these tasks will be planning, communication and cost control, critically in the area of direct reports and wider team members alike. This will be carried out in close collaboration with the finance function, a nominated relationship manager, management accountant or financial controller.

To aid the process of budgeting, apportionment, forecasting and cost control. Companies will generally have a standardised costing basis and in the main it will encompass the following activities:

- External costs:
  - consultancy services
  - training providers/services

16 Managing the cost base of the purchasing function

- sub-contracted activity
- interim staff
- temporary/interim staff
- consumables (stationary, telephones, and so on)
- IT (depending on how the service is delivered)
- advertising costs
- accommodation
- travel and subsistence
- catering (meetings, and so on)
- equipment
- miscellaneous expenses.
- Internal costs:
  - internal salaried staff
  - pensions provision
  - National Insurance/medical/dental costs
  - bonuses/pay rises
  - cars/transport
  - office space, and so on
  - Facilities Management (FM) charges
  - overhead allocation/cross charges from other departments, for example finance, legal, HR, and so on.

Some organisations will also need to consider how they will handle VAT, or for overseas transactions federal/state/regional taxes, and so forth, on any externally or internally charged resources, as this will affect project or programme costs.

There are many definitions of overheads. The NAO in its report on the BBC (June 2006) simply defines overheads as:

'Overheads are those costs such as general administration and support services, which cannot easily be associated with particular products or services. There is, however, no standard classification of the costs that make up "overheads". Although overheads tend to be seen as a "bad" cost, some level of overhead is needed to run an organisation and spending on overheads does not necessarily represent a poor use of resources.'

The report also makes reference to some 14,000 account codes within its expenditure portfolio. It is also interesting to note that the BBC does not have an automated process for allocating overheads! We will return to this fact later.

Apportionment methods

The following represents one approach to how apportionment can be achieved. However, it should be acknowledged that most companies have an established methodology and this should be followed unless agreed otherwise well in advance of making any budgets, charges or the like.

Step 1

Calculate the number of days a full- or part-time member of staff will work in a whole year, for example:

Finance for Purchasers

5 working days per week × 52 weeks = 260 days

Less public holidays: −10 days

Less annual leave: −30 days

Total working days = 220 days

Therefore there is no allocation for downtime or sickness.

Step 2

From step 1, which establishes the number of actual working days, you can proceed to calculate the number of hours worked per year, based on the agreed contractual day (say 37.5 hours/week = 7.5 hours/day).

220 days × 7.5 hours per day = 1,650 hours per year

Step 3

Divide the number of actual hours, established in step 2, by the total cost from the period actually worked and it will give you the hourly rate (remembering to include NI contributions, pensions, agreed/predicted bonuses, cost of car/transport allowance, medical provision, and so forth – this being referred to as the 'on-costs').

Example:

Total salary with all 'on costs' as identified above that *actually* apply for the year, which for the purposes of the exercise we will assume is £64,376, divided by the actual hours per year will give a rounded rate of £39.02 per hour.

Step 4

Assuming there is a general cross-charge to the department for all other departments and services from the classification of general overheads, then this can be calculated as a percentage of the overall actual salary/payroll cost for the year and defined as a percentage on cost. For the purposes of this exercise we will assume this is 4.62%.

Therefore the new hourly rate will rise to £39.02 × 104.62% = £ 40.82 per hour.

Step 5

The final exercise other than the allocation of actual costs is that of space/office/FM costs related to the staff member.

Step 5.1

Calculate the percentage of available space used by the department (or project). This should exclude communal space (corridors, toilers, canteens, general admin, reception space, and so on).

Department space/total space × 100 = % used.

Total weeks used/52 weeks × hours used/37.5 hours × 100 = % used.

Multiply the two usage percentages together.

Example: (460 m²/6,728m² × 100) × (44 weeks/52 weeks × 22.5 hours/37.5 hours × 100) = 3.47% utilisation and allocation of total cost.

Assuming this total cost was £ 240,565 this would be treated as follows to allow an hourly rate calculation:

£ 240,565 × 3.47%/1,650 hours = £5.06 per hour

Step 6

This would give a final charge-out rate for the staff member based on the project/activity illustrated above of:

£40.82 + £5.06 = £45.88 per hour + all other expenses (travel, accommodation, and so on).

Learning activity 16.1

Taking the example above of apportionment for determining an hourly cost, use the following new pieces of data to achieve the hourly rate:

- 8 days of public holiday
- 25 days of annual holiday
- 40 hours per week
- total salary with all on-costs of £112,786.

Feedback on page 273

Now try self-assessment question 16.1 below.

Self-assessment question 16.1

Complete a worked example of an overhead costing using the methodology outlined based on your place of study, using an actual or fictional salary, with real 'on-costs' and real assessment of your own area of study, costs to attend and/or carry study as a proportion of the total estimated hours for the course.

Feedback on page 275

16.2 Forecasting

The principal activity of forecasting will be that of the annual budget/overhead preparations and will be strongly allied to staff levels, capital

Finance for Purchasers

projects to be implemented, commitments made by the company to shareholders and so on. Generally speaking this will be an iterative process and will begin months before year end is in sight! Forecasting is also part of the ongoing weekly/monthly activities such as projects, programmes, cash flows, and so on.

Many factors will affect the timescales, especially if there is a multinational dimension to the organisation requiring cross-country/cross-region coordination to market factors, changes in legislation, and so on. The whole process might look something like this (but will vary from organisation to organisation):

- Week 1: Objectives defined and communicated.
- Week 2: Key projects prioritised and ongoing activities confirmed.
- Week 3: Overall company budget levels set and cost reduction targets defined by business unit/country, and so forth.
- Week 4/5: Business heads agree cross-border collaboration needed to deliver company objectives and meet cost reduction targets, and so forth.
- Week 6: First draft of budgets prepared based upon empirical data and assumptions and projections.
- Week 7/8: Business heads agree outline of budget structures.
- Week 9/10: First draft of budgets submitted to Finance to assimilate and cross-reference.
- Week 11/12: First draft of budgets returned with initial comments and clarifications for action by business heads.
- Week 13/14: Second draft of budgets submitted to finance for assimilation and cross-referencing and preparation of first round board packs.
- Week 15: Board review and recommendations/requirements.
- Week 16/17: Business heads in collaboration with Finance resolve final board requirements and prepare final board packs for board sign-off and approval.
- Week 18: Preparation of board packs for sign-off, external or internal communications and budget cascade across the organisation.
- Week 19: Board sign-off.
- Week 20: Communication cascade and budget release.

While the above timetable may be exaggerated to an extent, it is certainly likely that the whole process will take between 12 and 20 weeks from start to finish. Underlying the whole process will be the need to ensure that any forecasts and/or budgets are underpinned by the empirical data the company has, as well as market sector benchmarking, to ensure competitive advantage as well as developing a leading-edge approach so that the optimum competitive position is taken by the company. In this regard the purchasing professional has a key role to play in engaging with internal stakeholders and clients in agreeing the forthcoming targets and action plans, as well as reaching into the supply chain to deliver the necessary innovative and/or performance improvements needed to keep the organisation at the forefront of its sector.

As stated earlier, the need for ongoing forecasting is just as important, as the business needs to know where its likely position is going to be on all manner

16 Managing the cost base of the purchasing function

of different metrics, such as cash flows, order volumes, manufacturing volumes, and so on. Furthermore, these comparisons need to use as much actual and empirical historical data as possible to improve the accuracy levels, as planned activity will be based on these forecasts.

Learning activity 16.2

Compare your company's forecasting schedule or that of a reported public/ government body against the one detailed above in the text and explain what are the critical path and bottlenecks (these subjects have been covered in mandatory study session 'Leading and Influencing in Purchasing' – study sessions 4, 13, and 17) that are experienced by your own company or chosen quoted example.

Feedback on page 275

Now try the following self-assessment question.

Self-assessment question 16.2

Develop a communications and action plan (in no more than 1,500 words) for dealing with the annual budget activity as highlighted in the learning activity, including key memos, email bulletins, and so on.

Feedback on page 275

16.3 Reporting and management actions

Compare real documents or procedures from the workplace with given models or principles, noting the importance of delegation and clear lines of responsibility and ownership.

The way budgets are reported will vary from organisation to organisation, depending upon whether it's within the public or private sector and whether it's from a listed/quoted company or a privately owned company. This learning activity will focus on the three most visible sectors:

- public/government related/influenced body
- listed/quoted company of a recognised stock exchange, such as FTSE, NASDAQ, DOW, NIKKEI, DAX, CAC (further research on world stock markets can be found on the Web, for instance at Financial Times: http://www.ft.com)
- large private entities, that is to say, not publicly traded companies

For example, consider the report from the UK's NAO on the BBC in June 2006, which seeks to ensure that the governance requirements of the

16

269

Finance for Purchasers

BBC are met as well as ensuring that UK taxpayers have a transparent view of the primary TV/media licensing body for all UK citizens. This is further complicated by the Charter status that is 'enjoyed' by the BBC, which is set for renewal in 2007. It is reported that the BBC's overheads have reduced from 24% to 12% since the objectives were set in 2000. The report openly recognises the contribution from major initiatives by Procurement, Technology and Finance.

This clearly demonstrated that management actions needed to be taken as well as communicated to a wide audience, stating that in simple terms what the BBC's Governors wanted was 'Value for Money', with one of the key remarks being that clearer reporting to stakeholders was necessary to achieve the results. Like many other reports it sets out definitive actions for management to take to achieve optimum results, namely:

1   Measurement and control of the overheads (in relation to service/ product provision).
2   Clearer reporting:
     (a) better communication
     (b) clear roles and responsibilities
     (c) effective delegation.
3   Ownership of the costs.
4   Challenge to the 'status quo' to ensure a true/real need for a cost to be incurred.
5   Market alignment/parity and preferably upper quartile performance.

A need for caution is required when carrying out benchmarking exercises as we have already established that a standard practice or code does not exist for allocating or quantifying and subsequent reporting of overheads. Therefore the need for detailed cost breakdowns is essential; as in all procurement exercises, 'the devil is in the detail' and this is just as true in this activity. Equally, the need to ensure that a company determines how it will record, code, allocate and process lines of expenditure is critical at the outset. Equally a common misconception that installing an 'industrial strength' standard software package will cure the problem is simply not true, as the recipient organisation needs to determine the code structure and reporting suites not the other way around!

The 'bottom line', so to speak, is that the role in part of the business head, budget holder, director or governor is to take responsibility and accountability for an organisation's costs, none more so than its overheads. It is the overheads alone that can make or break a company, as well as whether they are accurately reported and communicated. Strict rules apply to all company officers and directors of listed/quoted companies on a recognised stock exchange.

We also need to recognise that all reporting is governed by the Financial Reporting Standards (FRS) to ensure consistency and clarity in the way data interpretation is made by all organisations so that any report indices, indicators, ratios, metrics and the like can be compared against a 'benchmark' and similar organisations within the sector, whether private or public. These can be accessed by visiting the website of the audit commission for the UK (Audit Commission: http://www.audit-

16 Managing the cost base of the purchasing function

commission.gov.uk. This organisation also sets out the key criteria for carrying out audits, from system requirements to the final reporting itself.

The area of cost reporting, interpretation, measurement and guidance on reporting is usually the domain of trained and qualified management accountants (through the recognised professional body CIMA in the UK).

A procurement professional, whose primary skills/attributes should include that of an effective communicator and facilitator, should have a key role in the whole budgetary process from start to finish a role that should not be limited to just that of the procurement function itself.

Learning activity 16.3

1 Define the four key objectives of *FRS 18 – Accounting policies.*
2 State which reporting standards cover:
   - reporting financial performance
   - capital instruments
   - provisions, contingent liabilities, and contingent assets
   - earnings per share
   - tangible fixed assets.

Feedback on page 277

Now try self-assessment question 16.3 below.

Self-assessment question 16.3

Identify the key requirements of an effective performance information system.

Feedback on page 277

Revision question

There is no revision question for this session.

Summary

This study session will have provided only a limited insight into the whole process of budgeting and how costs can be controlled and communicated. As stated earlier in the study session, many large companies will have set procedures already in place. Accordingly you will need to ensure you understand these and set them in context with what you have learned in this study session. Equally, most management accountants will be only to willing to ensure you understand the way the company conducts the whole process as well as how you can proactively engage with the other business units/functions and/or the finance function.

Some of the key messages from this session are as follows:

- Overhead definition: 'Overheads are those costs such as general administration and support services, which cannot easily be associated with particular products or services. There is, however, no standard classification of the costs that make up "overheads". Although overheads tend to be seen as a "bad" cost, some level of overhead is needed to run an organisation and spending on overheads does not necessarily represent a poor use of resources.'
- It is critical that the following key constituents are in place before proceeding with a budget, cross-charging or any other such activity:
  - an agreed process/methodology for cost allocation and budgets (this could be simpler or more complex)
  - good communication between the parties
  - cost control and monitoring once activities in progress
  - clear evidence of costs incurred, especially 'expenses'
  - fully auditable process
  - being prepared to do forecasting and sensitivity analysis at all phases of a project/activity.

In forecasting, many factors will affect the timescales, especially if there is a multinational dimension to the organisation, requiring cross-country/cross-region coordination to market factors, changes in legislation, and so on.

- Forecasting will only ever be effective if good cost control is in place as well as having a clear focus on what the key drivers are, how they might impact the organisation or project and what mitigating measures can be deployed to maintain control.
- Clear reporting is a an essential to stakeholders to achieve results, with definitive actions for management to take to achieve optimum results, namely:
  - measurement and control of the overheads (in relation to service/product provision)
  - clearer reporting;
  - better communication
  - clear roles and responsibilities.
- Effective delegation:
  - ownership of the costs
  - challenge to the 'status quo' to ensure a true/real need for a cost to be incurred
  - market alignment/parity and preferably upper quartile performance.
- Recognition that all reporting is governed by the Financial Reporting Standards (FRS) to ensure consistency and clarity in the way data interpretation is made by all organisations so that any report indices, indicators, ratios, metrics and the like can be compared against a 'benchmark' and similar organisations within the sector, whether private or public.

Suggested further reading

- Audit Commission: http://www.audit-commission.gov.uk – this will be needed to respond to the self-assessment questions and learning activities.

- CIPS: http://www.cips.org Research and practice papers relevant to the subject matter – these are frequently revised and updated and need to be viewed at the time of study.
- CIMA: http://www.cimaglobal.com Research and practice papers relevant to the subject matter – these are frequently revised and updated and need to be viewed at the time of study.
- Holmes, G, A Sugden and P Gee (2004) *Interpreting Company Reports and Accounts*, 9th edition. Harlow: FT Prentice Hall.
- NAO review presented to the BBC Governors' Audit Committee, June 2006, by the Comptroller and Auditor General, and a response to the review from the BBC.

Feedback on learning activities and self-assessment questions

Feedback on learning activity 16.1

As you will recognise from this learning activity, it is critical that there are the following key constituents in place before proceeding with a budget, cross-charging or any other such activity:

- an agreed process/methodology for cost allocation and budgets (this could be simpler or more complex)
- good communication between the parties
- cost control and monitoring once activities in progress
- clear evidence of costs incurred, especially 'expenses'
- fully auditable process
- being prepared to do forecasting and sensitivity analysis at all phases of a project/activity.

As you will see from the list above, cost control will be critical in maintaining credibility with clients, stakeholders and other departments. There are a number of ways this can be done. However, the best method will always be SMART and as simple, transparent and straightforward as possible.

The new hourly rate should be £69.30 per hour, based on the following steps:

Step 1

Calculate the number of days a full or part time member of staff will work in a whole year, for example:

5 working days per week × 52 weeks = 260 days

Less public holidays: −8 days

Less annual leave: −25 days

Total working days = 227 days

Therefore there is no allocation for downtime or sickness.

Step 2

From step 1, which establishes the number of actual working days you can proceed to calculate the number of hours worked per year, based on the agreed contractual day (say 40 hours/week = 8 hours/day).

227 days × 8 hours per day = 1816 hours per year

Step 3

Divide the number of actual hours, established in step 2 by the total cost from the period actually worked and it will give you the hourly rate.

Total salary with all 'on-costs' as identified above that *actually* apply for the year which for the purposes of the question is £112,786, divided by the actual hours per year will give a rounded rate of £112,786/1,816 = £ 62.11 per hour.

Step 4

Assuming there is a general cross-charge to the department for all other departments and services from the classification of general overheads, then this can be calculated as a percentage of the overall actual salary/payroll cost for the year and defined as a percentage on cost. For the purposes of this exercise we will assume this is 4.62%.

Therefore the new hourly rate will rise to £62.11 × 104.62% = £64.98 per hour.

Step 5

The final exercise other than the allocation of actual costs is that of space/office/FM costs related to the staff member.

Step 5.1

Calculate the percentage of available space used by the department (or project). This should exclude communal space (corridors, toilers, canteens, general admin, reception space, and so on).

Department space/total space × 100 = % used.

Total weeks used/52 weeks × hours used/37.5 hours × 100 = % used.

Multiply the two usage percentages together.

Example: (460 m²/6,728m² × 100) × (44 weeks/52 weeks × 22.5 hours/40 hours × 100) = 3.26% utilisation and allocation of total cost.

Assuming this total cost was £240,565 this would be treated as follows to allow an hourly rate calculation:

£240,565 × 3.26%/1,816 hours = £4.32 per hour.

Step 6

This would give a final charge-out rate for the staff member based on the project/activity illustrated above of: £64.98 + £4.32 = £69.30 per hour + all other expenses (travel, accommodation, and so on).

Feedback on self-assessment question 16.1

The worked example should show some thought to how as to tackle the worked example in any environment as well as researching *real* costs and charges for 'on-costs' and how this is presented back with all the necessary workings and logic, not just an hourly rate!

Feedback on learning activity 16.2

The whole process of forecasting either at the company level or project level is an exacting and critical task of the purchasing professional, which should not be taken lightly, but equally represents a key opportunity for the profession to engage with the whole organisation and shape the direction of the business by its proactive thinking and innovative approach to maintaining and developing a profitable enterprise and become a true business partner and not just an overhead!

Forecasting will only ever be effective if good cost control is in place as well as having a clear focus on what the key drivers are, how they might impact the organisation or project and what mitigating measures can be deployed to maintain control.

It is also important to stress the need to ensure early communication to all parties if planned actions and/or costs are likely to alter from forecast to any material extent. Equally, collateral ownership of budgets, costs and actions will provide the highest possible probability of success than if sole ownership is assumed by any party.

In conclusion, there will always be the unforeseen, like deregulation of an industry, thereby creating an unstable market. Again, this may present the procurement professional to 'shine' by using the strong supplier relationships established to mitigate any potential adverse affects, even this defers an inevitable price increase into the next budget cycle!

Feedback on self-assessment question 16.2

I would expect to see a matrix developed that resembled table 16.1.

Table 16.1

Recipient	Content	Method	Frequency	Action/ Information
Board of Directors	Executive summary of business plan for approval, key changes from	Board meeting, 1:1 briefing	As required	Project sponsor

(continued on next page)

Finance for Purchasers

Table 16.1 *(continued)*

Recipient	Content	Method	Frequency	Action/Information
	business plan, close out			
Project sponsor	Project status, budget monitoring, timings, barriers/blockers	Team meeting, scheduled briefings	Monthly minimum	Team leader
Team leader	Project status, key decisions, key processes, strategy, KPIs	Team meetings, scheduled project meetings	Weekly or as required	Team members
Project team	Business case approval, objectives, key measures, supplier appointment	Team meetings, sub-group meetings, email	Weekly or as required	Team leader or sub-group leader or specialist
Specialists	Objectives, relevant issues and KPIs	Specific briefings, email	As required	Team leader or sub-group leader
Organisation	Project objectives, KPIs, specific issues, changes	Conference, email	As required	Project sponsor and/or team leader
External – news bulletin	Project objectives and benefits summary	Conference, press release	As required	Project sponsor and/or team leader
Suppliers	Detail issues, objectives, key measures, supplier appointment, etc	Specific briefings, email	As required	Team leader or sub group leader
Authorities	Project status, key decisions, key processes, strategy		As required	Project sponsor and/or team leader
Local contacts	Project status, key decisions, key processes, strategy		As required	Project sponsor and/or team leader

This could include the following methods of communication:

- newsletter
- video
- poster
- advertisement
- face to face
- email
- internal notice board

- conference
- presentation
- newspapers/periodicals.

Feedback on learning activity 16.3

1   The four key objectives of *FRS 18 – Accounting policies* are:
    - relevance
    - reliability
    - comparability
    - 'understandability'.
2   The reporting standards that cover the following areas are:
    - *3 – Reporting financial performance*
    - *4 – Capital instruments*
    - *12 – Provisions, contingent liabilities, and contingent assets*
    - *14 – Earnings per share*
    - *15 – Tangible fixed assets.*

Feedback on self-assessment question 16.3

This should closely mirror the findings set out in the list provided by

NAO performance information: http://www.nao.org.uk/guidance/focus/ fabric.pdf.

In summary these should be;

- focused
- appropriate
- balanced
- robust
- integrated
- cost-effective.

Finance for Purchasers

Study session 17

Investment decision making using a range of methods

Introduction

Organisations often have to consider proposals for capital investment, and may have to choose from a variety of different options. In order to make such decisions, financial information will need to be examined.

A typical capital investment will:

- produce returns over a number of years
- require considerable up-front expenditure.

The hope is that the returns will ultimately outweigh the original investment.

The decision as to whether to make a capital investment, or which one to choose if there are options, is therefore crucial to the success of a business, especially as relatively large sums of money are often involved and the assets acquired last a long time.

This session will outline the main techniques that are used to evaluate projects, and will illustrate the techniques using the same figures to highlight the relative strengths and weaknesses of the different approaches.

The decision to go ahead with any major capital expenditure involves spending a large sum of money. The more effort that goes into the evaluation of the investment, the better the chances of success. The evaluation, though, is largely based on forecasts and estimates, and is therefore highly subjective. It is not an exact science.

Session learning objectives

After completing this session you should be able to:

17.1 Describe profit-based techniques – accounting rate of return (ARR).
17.2 Apply payback-based techniques – payback period (PP).
17.3 Apply discounted cash flow (DCF) based techniques.
17.4 Apply the cost of capital to the DCF techniques.
17.5 Describe the impact of depreciation on running costs.

Unit content coverage

This study session covers the following topics from the official CIPS unit content document:

Learning objective

5.1 Evaluate the nature and importance of investment decision making for home and international markets.
- Accounting rate of return (ARR)
- Payback period (PP)
- Discounted cash flow (DCF)
- Net present value (NPV)

17

279

Finance for Purchasers

- Internal rate of return (IRR)
- Opportunity costs of capital
- The impact of depreciation on running costs

Prior knowledge

Study sessions 1 to 16.

Resources

Atrill, P (2006) *Financial Management for Decision Makers*, 4th edition, chapter 4. Harlow: FT Prentice Hall.

Timing

You should set aside about 8 hours to read and complete this session, including learning activities, self-assessment questions, the suggested further reading (if any) from the essential textbook for this unit and the revision question.

17.1 Profit-based techniques

An investment project can be evaluated using a number of different techniques, which will be described within this session. Most of these techniques are based on an analysis of the cash flows that the project is likely to trigger – in other words on the basis of cash going out and cash coming back in.

We will start, though, by looking at assessing investment projects in terms of their *accounting profit*. Accounting profit is different to cash flow, as it is based on the accruals concept and – importantly in the context of investment decisions – will involve the charging of depreciation.

The main accounting-based evaluation technique is known as ARR ('accounting rate of return'). The technique is also sometimes referred to as ROI ('return on investment').

The use of the word 'return' here is significant. The technique essentially describes how much of a profit (in other words, 'return') is to be made on the proposed investment amount. It is expressed as a percentage.

Learning activity 17.1

A company is making a significant investment in a new technology project. The company has decided to evaluate the project in the same 'return on investment' way that it reports performance within the organisation. It plans therefore to forecast what the average annual profit will be (after deducting depreciation) and then express this as a percentage of the average book value of the IT investment.

(continued on next page)

17 Investment decision making using a range of methods

Learning activity 17.1 *(continued)*

What do you consider would be the potential drawbacks of using the above profit-based approach to make an investment decision?

Feedback on page 295

We will now look at some basic figures. Let us suppose that a company is considering investing £200,000. It has two choices, project A and project B. The projects are both expected to last for five years, after which time no further costs or revenues are expected. The fixed assets will be depreciated on a straight-line basis, with no residual values.

The projected annual profits (*after* deducting depreciation) for the two investments are as shown in table 17.1.

Table 17.1

Year	Project A (forecast profit)	Project B (forecast profit)
1	56,000	(20,000)
2	44,000	(10,000)
3	20,000	60,000
4	20,000	60,000
5	0	100,000

The two projects have very different profiles. Project A's profits are weighted towards the earlier years, whereas with project B most of the benefit is expected to be derived in the later years.

To work out the average return on investment (ROI), or the accounting rate of return (ARR) we need to do two things. First, we need to work out the average profit over the period. Second, we need to express this as a percentage of the average investment amount.

The average profit will be:

Project A = 56,000 + 44,000 + 20,000 + 20,000 + 0 = 140,000/5 = £28,000

Project B = -20,000 − 10,000 + 60,000 + 60,000 + 100,000 = 190,000/5 = £38,000

The average investment will be based on the book value of the investment at the beginning of the project and at the end of each subsequent year. It will be the same for both projects in this example (see table 17.2).

Table 17.2

	£
Opening value	200,000
At end of year 1 (cost minus depreciation to date) = 200,000 − 40,000 =	160,000
At end of year 2 (cost minus depreciation to date) = 200,000 − 80,000 =	120,000
At end of year 3 (cost minus depreciation to date) = 200,000 − 120,000 =	80,000
At end of year 4 (cost minus depreciation to date) = 200,000 − 160,000 =	40,000
At end of year 5 (cost minus depreciation to date) = 200,000 − 200,000 =	Nil

Finance for Purchasers

So the average book value will be:

200,000 + 160,000 + 120,000 + 80,000 + 40,000 + nil = 600,000/6 = £100,000

(NB an easier way of calculating the above would be to take the average of the opening and closing values, so £200,000 + nil = £200,000/2 = £100,000.)

The ARR (accounting rate of return) on the respective projects will therefore be:

- Project A: 44,000/100,000 = 44%
- Project B: 38,000/100,000 = 38%

Project A thus has a higher, and therefore better, accounting rate of return.

Self-assessment question 17.1

Note that the data for this exercise will be carried forward into the remaining exercises in this session.

Company X is considering the national launch of a new corn chip product – 'Sombreros' – tortilla chips with a rounder shape. They are to be sold initially in larger individual-sized 45g bags. Sombreros are potentially important to the development of Company X's product range, as it has so far not been involved in the fast-growing tortilla part of the food snack market.

Prior to the commitment of major funds to the project, the product has been tested regionally with encouraging results. The net cost of the trial has been calculated at £185,000.

A national launch will require:

- additional new manufacturing equipment costing £900,000
- upgraded existing production facilities costing £300,000.

Both these would be paid for at the outset and would be depreciated in the accounts over a five-year period (straight-line) with a residual value of £200,000.

Forecast cash flows from the project over the next five years are as shown in table 17.3.

Table 17.3

Year	Unit sales
1	6,000,000
2	8,000,000
3	8,000,000
4	9,000,000
5	9,000,000

- The net sales price to retailers in the first year will be 20p per bag (in other words, after any discounts or incentives to get the products on the shelves). Thereafter, the net sales price is expected to be 25p per bag.

(continued on next page)

Self-assessment question 17.1 *(continued)*

- The direct costs of producing one bag are 15p.
- Distribution costs will be 6% of net sales (based on the 25p/bag price).
- A further £100,000 incremental costs will be incurred each year (that is, additional running costs specific to this product launch)
- Advertising spend will be £250,000 in each of the first two years, £100,000 in each subsequent year.
- Assume no substitution of other *existing* Company X.

Ignoring taxation:

1. Work out the forecast annual profit for this project (by completing the table below).
2. Work out the accounting rate of return.

Table 17.4

	Year 1	Year 2	Year 3	Year 4	Year 5
Unit sales					
Price					
Sales revenue					
Direct costs					
Depreciation					
Distribution					
Advertising					
Other costs					
Profit					

Average value of investment = (opening value + closing value)/2 =

Feedback on page 296

17.2 Payback period (PP)

An alternative approach to evaluating investments is to consider how quickly the investment amount will be recouped.

The technique is known as the 'payback' method, and is essentially a very simple approach.

The calculation involves forecasting how quickly the original investment amount will be repaid – in other words, at what point in time will the project break even?

A very important aspect of this and all the other remaining techniques is that we need to use cash flow figures rather than profit figures.

The most significant factor that this highlights is that depreciation is not a cash flow. In order to convert the profit forecasts into cash flows we need therefore to add back the depreciation amounts.

Returning to the example used earlier in this session, we had used the *profit* forecasts shown in table 17.6.

Finance for Purchasers

Table 17.6

Year	Project A (forecast profit)	Project B (forecast profit)
	£	£
1	56,000	(20,000)
2	44,000	(10,000)
3	20,000	60,000
4	20,000	60,000
5	0	100,000

We also know that the annual depreciation in both cases was £40,000, based on the investment amount of £200,000 spread over five years.

Our cash flow forecast for the two projects, including the initial investment amount to be made at the outset (Year 0), would be as shown in table 17.7.

Table 17.7

Year	Project A (forecast cash flow)	Project B (forecast cash flow)
	£	£
0	(200,000)	(200,000)
1	96,000	20,000
2	84,000	30,000
3	60,000	100,000
4	60,000	100,000
5	40,000	140,000

We can now work out the respective payback periods of the two projects.

For project A, we get back £96,000 in the first year, and a further £84,000 in the second. That totals £180,000, so we need another £20,000. If we assume the cash flows arrive on a steady basis, the project should have paid back a third of the way through Year 3. So we can describe the payback period as 2.33 years.

Applying the same logic, we can calculate the payback period for project B to be 3.5 years.

Thus, project A has a quicker payback period than project B.

Learning activity 17.2

We have just looked at 'payback period' as a basis for evaluating investment decisions.

1 Try to identify some flaws in 'payback period' as a robust method of evaluating investments.
2 Thinking of 'real world' situations, can you identify circumstances in which 'payback period' would have a genuinely useful part to play in investment decisions?

Feedback on page 296

As highlighted by the above learning activity, the payback method has some advantages and some disadvantages. They can be summarised as follows:

Advantages

- The technique is relatively simple, and therefore popular.
- There are circumstances where quick payback is essential – for example, IT projects need to make a quicker than average return, as the assets themselves become quickly obsolete. Quick payback may also be especially desirable for higher risk investments.
- It can be an important consideration in an environment where short-term returns are demanded. UK investors and analysts have often been criticised for being too 'short-termist', but if there is a need to meet their expectations, the 'payback period' is a useful measure.
- As with all other techniques, it looks at an investment from a particular standpoint. Used in conjunction with other techniques, it helps provide a balanced view.

Disadvantages

- Its simplicity and popularity suggest, probably correctly, that it is not a very sophisticated technique.
- It pays less attention to cash flows received after the payback point.
- It ignores the time value of money.
- Determining an acceptable payback period may be fairly arbitrary.

Self-assessment question 17.2

Convert the Sombreros profit data to cash flows, by completing table 17.8.

Table 17.8

	Year 1	Year 2	Year 3	Year 4	Year 5
Profit	−340	130	280	365	365
Depreciation					
Cash flow					

What is the payback period for the Sombreros project?

Feedback on page 296

17.3 Discounted cash flow (DCF) techniques

As highlighted in section 17.2, one of the limitations of using the basic payback method was that it did not consider what happened after the payback point. Another weakness was that it did not take account of the 'time value of money'. We will therefore now have a look at an approach that addresses these issues.

First, we should consider in general terms the idea that money has a 'time value' What this means is that the earlier money is received (or paid out), the more value it has. If you were asked whether you would rather have

Finance for Purchasers

£10,000 today, or in a year's time, you are likely to choose the 'today' option.

There may be a number of reasons for this – but the main financial one is that you would have the opportunity of earning a return on your money such that, in a year's time, you had more than £10,000. Putting taxation and inflation to one side for the moment, you might earn 5% interest so that in one year you had turned your £10,000 into £10,500.

Thus it can be seen that the earlier cash is received, the more value it has in today's terms. £10,000 received today has a different value to £10,000 received in a year's time. In fact, the value of £10,000 received in a year's time might only be something like £9524 today. That is the amount that, if placed on deposit at 5% for a year, would have grown to £10,000 12 months later.

A key investment appraisal technique that applies the concept of the time value of money is 'net present value' (NPV). This technique involves restating the projected cash flows at their value *in today's terms*. It does this by what is known as *discounting* the cash flows.

If we return to our two projects, A and B, we can apply the NPV technique.

First we need a discount rate, and we will use 10% for illustrative purposes (and what the rate should be and where it comes from will be discussed later).

We can then use this 10% rate to discount the cash flows to their value today. This will involve multiplying the cash flows by what is known as the *discount factor*. If the money is received today, the discount factor will be 1 – because it is today. If it is to be received in a year's time, the discount factor will be: $1/1.1 = 0.909$.

So, receiving £1000 in a year's time is the equivalent of having £1000 × 0.909 = £909 now, assuming 10% is an appropriate rate.

Money to be received (or paid out) in two years' time will be multiplied by: $1/1.1^2 = 0.826$.

And so on. A table of discount factors is set out in table 17.10.

Table 17.10 Discount factors

	5%	6%	7%	8%	9%	10%	11%	12%
Year 1	0.9524	0.9434	0.9346	0.9259	0.9174	0.9091	0.9009	0.8929
2	0.9070	0.8900	0.8734	0.8573	0.8417	0.8264	0.8116	0.7972
3	0.8638	0.8396	0.8163	0.7938	0.7722	0.7513	0.7312	0.7118
4	0.8227	0.7921	0.7629	0.7350	0.7084	0.6830	0.6587	0.6355
5	0.7835	0.7473	0.7130	0.6806	0.6499	0.6209	0.5935	0.5674
6	0.7462	0.7050	0.6663	0.6302	0.5963	0.5645	0.5346	0.5066
7	0.7107	0.6651	0.6227	0.5835	0.5470	0.5132	0.4817	0.4523
8	0.6768	0.6274	0.5820	0.5403	0.5019	0.4665	0.4339	0.4039
9	0.6446	0.5919	0.5439	0.5002	0.4604	0.4241	0.3909	0.3606
10	0.6139	0.5584	0.5083	0.4632	0.4224	0.3855	0.3522	0.3220
	13%	14%	15%	16%	17%	18%	18%	20%
Year 1	0.8850	0.8772	0.8696	0.8621	0.8547	0.8475	0.8475	0.8333

(continued on next page)

Table 17.10 *(continued)*

	14%	15%	16%	17%	18%	19%	19%	20%
2	0.7831	0.7695	0.7561	0.7432	0.7305	0.7182	0.7182	0.6944
3	0.6931	0.6750	0.6575	0.6407	0.6244	0.6086	0.6086	0.5787
4	0.6133	0.5921	0.5718	0.5523	0.5337	0.5158	0.5158	0.4823
5	0.5428	0.5194	0.4972	0.4761	0.4561	0.4371	0.4371	0.4019
6	0.4803	0.4556	0.4323	0.4104	0.3898	0.3704	0.3704	0.3349
7	0.4251	0.3996	0.3759	0.3538	0.3332	0.3139	0.3139	0.2791
8	0.3762	0.3506	0.3269	0.3050	0.2848	0.2660	0.2660	0.2326
9	0.3329	0.3075	0.2843	0.2630	0.2434	0.2255	0.2255	0.1938
10	0.2946	0.2697	0.2472	0.2267	0.2080	0.1911	0.1911	0.1615

	21%	22%	23%	24%	25%	26%	27%	28%
Year 1	0.8264	0.8197	0.8130	0.8065	0.8000	0.7937	0.7874	0.7813
2	0.6830	0.6719	0.6610	0.6504	0.6400	0.6299	0.6200	0.6104
3	0.5645	0.5507	0.5374	0.5245	0.5120	0.4999	0.4882	0.4768
4	0.4665	0.4514	0.4369	0.4230	0.4096	0.3968	0.3844	0.3725
5	0.3855	0.3700	0.3552	0.3411	0.3277	0.3149	0.3027	0.2910
6	0.3186	0.3033	0.2888	0.2751	0.2621	0.2499	0.2383	0.2274
7	0.2633	0.2486	0.2348	0.2218	0.2097	0.1983	0.1877	0.1776
8	0.2176	0.2038	0.1909	0.1789	0.1678	0.1574	0.1478	0.1388
9	0.1799	0.1670	0.1552	0.1443	0.1342	0.1249	0.1164	0.1084
10	0.1486	0.1369	0.1262	0.1164	0.1074	0.0992	0.0916	0.0847

The net present value (NPV) of an investment is the total of all the discounted cash flows, including the original investment, expressed as a cash amount. A positive NPV means that the project should be undertaken. When comparing projects, the one with the highest NPV should be selected. So for projects A and B the figures are as shown in table 17.11.

Table 17.11

Year	Project A	Discount factor	Discounted cash flow	Project B	Discount factor	Discounted cash flow
	£	10%		£	10%	
0	(200,000)	1.0000	(200,000)	(200,000)	1.0000	(200,000)
1	96,000	0.9091	87,274	20,000	0.9091	18,182
2	84,000	0.8264	69,418	30,000	0.8264	24,792
3	60,000	0.7513	45,078	100,000	0.7513	75,130
4	60,000	0.6830	40,980	100,000	0.6830	68,300
5	40,000	0.6209	24,836	140,000	0.6209	86,926
		NPV =	67,586		NPV =	73,330

Having applied an appropriate discount rate to the two projects and converted the cash flows to their value today, we add up the cash flows for each project (including the initial investment amount) to arrive at the net present value – which is expressed as a cash amount. Project A's NPV is £67,586 and project B's is £73,330. What does this tell us?

It tells us that:

- Both projects have *positive* NPVs. This means that the discounted value of the projected cashflows is net positive. In other words, assuming the forecasts are correct, the investment will benefit the organisation financially. Both projects are attractive.
- Project B is more attractive than project A. It has a higher NPV, so investment in this project will be financially more beneficial (again, this assumes the forecasts are correct).

NPV is generally considered a superior technique to the other two so far considered. This is because:

- NPV takes account of the time value of money
- NPV takes account of all the cash flows of a project
- NPV is expressed as an amount of money, which represents the value of the project and the extent to which it will increase the wealth of the shareholders in the investing company.

It is, however, very dependent on the following important factors:

- As with all these techniques, it is only as good as the data being evaluated. If the forecasts are flawed, the NPV will not be meaningful.
- It is also dependent on the discount rate being appropriate. This is an important aspect of NPV, which we shall look at later in this session.

Learning activity 17.3

A number of surveys have been conducted, both in the UK and internationally, to determine the extent to which companies use the various techniques described so far.

Results increasingly suggest that discounted cash flow (DCF) techniques are used more than both payback and, especially, ARR.

Summarise the reasons why this might be.

Feedback on page 297

As far as DCF techniques are concerned, we have so far looked at NPV. An alternative technique is the 'internal rate of return' (IRR).

IRR represents the discount rate that would have to be used to arrive at an NPV of zero. It is expressed, therefore, in percentage terms.

It is probably best illustrated using projects A and B again. In the first instance, we shall just look at project A. We arrived at an NPV of £67,586, having applied a discount rate of 10% as shown in table 17.12.

Table 17.12

Year	Project A	Discount factor	Discounted cash flow
	£	10%	
0	(200,000)	1.0000	(200,000)
1	96,000	0.9091	87,274
2	84,000	0.8264	69,418
3	60,000	0.7513	45,078
4	60,000	0.6830	40,980
5	40,000	0.6209	24,836
		NPV =	67,586

The question now concerns the discount rate we would need to us for that £67,586 to be reduced to zero.

There is no magic formula for working this out, and it can only be done through a process of iteration. In practice, a spreadsheet package can quickly work out the figure, but here we should briefly consider how it is done.

If 10% gives us a positive NPV, the IRR will need to be more than 10%. We need first to make a sensible guess as to what the figure might be, and identify a rate that is likely to produce a negative result.

If we try 28%, the figures would look like those in table 17.13.

Table 17.13

Year	Project A	Discount factor	Discounted cash flow
	£	28%	
0	(200,000)	1.0000	(200,000)
1	96,000	0.7812	74,995
2	84,000	0.6104	51,274
3	60,000	0.4768	28,608
4	60,000	0.3725	22,350
5	40,000	0.2910	11,640
		NPV =	(11,133)

We have a negative NPV £11,133.

This means that the IRR is somewhere between 10% and 28%. The iteration process requires the following calculation:

- Using 10% we get a positive NPV of £67,586
- Using 28% we get a negative NPV of £11,133
- The difference between the two rates is 18%
- The sum of the two NPVs (ignore negatives) is £78,719
- The IRR is 10 + (18 × (67,586/78,719)) = 25.46%.

If we applied the same approach to project B, we would arrive at an IRR of around 20%.

These are approximate results, as the figure will be influenced by the rates that are guessed at in this way. In reality, spreadsheet models are used and a more accurate result can thus be obtained.

The key issues, though, concern what the measure means and how it is applied.

An IRR of 25%, as in this example, would be compared with a minimum rate that projects should achieve. This is often referred to in organisations as the 'hurdle rate', and only projects that exceed this rate will be acceptable. The hurdle rate itself is likely to be linked to what is known as the company's 'cost of capital' – how much it costs the company to have access to the money it is using to invest.

Put simply, if the company's cost of capital is 10%, and the IRR of a project is 25%, it potentially looks an attractive proposition. IRR can,

Finance for Purchasers

though, be used to compare projects with each other – so if alternatives are showing 30% and 45%, then 25% will look less attractive.

The above point introduces the idea of project ranking, and how organisations choose from a range of projects, especially when financial resources are limited. IRR is often used, but an alternative approach is to express the NPV as a percentage of the initial investment. This is sometimes known as the profitability index or profitability ratio. For projects A and B the measure would be as shown in table 17.14.

Table 17.14

	Project A	Project B
Investment £	200,000	200,000
NPV	67,586	73,330
Profitability ratio	33.8%	36.7%

These figures become more meaningful where different investment amounts are being proposed for different projects.

Self-assessment question 17.3

Using a rate of 9%, complete table 17.15 by inserting appropriate discount factors, and calculating the discounted cash flows.

Table 17.15

	Year 0	Year 1	Year 2	Year 3	Year 4	Year 5
Cash flow	−1200	−140	330	480	565	565
Discount factor						
Discounted cash flow						

1. What is the NPV of the project?
2. What is the discounted payback period?
3. What is the project's profitability ratio?
4. In which bracket do you think the IRR falls?
   - 0–5%
   - 5–10%
   - 10–15%
   - 15–20%

Feedback on page 297

17.4 The cost of capital and other issues

Cost of capital

The earlier part of this session has made reference to discount rates and the 'cost of capital', without looking too deeply about what these terms mean and how appropriate figures might be arrived at.

17 Investment decision making using a range of methods

Clearly, though, the discount rate used in DCF calculations is an important part of the overall evaluation. Different discount rates will produce different NPV results, and perhaps different investment decisions.

The discount rate that should be used is heavily influenced by how much it costs an organisation to raise money for investment purposes.

As discussed elsewhere in this course, companies raise capital from two main sources – shareholders and lenders. The capital from these two sources is known, respectively, as equity and debt. Existing cash resources might also be used, of course, in which case the cost is the interest that would otherwise have been earned on the money – the 'opportunity cost'.

Both equity and debt have a cost. There are a number of different models that are used to calculate the cost of equity capital – some use dividends as the basis, others are more concerned with an overall risk and return calculation – what sort of return are shareholders expecting, to compensate them for the risk of investing in that company?

The cost of debt is normally more straightforward, being based on the interest rate that is being paid.

The different types of capital give rise to the need for an overall cost of capital to be calculated. This is known as the weighted average cost of capital (WACC). It looks at the different types of capital that exist in a company, their relative size and their individual cost. A simple calculation might involve something like table 17.17.

Table 17.17

Type of capital	Value (£ million)	Proportion of total	Cost %	Contribution to WACC
Ordinary share capital	12	12/30 = 40%	11	11 × 0.4 = 4.4%
Preference share capital	3	3/30 = 10%	9	9 × 0.1 = 0.9%
Loan capital	15	15/30 = 50%	7.5	7.5 × 0.5 = 3.75%
Total	30	100%		WACC = 9.05%

For the above company, then, the 9.05% figure would underpin any discount rate that would be used to evaluate projects. There may well be other factors to additionally consider, including the possible need for some margin of safety to be added, as well as a possible risk premium for particular types of investment.

Learning activity 17.4

At your own place of work, try to establish:

- what cost of capital is applied to investment projects and
- how the figure is arrived at
- how the figure is used in evaluating projects.

Feedback on page 298

Taxation

The techniques described thus far have made no mention of taxation. Tax, however, has in practice a major role to play in the evaluation of investment projects. It will impact in the following ways:

- Capital investments will often attract capital allowances. These allow a business to offset the cost of an investment against its overall tax bill. The cash benefit of these allowances will be built into the project cash flow forecasts.
- Any profits that an investment generates are likely to be taxable. The cash outflows of these should also be built into the overall cash forecasts before being discounted.
- Interest is a tax-deductible expense. When building the cost of debt into the WACC model illustrated above, it should be an after-tax cost. For example, if the nominal interest rate on a loan is 9%, and the corporation tax rate is 30%, the true cost of the loan is $9 - (9 \times 0.3) = 6.3\%$

Inflation

A common misunderstanding is that DCF techniques in themselves deal with the issue of inflation. They don't, and inflation has to be dealt with as an additional step.

A key part of this is to appreciate that the prevailing interest rate at any time is normally quoted in 'nominal' terms. If that rate is 5%, and inflation is running at 2%, then the 'real' rate is: $1.05/1.02 = 1.03 = 3\%$

When applying investment evaluation techniques it is important to be consistent. A company needs to do one of the following when working out measures such as NPV:

- Don't build inflation into the cash flow forecasts, and use a 'real' discount rate.
- Build inflation into the cash flow forecasts, and use a 'nominal' discount rate.

If we go back to project A, the NPV data was as shown in table 17.18.

Table 17.18

Year	Project A	Discount factor	Discounted cash flow
	£	10%	
0	(200,000)	1.0000	(200,000)
1	96,000	0.9091	87,274
2	84,000	0.8264	69,418
3	60,000	0.7513	45,078
4	60,000	0.6830	40,980
5	40,000	0.6209	24,836
		NPV =	67,586

Let us assume these figures have used a real rate, and have no inflation built into them. Assume inflation is running at 5% per annum. The nominal rate to be used would therefore be:

1.1 × 1.05 = 1.155 = 15.5%

If we also build in to the cash flows 5% annual inflation, the NPV calculation would look like table 17.19.

Table 17.19

Year	Project A	Discount factor	Discounted cash flow
	£	15.5%	
0	(200,000)	1.0000	(200,000)
1	100,800	0.8568	87,273
2	92,610	0.7496	69,421
3	69,458	0.6490	45,079
4	72,930	0.5619	40,981
5	51,051	0.4865	24,837
		NPV =	67,591

The result is, barring rounding differences, identical.

Risk

Risk as a topic will be looked at in two later sessions. However, it is worth considering the topic of risk in the context of investment appraisal specifically. Investment projects will always have elements of risk. The question is how to address the risks, and there are four main options as shown in figure 17.1.

Figure 17.1

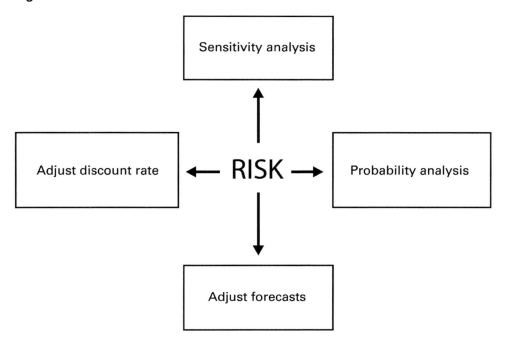

Sensitivity analysis involves doing a number of 'what-if?' type calculations. For example, how sensitive is the NPV to changes in the price of a new product to be launched? How sensitive is it to the life of the project? How sensitive to the initial investment amount? How sensitive to the discount rate itself?

Finance for Purchasers

Adjusting the discount rate involves building some risk premium into the discount rate being used. For example, an investment project in a politically unstable part of the world might apply a higher rate than a home based investment.

Probability analysis involves, for example, working out the NPV for more than one possible outcome and then applying a probability to that outcome. A weighted average 'expected NPV' can then be calculated along the lines of table 17.20.

Table 17.20

Outcome	Pessimistic	Neutral	Optimistic
NPV (£)	(2 million)	1 million	2.5 million
Probability	20%	70%	10%
NPV weighting	(400,000)	700,000	250,000

The 'expected' NPV of the above project would be:

$-400 + 700 + 250 = £550,000$

Adjusting forecasts involves taking a less optimistic view with elements of the cash flow for which risks exist — for example underestimating revenues, or taking a pessimistic view of more risky elements of cost, and then evaluating the figures.

Other issues

Another issue that can hamper accurate financial evaluation of projects concerns the ability to make accurate forecasts. As has been seen, the techniques used are applied to cash flow forecasts of the costs and benefits of investing in a project. Getting these forecasts right can be problematic.

A good example of this concerns an area of very significant investment — IT projects. While the costs of the initial investment might be relatively straightforward to predict, the financial value of the benefits can be less clear-cut.

New IT investment may speed up processes, may provide better and more reliable information, may help to attract staff, and may mean that the company doesn't get left behind in the way it does things. Putting a financial value on all these very real benefits is far from easy.

Self-assessment question 17.4

The following questions apply to the whole of this session:

1 The accounting rate of return (ARR) method uses the concept of 'profit' and is therefore a more objective approach than NPV and IRR. True/false?
2 Using discounted cash flow techniques is all about dealing with inflation, and the purchasing power of money. True/false?

(continued on next page)

Self-assessment question 17.4 (continued)

3 Rising interest rates make investment projects less likely to go ahead. True/false?

4 Although there are a number of different techniques, companies have to choose a preferred method which they will use to make a final decision. True/false?

Feedback on page 298

17.5 The impact of depreciation on running costs

The impact of depreciation is covered in section 4.1 in study session 4.

Revision question

Now try the revision question for this session on page 347.

Summary

In this session we have looked at a range of different tools that are used to appraise investment projects. They included the profit based accounting rate of return, the payback method and two techniques that involved discounting cash flows – the net present value and the internal rate of return.

We also looked at a number of issues that affect the application of these techniques – including risk factors, inflation and taxation.

All the techniques are in common usage, and many companies will apply all the techniques as part of their decision making process, which will also include non-financial criteria.

Suggested further reading

Atrill, P (2005) *Financial Management for Decision Makers*, 4th edition, chapters 4, 5 and 8. Harlow: FT Prentice Hall,.

Feedback on learning activities and self-assessment questions

Feedback on learning activity 17.1

The major problem with accounting/profit-based measures is that they are based on concepts that are often influenced by subjective and potentially arbitrary policies – for example the selection of depreciation policy. The depreciation applied to the investment will have a significant impact on the forecast annual profit of the project, and on the book value of the asset. An investment could be made to look more attractive simply by adopting a more advantageous depreciation approach.

In addition, book values and accounting profit do not reflect what is known as the *time value of money* – the earlier money is received, the more value

Finance for Purchasers

it has. For this reason, various adjustments need to be made if meaningful results are to be achieved, and we will be exploring these later in this session.

Feedback on self-assessment question 17.1

Table 17.5

	Year 1	Year 2	Year 3	Year 4	Year 5
Unit sales	6000	8000	8000	9000	9000
Price	20p	25p	25p	25p	25p
	£000	£000	£000	£000	£000
Sales revenue	1200	2000	2000	2250	2250
Direct costs	−900	−1200	−1200	−1350	−1350
Depreciation	−200	−200	−200	−200	−200
Distribution	−90	−120	−120	−135	−135
Advertising	−250	−250	−100	−100	−100
Other costs	−100	−100	−100	−100	−100
Profit	−340	130	280	365	365

Average profit = −340 + 130 + 280 + 365 + 365 = 800/5 = £160,000

Average value of investment = £1.2 million + £0.2 million = £1.4 million/2 = £700,000

Accounting rate of return = 160/700 = 22.9%

Feedback on learning activity 17.2

Payback has a number of flaws, some of which are addressed by the other approaches illustrated in this session.

A major weakness is that it does not consider anything that happens after the payback point. Evaluating a project on the basis of how long it takes to recover its costs misses out on a potentially vital ingredient – how much money will it make for us?

Another significant flaw is that it tends to lead to short-term decisions. If investment decisions were based solely on how quickly they paid for themselves, it might tend to discourage longer-term thinking.

A third weakness is the fact that the payback method, as described so far, ignores a very important finance concept – the 'time value of money'. This brings into play the idea that the earlier money is received, or paid out, the higher its value. Alternative techniques bring this vital factor into play.

Feedback on self-assessment question 17.2

Table 17.9

	Year 1	Year 2	Year 3	Year 4	Year 5
Profit	−340	130	280	365	365
Depreciation	200	200	200	200	200
Cash flow	−140	330	480	565	565

The initial investment is £1.2 million.

After 1 year the project has recouped −140,000

After 2 years the project has recouped −140,000 + 330,000 = 190,000

After 3 years the project has recouped −140,000 + 330,000 + 480,000 = 670,000

After 4 years the project has recouped −140,000 + 330,000 + 480,000 + 565,000 = 1235,000

So the payback point is towards the end of Year 4. At the beginning of Year 4 we were £530,000 short of payback. £565,000 is forecast to be received in Year 4, so the precise payback period is 4.94 years.

Given that this is an investment in a new consumer product, a shorter payback period than 4.94 years would probably be sought. With faster-moving products, and where consumer tastes can quickly change, a much quicker payback period – perhaps under three years – would be more appropriate.

Feedback on learning activity 17.3

Data on the frequency of use can be found in Chapter 4 of Atrill (2006).

NPV and IRR are more sophisticated techniques because they build into play the concept of the time value of money, They also address the key issue of whether the return from a project will be greater than the cost of capital being used for the project. Thus they are more commonly used, especially by larger organisations who are more likely to have the resources available to utilise such techniques.

ARR is the least commonly used. It is a very useful measure when reporting performance, but as a decision-making tool it lacks the robustness of DCF techniques.

Feedback on self-assessment question 17.3

Table 17.16

	Year 0	Year 1	Year 2	Year 3	Year 4	Year 5
Cash flow £K	−1200	−140	330	480	565	565
Discount factor	1	0.9174	0.8417	0.7722	0.7084	0.6499
DCF £K	−1200	−128.44	277.76	370.66	400.25	367.19

1 £87,400
2 4.76 years
3 £87.4/1200 = 7.3%
4 We have a positive NPV using a discount rate of 9%, so the IRR is going to be higher than this figure.
   If we applied a discount rate of 15%, we would get a *negative* NPV of £152,700.

So, using the iteration process, we can establish an approximate IRR of:
$9 + [6 \times (87.4/240.1)] = 11.2\%$

Feedback on learning activity 17.4

Most larger organisations will devote resources to working out and monitoring the cost of capital. The most complex aspect tends to be assessing the cost of equity capital – different models may be used, but they are quite theoretical and in practice some fairly broad assumptions may be made about the cost of equity.

Once the cost of capital has been identified, seeing how it is applied will also be interesting. Is this the figure used to evaluate projects, or are other elements – for example to address risk – built in too? Is the same figure used as the 'hurdle rate' for IRR evaluations?

Feedback on self-assessment question 17.4

1   False. The opposite is true, since profit is a highly subjective concept. This makes the ARR a less useful technique in practice.
2   False. The process of discounting deals with the fact that money has a time value and that a real return can be earned on cash which makes its early receipt financially valuable. This would apply even in periods of very low or even non-existent inflation.
3   True. Rising interest rates will increase companies' cost of capital. The higher the discount rate used, the less likely the project is to be viable.
4   False. Many companies apply all the techniques, and come up with a decision which may be based on other factors entirely. Investment appraisal techniques should be seen as aids to decision making, not decision makers in themselves.

Study session 18
Functions of an organisation – reduction and control of costs

Introduction

In previous sessions we have considered the various technical and inter-related activities of the purchasing function and the finance function in particular. Now we must turn our attention to the whole organisation and all the different levels, objectives, drivers and obstacles that we must both understand and specifically influence if we are to be successful at what we do as purchasing professionals.

Also it is equally appropriate that we consider the well-known phrase: 'If you are not adding value then you are just an overhead burden' – and we all know what happens to them!

So you don't know who does what, where and when! Make it your business, as you need to know.

Session learning objectives

After completing this session you should be able to:

18.1 Describe the functions of an organisation, and how they inter-relate.
18.2 Describe the importance of cross-functional working.
18.3 Highlight key aspects of good planning as a means of setting targets and controlling resources.
18.4 Demonstrate how project management tools and techniques can be used to reduce and control costs in procurement.

Unit content coverage

This study session covers the following topics from the official CIPS unit content document:

Learning objective

5.4 Evaluate the roles of the funcions of an organisation in the reduction and control of costs.
- Design and engineering
- Purchasing
- Marketing
- Distribution
- Finance

Prior knowledge

Study sessions 1 to 17, especially study sessions 15 and 16.

Finance for Purchasers

Resources

Obtain a number of organisation charts/diagrams (job titles/descriptions only) both from your own organisation and that of a number of well-respected blue chip organisations, and a copy of the companies' overhead breakdown or those of another organisation that will give you access/permission to use them for comparison/research purposes. You may also obtain a publicly available example for reference.

Timing

You should set aside about 4 hours to read and complete this session, including learning activities, self-assessment questions, the suggested further reading (if any) from the essential textbook for this unit and the revision question.

18.1 Understanding the key functions of an organisation and how they relate to purchasing

At the end of this section you should be able to answer for yourself the following questions about your own organisation:

- Who are the decision makers?
- Who are the budget holders?
- What are the principal functions of the organisation and how do they interact, overlap, engage, and so on?
- What are the primary objectives and targets of each primary job role and department/function?
- Who are the 'promoters' and who are the 'blockers' for change, procurement, and so on?
- In respect of overheads: the where, what, how, when, who questions (to understand where the priorities might lie).

Having done this you should now be in a position to overlay what you and the procurement function are trying to achieve for the greater good of the company and from this develop a 'road map' of how you can plan to achieve the set targets and objectives for the company.

In order to do this we should apply the same analytical tools that are applied to any category of spend by adopting a matrix weighting and scoring approach set against your own targets and objectives. For instance, if you are the category manager for capital expenditure in your organisation then this might typical involve the areas of:

- fleet
- plant and equipment
- IT
- buildings.

Next we will need to decide what your targets and objectives are relative to these areas and, again, what importance or weighting they carry in relation to the overall objective. This should be broken down into parts/percentage of 100(%). This exercise will involve you identifying what is important to the business (these will be prioritised with the companies objectives and plan) and will therefore mean that you should follow the lead already set by the board. Equally, providing the right weighting to individual tasks will mean that the higher the weighting, the more likely it is that they rank at the top of the list and become a natural priority for you and your team(s) to focus upon.

From your own organisation you will begin to determine who the ultimate budget holders and decision makers are and where the company currently commits its expenditure to in terms of the supply base. From all these factors you should then be able to determine a 'picture' of where the priorities and opportunities lie within your own company or a case study organisation. Generally this will enable you to construct a series of clear targets and subsequent action plan as to what 'targets' and areas of the business need the most focus and will deliver the maximum results for both you and the organisation. Some organisations take the formal approach of category management to define these into:

1 cost/price-sensitive
2 speed and consistency of delivery of goods and/or services
3 the quality of the product/service – delivered at a declared and consistent level
4 the level of customer service offered by the provider
5 whether all the legal and standards requirements are met in full
6 whether the supplier/service provider can deliver R&D that will benefit the organisation.

From this base data-gathering exercise you will also be building the foundation blocks for the Communications and Business Case elements we tackled earlier in study session 14.

Remember, you can evaluate the various elements in terms of a score, or by ranking or weighting:

- High/Medium/Low
- 1–10 or 1–5
- percentage
- 0, 5 or 10 (Kypner Trigo technique – which is designed to drive results apart by awarding only three extreme scores as shown)

The company objectives will generally be quite broad and will speak in terms of:

- better margins on existing business
- further expansion of existing activities in a certain location(s)
- diversification within a market sector(s)
- acquisition
- exports
- international growth
- new product development
- re-investing profits
- shareholder returns maximised

Finance for Purchasers

- specific focus on:
  - CSR
  - environment
  - ethical trading
  - new technology.

You should understand what these mean in terms of specific actions as this is what the executive directors (the Board) and senior managers will be measured upon. More critical for the purchasing function is how they need to align themselves and their objectives in order to be supportive and successful in what they do and achieve as a whole. As part of any data-gathering exercise the purchasing professional should obtain the following:

- mission statement
- corporate strategy
- business unit strategy
- IT policy
- technical standards
- CSR policy
- environmental policy
- product and marketing plans
- NPD plans
- sales plans/campaigns
- operating plans.

Learning activity 18.1

Assess the three objectives defined below for your own or another published organisation and construct a matrix model with weightings, scorings or rankings to highlight the area of focus that will deliver the maximum benefit from working across an organisation, with four or five action points for addressing each of the key objectives:

- better margins on existing business
- new product development
- specific focus on ethical trading.

From this the purchasing head will be expected to develop a strategy and set of objectives and action plans that support the board/company and will be directly allied to the themes and their importance within the organisation.

This will typically result in planned set of objectives being drawn up, together with a view on what stakeholders need to be influenced, how many suppliers are involved, how much spend will be impacted and the risks and issues associated with delivering these objectives for the purchasing function.

A typical set of plan headings might look something like that shown in table 18.1.

Table 18.1

Purchasing objective	Purchasing target	Number of stakeholders	Current spend	Number of suppliers	Board support for	Risk	H&S issue	New product development (NPD)	Technology

(continued on next page)

18 Functions of an organisation – reduction and control of costs

Learning activity 18.1 *(continued)*

purchasing
objective

Feedback on page 310

Now attempt self-assessment question 18.1 below.

Self-assessment question 18.1

Answer yes or no to the following questions;

1 Will the plan and approach to each company be the same?
2 Will there always be a maximum number of stakeholders?
3 Should health and safety be put behind costs issues?
4 Will all directors respond the same?
5 Will the solution to delivering the CSR agenda be same for all?

Feedback on page 311

18.2 The importance of cross-functional team working

Recognising how different functions impact on each other, and the need for early (from the outset) collaboration between functions, is vital and certainly critical to success. Procurement professionals must also consider and develop effective communication and coordination between functions in their role as a 'facilitator'.

We must first reflect on and consider what, why and where conflict may occur and what we can do to mitigate this. Consider the examples in table 18.3 and relate them to key stakeholders in your own organisation.

Table 18.3

	Potential conflict	Mitigating action(s)
1	Lack of conviction that a new way of doing something is needed	Share objectives and relate them to those of the stakeholder.
		Share the size of the potential prize for implementing a new way.
2	Just don't like change	Involve people early.
		Discuss and share options.
		Ensure facts and data are effectively communicated.
3	Fear of the unknown	Early effective and concise communication.
		Training.

(continued on next page)

303

Finance for Purchasers

Table 18.3 *(continued)*

	Potential conflict	Mitigating action(s)
		Support for the individual/team.
4	Fear of failure	Active listening to determine the *real* issues.
		Effective training – eg learning by doing.
		Support at all stages, especially post implementation.
5	Lack of respect in the person driving and/or delivering the change	There is a need to gain/regain respect either through peer group promotion, senior intervention and/or performance. But probably a combination of all three!
		Professional and objective approach at all times.
		Deliver what you promise.
		Don't over-promise and under-deliver; it should be the opposite to gain early trust.
6	Unpopular issue	Effectively communicate the objectives and how they align with the stakeholder.
		Emphasise the size of the prize, and not just in monetary terms, as the stakeholder may justifiably have another higher priority or agenda.
		Again, be professional and objective.
7	Tried to do it before and failed	Ensure you actively listen and understand the issues and the stakeholders' involvement and position before you engage. Especially the facts and data behind a past change and/or project.
		You must then use facts and data to objectively define the differences and the new method of approach, new business environment, and so forth.

Having identified the people you need to engage with and those you need to work with as a cross-functional team, this will require discipline, a sound method of working and a logical set of well communicated steps to get you there. *In no particular order* you need to consider the following tools and techniques in moving from the current order to a new order (note that you will be asked to discuss these with your fellow students, lecturer or mentor and order these as part of the self-assessment questions):

1   communication plan
2   stakeholder mapping
3   team charter
4   benefits plan
5   strategy
6   collect facts and data

7 define the measurement tools
8 agree upon a sponsor
9 pilot project
10 develop 'what if' scenarios
11 opportunity analysis
12 training plan
13 support network
14 project plan
15 business requirements analysis
16 supplier research
17 RFI/RFQ
18 supplier financial analysis
19 SWOT analysis
20 contract award.

In terms of ranking objectives, risks, or evaluating support from board directors, this can either be done by a relative method or an analytical method. The former will involve you in subjectively evaluating each issue against a known benchmark of low, medium or high levels of difficulty, risk. It might be easier to convince your friend of a good idea as opposed to the CEO of your organisation, as the friend will already be sympathetic towards you. Conversely, analytical methods by their very title will require you to objectively evaluate key criteria, score them from known data and bring to a conclusion the final value. So, for example, a risk issue may be broken down into a number of risk areas: publicity, fire, loss of sales, production, loss of key staff, research failure, and so on, so that against each heading the procurement specialist, usually with the help of specialists or cross-functional teams, will score each heading to develop an overall score as a value against a theoretical maximum score and hence a ranking of H, M or L.

Learning activity 18.2

Keep a diary or log of the areas of cross-functional conflict within your own organisation and categorise them using the seven heading examples shown below, or any others that seem appropriate to you. Rank them in terms of frequency and at what level in the organisation they occur.

- Lack of conviction that a new way of doing something is needed
- Just don't like change
- Fear of the unknown
- Fear of failure
- Lack of respect in the person driving and/or delivering the change
- Unpopular issue
- Tried to do it before and failed.

Feedback on page 311

Now attempt self-assessment question 18.2 below.

Finance for Purchasers

Self-assessment question 18.2

Consider the 20 tools and techniques below and place them in the order they should be performed.

1 communication plan
2 stakeholder mapping
3 team charter
4 benefits plan
5 strategy
6 collect facts and data
7 define the measurement tools
8 agree upon a sponsor
9 pilot project
10 develop what if scenarios
11 opportunity analysis
12 training plan
13 support network
14 project plan
15 business requirements analysis
16 supplier research
17 RFI/RFQ
18 supplier financial analysis
19 SWOT analysis
20 contract award.

Feedback on page 311

18.3 The monitoring and control cycle

The planning stage

Consider what steps are necessary to both control and reduce, on a pro-rata basis, one of the single greatest costs to a business, its *overheads*. In short, the main cost drivers (and asset) of an organisation are its people and the buildings and equipment they occupy and use. Accountants spend countless days and weeks calculating, forecasting, revising and analysing the overheads of a business, but this is usually in response to the actions of directors and managers within the business. One of the prime functions of procurement professionals is to support business heads in managing the budgets and cost of goods and services effectively to deliver the business objectives, and in so doing becoming a true business partner.

This all begins, or should begin, at the planning stage of an annual budget, for example where common/shared actions and activities are owned in partnership by the business heads and the procurement professional. This must include any revisions that are made and an open and transparent sharing of the information and actions/activities involved from formal sign off to year-end delivery.

Performance monitoring and control

This is exactly what it states in the title and no more! Having set and agreed a budget/plan with the board or business unit, there is then a form of contract between the two internally to deliver against that plan, recognising that the cash flow of the expenditure may not be linear and in reality will be linked to a series of business activities, projects and external factors as well.

Different functions will want to monitor and control in different ways and will range from completely hands-on to the complete opposite. However, in essence you need to agree what 'line items' you are going to measure and how from the outset before the year begins; equally how the *ownership* of a plan will be placed in the hands of those that can control and influence it throughout the year – for example, travel budgets, overhead count, and so on.

It should also be noted that this is an activity that needs to be carried out regularly (that is to say, monthly for projects) to ensure that when the next occasion the performance monitoring is carried out any deviations to plan can be quickly an efficiently corrected with hopefully minimal impact to the budget/plan being monitored. This will also avoid more severe escalation measures being taken due to infrequent or ad-hoc monitoring.

Learning activity 18.3

With reference to your own organisations, research the following key questions:

- How are plans agreed?
- How are they used to monitor performance and control resources and what methods may be employed to visually record them?

Feedback on page 312

Now attempt self-assessment question 18.3 below.

Self-assessment question 18.3

Take your own or a fictional business unit previous year budget (so that you have both planned and actual expenditure) and find ways to graphically represent all items so that they are true to the primary objectives of reporting, for example:

- specific
- measurable
- actionable
- relevant
- time-related.

Feedback on page 312

18.4 Cost coding and reporting:c cost overruns

Cost coding

Most organisations will use a cost coding system as a means of consistently categorising costs in order to both manage their business and comply with accounting standards. This is especially relevant for stock market listed companies and medium to large enterprises. An example of coding might reflect Capex or Opex/Function/year and period/SIC, and therefore the code in alphanumeric terms might look like the following:

- C/Mktg/0609/123456 for a Capex spend in Marketing

or

- O/Fin/0609/123456 for an expense item spend in the Finance department.

Without this discipline in the accounting function the purchasing professional would not be able to engage with accounts payable function in a business and obtain meaningful data. This data would normally allow the purchasing professional to determine:

- *Who* we buy products and services from.
- *Why* we buy such products and services as defined by the purchase order, call-off schedule, framework agreement, and so on.
- *Where* we consume the goods or services.
- *When* we consume the goods and services and at what frequency.
- *How* the goods and services are delivered.

This invaluable source of data will enable us to understand how the organisation functions on a real-time basis and along with the management accountants forecast the trends both up and down of those products and services.

Each product or service has a pre-allocated Standard Industry Code (SIC) which will allow us to compare business units and/or comparable organisations to evaluate and generate options and strategies for effective purchasing plans.

Many proprietary software finance systems have been developed around the world to make the processing of this information more efficient and effective as well as providing the ability to link and integrate it with other elements of the business such as planning, logistics, sales, and so on.

Reporting cost overruns

It is vital that any cost overruns are reported as and when they occur in the agreed format and to the relevant parties. Equally, what mitigating actions can be taken and the probability of their success should be evaluated an communicated immediately. Failure to recognise this essential communication could have serious consequences on a project, depending on the magnitude and timing of the issue and inevitable lack of action or mitigation.

It should also be noted that this is an activity that needs to be carried out regularly (monthly for projects and similar) to ensure that when the next time a cost overrun is identified any deviations to plan can be quickly and efficiently corrected, with hopefully minimal impact to the budget/plan being monitored. This will also avoid more severe escalation measures being taken due to infrequent or ad-hoc monitoring. The essence of this is to maintain control at all times.

Looking at the risk of cost overruns was part of an extensive investigation that the UK HM Treasury carried out and resulted in a major publication referred to as the Green Book, which looked at reasons for cost overruns and mitigating factors. The work encourages a focus on avoidance measures through effective planning and control and the understanding of risk factors so that they are understood from the outset of a project or investment and are then managed as opposed to events that cause cost overruns among many other things.

Learning activity 18.4

Using the UK HM Treasury Green Book Guide (Green Book online: http://.greenbook/hm-treasury.gov.uk), state what the 20 general types of risk are (Annex 4, Box 4.3) and five of the recommended actions for mitigation.

Feedback on page 313

Now attempt self-assessment question 18.4 below.

Self-assessment question 18.4

Read the section on Funding, Procurement and Technology risk in the Green Book and summarise the key points.

Feedback on page 313

Revision question

There is no revision question for this session.

Summary

The business cannot succeed through the excellence of one department or function alone. Many sayings and quotes over the centuries have reinforced the need to act as a cohesive enterprise, as value can only be realised as a complete entity and any weak link will ultimately pull the rest of the organisation down. The hub of this will always be clear and effective communication, with every individual contributing in a defined

Finance for Purchasers

and orchestrated manner. Therefore, by understanding the organisation you work in, the sector and the products, and actively engaging in cross-functional activities to achieve defined targets you will be part of a successful company.

Suggested further reading

- HM Treasury (2003) *Green Book*. HMSO
- Holmes, G, A Sugden and P Gee (2004) *Interpreting Company Reports and Accounts*, 9th edition. Harlow: FT/Prentice Hall.
- Knowledge and practice papers from CIPS: http://www.cips.org

Feedback on learning activities and self-assessment questions

Feedback on learning activity 18.1

An example of this might look like table 18.2. However, it is the rational approach and identification of key strategies and actions that is the critical part of this exercise. The table should be more comprehensive and detailed at the next level to crystallise the precise key targets and actions. In short, this is the business requirements analysis from a purchasing perspective.

Table 18.2

Purchasing objective	Purchasing target	Number of stakeholders	Current spend	Number of suppliers	Board support for purchasing objective	Risk	H&S issue	New product development (NPD)	Technology
Supply base reduction from 10,000 > 2,500	20%	8	£500 million	10,000	5 out of 7	M	L	L	L
Create operational savings from transactional business processes	15%	3	£500 million	10,000	4 out of 7	M	L	L	H
Increase the fleet choice but keep costs within budget	5%	150	£40 million	22	7 out of 7	H	H	L	M
Target each of your top 20 suppliers to deliver a piece of innovation that will create value for the company	5%	12	£400 million	20	5 out of 7	H	L	M	L-H
Ensure all key suppliers and service providers have an ethical trading plan and audit it regularly	5%	12	£450 million	250	5 out of 7	M	L	L	L
Greater awareness of the purchasing function and the people within it	0.5%	10,000	£0 million	0	0 out of 7	L	L	L	L

18 Functions of an organisation – reduction and control of costs

As priorities diminish and the impact and risk increase as well as tangible benefit reduces, the smaller the effort and/or the need to be pragmatic as to what extent these objectives/targets will be pursued or indeed incorporated into the key areas.

Feedback on self-assessment question 18.1

The answers in the section should be as follows.

1   No.
2   No.
3   No.
4   No.
5   No.

Feedback on learning activity 18.2

In essence your main task will be to deal with the 'blockers' and the negative aspects of a new way of working or change, while ensuring that supporters are not left behind and are used to good effect in helping you deal with the other stakeholders who are not 100% supportive. Your answer might be presented as in table 18.4.

Table 18.4

Frequency ranking	Potential conflict	Where did this occur
	Lack of conviction that a new way of doing something is needed	eg CEO, Head of X, Manager, etc
	Just don't like change	
	Fear of the unknown	
	Fear of failure	
	Lack of respect in the person driving and/or delivering the change	
	Unpopular issue	
	Tried to do it before and failed	

Keeping a healthy balance will ensure you have good cross-functional team working, no matter how large or small the role is for each member of the team.

Feedback on self-assessment question 18.2

The order should be:

1   agree upon a sponsor
2   strategy
3   stakeholder mapping
4   team charter
5   communication plan
6   project plan
7   collect facts and data
8   business requirements analysis
9   benefits plan

Finance for Purchasers

10 define the measurement tools
11 opportunity analysis
12 develop what if scenarios
13 SWOT analysis
14 supplier research
15 RFI/RFQ
16 supplier financial analysis
17 contract award
18 pilot project
19 training plan
20 support network.

Depending on your own organisation there may be a preference to slightly re-order some of the items. However, this list follows accepted practice for purchasing category management.

Feedback on learning activity 18.3

Plans are normally agreed by consensus, as this then ensures ownership across a broad community. Typically plans are agreed at board level and then cascaded down organisations for implementation.

It should be noted that the management accountant can play a vital role here in translating detailed company accounting plans into a working document from which the business head and purchasing professional can effectively control all the aspects of the budget as set and agreed by the board of directors.

The preference may be to turn the cost of staff into a Gantt chart, which categorises individuals, full-time or external interim/consulting resources as discrete tasks and deliverables set against milestone activities/dates, for example. Travel and accommodation may be set against a target and actual cost line displayed on an intranet for purchasing or the appropriate business unit. The same would be true for a training budget or any other cost/line item in the budget.

All of these can be broken down further by geographical location, project, region, and so on, so that they have relevance and ownership,

Feedback on self-assessment question 18.3

Your answer should consist of an example of data turned into either:

- bar graph
- pie chart
- graduated bar
- barometer
- red, amber, green status report (RAG)
- dashboard report (key metrics visually displayed on one chart/table).

As an example, a summary report to a board of directors would best suit a RAG report as it is a quick visual aid to allow senior members to focus on the important items and debate those first.

Feedback on learning activity 18.4

For each and every project a risk register is kept, and updated regularly together with the appropriate risk analysis recorded in it. Only following this can an informed risk management review take place. The HM Treasury Green Book has been an authoritative guide on risk evaluation procedures. The 20 types of general risk as defined by the Green Book are:

- availability
- business
- construction
- decant
- demand
- design
- economic
- environment
- funding
- legislative
- maintenance
- occupancy
- operational
- planning
- policy
- procurement
- project intelligence
- reputational
- residual value
- technology
- volume.

We can also see that the discipline of cost coding provides one of the primary cornerstones of purchasing category management, that of gathering the facts and data of what an organisation spends:

- with whom
- when/how often
- how much
- where in the organisation and
- why.

Without this upfront activity the organisation will simply be at the mercy of each and every supplier.

Feedback on self-assessment question 18.4

- Funding risk: Where project delays or changes in scope occur as a result of the availability of funding.
- Procurement risk: Where a contractor is engaged, risk can arise from the contract between the two parties, the capabilities of the contractor, and when a dispute occurs.
- Technology risk: The risk that changes in technology result in services being provided using non-optimal technology.

Finance for Purchasers

Study session 19
Evaluating risks and their impact

Introduction

When considering the concept of 'risk' it is useful to first determine what area of risk is being assessed.

Risk is everywhere, but we can achieve nothing without taking risks.

Some aspects of risk relate to the wider environment in which a business is operating. Thus wider factors such as political risk and country risk, and the global economic situation, have to be addressed before considering the specific risks within the organisation, or associated with its suppliers or customers and the local economy.

Additionally, more specific aspects of risk face organisations on a day-to-day basis. Among these are the financial and commercial risks involved when purchasing from a particular company. How financially sound is the supplier? How likely is it still to be in business in a year's time? Is it financially robust enough to be able to fulfil a contract satisfactorily. These are the types of question that will be addressed in the main section of this session, when we consider the area of supplier appraisal.

Risk management through insurance will also be considered in this session, while other commonly used tools to manage risk will be explored in study session 20.

Session learning objectives

After completing this session you should be able to:

19.1 Give examples of different types of risk (such as business risk, project risk, operational risk, country risk, financial risk).
19.2 Carry out a financial appraisal, using a range of financial performance and efficiency ratios:.
19.3 Describe investment ratios and their usefulness in the purchasing context.

Unit content coverage

This study session covers the following topics from the official CIPS unit content document:

Learning objective

6.1 Assess the different types of risk and their impact on each of the following:
- Suppliers
- Own organisation
- Customers

Finance for Purchasers

Prior knowledge

Study sessions 1 to 18.

Timing

You should set aside about 6 hours to read and complete this session, including learning activities, self-assessment questions, the suggested further reading (if any) from the essential textbook for this unit and the revision question.

19.1 Different types of risk

Risk is everywhere, and different types and levels of risk face any organisation at all times.

Some risks are easier than others to predict and manage. Most companies, for example, are exposed to global and regional economic factors. Large multinational companies can to an extent manage the risks by having a well-spread portfolio of operations around the world, and by having the capacity to be able to invest in economies where growth prospects are favourable, and to divest where the prospects are less good.

They can also assess country risk and political risk factors when making investment decisions around the world.

Smaller companies, by contrast, tend to be exposed to local economic and political risk factors, to which they are fully exposed. And it is on the individual organisation level – the 'micro' level – that this session will focus.

Learning activity 19.1

For a supplier with whose business you are broadly familiar, list three potential areas of risk that the supplier faces and highlight the potential impact (on your organisation, as a purchaser) of each risk.

Feedback on page 329

Among the risks faced by an individual organisation – or by the individual trading partners (such as suppliers and customers) in which they are stakeholders – are included:

- strategic risk
- business risk
- operational risk
- project risk
- country risk

- external/regulatory risk
- financial risk.

Strategic risk will be about the factors that might impact on the strategic direction a company is taking. For example, new suppliers entering the market could prevent a supplier from achieving its longer-term strategic goals.

'Business' or 'operational' risk describes the variability of operating profits. One key element of this was considered in study session 7 when we looked at marginal costing. 'Operational gearing' is a term that describes how sensitive a company's profits are to changing levels of revenue. As we saw in study session 7, the higher a company's fixed costs are, the more sensitive it is to changes in sales and output.

Operational risk can, though, include any risks that might undermine the operational capabilities of the organisation – for example the loss of key staff. They might also encompass what is known as 'reputational risk', where particular actions by a company can sully its reputation and thereby damage its commercial prospects.

Country risk concerns the particular risks that are presented by trading with organisations in a particular part of the world. There may be (among other things) political uncertainty, economic weakness, war risk or even the greater potential for natural disasters.

'Financial risk' describes risk additional to the business risk, and considers those risks inherent in a company's financial position and performance. These include:

- *Liquidity risk:* The risk that a company will, effectively, run out of cash and therefore not be able to operate.
- *Credit risk:* The risk that a company to whom credit has been granted (either by lending money, or offering trade credit) is unable to make payment.
- *Capital structure risk:* The risk that the capital structure of a business is too heavily reliant on debt, an issue we will look at more specifically in study session 20.

In reality, many of the risks highlighted above will overlap. Strategic risk, for example, will impact on certain financial risk factors.

Self-assessment question 19.1

If we categorise risk under by following headings:

- strategic risk
- business risk
- operational risk
- project risk
- country risk
- external/regulatory risk
- financial risk,

(continued on next page)

Finance for Purchasers

Self-assessment question 19.1 *(continued)*

which type of risk do the following most logically represent?

1 The arrangement of a new loan.
2 A business for whom 90% of costs are fixed.
3 A business operating in an industry with low entry barriers.
4 The ability to construct a building on time.
5 The unpopularity of the government in a country to which a company is exporting.
6 The reliance on the charisma of a chief executive.

Feedback on page 330

19.2 Financial appraisal, using a range of financial performance and efficiency ratios

When considering the risk factors involved in trading with another organisation, it can be useful to review the other party's financial accounting reports.

Ratio analysis can be applied to financial accounts to help identify where risks might exist, and to otherwise answer questions about the company's financial position:

- *Performance:* How well is the business performing? How profitable is it? How well is it controlling its costs? How does the business compare with its competitors? Is performance improving or deteriorating?
- *Financial status:* How financially sound is the company? Is the company solvent? How liquid is it?
- *Efficiency:* How quickly does the company move its stock? How quickly does it collect payment from customers? How quickly does it pay its bills?

When going through these measures, we shall apply them to some financial data that we have looked at before – those of UK Enterprise plc.

Its profit and loss account and balance sheet are reproduced in table 19.1 and table 19.2 below.

Table 19.1

UK Enterprise plc	2006	2005
Profit and loss account Y/E 31 March		
	£000	£000
Turnover	20,874	17,238
Cost of sales	(16,156)	(13,256)
Gross profit	4,718	3,892
Distribution expenses	(1,962)	(1,604)
Administration expenses	(898)	(724)
Operating profit	1,858	1,654
Interest payable	(598)	(488)
Profit before tax	1,260	1,166
Taxation	(416)	(386)
Profit for the year	844	780

(continued on next page)

Table 19.1 *(continued)*

UK Enterprise plc	2006	2005
Dividends	(308)	(262)
Retained profit	536	518

Table 19.2

UK Enterprise Plc	2006	2005
Balance sheet as at 31 March		
	£000	£000
Fixed assets		
Tangible assets	10,652	8,890
Current assets		
Stock	2,482	1,906
Debtors	3,122	2,382
Cash	30	40
	5,634	4,328
Creditors due in less than 1 year		
Creditors	(2,246)	(1,838)
Bank overdraft	(1,774)	(1,226)
Taxation	(416)	(386)
Proposed dividend	(308)	(262)
	(4,744)	(3,712)
Net current assets	890	616
Total assets less current liabilities	11,542	9,506
Long-term liabilities (loans)	(6,000)	(4,500)
Net assets	5,542	5,006
Shareholders' equity		
Share capital (Ordinary £1 shares)	2,000	2,000
Share premium	650	650
Retained profit	2,892	2,356
Shareholders' funds	5,542	5,006

Performance ratios

Return on capital employed

Operating profit/Long-term capital employed (expressed as a percentage).

Return on capital employed is one of several 'rate of return' measures. It is usually measured using profit before interest and tax (that is, the *operating* profit) and expressing this figure as a percentage of all the long-term capital employed by the business. This latter figure would usually include the shareholders' funds (including retained profits) as well as any long-term loans or bonds.

What is an acceptable return? Much depends on the nature of the business. A company that is capital-intensive (such as many manufacturing businesses) is likely to have a lower return on capital than one with fewer tangible assets (such as a PR consultancy). In general terms, though, the

Finance for Purchasers

ratio should over a period of time be higher than the company's cost of capital.

For UK Enterprise the appropriate figures are shown in table 19.3.

Table 19.3

	2006	2005
	£000	£000
Operating profit	1,858	1,654
Long-term capital employed:		
Shareholders' funds	5,542	5,006
+ Loan capital	6,000	4,500
= Total capital employed	11,542	9,506
ROCE	16.1%	17.4%

You will note here that the ratio has declined. Although profits have risen, they have not increased relative to the capital employed in the business. The latter figure has increased significantly as a result of extra borrowing that is now in place.

Fixed asset turnover

Sales/Fixed assets (expressed as a multiple).

Fixed asset turnover is a measure of efficiency in terms of the use of available capacity – in other words, how well the company is using its fixed assets to generate sales. If the figure declines, it might suggest a decline in efficiency – for example an increase in assets not being matched by a proportionate increase in sales. However, an apparently 'improved' ratio could be achieved if a company failed to keep its plant and machinery up to date by not replacing old fixed assets.

Operating profit margin

Operating profit/Sales or 'turnover' (expressed as a percentage).

The profit margin – also known as 'return on sales' – identifies what type of a return the company is getting on the sales it makes. What constitutes a high profit margin depends entirely on the industry in question. Generally speaking, increasing profit margins are good news for a business.

In the case of UK Enterprise plc, the figures are as shown in table 19.4.

Table 19.4

	2006		2005
	£K		£K
Operating profit	1,858		1,654
Sales	20,874	17,238	
Operating profit margin	8.9%		9.6%

Financial status or 'liquidity' ratios

Current ratio

Current assets/Current liabilities (expressed as a multiple or ratio, for example 2 or 2:1).

The **current ratio** measures the extent to which short-term assets are adequate to cover short-term liabilities. A 'normal' figure (if such a thing exists) for the current ratio might be about 1.2. However, just as too low a figure raises questions about liquidity, too high a figure might prompt questions about how efficiently the company is being run. Money invested in current assets may tie up funds that could be better used elsewhere.

'Acid test' ratio

Liquid assets (current assets excluding stock)/Current liabilities (expressed as a multiple or ratio, for instance 2 or 2:1).

The **acid test** is a more rigorous test of liquidity than the current ratio, as it only uses what are known as liquid (or 'quick') assets. This refers to current assets which are quickly convertible into cash, and for this reason would normally exclude stocks – which may not always be easily saleable.

If this ratio comes out as above 1, this is normally considered a comfortable situation. For both the 'current ratio' and the 'acid test', falling ratios are a sign of deteriorating liquidity.

If we look at the relevant part of the UK Enterprise balance sheet we can work out the ratios (see table 19.5).

Table 19.5

	2006	2005
Current assets		
Stock	2,482	1,906
Debtors	3,122	2,382
Cash	30	40
	5,634	4,328
Creditors due in less than 1 year		
Creditors	(2,246)	(1,838)
Bank overdraft	(1,774)	(1,226)
Taxation	(416)	(386)
Proposed dividend	(308)	(262)
	(4,744)	(3,712)

The current ratio would be:

- 2005: 4,328/3,712 = 1.17 (or 1.17:1)
- 2006: 5,634/4,744 = 1.19 (or 1.19:1).

The acid test ratio would be:

- 2005: 4,328 – 1,906 = 2,422/3,712 = 0.65 (or 0.65:1)
- 2006: 5,634 – 2,482 = 3,152/4,744 = 0.66 (or 0.66:1).

In both cases the ratios are very similar, and marginally higher for the latest year. Whether the ratios themselves were acceptable, or a cause for concern, would very much depend on the industry in question. For many retailers, for example, the above ratios would be relatively comfortable. For a manufacturing business, this is less likely to be the case.

Working capital or 'efficiency' ratios

When considering sources of finance in study session 11, we looked at working capital management as a means of generating internal finance. When appraising a supplier, we can consider similar issues and assess how well they are managing their own resources:

Stock turnover days

(Average stock/Cost of sales) × 365 (expressed as a number of days).

Stock turnover measures how quickly goods move through the business – usually the quicker the better. The stock figure used must be viewed with caution, particularly in a seasonal business.

Debtor days

(Trade debtors/Turnover) × 365 (expressed as a number of days).

Debtor days shows how long, on average, it takes for the company to get paid for the goods it sells. Strictly speaking, only credit sales should be used for a company that sells some goods for cash.

Creditor days

(Trade creditors/Purchases (or cost of sales)) × 365 (expressed as a number of days).

Creditor days measures how long the company is taking to pay its suppliers. An increase in the number of days could indicate some pressure, but might also mean simply that the company is managing its cash flow better by delaying payment.

The ratios for UK Enterprise would work out as shown in table 19.6.

Table 19.6

	2006	2005
Stock days	(2,482/16,156) × 365 = 56	(1,906/13,256) × 365 = 52
Debtor days	(3,122/20,874) × 365 = 55	(2,382/17,238) × 365 = 50
Creditor days	(2,246/16,156) × 365 = 51	(1,838/13,256) × 365 = 51

These ratios suggest a slight deterioration, although it should be remembered that the ratios themselves can only really identify broad trends. It appears to be taking UK Enterprise four days longer to sell its stock, and a further extra five days to then get paid – overall a nine-day deterioration, which has not been offset by any increase in time taken to pay suppliers.

There are two main risks associated with working capital. First, there is the risk of over-capitalisation. This occurs when a business actually has more invested in working capital than it really needs. This could take the form of having too much stock, for example, or a disproportionately high level of debtors. Such a situation suggests inefficiency, and – because it ties up capital that is of no real benefit – has a financial price.

The second risk factor, though, concerns almost the opposite scenario. If a company expands, but does not invest sufficiently in the extra working capital needs that go along with expansion, it may find itself what is known as 'overtrading'. Here the risk is that cash flows coming into a business are insufficient to meet payment obligations when they arise.

Employee ratios

Other frequently used measures consider financial results compared with the number of employees in a business, for example:

- sales per employee
- operating profit per employee
- output per employee.

These three measure are calculated simply by dividing the appropriate figure (eg sales) by the number of employees as disclosed in the financial accounts.

Growth ratios

Additionally, measures that reflect the growth of a business can often be useful. These are often referred to as 'growth ratios', and involve measuring the year-on-year growth of particular aspects of a business – for example sales growth, profit growth and net asset growth.

Cash flow ratios

Most traditional ratios focus on the profit and loss account/balance sheet relationship, and pay less attention the cash flow statement. There are, however, a number of ratios which have become more widely used in recent times and which bring cash flow figures into play.

Cash flow to current liabilities

(Net cash flow from operating activities/Average current liabilities) × 100.

This measure considers how easily a business is able to meet its current liabilities out of the cash it generates from its operations – an extension to the liquidity theme discussed above.

Cash flow per share

(Cash flow/Weighted average number of shares).

This looks at how much cash is generated per share that exists in the company. An increase therefore suggests improvement. The 'cash flow' figure used will depend on what is being examined – for example, one could consider the total cash flow, but alternatively limit it to the cash flow generated from operations.

Capex per share

(Capital expenditure/Weighted average number of shares) × 100.

Learning activity 19.2

Summarised financial data is shown in table 19.7 in the form one might see if it were acquired from a credit information provider.

(continued on next page)

Finance for Purchasers

Learning activity 19.2 *(continued)*

Review the data. Are the trends indicated generally positive or negative? What are the limitations of the data shown? Which measures would be of particular interest to a purchaser?

Table 19.7

	31 Dec X6	31 Dec X5	31 Dec X4	31 Dec X3	31 Dec X2
Profitability					
Profit margin %	7.1	6.9	8.1	8.6	8.9
Return on capital %	15.5	15.3	16.2	16.8	18.9
Liquidity					
Current ratio (x)	1.32	1.21	1.25	1.22	1.41
Acid test (x)	1.08	0.94	1.00	1.20	1.05
Working capital					
Stock turnover days	22.3	24.9	24.2	24.0	23.0
Debtor days	43.1	44.3	43.1	39.5	38.6
Creditor days	37.0	41.8	39.0	37.1	37.1
Employee					
Sales/employee	65.5	60.1	52.1	47.5	44.5
Profit/employee	4.70	4.57	4,58	4.64	4.37
Growth rates					
Turnover	+2.1%	+10.0%	+5.2%	+5.1%	+5.2%
Operating profit	-2.9%	-4.6%	-5.1%	+4.5%	+4.2%
Net assets	-8.4%	-1.0%	28%	+5.4%	+3.5%

Feedback on page 330

Learning activity 19.2 above involved appraising ratios that had already been calculated. Self-assessment question 19.2 below involves additionally calculating the ratios from some given data.

Self-assessment question 19.2

The profit and loss account and balance sheet of TVS Ltd are set out in table 19.8 and table 19.9.

Draw up a ratios table similar to table 19.10, and list the key issues that might concern a potential purchaser.

Table 19.8

TVS PLC Profit and loss account Y/E 31 December	2005	2004
	£000	£000
Turnover	3500	2025
Cost of Sales	(3049)	(1701)
Gross Profit	451	324
Other expenses	(283)	(201)
Operating Profit	168	123
Interest Payable	(26)	(6)
Profit before tax	142	117
Taxation	(60)	(51)
Profit after tax	82	66

(continued on next page)

Self-assessment question 19.2 *(continued)*

TVS PLC

Profit and loss account Y/E 31 December	2005	2004
Dividends	(63)	(31)
Retained Profit	19	35

Table 19.9

TVS PLC

Balance sheet as at 31 December	2005	2004
	£000	£000
Fixed assets		
Tangible assets	430	262
Investment	15	0
	445	262
Current assets		
Stock	703	262
Debtors	611	294
Cash	0	10
	1314	566
Creditors due in less than 1 year*	(892)	(280)
Net current assets	422	286
Total assets less current liabilities	867	548
Long-term loans	(50)	(50)
Net assets	817	498
Ordinary share capital	450	250
Share premium	100	0
Retained profits	267	248
Shareholders' funds	817	498

Creditors due in less than 1 year includes trade creditors of £495,000 (2005) and £170,000 (2004).

Calculate the key ratios.

Table 19.10

TVS plc – Ratios Worksheet		2005	2004
Return on capital employed	%		
Operating profit/(Shareholders' funds + Long-term loans)			
Return on sales	%		
Operating profit/Sales (or turnover)			
Current ratio	ratio		
Current assets/Current liabilities (or creditors due within 1 year)			
Acid test	ratio		

(continued on next page)

Finance for Purchasers

Self-assessment question 19.2 *(continued)*

TVS plc – Ratios Worksheet	2005	2004
Current assets (excluding stock)/Current liabilities (or creditors due within 1 year)		
Stock days	no of days	
(Stock/Cost of sales) × 365		
Debtor days	no of days	
(Debtors. Sales (or 'turnover')) × 365		
Creditor days	no of days	
(Trade creditors/Cost of sales) × 365		

Feedback on page 331

19.3 Investment ratios and their usefulness in the purchasing context

Another category of ratios relate to share prices and are normally calculated with the shareholder and investors in mind. They will form a key part of an investor's decision making – whether to buy or sell shares in a particular company.

One might therefore think that they are of less relevance to purchasers. However, they are often good indicators of the overall financial status of a company. Some of the ratios reflect the market's view of a company, which can be a good indicator of future prospects.

In looking at these measures, we will use data from Perco Plc, a fictitious UK listed company. Perco has recently announced its results. The following data is relevant:

- Perco made a profit after tax of £70 million.
- The average number of ordinary shares in the company over the last year was 500 million.
- The company's latest annual dividend is 8p per share.
- The latest share price is £1.60.
- There are no preference dividends.

Earnings per share

Earnings per share (EPS) is the profit attributable to shareholders divided by the number of ordinary shares in issue (expressed in cash amount).

So, in the case of Perco, the EPS will be:

£70 million/500 million shares = 14p.

In other words, for every share that exists in the company, 14p profit has been made.

The earnings per share (EPS) figure is not itself a ratio, but it is a figure that is central to the next ratio we look at, the price/earnings ratio.

EPS is a figure that is published as part of a company's annual results, and describes how much profit has been made by the company for each share it has issued. The 'profit' element – or 'earnings' – is the profit that is attributable to the ordinary shareholders of the company. Thus it is the profit that has been made after interest and tax have been deducted – but also after any preference dividends, as they are not payable to the ordinary shareholders.

Price/earnings ratio.

The **price/earnings (P/E) ratio** is the market price per share divided by the EPS (expressed as a multiple).

The **P/E ratio** shows how much of a multiple of EPS one has to pay when acquiring shares in a particular company. In other words, how many years it will take to recoup (in the form of profits) the price paid for the shares – assuming that future profitability remains the same.

This ratio can be 'historic' (based on the most recent published financial results) or 'prospective' (based on expected future EPS). It is a useful measure of comparison between companies, and is often used to assess value in a share price. For example, if the P/E ratio is relatively low, the shares *might* represent value at the prevailing price. Interpretation of P/E ratios requires particular caution, however. A company with a high P/E ratio is not necessarily better than one with a low one. It simply means that the shares are more highly rated, based often on expectations of future growth.

In the case of Perco, the following figures are relevant:

- Latest share price: 160p
- Latest EPS: 14p
- P/E ratio = 160/14 = 11.4 times.

In other words, somebody buying Perco shares at 160p is paying 11.4 times the amount of profit made for each share in the company. Put another way, each penny of Perco profits will cost a new shareholder 11.4p if buying the shares at this point in time. And, putting it another way still, it will take an investor 11.4 years to recoup the amount invested if future profits remain the same.

Dividend yield

Dividend yield is the dividend per share divided by the market price per share (expressed as a percentage).

So far we have looked at measures that consider the overall profit made for shareholders. We will now consider the part of that profit that is paid out to shareholders – the dividend. This is the cash amount that is paid out to shareholders, and it represents that part of the profit that the company is distributing rather than retaining in the business.

Dividend yield measures the percentage return on the market price of a share, in terms of the dividend paid. Whereas EPS looks at the *profit* made per share, this measure looks at the relationship between the latest *dividend* paid out per share, and the price of that share.

Finance for Purchasers

A high dividend yield can represent an attractive investment – but it may just reflect a falling share price. The falling share price in turn may suggest difficulties – and possibly reduced dividends in the future.

In the case of Perco, we are told that the dividend being paid is 8p per share. This needs to be compared to the latest share price:

8p/160p = 5%.

So, if an investor buys Perco shares at today's price of 160p, and future dividends stay at 8p, the cash return on the investment will be 5%.

Learning activity 19.3

Look at the share prices page from the *Financial Times* or other paper – and consider the investor ratios of some well known companies (see table 19.12). Why are the ratios as they are? How might the figures be explained?

NB: Although specific companies have been suggested, please feel free to work with figures of any companies of your choice.

Table 19.12

	easyJet	Tesco	Sage	Lloyds TSB
Latest share price				
Dividend yield				
P/E ratio				

Feedback on page 332

Dividend cover

Dividend cover indicates how well a dividend is covered by the company's earnings (that is, the profit attributable to shareholders). Where dividend cover is less than 1, dividends are being paid, at least partly, out of reserves (basically, profits made in previous years). Such an approach cannot continue indefinitely. The calculation works as follows:

Earnings per share (EPS)/Dividend per share (expressed as a multiple).

So, going back to Perco, the EPS was 14p and the dividend was 8p. Dividend cover is therefore:

14p/8p = 1.75 times

Profit levels are sufficient to cover the dividend payout – but less than half the profits made are being retained in the business.

Self-assessment question 19.3

The latest Company X share price is £4.90.

(continued on next page)

19 Evaluating risks and their impact

Self-assessment question 19.3 *(continued)*

The company has a total of 50,000,000 £1 ordinary shares in issue.

The latest profit statement included the data shown in table 19.13.

Table 19.13

	£ million
Operating profit	55.0
Interest	15.0
Profit before tax	40.0
Taxation	12.0
Profit after tax	28.0
Ordinary dividend	12.0
Preference dividend	6.0
Retained profit	6.0

Calculate:

1 The latest earnings per share.
2 The current P/E ratio.
3 The current dividend yield.

Feedback on page 332

Revision question

Now try the revision question for this session on page 347.

Summary

This session has considered a variety of the different types of risk organisations face. It then went on to look at particular finance-related risks, by using financial appraisal techniques – in particular, ratio analysis. These considered profitability, efficiency and liquidity. The session also covered ratios that apply specifically to stock market quoted companies, and which look at a business from the investor's perspective.

By applying these techniques to suppliers, customers and their own organisations, a purchaser can better understand some of the risks that any business faces in the course of carrying out its operations.

Feedback on learning activities and self-assessment questions

Feedback on learning activity 19.1

The risks identified might include:

- risks associated with the supplier's debt levels
- risks associated with the supplier's ability to pay its bills and survive on a day-to-day basis
- risks associated with the supplier's exposure to commodity prices

Finance for Purchasers

- risks associated with exposure to currency fluctuation
- risks associated with financial failure
- risks associated with other parties in the supply chain (for example, suppliers to the supplier).

The impact of the risks might range from increased prices (ie the supplier passes on the impact of their own risks) through to the financial failure of the supplier. This session looks specifically at techniques that can be used to evaluate the financial position of a supplier. Study session 20 will address some of the tools that are available to manage the risks identified.

Feedback on self-assessment question 19.1

Which type of risk do the following most logically represent:

1 Financial risk
2 Operational risk
3 Strategic risk
4 Project risk
5 Country risk
6 Operational risk

Feedback on learning activity 19.2

Are the trends indicated generally positive or negative?

- The figures show a mixed position, although some of the key measures are showing a gradual downward trend. The profit margin had declined each year until the most recent one, where a small increase was recorded. The same pattern shows itself for the return on capital measure. The company is clearly making profits, and the ratios themselves would need to be compared with other companies in the same industry, but the overall trend is adverse.
- The liquidity ratios seem reasonable, and fairly consistent. The acid test figure did dip below 1.0, but has subsequently risen again.
- The working capital ratios are generally showing somewhat adverse trends, although the latest year again indicates slight improvement – this time on the stock front. Debtor days is five days worse than the position five years ago, while creditor days have not moved in line with this.
- The employee measures indicate greater efficiency, perhaps from reducing the headcount.

What are the limitations of the data shown?

The limitations include:

- Ratios may highlight areas of concern, but they don't provide answers and cannot, in isolation, be used to make decisions.
- The ratios are only as reliable as the underlying data, and accounting data can be subject to creative presentation and manipulation.
- The ratios themselves are a little crude – for example, the working capital ratios use year-end figures (stock, debtors, and so on), which might not be representative of the year as a whole.

- The figures for one company in isolation can indicate trends, but without benchmarks (for example ratios for the industry in question as a whole) they might not be that useful.

Which measures would be of particular interest to a purchaser?

All the measures would be useful to a purchaser, and a view needs to be taken about the company as a whole. The ratio that might have most direct impact on the purchasing relationship might include the profit margin (as it, at least in part, is driven by the prices the company is able to achieve). However, a purchaser negotiating a longer term contract needs to be confident about the supplier's financial status, and ability to continue operating. Liquidity ratios can be a useful indicator of pressure in this area.

Feedback on self-assessment question 19.2

Table 19.11

TVS PLC – Ratios Worksheet		2005	2004
Return on capital employed	%	19.4	22.4
Operating profit/(Shareholders' funds + Long-term loans)			
Return on sales	%	4.8	6.1
Operating profit/Sales (or turnover)			
Current ratio	ratio	1.47:1	2.02:1
Current assets/Current liabilities (or creditors due within 1 year)			
Acid test	ratio	0.68:1	1.09:1
Current assets (excluding stock)/Current liabilities (or creditors due within 1 year)			
Stock days	no of days	84	56
(Stock/Cost of sales) × 365			
Debtor days	no of days	64	53
(Debtors. Sales (or 'turnover')) × 365			
Creditor days	no of days	59	36
(Trade creditors/Cost of sales) × 365			

While the company has grown (sales are up by over 70%), the above indicators show some causes for concern, including:

- Although the actual profit figure has increased, profitability (as expressed through return on capital and profit margin) have declined.
- Liquidity looks under pressure, with the acid test falling from above 1 to 0.68.

Finance for Purchasers

- Working capital management looks to have deteriorated – stock doesn't seem to be shifting and collection of cash has slowed. The payment period has increased – but this might be a result of greater pressure rather than more astute financial management.

From a purchasing perspective, these would be worrying trends. How likely is it that the company will still be trading in a few years' time? Have they expanded too quickly? Why are they holding such a large amount of stock? Will their payment record jeopardise their relationships with their own suppliers?

Feedback on learning activity 19.3

The dividend yield figures are likely to reveal a higher rate for the banking and retailing companies (mature businesses, traditionally high yield) compared with those that still have more obvious growth prospects (budget airlines, IT).

The P/E ratios are likely to show the reverse of this. The better the growth prospects, the higher the P/E ratios.

Individual company situations may override the above point, however, as it is a generalisation. A sharp fall in any company's share price would automatically trigger an increase in the stated yield.

Feedback on self-assessment question 19.3

1 First we have to arrive at the correct profit or 'earnings' figure. The profit after tax figure is £28 million, but we need to also deduct the preference dividend of £6 million, so:
   EPS = £22.0 million/50 million = 44.0p.
2 £4.90/44p = 11.1 times.
3 Dividend = £12 million/50 million = 24p per share = as a percentage of share price = 4.9%.

Study session 20

Evaluate and select risk management options

Introduction

As highlighted in study session 19, risk presents itself in a wide range of circumstances. This session looks at ways in which risk can be managed.

Session learning objectives

After completing this session you should be able to:

20.1 Give examples of debt, and evaluate the risks presented by debt.
20.2 Describe futures and derivatives, and explain how they can be used to manage risk.
20.3 Describe the role and need for insurance.

Unit content coverage

This study session covers the following topics from the official CIPS unit content document:

Learning objective

6.3 Evaluate and select financial risk management options.
  • Debt
  • Futures and derivatives
  • Insurance

Prior knowledge

Study sessions 1 to 19.

Resources

Holmes, G, Sugden, A and Gee, P (2005) *Interpreting Company Reports and Accounts*, 9th edition, chapter 14. Harlow: FT Prentice Hall.

Timing

You should set aside about 5 hours to read and complete this session, including learning activities, self-assessment questions, the suggested further

Many examples exist of poor risk management leading to serious financial damage – the collapse of Barings Bank, the fraudulent activities at Enron and the recall of chocolate bars by Cadbury-Schweppes. Companies must consider their total risks across their organisation, and develop ways of evaluating and managing them. At the same time, companies have to take risks to gain returns. The more they understand these risks, and how they can be managed, the better.

20

reading (if any) from the essential textbook for this unit and the revision question.

20.1 The risks presented by debt

In study session 11 we considered different sources of finance. Among the long-term external sources were various types of finance that involved borrowing money, and which could therefore be categorised as 'debt'. The two most significant such sources of finance are loans and bonds.

This session will revisit debt, and explore it in more detail. In particular, we will look at the risks associated with debt, how they can be measured and how they can be managed.

Measuring 'financial gearing'

A key measure used to assess the amount of debt a company has, and how risky that might be, is the 'gearing' ratio. This measure looks at the total level of borrowing in relation to the amount of money provided by shareholders – the shareholders' funds or 'equity' of the business.

The measure can be, and is, worked out in a number of different ways, which can be confusing. Some versions are also referred to as the 'debt/equity' ratio. The object, though, is to establish whether the proportion of debt to equity is a cause for concern.

The most common way of measuring financial gearing is to express long-term borrowed money – 'debt' – as a percentage of the total long-term capital being used by the business. This latter figure will normally be arrived at by adding the debt to the shareholders' funds.

If we revisit the balance sheet of UK Enterprise that we looked at in study session 5, we can consider their gearing ratio (see table 20.1).

Table 20.1

	2006	2005
	£000	£000
Fixed assets		
Tangible assets	10,652	8,890
Current assets		
Stock	2,482	1,906
Debtors	3,122	2,382
Cash	30	40
	5,634	4,328
Creditors due in less than 1 year		
Creditors	(2,246)	(1,838)
Bank overdraft	(1,774)	(1,226)
Taxation	(416)	(386)
Proposed dividend	(308)	(262)
	(4,744)	(3,712)
Net current assets	890	616

(continued on next page)

20 Evaluate and select risk management options

Table 20.1 *(continued)*

	2006	2005
Total assets less current liabilities	11,542	9,506
Long-term liabilities (Loans)	(6,000)	(4,500)
Net assets	5,542	5,006
Shareholders' Equity		
Share capital (Ordinary £1 shares)	2,000	2,000
Share premium	650	650
Retained profit	2,892	2,356
Shareholders' Funds	5,542	5,006

The gearing ratio for 2006 will be:

- Debt = 6,000
- Total capital: 6,000 (Debt) + 5,542 (Shareholders' funds) = 11,542
- Gearing ratio = 6,000/11.542 = 52%.

Comparative figures for 2005 are 4,500/9,506 = 47%, so the gearing ratio has increased over the period, and more than half the company's long-term capital has been borrowed.

Other methods of calculating gearing would include:

Expressing the debt as a percentage of the Shareholders' funds (rather than the total capital), the respective figures using the above data would then become:

- at March 2006: 6,000/5,542 = 108%
- at March 2005: 4,500/5,006 = 90%.

Using this approach, which is often referred to as the 'debt/equity ratio', one can get very high percentage figures – whereas using the earlier calculation there is a 100% ceiling.

An additional complication involves deciding what to include in the 'debt' element. So far, we have just included the long-term loans, but UK Enterprise has a significant overdraft in both years. Should we include that as well?

The answer is that there are no rules, and some users of accounts might consider it appropriate to include an overdraft, especially if it appears as if the company is using an overdraft facility on a permanent basis. If we include the overdraft, the gearing figure will increase accordingly.

The financial gearing effect

The gearing ratio is so called because of the effect it has on the profits a company makes for its shareholders. The 'gearing effect' describes the way in which the higher a company's gearing, the more sensitive the company is to prevailing interest rates.

Finance for Purchasers

Measuring 'interest cover'

Another ratio that can be used to assess an organisation's ability to manage its debt levels is interest cover. Here we consider a company's annual interest bill, and consider how comfortably the business is able to cover the interest amount out of the profits it is making. The ratio is therefore extracted entirely from the profit and loss account, as follows:

Profit before interest and tax/Interest (expressed as a number of times).

For example, if we consider the profit and loss account of UK Enterprise plc – the company we have used in various sessions already – we can work out the company's interest cover. Table 20.2 shows the profit and loss data.

Table 20.2

	2006	2005
	£000	£000
Turnover	20,874	17,238
Cost of sales	(16,156)	(13,256)
Gross profit	4,718	3,892
Distribution expenses	(1,962)	(1,604)
Administration expenses	(898)	(724)
Operating profit	1,858	1,654
Interest payable	(598)	(488)
Profit before tax	1,260	1,166
Taxation	(416)	(386)
Profit for the year	844	780
Dividends	(308)	(262)
Retained profit	536	518

Interest cover will be as shown in table 20.3.

Table 20.3

	2006	2005
Profit before interest and tax	1858	1654
Interest expense for year	598	488
	3.1 times	3.4 times

In other words, UK Enterprise is making sufficient profit before interest to be able to cover it quite comfortably (over 3 times). However, the cover has reduced a little in the most recent year.

Clearly, if the ratio is less than 1, the profit made does not cover the interest cost, and a loss will arise. And if the ratio is, say, 2 then a doubling of interest rates might be of significant concern if the company, especially if it is borrowing at variable rate.

Debt service coverage ratio

In study session 19 we looked at some 'cash flow' based ratios. Another one that has relevance here is the **Debt service coverage ratio**. It looks at ability to pay interest and to repay debt, using the following calculation:

20 Evaluate and select risk management options

EBITDA/annual debt repayments and interest (where EBITDA = earnings before interest, tax, depreciation and amortisation)

Debt v equity debate

A very important consideration for a company is the question of how it should be financed, and what the appropriate balance between debt and equity might be.

The choice between debt and equity will involve consideration of the following factors:

- Debt has to be repaid, equity is essentially a permanent source of finance.
- Interest has to be paid on borrowed money, whereas the cash cost of equity – the dividend paid to shareholders – is often discretionary. Companies, in hard times, may reduce the dividend or even not pay it at all.
- Linked to the above, though, is the fact that interest is a tax-deductible expense, whereas the dividend is not.
- Issuing new shares may dilute the ownership of the business, whereas debt will not have this effect. Dilution of ownership describes the situation where shareholders, as a result of a share issue, suffer a reduction in the proportion of shares that they own.
- It is usually cheaper to arrange debt finance than it is to arrange equity finance.
- With debt finance, security is often required (as discussed above). This is not the case with equity.

Learning activity 20.1

Table 20.4 shows some financial data for a selection of listed companies You are asked to rank them in terms of financial risk.

Table 20.4

	Company 1	Company 2	Company 3	Company 4
	£ million	£ million	£ million	£ million
Shareholders' funds	157	56	3293	80
Debt	852	38	1144	63
Profit before interest and tax	115	66	330	51
Interest	63	2	30	2

The data is based on figures extracted from the financial results of real UK listed companies.

Feedback on page 342

Now attempt self-assessment question 20.1 below.

Finance for Purchasers

Self-assessment question 20.1

Which of the following would be classed as 'debt' for the purposes of calculating the 'capital gearing' or 'debt equity' ratio?

(a) a bank overdraft facility, used for about three months of the year by a seasonal business
(b) a bank overdraft facility that is in permanent use
(c) a three-year term loan from a bank
(d) a bond due to mature in five years' time
(e) a credit factoring facility
(f) a bond due to mature in five *months'* time
(g) preference shares which pay an annual 5% dividend
(h) a three-month trade credit agreed with a supplier.

Feedback on page 342

20.2 Futures and derivatives

An increasingly common facet of many companies' risk management activity concerns the use of what are known as 'derivatives'.

A derivative is a financial instrument that derives – hence the name – its value from some other underlying item. These underlying items typically include things like:

- shares
- exchange rates
- interest rates
- commodity prices.

To understand the idea of derivatives, it is important to separate the above underlying items from the derivatives themselves. Examples of derivatives include:

- options
- futures
- forward contracts
- swaps.

So, for example, an investor may buy or sell shares, and a company may buy some foreign currency. These transactions would not in themselves involve the use of derivatives.

But if the investor held some shares, and wanted to protect himself against a drop in their value, he might make use of derivatives – for example, share options.

And if the company did not need the currency for a few months, but wanted to protect itself against adverse exchange movements in the

20 Evaluate and select risk management options

meantime, it might use derivatives – for example futures or forward contracts.

Learning activity 20.2

Consider an international airline. What risks might they face from movements in the following?

- the oil price
- exchange rates
- interest rates.

How might airlines attempt to manage the risks identified?

Feedback on page 343

We now look at derivatives in a little more detail.

Options give the holder the right, but not the obligation, to buy or sell an asset (for example some shares) at a pre-agreed price at some point in the future. The right to buy something is known as a 'call option', and the right to sell is a 'put option'.

A **forward contract** is an agreement to buy (in other words, here there is an obligation) or sell a particular asset at an agreed price on a specific future date. A **future** has similar characteristics, but an additional facet is that the contracts are standardised and traded on exchanges.

A **swap** is an agreement to exchange, with another party, an obligation to pay streams of cash over a given future period. Swaps are most commonly seen in the banking sector, and usually involve either loans or currency holdings.

Derivatives have four main characteristics:

- their value (that is, their price) is dependent on price movements of the underlying asset
- they require little or no initial outlay
- they are settled at a future date
- they are used for both hedging and speculation purposes.

The last point is an important one. Derivatives are an important part of many companies' risk management strategy. They are used to hedge against adverse movements in share prices, interest rates, exchange rates and the like. As such, they are used to reduce risk – and the popular assertion that derivatives are risky things to get involved with is not, in these circumstances, true. Derivatives used in this way represent a legitimate – and perhaps essential – risk management tool.

The term 'hedging' describes the techniques that can be used to reduce price risk. Organisations can use derivatives to take a position where the payoff

Finance for Purchasers

can, at least partly, offset adverse movements in the underlying exchange rate, interest rate or commodity prices to which they might be exposed.

However, there are others who simply trade in derivatives and try to make money by guessing which way the various markets will turn. This is simply speculation, and clearly in these circumstances derivatives *do* carry a high degree of risk.

Self-assessment question 20.2

For each of the following statements, decide whether they are true or false.

1   If a company sells a futures contract, it means it expects the price of the underlying asset to rise.
2   Using futures and options requires a big appetite for risk.
3   The price of an option is linked to the price of the underlying asset.
4   Buying currency on a forward contract means that the buyer will benefit if the exchange rate moves in their favour.

Feedback on page 343

20.3 Insurance

A more traditional approach to managing risk is to take out insurance against the risk occurring. Arrangements can be made with an insurer to protect against almost any risk that might exist. As long as the insurer can assess the likelihood of a particular outcome, it should, at a price, be able to offer cover.

For example, a contractor will be expected to have in place certain standard insurance cover such as Public Liability, Employers, Equipment, Third Party, and so forth.

Consideration should also be given to the following depending on the company's activities and the extent to which it might therefore be relevant:

* directors and officers – their acts in relation to employees and other companies/suppliers
* professional indemnity – cover that protects a professional in the event of professional negligence
* legal – protection against large legal costs set above a ceiling, for example £50,000
* medical/dental – employee-related
* key man – niche, specialist, unique skills or 'networked high profile' people
* special insurances, for example, marine insurance.

Larger companies (for example members of the FTSE-100 or Fortune 500) may well self-insure. The scale of their activities may make it financially worthwhile effectively to operate their own insurance business, especially

20 Evaluate and select risk management options

where the risks are relatively predictable. It is unlikely to be used in situations where the risk is potentially so damaging that it would threaten the business as a whole.

Learning activity 20.3

Consider a purchasing activity or project you are familiar with. Draw up a list of all the insurance cover that is associated with that activity of project.

Feedback on page 344

A purchaser, when appraising or monitoring a supplier, needs to be satisfied that the supplier is adequately insured against identifiable risk.

Circumstances will dictate precisely what cover needs to be in place, but it is unlikely that a major contract would be entered into without verification of suitable insurance cover.

The types of insurance that are likely to be required, depending on the circumstances, include:

- public liability insurance
- product liability insurance
- professional indemnity cover
- employer's liability insurance.

Self-assessment question 20.3

How might an organisation protect against:

1 the financial collapse of a customer
2 the financial collapse of a supplier
3 payment of an individual customer invoice
4 the rising cost of raw materials
5 the rising price of the currency of a country from which it is importing goods?

Feedback on page 344

Revision question

Now try the revision question for this session on page 348.

Summary

The session has built on the learning from study session 19 by highlighting and evaluating risks presented by debt. The session then looked at the growing area of derivatives and discussed the circumstances in which they

20

341

Finance for Purchasers

can be used as a risk management tool. Finally, the session gives an overview of a more traditional aspect of risk management – insurance.

Feedback on learning activities and self-assessment questions

Feedback on learning activity 20.1

If we work out the 'gearing' and 'interest cover' ratios, a clearer picture emerges (table 20.5).

Table 20.5

	Company 1	Company 2	Company 3	Company 4
Capital gearing	84%	40%	26%	44%
Interest cover	1.82 times	33 times	11 times	25 times

Company 3 has the highest amount of borrowings, but in relative terms the figures do not appear too risky and it has a gearing ratio of only 26%. Company 1 has by far the highest gearing – 84% of its capital has been borrowed.

Company 1 also has the lowest interest cover at 1.82 times – a figure that suggests it would be vulnerable to interest rate rises. The other three companies are, at present, very easily able to pay their interest costs, although the amount of debt in Company 3 suggests a higher interest cost (and lower cover) next time round.

Feedback on self-assessment question 20.1

There is no precisely right answer to this question. However, 'debt' is normally associated with longer-term capital on which interest is paid.

Examples (c) and (d) would therefore definitely be included in debt calculations.

Where the use is specifically short-term, related to day-to-day operational needs and part of the working capital cycle – as in the situations described in (a), (e) and (h) – they would not normally be treated as debt.

The others are debatable, but it would be reasonable to consider a permanent overdraft as, effectively, long-term funding and therefore to be classed as debt. The bond due to mature in five months' time is also debt – it is just that it will soon be repaid. So, (b) and (f) would be debt.

Preference shares paying a 5% dividend may or may not be debt. Technically, preference shares are equity not debt. However, recent accounting developments require that preference shares be treated (and accounted for) as debt if they contain certain debt-like characteristics – for example if there is a fixed rate of interest rate and an agreed repayment date. This would require them to be shown as a liability in the balance sheet.

There are many hybrid financial instruments in use today that include features of both debt and equity. These are known as compound instruments – and for accounting purposes they have to be split into their component (debt and equity) parts.

Feedback on learning activity 20.2

An airline will face risks in all three of these areas. The oil price will clearly have an impact on the price of jet fuel, which in turn represents a significant and unavoidable operating cost for an airline. The recent rise in the price of oil has had a major impact.

Different airlines have adopted different approaches to this issue, but most airlines will use hedging techniques of one sort or another. By buying oil futures contracts, for example, an airline will not suffer if prices rise further.

Another way of dealing with the risk might be to try to pass it on to the customer – and this is what many airlines have been doing with the introduction of fuel surcharges – an initiative that has proved quite controversial.

A recent report indicated that, while Lufthansa was 90% hedged against rises in oil prices, Ryanair had very little long-term hedging in place. Ryanair has also indicated that it would not resort to the increasing fuel surcharges applied by, among others, Lufthansa and British Airways.

An airline that is borrowing significant amounts (and most do) may look to using fixed rate borrowing as one means of protecting themselves against a rise in interest rates.

International airlines are likely to have flows of cash in and out in a wide range of different currencies. If the inflows and outflows of any currency are broadly matching then there may not any need to take action. However, where the airline is exposed to particularly high risk if the value of a currency were to change significantly, it is likely to enter into forward contracts.

Feedback on self-assessment question 20.2

1   False. If a company sells a futures contract, it expects the price of the underlying asset to fall. Selling a future means entering into an agreement to sell the asset at some time in the future, at a price agreed today. It would only do this if it expected the price of the underlying asset to fall.
2   False. The reverse is true, since these instruments were originally designed to help control risk. However, those with a big appetite for risk are also attracted to futures and options, as they offer a highly geared medium for speculation.
3   True. The price of an option will be influenced by the price of the underlying asset. It will also be influenced by the time left to expiry, the volatility of the underlying asset, and prevailing interest rates.
4   False. If the price of the US$, for instance, falls, the buyer of the forward contract will have paid a higher price than they otherwise might. They will, though, have been protected against a rise in the price of US$.

Feedback on learning activity 20.3

Answers will vary depending on the circumstances, but might usefully be split between insurance cover that would apply to any project (public liability cover, for instance) and that which relates specifically to the chosen activity.

Feedback on self-assessment question 20.3

1 The financial collapse of a customer can be directly protected against by taking out credit insurance. Less directly, the financial performance of the customer can be closely monitored and credit limits tightly observed and controlled, as a way of limiting potential financial damage.
2 The financial collapse of a supplier can be protected against by, as above, paying close attention to the supplier's financial status as a way of ensuring exposure is kept within manageable limits. Additionally, having a range of suppliers and therefore spreading the risk (and reducing reliance on a small number of suppliers) could form part of a risk management strategy.
3 Payment of an individual customer invoice can be managed via insurance, but also by the use of credit factoring and invoice discounting services – which themselves can incorporate credit insurance.
4 The rising cost of raw materials may (depending on what the materials are) be dealt with by buying on forward or futures contracts.
5 The rising price of the currency of a country from which it is importing goods can again be managed via currency forward contracts or future.

Revision questions

Revision question for study session 1

Compare and contrast the roles of management accounting and financial accounting in a private sector organisation.

Feedback on page 349

Revision question for study session 2

(a) Identify five types of stakeholder groups in private sector companies in the UK. Briefly discuss their financial and other objectives.
(b) Evaluate the ways in which good corporate governance procedures can help to manage the divergent objectives of the identified stakeholder groups.

Feedback on page 349

Revision question for study session 3

Predict the impact that the change to International Financial Reporting Standards (IFRS) is likely to have on procurement decision making.

Feedback on page 350

Revision question for study session 4

A company is considering investing in new IT equipment and systems at a cost of £4.5 million.

(a) Justify the view that, in the IT industry, 'reducing balance' is a more appropriate method of depreciating assets than 'straight-line'. Illustrate your answer by using the above £4.5 million investment as an example and by making (and stating) any assumptions you wish.
(b) A further £250,000 is to be spent on training staff in the use of the new system. Judge whether this expense should be treated as a capital item or a revenue expense.

Feedback on page 351

Revision question for study session 5

Compare and contrast the content, and the relative usefulness, of the three primary published financial accounting statements from the perspective of a purchaser assessing the financial strength of a potential supplier.

Feedback on page 352

345

Finance for Purchasers

Revision question for study session 6

Using as an example the purchase of drugs by a hospital or health department, compare and contrast the use of descriptive and inferential statistics as an effective aid to purchasing decisions.

Feedback on page 354

Revision question for study session 7

Critically evaluate the use of marginal costing and contribution analysis as a means of financial decision making.

Feedback on page 354

Revision question for study session 8

Company X has recently developed a new product for which they are now trying to establish an appropriate price. It has used cost plus 20% in the past.

The direct costs of producing one unit of the new product is as follows:

- Material costs: £12
- Labour costs: £16

Additionally, it is estimated that fixed overheads of £9 per unit will be incurred.

(a) Propose two different cost plus pricing approaches that could be adopted using the data provided, and explain an advantage and disadvantage of each method.
(b) Suggest another possible pricing strategy that could be used to price new products and describe the likely impact on the price of the product.

Feedback on page 356

Revision question for study session 11

An established quoted company is looking to expand its operations, partly by purchasing new premises. It is also looking to invest in new plant, as well as IT equipment and systems.

(a) Propose three different sources of finance that might be appropriate, and assess the advantages and disadvantages to the company of each method of finance.
(b) Identify and explain three conditions that would need to be agreed with a lender before any long-term loan funding could be agreed.

Feedback on page 357

346

Revision questions

Revision question for study session 12

(a) Critically assess the view that traditional budgeting processes are no longer relevant in today's organisations
(b) Evaluate an alternative process.

Feedback on page 358

Revision question for study session 17

The information in table 21.4 relates to three possible expenditure projects being considered by a company. The company has limited funds available for investment, and can therefore only carry out one of the three projects. Its cost of capital is 9%.

Table 21.4

	Project A	Project B	Project C
Initial cost	£230,000	£205,000	£180,000
Expected life	5 years	5 years	4 years
Expected cash inflows			
Year 1	£90,000	£100,000	£40,000
Year 2	£80,000	£80,000	£65,000
Year 3	£80,000	£50,000	£95,000
Year 4	£60,000	£50,000	£100,000
Year 5	£55,000	£50,000	

(a) Calculate:
- the payback period for each project
- the net present value (NPV) of each project
- the profitability ratio for each project.
(b) Which project should be accepted, and why?
(c) Discuss the factors that management would need to consider in addition to the financial factors before making a decision on the project.

Feedback on page 359

Revision question for study session 19

Set out in table 21.6 and table 21.7 are profit and loss and balance sheet data for two companies operating in the same industry.

Table 21.6

Profit & Loss Account
Y/E 31 March 2006

	Company A £ million	Company B £ million
Turnover	400	320
Cost of good sold	(325)	(239)
Gross profit	75	81
Operating expenses	(43)	(52)
Operating profit	32	29
Interest payable	(6)	(1)
Profit before tax	26	28

(continued on next page)

347

Finance for Purchasers

Table 21.6 *(continued)*

Profit & Loss Account
Y/E 31 March 2006

Taxation	(8)	(8)
Profit for the year	18	20
Dividends	(8)	(16)
Retained profit	10	4

Table 21.7

Balance Sheet as at 31 March 2006	Company A	Company B
	£ million	£ million
Fixed assets		
Tangible assets	144	205
Current assets		
Stock	70	80
Debtors	45	41
	115	121
Creditors due in less than 1 year		
Creditors	41	75
Taxation	2	42
Bank overdraft	10	8
Proposed dividend	8	16
	61	141
Net current assets ('Working capital')	54	(20)
Total assets less current liabilities	198	185
Long-term liabilities (Loans)	(52)	0
Net assets	146	185
Shareholders' Equity		
Share capital	83	128
Retained profit	63	57
Shareholders' Funds	146	185

(a) Assess the relative performance and working capital efficiency of the two companies using appropriate ratios.

(b) Evaluate the usefulness of using ratio analysis from the perspective of a purchaser looking at the published accounts of a potential supplier.

(c) Evaluate the additional usefulness of a cash flow statement in the context of financial ratio analysis.

Feedback on page 361

Revision question for study session 20

Critically evaluate the application of the (capital) gearing ratio to financial accounts as a means of assessing risk in a particular company from a procurement perspective.

Feedback on page 364

Feedback on revision questions

Feedback on revision question for study session 1

This question would ideally be answered by looking at the two accounting roles against the different aspects set out in table 1.1.

This suggested seven different angles to consider:

1   The main purpose of financial accounting is that it is a mechanism for *reporting to shareholders*, and to other users of published accounts such as lenders, suppliers, unions and government. This contrasts with the main purpose of management accounting, which is to aid management.
2   The users of financial accounting information tend to be *external*, compared to management accounting, whose users are *internal*.
3   Financial accounting is driven by *legal requirements*. Management accounting is whatever the organisation will find useful. Linked to this is the fact that financial accounts also need to conform to professional standards and regulatory needs – whilst management accounting can be presented in whatever way is managerially useful.
4   The *focus* of financial accounting tends to be on the whole organisation, with the ultimate production of 'consolidated' or 'group' accounts. Management accounting, by contrast, is likely to involve information about much more narrowly defined and separated parts of the organisation.
5   Financial accounts must conform to *accounting principles*, for example UK GAAP (Generally Accepted Accounting Principles), whereas management accounts need not.
6   Another key aspect is the *time horizon*. Financial accounting is largely historic and backward looking. Management accounting will also include the reporting of past performance, but it also involves looking forward, for example via forecasts, plans, budgets and project appraisals.
7   The *reporting frequency* of financial accounting is again driven by external requirements (for example to produce annual and half-yearly figures), whilst no such requirement exists for management accounting.

Feedback on revision question for study session 2

(a) Your answer should highlight five different stakeholders. Examples would be:
   - Shareholders, whose main objective is wealth maximisation.
   - Lenders look to receive payment of interest and repayment of loan capital.

- Management objectives are to run the company for the benefit of shareholders, but will also have possibly separate objectives (maximising their own remuneration, career prospects and so on).
- Employees are interested in salary levels, working environment, security of employment.
- Suppliers and customers will have their own objectives (for example, profitability for the supplier, product satisfaction for the customer) that will depend on their relationships with perhaps several different organisations, not just the one in question. They are likely, though, to have specific objectives in relation to quality, lead times, price and so on.
- Local community groups will have objectives that link to the impact the company has on the local environment.

(b) The emphasis of recent UK corporate governance initiatives has been on disclosure requirements, and the encouragement of the demonstrable use of best practice.

Recent developments have included:
- quality and quantity of non-executive directors
- the appointment of remuneration committees
- greater disclosure of remuneration and share options information
- the separation of the role of chairman and chief executive (to avoid concentration of power).

The focus of corporate governance has therefore been on the way in which organisations are directed and controlled, and it is the directors of an organisation who make decisions about which of the divergent stakeholder interests described in (a) should have priority, and how they should be managed.

The argument is therefore that this need for greater accountability and transparency is in the interests of all stakeholder groups. Whilst directors still have to make choices about the way different stakeholder groups are managed, they do so against a backdrop of much greater accountability.

Feedback on revision question for study session 3

Your answer should first consider the extent to which procurement decision making is influenced by accounting standards per se. The impact of the switch to IFRS can only be significant if published financial accounts are part of the procurement decision making process.

The analysis of company accounts should, though, be part of any major purchasing decision, and the switch to IFRS may have a number of effects, including the following.

The switch to a new set of standards will require procurement decision-makers to be aware of (or able to access analysis done by people that are aware of) the technical differences between the new and old standards being used. Although there are many similarities in the standards, there are also some key changes in emphasis in areas such as fair value accounting and accounting for derivatives.

Revision questions

There are also changes in terminology and layout which those analysing accounts on behalf of procurement decision makers will need to be familiar with. Examples include the following.

Key differences include the use of the term 'Income Statement' (as opposed to 'Profit & Loss Account'). Other significant terminology differences include those shown in table 21.1.

Table 21.1

UK term	IAS term
Fixed assets	Non-current assets
Stock	Inventories
Debtors	Receivables
Creditors	Payables

The switch to IFRS will in theory have a beneficial impact to the extent that it is a move towards a global set of rules. This in time should allow easier comparison between different companies around the world, although true global convergence is still some way off – convergence with US standards being an example. But the adoption of IFRS by all European Union listed companies is an example of a move towards greater consistency in approach that can only be of positive use when it comes to procurement decisions being made.

Feedback on revision question for study session 4

(a) There are several methods of depreciating assets, including straight-line depreciation and reducing balance depreciation. You would be expected here to describe how these two methods apply, and illustrate your answer with appropriate figures.

With straight-line depreciation, two additional judgments have to be made. What is the expected life of the asset, and how much will it be worth at the end of that time period?

We might assume, therefore, a life of four years and a residual value of £0.5 million.

In that case the annual depreciation would be £4.5 million – £0.5 million = £4 million/4 = £1 million.

The annual figures would look like table 21.2.

Table 21.2

	Balance sheet value at start of year	Annual depreciation	Balance sheet value at end of year
Year 1	4,500,000	1,000,000	3,500,000
Year 2	3,500,000	1,000,000	2,500,000
Year 3	2,500,000	1,000,000	1,500,000
Year 4	1,500,000	1,000,000	500,000

Finance for Purchasers

Using reducing balance, there is no requirement to forecast a residual value, but an appropriate percentage rate needs to be determined. Reducing balance depreciation implies more productive use of an asset in its early years, and the rate used will reflect the extent to which that is the case.

If we use 40%, the figures over the first four years will be as shown in table 21.3.

Table 21.3

	Balance sheet value at start of year	Annual depreciation	Balance sheet value at end of year
Year 1	4,500,000	1,800,000	2,700,000
Year 2	2,700,000	1.080,000	1,620,000
Year 3	1,620,000	648,000	972,000
Year 4	972,000	388,800	583,200

The key point here is that, using 40% reducing balance depreciation, we have loaded the depreciation more heavily in the earlier years and this might more accurately reflect the use of a new IT system, and will certainly more accurately reflect its year end valuation. It is the percentage rate used, though, rather than the method itself that brings this result. Using 20%, for example, would have had the opposite effect.

(b) Training expenditure would usually not be capitalised as it is an ongoing running cost for a business with no tangible asset value that could be depreciated in future years.

The £250,000 training spend in this case, however, could reasonably be deemed a part of the overall investment and as such could be treated as capital and depreciated alongside the £4.5 million main asset cost.

Feedback on revision question for study session 5

The three main published financial statements are:

- profit & loss account (income statement)
- balance sheet
- cash flow statement.

The profit & loss account (P&L) is a summary of the organisation's profit generating performance over a period of time (for example a year). It therefore records revenues for the period, and deducts costs incurred in generating those revenues. As well as operational costs, the statement also reports finance costs and taxation (and, under UK GAAP, it also highlights the dividend to be paid on the year's activities).

The balance sheet is a snapshot of the organisation's financial position as at a particular point in time. It lists the company's assets – the things it owns – and its liabilities – the amount it owes at that time. The net assets of the business represent the difference between the assets and the liabilities. The balance sheet also describes how these net assets have been financed by

Revision questions

the shareholders – typically through share issues and through shareholders agreeing to leave profits in the business.

Also, by breaking down assets and liabilities according to whether they are long-term or short-term in nature, a balance sheet allows users to assess the shorter-term viability of a business. The difference between the current (short-term) assets and the current (short-term) liabilities is shown in the balance sheet, and described as 'net current assets'. This is sometimes also referred to as 'working capital', and shows the extent to which short-term liabilities are covered by short-term assets – an indicator of 'liquidity'.

The cash flow statement is similar to the profit & loss account in that it describes what has happened over the year – this time, in terms of movements of cash. Thus it describes the cash generated from operating activities, but also tracks cash flows stemming from taxation, interest, dividend payments, capital expenditure and the raising or repayment of finance.

All three statements are useful in their own right, given that they describe the financial performance of a business from three different perspectives. From a purchasing perspective, sight of all three statements would be vital. The profit and loss account gives an indication of underlying business performance, and can offer useful information about aspects such as revenue growth, profit margins, cost control etc. It should be noted, though, that the P&L contains some subjectivity (for example with depreciation, or with bad debt provisions).

The balance sheet also contains some subjective elements that need to be treated with care, but the purchaser can gain a view of the financial strength of the business – what the underlying assets are, how liquid the business is, how well it is managing its working capital, how much it is borrowing.

The cash flow statement is often cited as being the most useful, as it deals in real cash and as such is a more reliable reflection of the underlying strength of the business – and from the perspective of a purchaser, a degree of comfort about cash flow is likely to be essential, given that most business failures are caused by cash flow shortfalls.

All three statements have their uses, but a clearer picture tends to emerge when financial ratios are applied to the data. This process involves looking at figures from different statements (for example looking at profit in relation to the asset base of the business), and endorses the idea that all three statements are useful, particularly when looked at in conjunction with each other.

The usefulness of financial accounts must, though, also be considered in the context of the 'historical age' of the figures being reviewed. A limited company (Ltd) has 10 months after its accounting date in which to file its accounts at Companies House, whilst a PLC has to file within 6 months. This can lead to situations where the accounts being reviewed are significantly out of date. This, compounded by the fact that the data is in any case historical and usually not adjusted for inflation, can compromise their usefulness – especially in circumstances where decisions are being made about a future relationship.

353

Finance for Purchasers

Feedback on revision question for study session 6

Your answer here might first highlight the differences between descriptive and inferential statistics.

Descriptive statistics merely present data without drawing conclusions, but the key to their effectiveness as an aid to decision making lies in the way the data is presented and summarised.

Data presented in a useful order, or through the use of graphical techniques such as bar charts and pie charts, can highlight trends or facets that may otherwise not be easily identifiable.

Descriptive data can also be summarised via measures of central tendency such as the mean and the standard deviation, median (and upper and lower quartile ranges) and the mode.

Inferential statistics, by contrast, involve the presentation of data in a way that draws conclusions via the making of informed guesses from, typically, data extracted from a statistically significant sample.

Turning to the example of drugs for the healthcare industry, any number of particular examples might be suggested. The important aspect is to draw a distinction as to whether the data is merely descriptive, or whether it is drawing some particular conclusion – usually as a result of some testing that has been done. Also, when being used to aid decision making, how clearly the data is presented is also key.

Here are some examples of *descriptive* statistics that might be used to inform a purchasing decision of this type:

- descriptive data summarising currently available drugs
- data describing recent performance and reliability of different suppliers of drugs
- data highlighting drug prices, drug availability, drug delivery
- data describing current usage levels of different drugs
- data describing recent trends in health and in the frequency of occurrence of particular conditions
- age profiles of the population.

By contrast, examples of *inferential* statistics that would aid a purchasing decision in this context would include:

- statistics drawing conclusions about possible future trends in the occurrence of particular illnesses or conditions
- conclusions drawn from tests carried out to demonstrate the efficacy of particular drugs
- conclusions drawn from clinical trials about the potential side effects of particular drugs.

Feedback on revision question for study session 7

Your answer here might usefully start by describing what contribution analysis is, how 'contribution' is worked out, and the types of financial decisions that can be made using the analysis.

Contribution is the difference between sales and variable costs. This can be presented on a 'per unit' basis, or alternatively for the business as a whole for a specified (normally future) period.

Contribution analysis also requires a figure representing the overall fixed costs of a business (for a specified period).

Contribution analysis can then provide decision-making data that link to levels of sales required to break-even, or to achieve particular levels of profit. For example, the break-even point of a business is where sufficient contribution is being made to cover the fixed costs of the operation.

To illustrate this point, a company might sell a product for £10. If the variable costs of making that product are £7, then the contribution per unit will be (£10 – £7) = £3.

If the fixed costs of the business are £30,000 for a given period, the company will in the same period have to sell 30,000/3 = 10,000 units.

This basic model can be extended to aid decisions such as:

- Should we make something in-house, or buy it from outside?
- Should we close down a loss-making operation, or keep it open?
- What product should we concentrate on if there is some limiting factor that is constraining out activities?

All the above decisions can be aided by separating variable costs from fixed costs and by assessing activities on the basis of their contribution rather than their overall profit after fixed costs.

The critical evaluation should address some of the weaknesses inherent in the process, which are mainly driven by the unrealistic assumptions that have to be made and the practical difficulties involved in applying what is a very simply model to what tend to be far more complex real world scenarios. These weaknesses are highlighted in the study guide, and include:

- The unrealistic assumption that selling prices remain constant at different levels of activity.
- The unrealistic assumption that costs behave in a linear way – for instance, that variable costs will rise on a constant basis in line with sales. In reality, costs per unit are likely to decrease with volume buying, as discounts will be available. Fixed costs, also, can easily change even in the short-term.
- The unrealistic assumption that costs can easily be categorised as either fixed or variable. Many costs in practice fall somewhere between the two.
- The unrealistic assumption that, where companies have several products, the sales mix remains constant.
- A lot of contribution based decision making involves making subjective estimates.
- The concept unrealistically assumes that what is manufactured is sold.

Finance for Purchasers

Contribution analysis is a useful aid to decision making, and more sophisticated models can be developed to deal with many of the weaknesses highlighted above. But that then compromises one of the concepts greatest strengths – its simplicity.

Feedback on revision question for study session 8

(a) Two different cost plus pricing strategies could be:
Variable cost + 20%
Assuming material and labour costs are variable, the price of the product would be:
12 + 16 = 28 + 20% = £33.60
Total cost + 20%
This will also include the fixed overhead of £9 per unit:
12 + 16 + 9 = 37 + 20% = £44.40
The main advantage of 'variable cost plus' is that it avoids any arbitrary allocations (ie the fixed overhead part) and concentrates on short-term relevant costs. It is also a very simple method. The actual percentage rate applied to variable costs can be increased/decreased to enable the overall fixed costs of the business to be covered.
The disadvantages are that it represents only part of the overall costs, is very short-term oriented, and ignores the price/demand relationships. 'Total cost plus' attempts to include all costs and thereby reduces the possibility that fixed costs won't be covered. Its simplicity, again, is a positive factor. The main disadvantage is the fact that total cost by definition includes some arbitrary apportionments of cost. This method also ignores price/demand factors.

(b) *Price skimming'* is one option, and is likely to lead to a higher initial price.
Price skimming raises the price artificially in an attempt to quickly recoup costs and generate an early profit. It tends to be a successful approach for products that are in demand or where there are few competitors – certain types of electronic equipment for example. The product needs to be something that has some unique characteristic or prestige associated with it. In relation to the product life cycle, a price skimming approach is most likely when the product is in its growth stage, as demand is likely to be high, so it may be appropriate for pricing a new product.
The advantage of price skimming is that it enables the selling company to exploit demand to the full at a stage when certain consumers may be less price-sensitive. A potential disadvantage is that charging a high price may attract new entrants to the market who may offer more realistic prices and thus take away market share. Also, where consumers perceive 'price skimming' to have taken place, there could be reputational damage and longer term customer relationships might be adversely affected.
An alternative approach is *'price penetration'*. This, in contrast to price penetration, is likely to lead to a lower initial price. Again, this approach tends to occur at an early stage of a product's life cycle – typically the introductory stage – and is therefore relevant to a new product.
Price penetration enables the product to get a foothold in the market. Prices are artificially reduced to attract the largest possible market.

The main potential advantage is that it can prevent or discourage competition. The main disadvantage, though, is that the low pricing strategy may put so much pressure on margins that the product is not profitable, and also that – once a low price has been set – it can be very hard to raise it at a later stage.

Feedback on revision question for study session 11

(a) A key factor here is the need for finance suggestions to be linked to the purpose for which they are being used. This company buying premises, and also investing in other medium/long-term assets and therefore the finance used should also be of a medium/long-term nature.

This would therefore effectively rule out most short-term finance such as an overdraft facility or credit factoring.

Three different longer term types of finance that might apply are:

- *Share issue*. A share issue is certainly long-term in nature, and is potentially appropriate for the purposes quoted although it would be more likely in practice to be used, for example, to finance the takeover of another business.

  It is likely that, in the case outlined, a rights issue would be made. This involves offering new shares to existing shareholders. One advantage of issuing shares is that the dividend paid to shareholders is (with ordinary shares) discretionary, although the success or otherwise of a share issue might be influenced by the expectation of future dividends. Another advantage is that the cash raised does not have to be repaid – it is effectively permanent capital and subscribers to the share issue can get their money back by selling their shares to another investor.

  Disadvantages include the fact that share issues themselves are relatively difficult and expensive from an administrative point of view. More specifically, dividends paid to shareholders are not tax-deductible, which contributes to the view that equity is a more expensive source of finance than debt. There is the danger, too, that the share issue may not be sufficiently attractive to investors and that (if not underwritten) the finance may not be raised.

  The company may wish to borrow money to finance the assets being acquired. In the case of the premises, a *commercial mortgage* may be appropriate, where a bank or other lender provides debt finance secured specifically against the asset (the premises) being acquired.

- *Term loans* might represent an easier and cheaper source of finance, although the company's existing gearing level will have a bearing on this. Loans can be geared specifically to the purpose to which they are being used – in terms of timescales and also in terms of potential collateral for the lender. Another advantage is that interest is tax-deductible.

  Disadvantages of loan capital include interest rate risk (unless a fixed rate is agreed – and then there is the risk that rates subsequently fall), as well as the need to meet the loans terms and conditions which may be onerous.

- *Debentures* are similar to long-term loans, although they have some additional features. Firstly, they are usually secured against some

357

Finance for Purchasers

(for example the premises being bought in this example) or all of the borrowing company's assets. Secondly, they are issued in units, which can subsequently be traded.

- *Hire purchase* (HP) finance may be an option with the plant and IT investments, though often a relatively expensive one. Here the assets belong to the HP company, which allows the hirer to use the assets in exchange for a series of regular payments. The payments effectively cover capital repayment and interest charges. The HP company is protected against non-payment through the fact that it always owns the assets being used.

- *Leasing* is similar to taking out a loan (and financial accounting treats finance leases as if they were effectively loans), and acquiring plant and IT equipment would often be done through leasing arrangements. The technical difference is that the leasing company owns the asset, and the lessee (the company in need of the finance) makes regular payments in return for the right to use the asset. One advantage of leasing assets is that payments to service the lease can be closely matched to the benefits derived from using the leased asset.

  There is a distinction to be drawn between operating leases (where the lessee is committed only to a short-term contract) and finance leases (where the commitment typically covers the major part of the asset's useful life). In the case of operating leases, therefore, another benefit is that the risk of obsolescence is borne by another party. All leases, though, enjoy the benefit of certainty in terms of amounts to be paid out, with financing costs agreed at the outset and built into the regular lease payments made.

(b) Three conditions that would need to be agreed with a lender before any long-term loan funding could be agreed might include:

- interest rates
- term (duration) of loan
- security to be used as collateral for loan.

When a lender commits to longer-term financing, it is likely that they will want to protect themselves more tightly given the lengthy commitment being undertaken. Thus, the terms and conditions associated with longer term lending might include some broader obligations on the borrower, including agreements concerning:

- additional borrowing restrictions
- regular information flows from borrower to lender
- agreements to keep financial accounts within certain agreed parameters – often based on financial ratios such as gearing and interest cover.

Feedback on revision question for study session 12

(a) Supporters of budgeting processes will highlight the various benefits that can be derived if the process is working well. These include ideas such as:

- Budgeting processes force people to plan and think ahead.
- Budgets can help in achieving corporate objectives.
- Budgets are a useful control mechanism.
- Budgets allow agreement on objectives and resource allocation.

358

Revision questions

- Budgets encourage communication and co-ordination.
- Budgets can act as a performance measurement tool.
- Budgeting systems can quickly highlight problem areas, and budgetary control processes encourage appropriate corrective action.
- Budgets can be devolved in a way that gives more people responsibility and motivation.

Opponents of traditional budgeting processes pick up on the ways in which budgets can be abused. They will point to the ways in which budgets can cause internal conflict and can lead to dysfunctional behaviour. They will criticise the over-reliance on financial information as a performance measurement tool. They will highlight the fact that many of the benefits touted (for example regarding communication and motivation) simply don't work in practice – and that budgets can in fact be very demotivating as they tend to stifle creative behaviour.

They will argue that budgets actually add little value, are often based on guesswork and take up excessive amounts of management time and act as a constraint to the kind of innovative ideas that might be vital in a fast-changing environment. Budgets can be, and often are, inflexible. Another issue concerns the changing nature of business. Most traditional budgeting processes have their roots in relatively uncomplicated businesses, often manufacturing based. Drawing up a budget for such a business might be more straightforward than for many modern, multi-faceted and quickly changing businesses today.

(b)   Alternative approaches are many and varied, but there remain questions about the fact that disbanding traditional budgets runs the risk of giving up many of the real benefits around planning, control and performance measurement that traditional budgets offer.

One example is the 'beyond budgeting' model, which judges performance using relative measures such as comparison with competitors, or relative financial indicators (such as return on investment) as opposed to an absolute cash figure. There is no use of fixed targets and performance is judged against conditions that actually occurred (as opposed to those that were forecast).

Key questions that are asked in challenging such an approach would include the impact on management of losing aspects of traditional budgeting which would be replaced, but which might be deemed vital. For example, will control over spending be lost? How would scarce resources be allocated? How much does the success of such an approach depend on the quality and attitudes of staff in the company? Benefits might be the freeing up of management time for more productive activities.

The 'Balanced Scorecard' model, whilst not an alternative model to budgeting, does offer a more broadly based performance measurement tool that does not look purely at financial indicators. As such, it is an approach that does address some of the criticisms of over-reliance on traditional budgeting processes.

Feedback on revision question for study session 17

(a)   Workings. Table 21.5 sets out the discounted cash flows (at 9%) of the three projects. It then calculates the NPV of each project, the payback period of each project (using undiscounted cash flows) and

359

Finance for Purchasers

the 'profitability ratio' which expresses the NPV as a percentage or the initial investment amount.

Table 21.5

	Discount factor 9%	Project A cash flows	Project A DCF	Project B cash flows	Project B DCF	Project C cash flows	Project C DCF
0	1.000	−230,000	−230,000	−205,000	−205,000	−180,000	−180,000
1	0.917	90,000	82,530	100,000	91,700	40,000	36,680
2	0.842	80,000	67,360	80,000	67,360	65,000	54,730
3	0.772	80,000	61,760	50,000	38,600	95,000	73,340
4	0.708	60,000	42,480	50,000	35,400	100,000	70,800
5	0.650	55,000	35,750	50,000	32,500		
		NPV =	59,880	NPV =	60,560	NPV =	55,550
Payback period			2.75 years		2.5 years		2.79 years
Profitability ratio			26%		29.5%		30.9%

(b) Given the 'limited funds' scenario, students should highlight the merits of Project C. Although it has the lowest NPV, it has the highest profitability index and may therefore be the one that optimises the use of limited funds.

(c) The techniques applied suggest that there is little to choose between the projects from a purely financial perspective. Management will need to consider a range of other factors before making a decision. Students should be raising issues such as:

- The relative risks of the projects. Projects with higher risks need to be more financially attractive to compensate for the risks.
- Whether risk factors have been built into any of the figures. Risk factors as mentioned above can be built into the forecast cash flows (or into discount rates used).
- The implications of one project having a shorter life than the other two. Selecting the shortest project may free up resources to invest in other projects at an earlier stage.
- The extent to which the projects fall in line with corporate strategy. This will have a bearing on any decision, and may override a decision based purely on the figures, as will factors such as the need to make investments to comply with legal requirements or safety factors, or to gain market share via a loss-making (for example 'price penetration') strategy.
- The confidence with which the cash flows have been prepared. Whilst the calculations may appear very detailed, the results (such as the NPV) are only as good as the data being used to make the calculations. The original cash flows are only forecasts and as such

may not be reliable – making the value of the NPV figure very limited.

Feedback on revision question for study session 19

(a) Assess the relative performance and working capital efficiency of the two companies using appropriate ratios.
Performance ratios that could be used include:

Return on capital employed

Operating Profit/Long-term capital employed (%)

Company A:

32/146 + 52 = 16.2%

Company B:

29/185 = 15.7%

Gross profit margin

Gross profit/Sales (or turnover) (%)

Company A:

75/400 = 18.8%

Company B:

81/320 = 25.3%

Return on sales (operating profit margin)

Operating profit/Sales (or turnover) (%)

Company A:

32/400 = 8.0%

Company B:

29/320 = 9.1%

Fixed asset turnover

Sales/Fixed assets

Company A:

400/144 = 2.8 times

Company B:

320/205 = 1.6 times

Working capital efficiency ratios include:

Stock turnover (days)

(Stock/Cost of sales) × 365 (expressed as a number of days)

Company A:

(70/325) × 365 = 79 days

Company B:

(80/239) × 365 = 122 days

Debtor days

(Trade debtors/Turnover) × 365 (expressed as a number of days)

Company A:

45/400 × 365 = 41 days

Company B:

(41/320) × 365 = 47 days

Creditor days

(Trade creditors/Purchases (or cost of sales)) × 365 (expressed as a number of days)

Company A:

(41/325) × 365 = 46 days

Company B:

(75/239) × 365 = 115 days

We can summarise the results (table 21.8).

Table 21.8

	Company A	Company B
ROCE	16.2%	15.7%
Gross margin	18.8%	25.3%
Operating margin	8.0%	9.1%
Fixed asset turnover	2.8 ×	1.6 ×
Stock days	79 days	122 days
Debtor days	41 days	47 days
Creditor days	46 days	115 days

ROCE is similar for both companies, with A marginally the better. On the profit margin front, however, B is doing significantly better. This is particularly evident at the gross margin level; it may be able to charge more for similar goods, it may be able to source and make goods more cheaply – or perhaps a combination of the two is taking place.

On the working capital efficiency front, however, a different picture emerges. A is able to shift stock much more quickly than B, and subsequently get paid for it sooner. This suggests greater efficiency, and raises questions about B's stock levels.

B is taking much longer to pay suppliers than A, however. This might be down to a tougher negotiating approach – but could equally be a sign of further inefficiencies that could antagonise suppliers.

(b) Ratios are useful to purchasers in a number of ways.

They look at the relationship between different figures in the accounts in a way that highlights strengths and weaknesses, and also flags issues that may require further investigation.

Thus the data above highlights various factors set out in part (a) which would have been less obvious had the ratios not been applied.

Ratios do not, however, necessarily provide any answers. Rather, they prompt questions (for example, concerning Company B's slow-moving stock and excessive time to pay creditors).

More general weaknesses of ratio analysis concern the fact that they are usually based on historical financial accounting data, when a purchaser is more interested in future projections.

Ratio analysis applied to financial accounting data also suffers from all the weaknesses inherent in the data itself – the subjectivity of financial accounting statements, the fact that they are historic and out of date, the possibility that figures have been massaged or manipulated to present a better picture than should be the case.

Individual ratios themselves might also contain weaknesses. A measure like stock days might be significantly influenced by seasonal factors. Others, such as creditor days, often aren't able (because of the limitations of financial accounts) to offer more than a fairly crude estimate of the trend that is taking place.

(c) Evaluate the additional usefulness of a cash flow statement in the context of financial ratio analysis.

Most traditional financial ratios are applied to the profit & loss account and the balance sheet. Recent years have seen the development (via FRS1) of the cash flow statement, which is seen as an important statement to examine when assessing a business. Its usefulness stems from the fact that it highlights real movements of cash, and is not the result of the kind of subjective judgments and estimates that can play a large part in the preparation of the other two primary statements.

Ratio analysis can therefore also be applied to cash flow statements, sometimes in conjunction with aspects of the profit & loss account and the balance sheet.

The cash flow ratios outlined in the text, and which would usefully be brought into an answer to this question, were:

Cash flow to current liabilities

(Net cash flow from operating activities/Average current liabilities) × 100

Cash flow per share

Cash flow/Weighted average number of shares

Capex per share

(Capital expenditure/ Weighted average no. of shares) × 100

Feedback on revision question for study session 20

Your answer might begin with a definition of the gearing ratio as:

Debt/(Debt + equity) (%)

Issues that the evaluation could cover include:

Defining the ratio. The above ratio is commonly used, but so is a similar measure as follows:

Debt/Equity (%)

Whilst the above ratio is often termed the 'debt/equity' ratio, it is still also referred to as the 'gearing' ratio.

There is also the issue of defining what is meant by debt. This raises questions about what should be included. Traditional long-term loans and bonds would be in there, but the increasing prevalence of hybrid instruments that are part debt, part equity make precise definitions difficult. Similar problems are presented by financial instruments that are debt now, but are convertible to shares in the future, and by preference shares which, though technically shares, have many of the attributes of debt (such as a fixed percentage dividend).

The gearing ratio might also exclude an overdraft from the calculation, on the basis that it is short-term in nature. That might be contentious if the overdraft being used is essentially a permanent one.

The equity side of the equation can also lead to difficulties in interpretation. A company that has had to write-off the value of investments made, resulting in large accounting losses which will reduce the retained profits element of the business. This will lead to a rise in the gearing ratio, all other things being equal, but has the risk in the business really increased as a result of a one-off accounting transaction?

In addition to the above technical weaknesses, there is the issue of interpreting the ratio. An accepted principle of finance is that debt is cheaper than equity for a number of reasons, including the fact that interest is a tax-deductible expense. It follows that companies may therefore wish to borrow to make their financing more efficient – ie they will deliberately increase the gearing ratio. At some point, that may increase the overall risk – but determining that point is not an exact science.

Additional factors that might be included in an answer here include factors that relate to all financial accounting ratios – the fact that they are historic (and a procurement decision is most likely to be looking to the future), the fact that the balance sheet just relates to one moment in time, the fact that creative accounting techniques could lead to some misleading figures being present. Here, in the context of gearing, some debt might be 'off balance sheet' – some recent financial scandals included elements of debt not being reported within the accounts.

But the ratio can be a useful indicator of risk. If the gearing ratio is increasing to the extent that a significant majority of the financing is borrowed, then questions need to be asked. Gearing is a commonly used indicator by finance providers – investors and lenders – and in this context a ratio of 50% is often seen as a useful benchmark. A bank might, for example, like to see the provision of new lending matched by a similar contribution from the owners of a business to maintain the ratio at around the 50% mark.

It is useful, also, to look at the gearing ratio alongside other borrowing ratios so that a clearer picture might emerge – and measures that would be useful to raise here include 'interest cover' and the 'debt service coverage' ratio.

An important additional point to make is that the gearing ratio only considers one aspect of financial risk, and financial risk is only one part of the overall risk range that procurement decisions need to have considered.

Finance for Purchasers

References and bibliography

References and bibliography

This section contains a complete A–Z listing of all publications, materials or websites referred to in this course book. Books, articles and research are listed under the first author's (or in some cases the editor's) surname. Where no author name has been given, the publication is listed under the name of the organisation that published it. Websites are listed under the name of the organisation providing the website.

Arnold, G (2002) *Corporate Financial Management*, 2nd Edition, FT Prentice Hall.

Association for Project Management (2006) *APM Body of Knowledge*, 5th edition. APM Publishing.

Association of Chartered Certified Accountants (2001) *Full Cost Accounting: An Agenda for Action*. ACCA.

Association of Chartered Certified Accountants: http://www.accaglobal.com

Atrill, P (2005) *Financial Management for Decision Makers*. FT Prentice Hall.

Audit Commission: http://www.audit-commission.gov.uk

BBC: http://www.bbc.co.uk

Black, G (2003) *Students' Guide to Accounting and Financial Reporting Standards*. FT Prentice Hall.

Bower, JL, and CG Gilbert (2005) *From Resource Allocation To Strategy*. Oxford University Press.

BPP (2002) *AAT Central Assessment Kit*. Units 8 and 9: Managing Costs and Allocating Resources. BPP Publishing.

BS ISO 15686 & BS EN 60300.

Butterick, R (2005) *Project Workout: A Toolkit for Reaping the Rewards of all your Business Projects*, 3rd edition. FT Prentice Hall.

Cadbury, A (1992) *The Report of the Committee on the Financial Aspects of Corporate Governance*, London: Gee.

CIMA: http://www.cimaglobal.com/

Davies, A, and M Hobday (2005) *The Business of Projects*. Cambridge University Press.

Devaux, SA (1999) *Total Project Control: A Manager's Guide to Integrated Project Planning, Measuring and Tracking*. New York: John Wiley.

Drury, C (2005) *Management Accounting for Business*, 3rd edition. Thompson.

Dyson, J (2001) *Accounting for Non-accounting* students, 3rd edition. FT Prentice Hall.

Edwards, S, E Bartlett and I Dickie (2000) *Whole life costing and life-cycle assessment for sustainable building design*. BRE Press.

Elliott, B, and J Elliott (2005) *Financial Accounting and Reporting*. FT Prentice Hall.

Financial Reporting Council: http://www.frc.org.uk/asb/

Financial Times: http://www.ft.com/indepth/accounting

Franco, G (2006) *Leading and Influencing in Purchasing*. Stamford: CIPS

FSA (2003) *The Revised Combined Code on Corporate Governance* (http://www.fsa.gov.uk/pubs/ukla/lr_comcode2003.pdf)

Graves, SB, and JL Ringuest (2002) *Models and Methods for Project Selection: Concepts From Management Science, Finance and Information Technology*. Berlin: Springer.

Greenbury, R (1995) *Directors Remuneration: Report of a Study Group Chaired by Sir Richard Greenbury*, London: Gee.

Hampel, R (1998) *Committee on Corporate Governance: Final Report*, London: Gee.

Higgs, D (2003) *Review of the Role and Effectiveness of Non-executive Director*, London: The Department of Trade and Industry.

HM Treasury (2003) *HM Treasury Green Book. Appraisal and Evaluation in Central Government*. London: TSO.

Private Finance Initiative via HM Treasury website: http://www.hm-treasury.gov.uk/documents/public_private_partnerships/ppp_links.cfm

Holmes, G, A Sugden and P Gee(2004) *Interpreting Company Reports and Accounts*, 9th edition. FT Prentice Hall.

Horngen, CT, SM Datar and G Foster (2005) *Cost Accounting: A Managerial Emphasis*, 12th edition. Prentice Hall.

House of Commons 2001 Research Paper 'The Private Finance Initiative': http://www.parliament.uk/commons/lib/research/rp2001/rp01-117.pdf

International Accounting Standards Board: http://www.iasb.org/Summaries+of+International+Financial+Reporting+Standards/

Institute of Chartered Accountants in England and Wales: http://www.icaew.co.uk

International Financial Reporting Standards: http://www.ifrs.co.uk

Lewis, JP (2006) *Project Planning, Scheduling, and Control: A Hands-on Guide to Bringing Projects in on Time and on Budget*, 4th revised edition. McGraw-Hill.

Lumby, S, and C Jones (1999) *Investment Appraisal and Financial Decisions*. 6th edition, chapters 3, 5 and 6. Chapman and Hall.

Max Wideman: http://www.maxwideman.com/papers/index.htm

McLaney, E (2002) *Business Finance: Theory and Practice*, 5th edition, chapters 4, 5 and 6. FT Prentice Hall.

NAO (2006) *Review presented to the BBC Governors' Audit Committee by the Comptroller and Auditor General, and a response to the review from the BBC.*

Private Finance Information Service, National Assembly for Wales: http://www.pfu.wales.gov.uk/

National Audit Office Recommendations Service Partnerships UK 4Ps: http://www.partnershipsuk.org.uk/

NFEA: http://www.smallbusinessadvice.org.uk/busplan/bpdownloads.asp

Office of Government Commerce, Procurement Guide 07: http://www.ogc.gov.uk/index.asp?id=35

OJEC Tenders Electronic Daily Website: http://ted.publications.eu.int/CD/application/pif/resources/shtml/common//home/home.html

Pennypacker, JS, and LD Dye (editors) (2002) *Managing Multiple Projects: Planning, Scheduling and Allocating Resources for Competitive Advantage*. Marcel Dekker.

Pike, R, and B Neale (1999) *Corporate Finance and Investment*, 3rd edition, chapters 5 and 7. FT Prentice Hall.

Pilkington Annual Report 2005 (http://www.pilkington.com)

PrivateFinance-i.com: http://www.privatefinance-i.com/

PPP Forum: http://www.pppforum.com

Rad, PF (2001) *Project Estimating and Cost Management*. Management Concepts.

Rexam Plc Annual Report 2005 (http://www.rexam.com)

Sato, Y, and JJ Kaufman (2005) *Value Analysis – Tear Down*, 1st edition. Industrial Press.

Financial Partnerships Unit, Scottish Executive: http://www.scotland.gov.uk/pfi

Schwindt, C (2005) *Resource Allocation in Project Management*. Springer-Verlag Berlin and Heidelberg GmbH.

Seal, W (2005) *Management Accounting*. McGraw Hill.

Serco Plc Annual Report 2005 (http://www.serco.com)

Smith, JA (2004) *Strategic Management Accounting in the Small Business, Handbook of Management Accounting*, 3rd edn (editor J Innes). Thomson and Gee.

Stuteley, R (2002) *The Definitive Business Plan*, 2nd edition. FT Prentice Hall.

Turner, JR, and SJ Simister (2000) *The Gower Handbook of Project Management*, 3rd edition. Gower Publishing.

Index

10-day deterioration in stock turnover, 187
10-day improvement in the collection period, 186
5-year summary, 68
ABC *see* activity-based costing
ACCA *see* Association of Chartered Certified Accountants
Accountancy Investigation and Disciplinary Board, 35
accounting rate of return (ARR), 127, 280
accounting standards, 33
    convergence, 39
    financial accounting, 3
    international issues, 33, 38, 59, 62
    role, 34
Accounting Standards Board (ASB), 34, 37
accounting terminology, 33
acid test ratio, 321
activity analysis, 250
activity-based costing (ABC), 93, 117
advertisements, 20, 49
Alcatel Austria v *Bundesministerium für Wissenshaft und Verkehr* [C-81/98], 23
apportionment, 264, 265
appraisal
    financial, 318
APQC, 251
arm's length price, 118
ARR *see* accounting rate of return
artificial inflation, 51
ASB *see* Accounting Standards Board
assets
    current assets/liabilities, 61, 323
    finance sources, 168, 177
    fixed, 60, 320
    net, 61
    turnover, 320

Association of Chartered Certified Accountants (ACCA), 2
audits/auditing
    Audit Commission, 270
    Audit Committees, 26
    Auditing Practices Board, 35
    expenditure types, 128, 133
average, 78
average deviation, 80
BAFO *see* Best and Final Offer
balanced scorecards, 6
balance of payments, 15, 16
balance sheets, 60, 62, 318
bank loans, 168
Bank of England Monetary Policy Committee, 17
base estimates, 242
benchmarking, 249
benefits realisation plans, 261
best and final offer (BAFO), 133
bonds, 175, 183
break-even data, 92
break-even point, 97
British Airways, 14
budgets/budgeting
    benefits, 200
    budget assumptions, 196
    budget centres, 195
    business plans, 195
    control, 192, 194, 195
    cost management, 264, 267, 269
    development and management, 191
    limitations, 200
business needs identification, 208, 212, 215
business plans, 195, 231
business risks, 317
Cadbury Report (1991), 25
Capex *see* capital expenditure
capital
    finance sources, 180

371

capital expenditure (Capex), 43,
129
depreciation impacts, 44
expense items, 49
per share, 323
capital investment, 279, 280, 283,
285, 290
capital projects
base estimates, 242
change control, 242
drivers, 126
capital spend *see* capital expenditure
capital structure risks, 317
cash budgets, 198
cash flows
current liabilities, 323
discounted cash flow technique,
286
forecasts, 198, 215
per share, 323
ratios, 323
statements, 64
category management, 301
central tendency, 78
change control, 242
Chartered Institute of Management
Accountants (CIMA), 2
Chartered Institute of Public
Finance and Accountancy
(CIPFA), 2
CIMA *see* Chartered Institute of
Management Accountants
CIPFA *see* Chartered Institute
of Public Finance and
Accountancy
closing cost gaps, 147
cluster sampling, 85
Combined Code on Corporate
Governance (2003), 25
commodity prices, 14
communication
business plans, 231
findings and recommendations,
225
key data, 226
community and CSR, 28
Companies House, 4
company secretaries, 8, 9
competitiveness, 112
Compliance Directive (as amended
by Services Directive 1992), 20,
24

Constructing the Team, 126
consumer prices index (CPI), 15
contingency planning, 246
contribution analysis, 95, 97, 99,
104
controllable items, 195
control of cost management, 299,
300, 303, 306, 308
convenience sampling, 85
convergence of accounting
standards and practices, 39
corporate governance, 10, 24
corporate plans, 192
corporate social responsibility
(CSR), 26
cost/time diagrams, 159
cost accountants, 8
cost base pricing, 115
cost behaviour, 93
cost coding, 308
cost estimating groups, 147
cost gap closure, 147
costing
pricing strategy
resource requirement
assessments, 215
cost management, 241, 242
benchmarking, 249
control, 299, 300, 303, 306,
308
planning, 243, 246
purchasing function, 263, 264,
267, 269
reduction and control, 299,
300, 303, 306, 308
review stages, 253
supply chains, 248
cost of capital, 290
cost overruns, 308
cost-plus pricing, 115, 197
costs
cost–volume–profit and break-
even data, 92
expense item impacts, 47
financial accounting statements,
56
cost–volume–profit, 92
country risks, 317
CPI (consumer prices index), 15
credit availability, 17
creditor days, 322
creditors, 171

credit risks, 317
cross-functional team working, 303
CSR *see* Corporate Social
    Responsibility
current assets/liabilities, 61, 323
current ratio, 321
data presentation and
    communication, 226
DCF *see* discounted cash flow
debentures, 175
debt
    balance sheets, 60
    debt service coverage ratio, 336
    equity, 337
    finance sources, 173
    investment, 291
    risk management, 334
debtor days, 322
debtor management, 170
decision making
    contribution analysis, 99
    evaluating project decision
        making, 141
    investments, 279, 280, 283,
        285, 290
    limiting factor effects, 102
    macro-economic factor
        impacts, 14
    marginal costing, 99
Department of Trade and Industry
    (DTI), 21
depreciation, 43, 44, 45
derivatives, 338
descriptive statistics, 76
development capital, 181
development costs, 48
deviation, 80
direct costs, 92
Directives on Public Procurement,
    18
discounted cash flow (DCF)
    techniques, 285
discount rates, 291
dividend cover, 328
dividends, 57
dividend yield, 327
DTI *see* Department of Trade and
    Industry
earnings per share (eps), 57
earnings per share (EPS), 326
economic growth, 13, 15
efficiency ratios, 318, 322

Egan report, 126
employee ratios, 323
employment, 15
environment and CSR, 28
eps *see* earnings per share
equity, 180, 291, 337
estimation
    cost management , 244
European Union (EU) Directives
    on Public Procurement, 18
evaluating risks *see* risk evaluation
evaluation
    EU Directives, 21
    project decision making, 141
expenditure, 43
    profitability impacts, 47
    see also, 43
    types, 125
external costs, 264
external factor impacts, 13
external pricing, 112
external sources of finance, 172,
    180
factoring, 177
Federal Accounting Standards
    Board, 38
finance
    accounting terminology, 33
    costs, 48
    external sources, 172, 180
    internal sources, 168
    leases, 49, 176
    public sector sources, 183
    resource requirement
        assessments, 215
    sources, 167
financial accounting
    accountant roles and
        responsibilities, 4, 7
    management accounting, 1, 2
    recent developments, 5
    statement production, 3
financial accounting statements
    5-year summary, 68
    balance sheets, 60
    cash flow statement, 64
    contents, 55
    profit and loss account, 56
    STORGL, 68
financial appraisals, 318
financial controllers, 8
financial gearing, 334, 335

Financial Reporting Council (FRC), 34
Financial Reporting Standards (FRS), 34, 270
financial risks, 317
financial status, 318, 320
fiscal policy, 17
five-year summary, 68
fixed assets, 60, 320
fixed budgets, 197
fixed costs, 93
flexible budgets, 197
forecasts
  cash flow, 64, 198, 202
  cost management, 245, 264, 267
  investment , 294
  resource requirement assessments, 215
forward contracts, 339
FRC *see* Financial Reporting Council
FRS *see* Financial Reporting Standards
full absorption costing, 93
futures, 338
GAAP *see* Generally Accepted Accounting Principles
Gantt charts, 312
GATT *see* General Agreement on Tariffs and Trade
GDP (gross domestic product), 14, 15
gearing, 94, 317, 334, 335
General Agreement on Tariffs and Trade (GATT), 22
Generally Accepted Accounting Principles (GAAP), 4
gilts, 183
global accounting standards, 39
GNP (gross national product), 15
good practice, 22
goodwill, 61
government monetary policy, 16
government policy, 14, 16
grants, 184
graphical descriptive statistics, 76
Greenbury Report (1995), 25
gross domestic product (GDP), 14, 15
gross national product (GNP), 15
gross profit, 57

growth rate measures, 15
growth ratios, 323
Hampel Report (1998), 25
hedging, 339
Higgs Report (2003), 25
human capital, 208, 212, 215
IAS *see* International Accounting Standards
IASB *see* International Accounting Standards Board
ICAEW *see* Institute of Chartered Accountants in England and Wales
ICAI *see* Institute of Chartered Accountants in Ireland
ICAS *see* Institute of Chartered Accountants in Scotland
IFRS *see* International Financial Reporting Standards
imports/exports, 15
income statements *see* profit and loss accounts
incremental budgeting, 197
indirect costs, 92
inferential statistics, 84, 86
inflation
  artificial, 51
  external factor impacts, 14, 15, 17, 30
  investment, 292
information technology (IT)
  equipment costs, 54
  investment, 294
innovative management accounting, 6
Institute of Chartered Accountants in England and Wales (ICAEW), 2
Institute of Chartered Accountants in Ireland (ICAI), 2
Institute of Chartered Accountants in Scotland (ICAS), 2
insurance, 340
interest
  cover measurements, 336
  financial accounting statements, 57
  rates, 13, 14, 16
internal costs, 265
internal pricing, 112
internal rate of return (IRR), 128, 288

internal sources of finance, 168
International Accounting Standards (IAS), 59, 62
International Accounting Standards Board (IASB), 38
International Financial Reporting Standards (IFRS), 33, 38
international issues in accounting standards, 33, 38, 59, 62
interquartile range, 80
investment decision making, 279, 280, 283, 285, 290
investment gateway process, 136
investment ratios, 326
investments and balance sheets, 60
invoice discounting, 179
IRR *see* internal rate of return
IT *see* information technology
job plans, 151
judgement sampling, 85
key financial statements, 55
Latham report, 126
leaseback, 177
leases, 49, 176
leasing costs, 49, 53
legal aspects, 13
lenders and investment, 291
liabilities, 61, 323
LIBOR – the London Interbank Offered Rate, 175
life cycle costing, 142
limiting factors, 102, 196
liquidity ratios, 320
liquidity risks, 317
loan capital, 60
loans, 186
London Interbank Offered Rate (LIBOR), 175
long-term business plans, 192
long-term liabilities, 61
long-term loan finance, 174
macro-economic factor impacts, 14
macro-environmental factors, 192
make or buy decisions, 91
management accounting, 1, 2, 6, 7
management actions in cost management, 269
managing costs *see* cost management
marginal costing, 95, 98, 99, 104
margin v mark-up, 117
marketing costs, 49

marketplace and CSR, 28
market pricing, 112
mark-up v margin, 117
mean, 78
mean deviation, 80
measure of central tendency, 78
median, 78
mode, 79
monetary policy, 16
money supply, 16
monitoring cost management, 306
Monte Carlo simulations, 247
National Audit Office (NAO) , 133
National Debt, 185
national income, 15
negotiated price, 111
negotiated tender procedure, 22
net assets, 61
net present value (NPV), 127, 286
new product development (NPD), 146
non-controllable items, 195
non-equity finance sources , 172
NPD *see* New Product Development
NPV *see* Net Present Value
null hypothesis, 86
OECD *see* Organisation for Economic Co-operation and Development
Official Journal of the European Communities (OJEC), 21
Open Standards Benchmarking Collaborative (OSBC), 252
open tender procedure, 22
operating activities and cash flows, 64
operating costs, 56
operating expenditure (Opex), 129
operating leases, 49
operating profit, 57, 320
operational gearing, 94, 317
operational risks, 317
Opex *see* operating expenditure
options, 339
ordinary share capital, 180
Organisation for Economic Co-operation and Development (OECD), 26
organisation functions, 299, 300, 303, 306, 308

375

OSBC *see* Open Standards
  Benchmarking Collaborative
overdrafts, 177, 186
overheads, 92, 265, 267, 306
P/E *see* price/earnings ratio
payback period (PP), 127, 283
PCF *see* Process Classification
  Framework
penetration pricing, 114
people
  resource requirements, 208,
    212, 215
performance
  financial appraisals, 318
  monitoring and control, 307
  ratios, 319
  targets, 192
PFI *see* Private Finance Initiative
PIN *see* prior indicative notices
planning
  cost management, 243
population, 85
PP *see* payback period
PPP *see* Public Private Partnerships
preference share capital, 181
presentation and communication,
  226, 231
price/earnings (P/E) ratio, 327
price elasticity of demand, 113
price skimming, 114
pricing strategies, 111
  cost-plus pricing, 115
  market pricing, 112
  transfer pricing, 118
principal budget factors, 196
principles of accounting standards,
  35, 39
prior indicative notices (PIN), 21
Private Finance Initiative (PFI),
  132, 183, 184
private money and public facilities,
  132
probability, 86, 294
Process Classification Framework
  (PCF), 251
procurement regulatory
  frameworks, 18
procurement spend authority levels,
  256
production costs, 116
product life cycles, 114
product range decisions, 91

Professional Oversight Board for
  Accountancy, 35
profit after tax, 57
profit and expenditure, 47
profit and loss accounts, 37
  expense item impacts, 47
  finance account statements, 56
  financial appraisals, 318
  International Accounting
    Standards, 59
profit attributable to shareholders,
  57
profit based investment techniques,
  280
profit margins, 320
project/programme evaluation by
  benchmarking, 249
project costing, 215
project decision making tools, 141
project development, 132
PSNCR *see* Public Sector Net Cash
  Requirement
public expenditure, 132
public facilities with private money,
  132
Public Private Partnerships (PPP),
  132, 183, 184
Public Procurement Directives, 18
Public Purchasing Remedies
  Directive 1989, 20
Public Sector Net Cash
  Requirement (PSNCR), 185
public sector sources of finance, 183
Public Services Directive, 20, 23
Public Supplies Directive, 20, 22
Public Works Directive, 20, 22
purchasing
  investment ratios, 326
  organisation key functions, 300
purchasing function and cost
  management, 263, 264, 267,
  269
qualitative characteristics of
  accounting standards, 36
quota sampling, 85
R&D *see* research and development
random sampling, 85
range, 80
recession, 15
reducing balance depreciation, 45

reports/reporting
    corporate governance, 25
    cost management, 269
    cost overruns, 308
    financial accounting, 3
research and development (R&D)
    expenditure, 48
reserves and balance sheets, 60
resource requirement assessments,
    207, 208, 212, 215
responsibility accounting, 195
restricted tender procedure, 22
retail prices index (RPI), 15
retained profits, 57, 186
Rethinking Construction, 126
return on capital employed
    (ROCE), 127, 319
return on investment (ROI), 280
revenue expenditure, 43, 47, 49
revenue reserves, 186
reverse engineering, 149
review stages of cost management,
    253
rights issue, 181
risk evaluation, 315, 316, 318, 326
risk management, 246, 333, 334,
    338, 340
risks
    investment, 293
    types, 316
ROCE *see* Return On Capital
    Employed
ROI (return on investment), 280
role of accounting standards, 34
roles and responsibilities of
    accountants, 4, 6, 7
RPI (retail prices index), 15
sale and leaseback, 177
sale of assets, 168
sales/turnover, 56
sampling, 85
Sarbanes-Oxley Act of 2002, 26, 54
sensitivity analysis, 136, 293
Services Directive 1992, 20, 24
share capital, 60, 180, 186
shareholders
    balance sheets, 62
    investment, 291
    profit and loss accounts, 57
share issues, 173, 186
short-term external finance, 177
short-term operating plans, 192

SIC *see* Standard Industry Code
significance levels, 87
skill profiling, 212
SMART analysis, 196
social responsibility *see* Corporate
    Social Responsibility
special purpose companies (SPC),
    132
Special Purpose Vehicles (SPV), 184
spread, 80
SPV *see* Special Purpose Vehicles
SSAPs (Statements of Standard
    Accounting Practice), 34
stakeholders and CSR, 27
standard deviation, 81, 82
Standard Industry Code (SIC), 308
standards *see* accounting standards
Statement of Principles, 35
statement of total recognised gains
    and losses (STORGL), 68
Statements of Standard Accounting
    Practice (SSAPs), 34
statistics
    descriptive, 76
    inferential, 84
stock management, 170
stock turnover days, 322
STORGL *see* statement of total
    recognised gains and losses
straight-line depreciation, 45
strategic risks, 317
summary statistics, 76
sum of the years digits, 46
supply chains and cost
    management, 248
swaps, 339
SWOT analysis, 192, 233
systematic sampling, 85
tabular descriptive statistics, 76
target costing, 118, 145
tax accountants, 8, 9
taxation, 14
    capital v expense items, 51
    financial accounting statements,
      57
    impacts on decision-making, 14
    investment, 292
    transfer pricing, 118
team working, 303
tear-down analysis, 149
ten-day deterioration in stock
    turnover, 187

377

ten-day improvement in the
collection period, 186
tender procedures, 22
terminology of finance and
accounting, 33
threat of substitutes, 113
thresholds (supplies, services,
works), 20
timescales and EU Directives, 21
total costs, 111, 116
traditional management accounting,
6
transfer pricing, 111, 118
Treasury stock, 183
Treaty of Rome (Article 86), 19
triangle of finite resources, 209
turnover, 56, 187, 320
unemployment, 15
Utilities Directive and Utilities
Regulations 2006, 20, 23
value analysis – tear-down (VA–
TD), 149
value engineering, 153
value for money (VFM), 156
value management, 153
variability, 80
variable costs, 93, 111, 116
variance, 81, 82
VA–TD, 149
venture capital, 181
VFM (value for money), 156
WACC *see* Weighted Average Cost
of Capital
WBS *see* Work Breakdown
Structure
weighted average cost of capital
(WACC), 291
whole life costing, 142
whole team approaches, 247
work breakdown structure (WBS),
244
working capital, 60, 61, 322
workplace and CSR, 28
World Trade Organization (WTO),
22
zero-based budgeting (ZBB) , 197